Diary of an Oxford Methodist

Benjamin Ingham, 1712–1772

Diary of an Oxford Methodist
Benjamin Ingham, 1733-1734

Edited by Richard P. Heitzenrater

Duke University Press   Durham 1985

© 1985 Duke University Press, all rights reserved
Printed in the United States of America

Library of Congress Cataloging in Publication Data
Ingham, Benjamin.
Diary of an Oxford Methodist, Benjamin Ingham, 1733–1734.
Bibliography: p.
Includes index.
1. Ingham, Benjamin.   2. Methodists—England—
Biography.   I. Heitzenrater, Richard P., 1939–
II. Title.
BX8495.I68A33   1984   287'.092'4 [B]   84–28635
ISBN 0–8223–0595–X

To Irving B. Holley and Harold Parker,
my mentors in history at Duke,
who introduced me to
the discipline of research,
the art of interpretation,
and the excitement of discovery

Contents

Diaries hold a special fascination for many people, be they faithful diarists or curious readers. The lure of these "archives of the memory" first captivated me fifteen years ago when I accepted the challenge of decoding the unpublished personal diaries of John Wesley. The tedium and consternation that naturally accompany such a project have been more than offset by the excitement of pioneer exploration into significant manuscript writings of a prominent historical figure and by the heartening conquests over a continuing succession of decipherment problems. The most elating moment in the whole process, however, came in the solitude of the Methodist Archives strongroom in London on the last day of July 1969. While scrutinizing individually each item on the shelves and in the boxes of that largely uncharted treasure trove, I opened a little notebook nearly identical in style and format (save the handwriting) to the Wesley diaries on which I had been laboring for months. Toward the front of the small leatherbound volume was an unobtrusive yet startling note: "Charles Wesley . . . taught me the following method of keeping a diary," followed by three pages, double-columned, containing a key to much of the Wesleyan system of abbreviations and symbols. Inside the front cover was another list of otherwise incomprehensible symbols along with their meanings. A quick scan of the notebook revealed that it was the diary of Benjamin Ingham, friend of the Wesleys and fellow Oxford Methodist. Subsequent examination and analysis of the document have proven invaluable in unlocking many of the mysteries of the Wesley "code" and in offering a wealth of detailed information regarding the "first rise of Methodism" at Oxford.

My main purpose in publishing this diary is to make available for the first time an Oxford Methodist diary that exhibits both the Wesleyan method of diary keeping and the life and thought of the Oxford Methodists during an important phase of their development. My first concern has been to provide an accurate transliteration of the diary text. Extensive annotations give the reader a view of the historical context and the specific implications of the diary entries. The Introduction is intended as a guide through the complexities of the diary. Oxford Methodism is described in enough detail to provide the necessary framework for an enhanced understanding of the diary text, as well as to demonstrate the way Ingham's diary itself contributes to both the form and substance of our knowledge of the Wesleyan movement at Oxford. Explanations of some basic referents regarding Oxford University and the North Country augment the entries but by no means sap the document of every interesting or useful inference. I would hope there will be others who find this diary a fruitful source for the study of eighteenth-century British life and thought.

The text of the diary has been modernized—the punctuation regularized, archaic spellings limited to the notes, and most of the prolific capitalization removed, except for references to university exercises and other appropriate terms. On any doubtful matter of style, the form of the manuscript was retained. Abbreviations in the text have been extended without the use of brackets unless a question of meaning remains. Entries transliterated from shorthand are underlined. The nature of the material requires extensive annotation. To reduce the number of notes and cross references, the "exacter" diary format is outlined in Appendix 1; individuals frequently mentioned in the text are listed in Appendix 2; books read by Ingham are listed in Appendix 3; and definitions of frequently used but unfamiliar terms are given in the Glossary. Citations of standard antiquarian sources published in multiple editions are noted by chapter, section, and/or paragraph rather than by page so that the reader may easily refer to any edition. Cross references within the diary are simply by day and month since the diary covers exactly one year, September 1733 through August 1734. The discrepancy between Julian and Gregorian calendars in use during this period accounts for the double reference, 1733/34, from 1 January to 25 March.

My work in preparing this volume has benefited from assistance and support from many quarters. I am grateful to The Methodist Church of Great Britain for their extraordinary kindness in making the Ingham and Wesley diaries accessible to me over several years of research and to their Archives Committee for permission to publish this diary. I also acknowledge my gratitude to the American Council of Learned Societies for fellowship assistance and to Centre College of Kentucky and Perkins School of Theology, Southern Methodist University, for research leaves and other substantial support of my work on the Oxford Methodist diaries.

Several persons deserve a special note of thanks: John C. Bowmer, former director of the Methodist Archives, who was the first to share my excitement at discovering the Ingham diary and whose gracious assistance helped lighten many of my research tasks over the years; William Leary, present Archivist of The Methodist Church in Great Britain; David W. Riley, Assistant Librarian at The John Rylands University Library of Manchester, where the Methodist Archives now reside; John Goodchild, Principal Local Studies Officer at the Wakefield Metropolitan District Council Library; Mrs. Beatrice Scott, who has directed me to many useful sources of information relating to Ingham; Miss R. F. Vyse, Assistant Archivist of the University Archives in the Bodleian Library; Dr. J. M. Kaye, Archivist and Law Tutor at Queen's College; Professor John Walsh, Fellow of Jesus College, and Professor V. H. H. Green, Fellow and Rector of Lincoln College, both of whom read parts of the book and shared with me many insights from their special expertise in Oxford history; and dozens of British friends, many whose names I never knew, who readily responded with more than polite interest to a wandering stranger's inquiries about local history.

I am particularly indebted to Frank Baker of Duke University and Albert C. Outler of Southern Methodist University, who have not only been a constant source of help and inspiration over the last two decades as my tutors and colleagues in Wesley studies but have also read the manuscript carefully and made many helpful suggestions; to Wanda W. Smith, my assistant, who has provided valuable research and secretarial assistance in the final stages of preparing this volume; to John Vickers, who prepared the index; and to my wife Karen, whose judicious editorial sense and persistent encouragement made possible the completion of this project.

R. P. H.
Southern Methodist University
Dallas, Texas

Abbreviations

B.C.P.   *The Book of Common Prayer,* London, 1662.

D.N.B.   *The Dictionary of National Biography,* ed. Leslie Stephen and Sidney Lee (Oxford: Oxford University Press, 1921–22), 22 vols.

Letters   *Letters,* I–VII, ed. Frank Baker, vols. 25–31 of *The Works of John Wesley.* Citation by volume and page for vols. I and II (Oxford: Clarendon Press, 1980–82); citation by date only for letters after 1755 (forthcoming volumes).

MA   Methodist Archives, The John Rylands University Library of Manchester.

OD   John Wesley, MS. Oxford Diaries, in the Colman Collection, Methodist Archives, MA. Citation by volume and page.

          OD I   5 April 1725–20 February 1727
          OD II   30 April 1729–16 June 1732
          OD III   17 June 1732–30 September 1733
          OD IV   1 October 1733–22 April 1734
          OD V   7 September 1734–28 February 1735

O.E.D.   *The Oxford English Dictionary,* ed. J. A. H. Murray, Henry Bradley, W. A. Craigie, C. T. Onions (Oxford: Clarendon Press, 1933), 13 vols.

Queen's
College   *Statutes of Queen's College, Oxford,* no. 4 in *Statutes of the*
Statutes   *Colleges of Oxford,* ed. E. A. Bond (London, 1853).

Sermon   *Sermons,* I–IV, ed. Albert C. Outler, vols. 1–4 of the forth-
              coming *The Works of John Wesley* (Nashville: Abingdon
              Press, 1984–). Citation by sermon number, title, part, and
              section as contained in this definitive edition (e.g., Sermon
              146, "The One Thing Needful," I.3).

Statutes   *The Caroline Code, or Laudian Statutes,* vol. I of *Oxford
              University Statutes,* ed. G. R. M. Ward (London: William
              Pickering, 1845). Citation by title, section, chapter (e.g.,
              VI.3.4).

V.C.H.   *The Victoria History of the County of Oxford,* vol. 4, *The
              City of Oxford,* ed. Alan Crossley (Oxford: Oxford Univer-
              sity Press, 1979).

Chronology

1712	June 11	Benjamin Ingham born at Ossett, Yorkshire
1728		Became usher at Batley Grammar School, Yorkshire
1730	Oct 10	Entered Queen's College, Oxford
1733	Apr 18	First met John Wesley
1733	Sept 1	Started to keep a diary
1734	Apr 12	Made "resignation" to God
1734	June 17	Stood for his B.A. degree at Oxford; the following week, went home to Ossett
1735	Feb	Went back to Oxford after eight months in Ossett
1735	June 1	Ordained by Bishop Potter in Christ Church cathedral, Oxford
1735	June 4	Went to London and Matching as schoolmaster and curate
1735	Oct 21	Set sail for Georgia (America) with the Wesleys
1736	Apr	Moved to "Irene" (near Savannah) to work with the Indians in America
1737	[Jan]	"Found rest to his soul"
1737	Feb 26	Set sail for England to recruit helpers for Georgia
1737	Sept	Returned home to Ossett
1737	Oct 16	Sermon at Wakefield, Yorkshire, caused an uproar
1738	June 13	Set sail for Herrnhut, Germany, with John Wesley
1738	July 4	At Marienborn his heart "burned within"
1739	June 6	Prohibited from preaching in diocese of York; began field preaching, soon had fifty societies
1740	Apr 26	Dewsbury riots, Yorkshire, attributed to Ingham's preaching

1740	May 22	Tried to moderate between Wesley and Moravians
1740	Aug 24	Experienced assurance of salvation
1741		Broke with John Wesley over entire sanctification
1741	Nov 12	Married Lady Margaret Hastings, sister of Selina, Countess of Huntingdon; moved to Aberford, Yorkshire
1742	July 30	Placed his societies under control of Moravians
1743	July	Attended Moravian Synod at Hirschberg, Germany
1744	Apr 27	Attended court of George II with Address from Moravians
1744		Bought Lamb's Hill (after 1763, "Fulneck") near Pudsey, Yorkshire, for Moravians
1745	Feb 15	A son, Ignatius, born to Lady Margaret and Benjamin Ingham
1747	Apr	Attended Moravian Synod at Herrnhaag, Germany
1748		Published *A Collection of Hymns for Societies*
1749		Tension with the Moravians
1753	May 22	Methodist Conference considered uniting with Ingham
1755	May 6	Sat in Methodist Conference at Leeds, no union; set up Inghamite Conference, began ordinations
1759		Influenced by Sandeman and Glas; controversy reduced Inghamites to thirteen societies
1763		Published *A Discourse on the Faith and Hope of the Gospel*
1768	Apr 30	Lady Margaret died
1772	Dec 2	Benjamin Ingham died

Diary of an Oxford Methodist

Introduction

MIRRORS AND WINDOWS

As the March sun's rays began melting the Sunday morning frost off Oxford's manicured lawns, Benjamin Ingham made his way from Queen's to Lincoln College. He had traced this five-minute route at least a dozen times since first meeting John Wesley the previous April. Never before, though, had Ingham come so early with so many questions on his mind.

Ingham's arrival interrupted the thirty-year-old Wesley just as he had begun reading Clement of Rome (in Wake's translation). The Methodist leader, called Primitive Christianity by some of his lighthearted associates, laid aside Wake's volume in order to advise his younger friend. For half an hour the conversation ranged over topics of peculiar concern to Ingham and his half-dozen companions at Queen's College who were trying, like Wesley, to develop and follow a pattern of holy living.

Thanks to Ingham's careful diary keeping at this point, we know the questions and topics covered in that early morning conference in the spring of 1734. Should Ingham and his friends go to the Castle, site of the county jail, to receive the Sacrament with the prisoners? Wesley would have them go. What guidelines should they follow to promote temperance in their eating? Wesley had a list of ten rules for them to follow, containing not only specific dietary restrictions but also the general injunction, "Before you sit at full table, pray for help." What method should they use in measuring their spiritual pulse and their "temper of devotion"? Wesley suggested a pattern of self-examination ("recollection") along with a scheme of symbols for recording the results in their diaries. It seems he had a method for everything.

As the sun streamed more brightly across the chapel quadrangle into Wesley's room, the two friends suspended their conversation long enough for Ingham to fetch John Robson, one of Wesley's students at Lincoln. Before sitting down to breakfast at seven, Wesley proposed that Ingham and Robson get together once a week in order to encourage each other in their religious endeavors. He had an agenda in mind: they were to talk only of themselves and their progress, and of their activities at St. Thomas's Workhouse. They were to talk about nothing else and to dispute nothing. The two agreed to meet every Monday evening.

Over the breakfast table, the three friends addressed theological questions. Again, Ingham's diary reveals the gist of their "religious talk": the "three states of man," namely, the natural, the legal, and the evangelical, of which only the last two could lead to salvation. The conversation then turned to more practical aspects of the Methodist pattern of holy living. Wesley stressed the importance of hourly self-examination, of continual recollection, and of mutual confession of one's faults. To this end he impressed upon them the advantages not only of keeping but also of comparing diaries.

On that note the conference ended, Wesley dressed for morning prayers in the Lincoln College chapel, and Ingham returned to Queen's College to do the same there. Ingham's attendance at morning and evening chapel services was unfalteringly regular during this period, but on this particular occasion it seems the prayers had already begun to echo throughout the magnificent new chapel at Queen's as Ingham slipped into his place. His tardiness was most likely the result of his having taken time while in his room to note in his diary the events of the preceding two hours.

The diary, a Methodist's constant companion and conscience, was for Ingham a ledger of the soul and a mirror for the spirit, recording and reflecting the progress and pitfalls of his struggle to advance along the path of holy living. For us, however, this amazing little volume, divulging its secrets two and a half centuries later, not only casts new light on one man's pilgrimage of faith, but also opens a new window into the sometimes obscured corners of life and thought in Georgian Oxford.

The vignette of the early morning conference portrayed here is only a brief glimpse of the sort of historical narrative that, with the help of other contemporary documents, can be drawn from the pages of Ingham's diary.[1] Ingham's concern for carefully recording his activities, using a coded method that John Wesley was developing, may have caused him to be late for chapel that Sunday morning in 1733. But his persistence and thoroughness in following that procedure have provided us today with a key document not only for depicting the young Mr. Ingham, but also for comprehending more fully the extant diaries of other Oxford Methodists including Wesley himself. From these materials we may glean information that helps us understand more clearly the nature and design of Oxford Methodism, the formulation and development of Wesleyan theology, and the manner and style of university life in early eighteenth-century England.

THE OXFORD METHODIST DIARIES

The eighteenth century was an age of diarists. Persons of all sorts had a penchant for jotting down personal observations in little notebooks, foot-holds for the memory. The purpose of such an exercise, however, at times went beyond the simple desire for easy recollection of times and events. The diarist often hoped that recording and reflecting upon past activities would prove a means of moral or spiritual improvement.[2] This is especially true of the religious diarist whose explicit intention was to record God's providential activity but whose real hope was to improve in holiness.

The diary of Benjamin Ingham is by intention a religious diary even though it records a great deal of information that would seem beyond the

1 In this instance John Wesley's personal diary (OD IV, 100) and the weather diary of Thomas Hearne (MS., Hearne's Diaries 147, p. 160, Bodleian Library, Oxford) provided helpful details, such as Hearne's note for 17 March: "A very fine day, but a frost in the morning." See plate 1 for a view of the Chapel.
2 Even the anticipation of recording one's actions might help, as James Boswell noted in the preface to his journal: "Knowing that I am to record my transactions will make me more careful to do well. Or if I should go wrong, it will assist me in resolutions of doing better." Boswell's London Journal, 1762–63, ed. Frederick A. Pottle (New York: McGraw-Hill, 1950), p. 39. An anonymous diarist in 1680 noted at the beginning of the fifth book of his record, "The particeular grace I will endever to obtain duering the righting this Booke is spirituall recolection or the constant consideration of the presence of God. The Lord give me his grace that at the end I may perceive some incres in this vertue." MS., Rawlinson Collection, Q.e. 26–28, Bodleian Library, Oxford.

scope of such a design.[3] Ingham's model was the Wesley diary. John Wesley had begun to keep a diary at Oxford in 1725, about the time he decided to enter holy orders, shortly after receiving his bachelor of arts degree. His intent was to follow Jeremy Taylor's first rule of holy living, care of one's time. The diary was to be a means both of promoting and of charting his progress in holy living. The system of notation Wesley developed for his diary soon became a personalized code. Abbreviations, symbols, and a complex cipher were woven together to allow secrecy for many of his entries. It was a complicated but useful system that also saved time and space. When Charles Wesley decided to keep a diary in 1729, it was to his older brother John that he looked for a method.

> What particulars am I to take notice of? Am I to give my thoughts and words as well as deeds a place in it? I'm to mark all the good and ill I do; and what besides? What cipher can I make use of? If you would direct me to the same or a like method with your own, I would gladly follow it for I'm fully convinced of the usefulness of such an undertaking.[4]

Charles was not the only person to look to John for guidance. While a tutor and fellow of Lincoln College, John Wesley gained as many as forty or fifty adherents to his pattern of holy living during the next five or six years. Most were not among the handful of persons who met regularly in a little society with Wesley, and not all of them followed every aspect of Wesley's own scheme of thought and activity. But from references in the extant diaries of three (John Wesley, Benjamin Ingham, and George Whitefield), we know that at least fifteen of the Oxford Methodists learned the coded system of diary keeping that Wesley was developing.[5] The reasons for using this "code" were secrecy and economy; the purpose of everyone's using the same system was to enable them to share and compare diaries.

Ingham noted in his diary that he learned the Wesleyan method of

---

[3] John Free attacked the Methodists in 1758, describing their origins in this manner: "The name was first given to a few persons who were so uncommonly methodical as to keep a diary of the most trivial actions of their lives—as how many slices of bread and butter they ate. . . ." (quoted in Wesley's letter to Dr. Free, 24 August 1758).

[4] *Letters*, I, 236 (22 January 1728/29). See plates 2 and 3.

[5] Whitefield's diary for 1736 is in Add. MSS. 34068, British Library, London; a fragment from his diary for 1735 is in the Congregational Trust Hall Library, London.

keeping a diary through Charles Wesley rather than John, an intriguing clue to the organizational pattern of Oxford Methodism. Although Charles's diary has not survived, we can surmise that it would match the style of both Ingham's and John Wesley's since the latter two are nearly identical.[6] And a comparison of changes in format in the extant diaries shows how the diary method, as well as many other aspects of Oxford Methodism, was transmitted from John Wesley to those around him. During the last week of January 1733/34, John changed his diary format from a paragraph style to a fuller and more precise ("exacter") columnar style. After using the new system for a few days, John met with Charles on a Friday afternoon in early February and "talked of diaries," no doubt focusing on the new format. Presumably Charles then adopted the new scheme in his own diary. On the first day of March, Charles began teaching this "exacter" diary method to Ingham and Richard Smith, who were meeting regularly to study in Charles's room. Three days later, the new style appears in Ingham's diary. Two weeks after adopting this columnar format, Ingham began talking about it with some friends who were meeting regularly with him at Queen's; within a few days he taught *them* this "exacter" method.

The Ingham notebook, then, contains his first attempts at diary keeping and also reflects some of the major changes in the Wesleyan diary method. Because Ingham was learning the system and teaching it to others at the same time, his diary tends to be more explicit and less complicated than John Wesley's even though both used the same method. As a result, the format and content of the Ingham diary present information that is useful in illuminating many of Wesley's diary entries as well as fascinating in its own right. On the same day that Ingham began the "exacter" diary method, he also transcribed several important lists into his diary. On some blank pages in the front, he began recording many abbreviations, signs, and symbols used in the Wesleyan system, along with their meanings. Inside the front cover Ingham noted more symbols, defining each. Since Wesley left no such key to his coded scheme of signs and symbols, these two lists in Ingham's diary help unlock parts of the Wesley code that would otherwise defy explanation.[7]

6 One minor variance is Ingham's frequent use of James Weston's shorthand method, which Wesley did not begin to use in his diary until early 1735 (see Appendix 3).
7 Wesley regularly used abbreviations for frequently used words, such as prepositions and pronouns, and occasionally listed these in the front of manuscript

Because Wesley also neglected to place headings at the top of each column in the "exacter" format, several vertical rows of cryptic entries on each page of his diary lie mute without a hint of their significance. Fortunately, Ingham identified each column in his diary with a heading, thereby revealing the topics of the corresponding rows in the Wesley entries: temper of devotion, degree of recollection, resolutions broken, resolutions kept, blessings.[8] The coded entries in both diaries now begin to make sense, disclosing an intricate record of self-examination that sheds new light on the spirit of religious contemplation that characterized the early Wesleyans.

Ingham's hourly description of his activities, besides being more explicit, tends to be fuller than Wesley's.[9] For example, Ingham frequently outlines the specific content of conversations, at times recounts the positions held in arguments among his friends, and often records the focus of his meditations or prayers. When Ingham visited Wesley on the morning of 17 March 1734 (described earlier), the latter simply noted in his diary, "Ingham, religious talk," followed by "Robson, tea, religious talk of diary." Ingham, on the other hand, delineated the details of the conference in an expanded version that occupies fourteen lines in his diary. This richness of description, along with the record of pervasive self-analysis and the keys to the Wesleyan method of diary keeping, makes the Ingham diary a most important document for understanding the life and thought of Oxford students and the early Methodists in the 1730s.

THE OXFORD METHODISTS

Organization

The picture of Oxford Methodism revealed by Ingham's diary bears little resemblance to the simplistic portrait of the "Holy Club" described in most studies of the Wesleyan movement. The image of a single group of

---

volumes that might be read by other persons, such as his commonplace book containing poetry (John Wesley MS., Colman Collection I, MA).

[8] See the description of the "exacter" diary method in Appendix 1.

[9] These diaries are neither absolutely precise nor totally exhaustive, however. Most entries are listed to the nearest quarter hour; in many instances the activity may have taken slightly more or less time than that noted, and in some cases may not have been the sole focus of that time period. Cf., for example, 10 December and note 121; 23 February, note 209.

Methodists meeting in John Wesley's room at Lincoln College is an impression that is incomplete and even misleading. Unfortunately, most descriptions of the first rise of Methodism resemble a collection of twice-told tales, and even recent attempts at revision are usually only reinterpretations of inaccurate and inadequate information.[1]

The old stereotyped image of the Holy Club was fixed as an icon in the Methodist memory by Marshal Claxton's painting, *The Institution of Methodism.*[2] His portrayal is based primarily on a letter written by John Wesley in October 1732.[3] The account as given in Wesley's letter is misleading in two ways—in the simplistic version of the origin of the group, supposedly in November 1729, and in the description of its structure, which was even then beginning to change. Wesley's own diary offers a corrective to the first problem, showing the complex early development of the group over a twenty-month period from the summer of 1729 to the fall of 1730.[4] Ingham's diary, together with Wesley's, helps solve the second problem by revealing the complicated network of relationships that was the matrix for Methodist activities after the middle of 1732.

Historians have been confused from the outset in trying to describe

1 The currently popular version of the story has Charles Wesley as the "first Methodist" organizing "the Holy Club" in May 1729, then turning the leadership of the "Methodists" over to his brother John on 22 November of that year. In fact, however, there was no *group* in May 1729 (Charles Wesley and William Morgan were simply studying and attending the Sacrament together); John Wesley returned to Oxford for two months in *June* 1729 (and engaged in the same activities he did later on his return in November); the term "Holy Club" was not coined until November *1730* (and dropped six months later); and the name "Methodist" does not appear until the summer of *1732*. For a survey of the literature on this topic, see Richard P. Heitzenrater, *The Elusive Mr. Wesley* (Nashville: Abingdon Press, 1984), vol. 2, part 2, especially pp. 204–7.

2 Marshal Claxton's misleading painting, done in the 1850s, has been reproduced many times, often with the caption "The Holy Club" or "The Rev John Wesley and his Friends at Oxford." See *Proceedings of the Wesley Historical Society* 2 (1899), p. 28. Major errors include the number of persons portrayed, the particular combination of persons at one place and time, and the location of the group in John Wesley's room as *the* meeting place.

3 *Letters,* I, 335–44. This letter to Richard Morgan, Sr., contains a description and defense of Wesley's activities up to that point; it is prefixed to most editions of Wesley's *Journal* (see note 6 below), sometimes under the title, "The Rise and Design of Oxford Methodism." See 26 October, note 66.

4 OD II, 5–66. See also Richard P. Heitzenrater, *John Wesley and the Oxford Methodists, 1725–1735* (Ph.D. diss., Duke University; Ann Arbor, Mich.: University Microfilms, 1972), pp. 46–125.

Oxford Methodism, especially during the period from 1732 to 1735. John Wesley would seem to be the one best suited to clarify any difficulties in that regard, but in fact his own attempts to do so merely set the pattern for much of the confusion that later prevailed. For instance, on the matter of how many Methodists belonged to the movement at Oxford, Wesley claimed in January 1734 that there were only four members in his little society, whereas his student, Richard Morgan, Jr., told his father that there were seven.[5] Wesley's diary confirms that there were only three people meeting with him at that time, making four in the group. Morgan seems to have included in his reckoning individuals who were associated with the Methodists but did not meet regularly with Wesley's own personal group. That is to say, Morgan answered the question, How many Methodists are at Oxford? whereas Wesley answered the question, How many persons meet with me in my little society? On the other hand, if Wesley's diary is used as the measure of historical accuracy, his later recollection that his little society grew to fourteen or fifteen by 1735 must have been calculated to answer the Morgan-type question, for his diary indicates that the group meeting with him in 1735 is no larger than seven or eight people at the most, although he would have known of at least as many more around the university who were following his methods.

Ingham's diary helps clear up the confusion. Oxford Methodism consisted not of one group but of many. The core society was indeed gathered around John Wesley and by the beginning of 1732 consisted of six persons. But this simple pattern of one group, complicated only by some fluctuation of membership, began to change in mid-1732 when John Clayton joined the Wesleyan movement. Clayton already had a "small flock" meeting with him at Brasenose College for study and devotion, and his joining with the Wesleyan company gave the Methodist movement a two-level structure, the Wesley group and the Clayton subgroup.[6] Another satellite group appeared in town in 1733 led by Miss Potter, to whom Wesley also provided guidance and with whom he occasionally

[5] *Letters,* I, 365, 368.

[6] Clayton encouraged his friends to engage their acquaintances in the work, "by which means," he told Wesley, "I hope in God we shall get at least an advocate for us, if not a brother and a fellow labourer, in every College in town." One of Clayton's pupils (William Nowell?) "promised to try what he can do with a cousin of his at Queen's" (Ingham?). *The Journal of the Rev. John Wesley,* ed. Nehemiah Curnock (London: Epworth Press, 1916), vol. 8, 281 (letter of 6 September 1732).

met. Ingham's diary indicates that in 1733 Charles Wesley also had at least one subgroup meeting with him at Christ Church, consisting first of himself and Ingham, and later including Richard Smith, Henry Evans, and Richard Carter, all Christ Church men except Ingham. Ingham, Smith, Evans, and Carter, like the persons in Clayton's subgroup, did not meet with John Wesley's small company but learned the Wesleyan pattern and methods through a member of Wesley's company who was the leader of their subgroup.

It is somewhat startling to discover that Benjamin Ingham, traditionally thought to be a member of the so-called Holy Club did not in fact attend the meetings of Wesley's little society. Equally startling, however, is the revelation in Ingham's diary that, having learned the Methodist pattern of living from Charles Wesley (with occasional consultations with John), Benjamin Ingham himself started several groups at Queen's College, faithfully attempting to duplicate Wesley's scheme in his own college. This represents a third level in the organization of Methodist cell groups at Oxford.

Ingham's descriptions of the meetings of these various clusters of persons constituting Oxford Methodism reflect some of the complexity and variety evident in the movement by 1733. For instance, the most common *time* for their meetings was from seven to nine o'clock in the evening, but some of the groups met at other times, such as one o'clock in the afternoon, for their reading and/or religious talk. The *purpose* of the meeting sometimes determined the schedule. Some groups met regularly at three in the afternoon on fast days for breakfast (to break the fast) as well as for study and discussion, and at least one small band prepared for Sundays by meeting late on Saturday evenings to "watch," pray, and read. Other groups met for purposes that did not necessarily determine their schedule: to read logic, to study experimental philosophy, to compare diaries, or to read the Greek Testament. The *frequency* of meeting also varied among the groups, some meeting only once a week, others meeting on a regular schedule as often as three or four times a week. The longevity of the groups varied widely. In some cases, four or five meetings were sufficient for them to accomplish a particular purpose such as reading a book together. In others, such as Ingham's Friday evening group or the Wednesday–Saturday–Sunday group, meetings persisted regularly for months in spite of several changes in focus and/or personnel. The *place* of meeting also differed from one group to the next. Many rotated their meetings among the rooms and colleges of the members, some on a fairly regular schedule, as did John Wesley's group, and others in a more random fashion. Some groups met consistently in the same place— Ingham's meetings with Charles Wesley's little band always took place in Charles's room, never in Ingham's room at Queen's or in the rooms of the two or three other Christ Church men in that group. The Friday night gathering at Queen's met almost exclusively at John Ford's room for five months before switching to Ingham's room in April 1734.

The *composition* of these groups is as varied as their patterns of meetings. The size of the groups generally ranged from three to six persons, although some regular meetings involved only two. Although most were men associated with the university, at least one woman, Miss Potter, was hosting (and perhaps leading) a group in town. Some combinations were mostly undergraduates; others included masters and bachelors, tutors and fellows. Although there was some identification of groups with specific colleges, there was no necessary limitation in this regard. Christ Church, Lincoln, Queen's, and Brasenose were the primary centers, but Merton, Exeter, Pembroke, and Magdalen had their Methodists as well. The diaries also reveal that considerable shifting and overlapping of personnel took place among as well as within the groups. Ingham, as noted, met with Charles Wesley's group at Christ Church, and although two of those Christ Church men (Wesley and Carter) never came to Ingham's groups, two others did begin to attend meetings at Queen's College (Smith and Evans). James Hervey of Lincoln College, often portrayed as a close associate of John Wesley in the Holy Club, appears more often in Ingham's diary than Wesley's, first as a member of a small company centered at Lincoln which included Ingham (but not Wesley!), and then as a new person "admitted" into the group of mostly Queen's College men that met on Wednesday–Saturday–Sunday. John Robson and Thomas Greives, also Lincoln College students and both associated with John Wesley's little society, also shifted their affiliation, at least for a time, to meet with one or another of Ingham's groups. Will Clements, one of John Wesley's students at Lincoln and a regular participant in his Methodist group, became piqued at his tutor early in 1733. Wesley noted in his diary that Clements was talking of "breaking up our society." Within days, he stopped meeting with Wesley and began attending Miss Potter's group.[7] The Ingham and Wesley diaries are sprinkled with notations of "prevailing" upon persons to join their activities or of "convincing" persons to

[7]   OD III, 66 (15 April 1733), 67 (19 April 1733).

adopt a particular notion or practice; other notations indicate when a friend had "revolted" or "left us," not wanting to meet with them anymore, or had "agreed" to meet with a group only if certain other parties would not be present. In some cases, Wesley himself seems to have instigated changes in the composition of groups in order to further certain individuals' progress in particular aspects of the Methodist design.

Many of the persons trying to live by the Methodist pattern were reluctant to adopt such practices as regular fasting, early rising, or meticulous diary keeping. Even the most active participants were guilty of occasional backsliding. "Membership" might therefore be too definite a category to use in trying to describe the ambiguities and complexities of an individual's relationship to the Methodist movement as seen in the diaries. There was no rite of initiation, no cause for exclusion. One's association was totally voluntary. In spite of their lists of resolutions and questions, the Methodists had no required regulations, no measurable parameters of membership, no single meeting place. Clayton had discouraged Wesley from organizing an avowed society with a set of rules, pointing out that "it would be no additional tie upon yourselves and perhaps [be] a snare for the conscience of those weak brethren that might choose to come among you."[8]

By 1733, the association of Wesley and his friends was no longer called a "club" and certainly had begun to assume a structure that belied such simplistic designations. The term "Methodist," first used the previous year, had appeared coincidentally with a new stage of complexity in their organizational pattern. From that point on, it is difficult to think in terms of "members" or "nonmembers"; it is not merely a matter of affiliation with a particular group or adherence to a particular standard. The primary requisite for being called a Methodist was the desire to work out one's salvation and to engage in the pursuit of perfection. To catch the essence of Methodism at Oxford is to recognize this impulse as well as the developing lifestyle that it elicited.[9] Accordingly, the diaries of the Oxford Methodists do not report clear-cut designations of who "belonged" to this blossoming movement so much as they display a diverse array of persons whose Methodist inclinations can and must be measured individually by their seriousness of intention and the degree of their participation in a Wesleyan pattern of life and thought.

8 *Letters,* I, 352 ([25] July 1733).
9 See Heitzenrater, *Oxford Methodists,* pp. 35–45.

Activities

The various activities that characterized the life of the Oxford Methodists, such as fasting, visiting the prisons, rising early, attending the Sacrament, helping the poor, and meeting for study and prayer, were not in themselves new or unique to the university scene, even in post-Restoration England. Samuel Wesley, father of John and Charles, had visited the prisons at Oxford when he was a student at Exeter College in the 1680s.[10] George Fothergill reports that he himself had gone frequently to his tutor's room at Queen's College in 1722 with other pupils for prayers at nine in the evening.[11] Tutors as well as preachers were enamored of various "methods" by which to inculcate their programs or ideas.[12] Certainly Methodists were not the only persons to attend the Sacrament at Christ Church and St. Mary's.[13] What made Oxford Methodism distinctive, however, was the peculiar combination of activities and personalities that composed the movement, and even more particularly, the intensity and persistence with which their "methods" permeated (or were intended to permeate) their lives.

The Wesleyans were, in the first instance, a small study group or literary society made up of persons with pietist inclinations. From their first setting out on the path of holy living, the Wesley brothers were doing little more than following diligently the stipulations and expectations of the university statutes with regard to the life and study of Oxford students. Charles's own personal "reformation" late in 1728 was in fact

10   *Letters,* I, 338 (Samuel Wesley to John Wesley, 28 September 1730).
11   *The Fothergills of Ravenstonedale,* ed. Catherine Thornton and Frances McLaughlin (London: William Heinemann, 1906), p. 67.
12   Ambrose Bonwicke, whose life of piety was one of several models imitated by the Oxford Methodists, wrote to his father shortly after arriving at St. John's College, Cambridge, "My tutor did not talk to me about a Method, etc., as I hear is customary; but I have (thinking it convenient) proposed to myself one." A schedule of weekly studies follows. Theological and homiletical "method" was the subject of many treatises, and the general concern for promoting Christian virtues through disciplined living is epitomized in the tract, *The Way of Living in a Method, and by Rule,* first published in 1722 and widely distributed by the Society for Promoting Christian Knowledge (S.P.C.K.) well into the next century (see Appendix 3).
13   Ingham adopted the convention of referring to the Eucharist as *the* Sacrament, a practice followed throughout this edition. Wesley frequently noted the attendance at St. Mary's for the Sacrament at the beginning of each term; the number was usually very low (see 9 October, note 50 and 23 April, note 38).

coincident with a resurgence of concern among many of the university officers that the tutors

> discharge their duty by double diligence in informing their respective pupils in their Christian duty, and . . . in recommending to them the frequent and careful reading [of] the Scriptures and such other books as may serve more effectually to promote Christianity, sound principles, and orthodox faith.[14]

Before the autumn of 1730, the two Wesley brothers and their one or two friends can be defined as a group only insofar as they were becoming of one mind in their intention to lead holy lives and, starting in the spring of that year, were meeting together regularly for study and "religious talk." The public did not take any notice of them until they began, toward the end of 1730, to attend regularly the Sacrament at Christ Church and to visit the prisons and the poor folk in town. To these public acts of piety and charity, which brought upon them the name Holy Club (succeeded shortly thereafter by the title Godly Club), they added in 1732 a pattern of disciplined religious practices modeled on the life and thought of the Early Church, most notably the observance of the Stationary fasts on Wednesdays and Fridays. These activities and the theology that lay behind them brought upon the group a new name, "Methodist," which soon found its way onto the printed page and thereby fastened itself on English minds and lips.[15]

14 Instructions given in a broadside beginning "At a General Meeting of the Vice-Chancellor, Heads of Houses, and Proctors of the University of Oxford, on Monday, Dec. 2nd, 1728. . . ." It should be remembered that most of the students at Oxford were preparing for holy orders; the university statutes required the tutors "to imbue the scholars committed to his tuition and rule with virtuous morals, and to instruct them in approved authors, and most of all in the rudiments of religion, and the articles of doctrine that were published in the Synod at London in the year 1562; and to the utmost of his power he is to make them conform to the discipline publicly received in the Church of England." *Statutes*, III.2.

15 The earliest use of the term "Methodist" in relation to the Wesleyans in any contemporary document is in a letter of 5 September 1732 from John Clayton to John Wesley. *Journal of John Wesley*, vol. 8, 281. See pp. 29f. below. The term was also used in the first published attack on Wesley and his comrades in *Fog's Weekly Journal* on 9 December 1732, and became fixed as their common title after the publication in February 1733 of an anonymous apologetic tract entitled *The Oxford Methodists*, which quoted at length Wesley's letter to Richard Morgan of October 1732 (see note 3 and Appendix 3).

By January 1733, then, the basic design of Oxford Methodism had emerged insofar as the main branches of its activities are concerned: study, devotion, charity. During the following two years the pattern was put to the test with several new adherents trying out the Wesleyan methods of pursuing inward and outward holiness. This increase in numbers was accompanied by more variety and intensity in their activities along with a certain amount of tension and conflict, both internal and external. These last two years the Wesleys spent in residence at the university represent the fullest expression of Oxford Methodism, and it is this period that is described in Ingham's diary.

SCHOLARSHIP   The scholarly concerns of the Wesleyan movement at this stage are clearly reflected in the pages of Ingham's diary. The range of books read by Ingham and his friends at Queen's is almost identical to the spectrum read by Wesley's group. The classical authors basic to an Oxford education are clearly evident: Homer, Cicero, Virgil, Juvenal. Other common textbooks in the Oxford curriculum appear regularly, such as those by Aldrich, Sanderson, Gravesande, and Kennet. At the same time, the type of devotion to be expected in a pietist reading bibliography is well represented in the works of Thomas à Kempis, Law, Taylor, Horneck, Goodman, and Francke. The sermons of Norris, Lucas, and Beveridge follow the same line. The meditative perspective is found in works by Hall, Ken, and Gerhard. Scougal, Scupoli, and Rodriguez bring a mystical element into the list. The lives of Bonnell, Bonwicke, and de Renty provide patterns of holy living, and *The Second Spira* (by Richard Sault) gives warning of consequences in the other direction. The writings of the Early Fathers of the Church appear frequently, as do works about them by Cave, Deacon, and Reeves. The Greek New Testament and Robert Nelson's *Fasts and Festivals* were staple reading for Ingham and his friends, and the *Country Parson's Advice to his Parishioners* was in many ways the foundation of their whole approach to covenantal holy living.[16]

Only a handful of authors appearing on Ingham's pages are not mentioned by Wesley during these years, including Robert Jenkin on the rea-

[16] See Appendix 3 for books read by Ingham. Ingham read through the *Country Parson's Advice* (1680) at least six times, sometimes alone, at other times with friends. His "resignation" to a holy life during Holy Week of 1734 was accompanied by a series of resolutions, largely "in the Country Parson's words," carefully transcribed into his diary (see pp. 165–69).

sonableness of Christianity, Johannes Leusden's edition of the Greek Testament, Simon Patrick on the Sacrament and on fasting, Thomas Ittig on the Early Fathers, and an apparently anonymous treatise entitled *The Penitential Office for the Sixteenth Day of the Month.*[17] Although works of divinity predominate in the readings at meetings of the Methodists during this period, providing the grist for their religious talk, the popular literature of the day is not completely disregarded by Ingham or, in fact, by Wesley. In the spring of 1734 Wesley had begun to advise some students against reading "secular" writings, including even the classics, but he never made it a general rule. Wesley never completely avoided such literature himself, content to "sanctify" his reading program by including a preponderance of good religious books.[18] And even though Ingham at one point "talked against [the] poets," we find no pervasive antipathy in him toward poets or secular writers.[19] His personal reading included not only the *Tatler, Guardian,* and *Spectator,* but also occasional reading from Voltaire, Pope, Vanbrugh, Milton, Herbert, and Young.

Religious writings nevertheless made up the core of the Methodists' reading program. When no published work was available that seemed in Wesley's mind to satisfy their needs, he circulated handwritten copies of material that he himself had composed on important subjects, just as he passed around various lists of rules, resolutions, and questions for his friends to ponder. It is not surprising that we find Ingham reading Wesley's crucial letter to Richard Morgan, Sr., which gives the rationale for the Methodists' development at Oxford, and Wesley's circular "letter of company." Ingham sometimes would read a Wesley sermon when meeting with his friends, such as the sermon on the Sacrament widely used by the Oxford Methodists.[20] In one instance, Ingham shared with his

17   See 16 May, note 128. This diary contains the only references to this treatise I have been able to find.
18   Wesley was supported on this point by the opinion of John Clayton. *Letters,* I, 391 (2 August 1734).
19   Ingham's confession on 7 August 1734 of having "indulged vain thoughts of being a fine poet" seems directed more against vanity than poetry.
20   This "sermon" was for the most part extracted from the works of Robert Nelson and William Beveridge on the necessity of frequent attendance upon the Sacrament, composed in 1732, as Wesley later said, "for the use of my pupils at Oxford." He later abridged his own extract even further, publishing it in his collected edition of sermons in 1788 as "The Duty of Constant Communion" (Sermon 101). Ingham also made copies of John Clayton's sermons; see 24 February.

friends a sermon Wesley had preached that very morning in St. Mary's. Another Wesley composition in manuscript form that received wide circulation, though not universal acceptance, was his essay ("treatise" or *genesis problematica*) on the Stationary fasts, written during the summer of 1733. Wesley eventually resorted to publishing some of the material that was circulating among the Methodists, such as his collection of prayers, which Ingham notes having read at Charles Wesley's in January 1734 only three days after John received the printed copies from London.[21]

Ingham also tried his hand at writing religious treatises. In addition to the exercises for his degree, which included writing *geneses*[22] on the Sacrament and on the Stationary fasts, he also wrote what he called "a short scheme of the reasonableness of our practices of rising, fasting, etc." as well as a "scheme for daily examination." The diary also shows him writing three sermons, beginning to compose the first one, on Matthew 19:17, by writing a *genesis problematica solitaria*. It appears, however, that Ingham did not distribute or use his own writings in his study groups.

The Methodist program often fused academic and devotional interests, as can be seen in their meetings, which consisted primarily of two types of activity: (1) study and discussion of useful books that would help them promote their common design, and (2) religious talk about their progress in holy living, which included praying ("the chief subject of which was charity" or love), reviewing their progress in holiness (which often included comparing diaries), considering their charitable activities, passing out "pious books" for their own and others' use, and determining the duties of the following day or days.[23] It appears that those who were more intensely involved in the Methodist design participated in the religious talk sessions, whereas the reading sessions were at times attended by a wider range of interested persons.[24]

Although the diaries never indicate explicitly that a meeting as such is

---

21 *A Collection of Forms of Prayer for Every Day in the Week,* John Wesley's first published book. See OD IV, 46 (17 January 1733/34).

22 See Glossary, s.v. "Genesis."

23 The agenda of a typical Methodist meeting, never fully outlined in the diaries, can be deduced from the descriptions of Richard Morgan, Jr., in a letter to his father (*Letters,* I, 365) and of John Gambold in "The Character of Mr John Wesley," *Methodist Magazine* 21 (March 1798), p. 119.

24 Richard Morgan, Jr., attended only the reading and study portion of Wesley's meetings since he was "so little experienced in piety and charity," as Wesley explained to the boy's father (or until he "had acquired a pretty good stock of religion," to quote the son's report to his father). *Letters,* I, 360, 365.

taking place, this usually can be deduced from the listing of those who are gathering, and the description of what they are doing and when the activity is taking place. We can tell for example that when Ingham is getting together with Watson, Washington, Smyth, and Ford every Friday evening from about seven to nine, reading William Law's *Serious Call,* and having "religious talk," they are having a Wesleyan-type meeting for scholarly study and discussion. The term "religious talk" in itself is not a clear indicator of a Methodist meeting, since its most common use is to describe the nature of simple conversations between two persons, noted several times each day in the diaries. But when Ingham meets with Robson on Monday nights for "religious talk," we know from earlier diary entries that they are discussing their spiritual progress and their charitable activities at the workhouse. There are many occasions when the time, place, and personnel indicate a Methodist meeting, but the description "religious talk" is not specific enough to determine the precise nature of their discussions.

DEVOTION   The various clusters of Wesleyans meeting around the university and city of Oxford were, in effect, following the *Country Parson's Advice* to unite in friendly societies, "engaging each other in their several and respective combinations to be helpful and serviceable to one another in all good Christian ways."[25] To that end, their corporate endeavors extended beyond the basic program of study and discussion. Confession was a part of their group experience: not only did they compare diaries at some of their meetings as a means of confessing their own sins, but they did not hesitate to point out the faults of others, howbeit striving to do so "with tenderness." Reprimands among friends for past sins were complemented by methods of encouraging proper conduct in the present— Ingham and his friends developed a series of hand signals to warn each other in public when they saw or heard one of their company saying or doing something that "did not tend to God's glory." The discussion at their meetings often focused on their progress in holy living, noted in Ingham's diary as "religious talk of ourselves and our friends." Ingham's

25   *Country Parson's Advice,* p. 81. In a letter to the editor of the *London Magazine* in 1760, John Wesley noted his having first read this work some thirty years before, quoting this passage and adding that "a few young gentlemen then at Oxford approved of and followed the advice. They were all zealous Churchmen, and . . . for their exact regularity they were soon nicknamed Methodists" (letter dated 12 December 1760).

daily entries exhibit a constant concern for friendship and friends, one recurring question in that regard being "how to manage 'em." John Wesley's letter of company, a document now lost, seems to have offered suggestions (a *method,* if you please) to the Methodists on how to promote holy living through the proper management of one's personal associations.[26]

The life of devotional piety encouraged and nurtured by the association of Wesleyans at Oxford was grounded in the personal and private exercises of meditation, self-examination, prayer, and Bible reading. The meditative practices used by the Methodists at this point were part of the mystic, holy living tradition that goes back to the Early Fathers of the Church, but which had been rationalized, regularized, and methodized in Europe during the fifteenth and sixteenth centuries.[27] Joseph Hall helped transmit this tradition to England through his *Art of Divine Meditation,* which Wesley abridged in 1733 and used with his friends.[28] Several other books of meditation (or containing meditations) were also used regularly by Ingham, Wesley, and their companions, including Johann Gerhard's *Meditations,* Thomas Ken's *Meditations,* Anthony Horneck's *Best Exercise,* Simon Patrick's *Christian Sacrifice,* Francis de Sales's *Introduction to a Devout Life,* Jeremy Taylor's *Holy Living* and *Holy Dying,* and Robert Nelson's *Practice of True Devotion* (see Appendix 3). The subjects of these meditations range from the life and death of Christ, the attributes of God, and the virtues desired by the Christian, to the follies of the world, the faults and infirmities of the sinner, and the impending judgment. At least an hour a day was set aside for meditating, the purpose of which was to help one develop self-knowledge and improve in virtue.[29] Charles Wesley advised Ingham that if he were "irrecollected"

[26] The idea that persons "become such as the company they keep" is a theme found in several works the Methodists read, such as Richard Lucas's sermon *The Influence of Conversation* (1707), sec. 1, and Robert Nelson's *Practice of True Devotion* (1698), I.vi (see Appendix 3).

[27] See Louis Martz, *The Poetry of Meditation* (New Haven: Yale University Press, 1954), pp. 4–13.

[28] Wesley was careful to include Hall's observation that it was more possible "to live without a heart than to be devout without meditation." John Wesley MS., Colman Collection VII, p. 29, MA. Cf. Joseph Hall, *The Art of Divine Meditation* (1607), ch. XXXVII (see Appendix 3).

[29] Wesley had set times for meditation during this period; Ingham was less regular, but generally meditated early in the morning or before his daily self-examination in the afternoon. John Gambold advised Ingham that meditation on

for two consecutive hours, he might use a book of meditations for at least a half-hour to recover a state of "recollection" or spiritual composure. The Wesley brothers had learned the importance of meditation from their mother, who also had pointed out to them in March 1734 that their schedule might include even more time for meditation, which she saw as "incomparably the best means to spiritualize our affections, confirm our judgments, and add strength to our pious resolutions of any exercise whatever."[30]

Meditation was at the heart of the spiritual exercises that the Methodists used to develop virtue, the wellspring of the holy life. Self-knowledge was an important goal of meditation, and self-examination was a primary means to that end. One facet of the scheme or method used by Wesley and the Methodists was similar to that outlined by Ignatius of Loyola in his *Spiritual Exercises*. A "general examination" demanded accountability for one's thoughts, words and actions on the basis of a list of questions:

Did I in the morning plan the business of the day?
Have I been simple and recollected in everything?
Have I been or seemed angry?
Have I used the ejaculations once an hour?

These and similar questions, numbering about fifteen in most of the Wesley brothers' various revisions of the list, were the framework for a daily examination of conscience, measuring how well one was adhering to the habits of holy living outlined therein.[31] Ingham used a general examination of this sort weekly (on Friday evenings) for several months before changing to a daily examination in January 1734. In March he copied the Wesleys' list of "general" questions into his diary and began using it as a basis for hourly examination throughout the day (recorded in the "exacter" diary format), still noting a "daily examination" every

God's omnipresence and peculiar care of us was one of the "best means to acquire all the virtues" (see 1 April).

30 See 20 June and *Letters*, I, 384.

31 OD II contains rough notes and resolutions at the front and back from which John Wesley drew up his list of General Questions; revisions of that list he subsequently transcribed into OD III and OD IV. Ingham's list, copied from Charles Wesley's and almost identical to John's, is found on pp. 119–20. Whitefield's diary for 1736 also contains this list of fifteen questions (Add. MSS. 34068, British Library, London, p. 2; cf. Arnold Dallimore, *George Whitefield* [London: Banner of Truth Trust, 1970], vol. 1, 80); see also Ignatius of Loyola, *Spiritual Exercises* (1548), secs. 24–31, "Particular and Daily Examen."

afternoon and using the term "General Examination" on Friday evening to designate his review of the previous week.

In addition to the list of General Questions, Wesley's scheme also contained lists of Particular Questions (in the Ignatian manner) which provided the basis for "particular examination."[32] This exercise featured the special virtues assigned for each day of the week, with lists of questions arranged under those virtues:

Sunday	Love of God
Monday	Love of Man
Tuesday	Humility
Wednesday	Mortification and Self-denial
Thursday	Resignation and Meekness
[Friday	Mortification and Self-denial][33]
Saturday	Thankfulness

The purpose of this endeavor was to ferret out specific sins and to plant in their place the corresponding virtue. These were not rules that demanded obedience; the emphasis was not on the performance of certain good works. Rather, the questions were designed to use the examination of one's performance as a measure of the development of virtue, and thus to gauge the inclination of one's heart and affections, an unfailingly inward focus.[34]

As with most forms of vital Christian spirituality, the Oxford Methodists' life of meditative piety was marked by regular, one could say constant, use of prayer. Ingham's daily activities, as noted in his diary, are bracketed by periods of prayer which become more and more frequent as the year passes. He is careful to differentiate various sorts of prayer. *Private prayer* is distinguished from *Public Prayers* (the service in the Church) but does not necessarily indicate spontaneous or personal prayers.

---

32 Wesley's lists can be found in OD III, OD IV, and OD V. Ingham seems not to have stressed this aspect of self-examination to the same extent that John Wesley did, although he certainly would have been familiar with the process from using the Wesleyan method and from having read William Law's *A Serious Call to a Devout and Holy Life* (1729), ch. XXIII (see Appendix 3).

33 The questions for Wednesday served also for Friday. See OD III, vii; OD IV, iii, and the pages preceding Wesley's November summary; OD V, v; and John Wesley, *A Collection of Forms of Prayer for Every Day in the Week* (1733) (see Appendix 3).

34 For a discussion of the theology that underlies this practice, see the section on theology below.

He frequently notes "private prayer" when in the company of his friends, and even when alone he used many prayers from various books of devotion. *Ejaculatory prayers,* short prayers of praise or petition, were used by many of the Methodists at the start of every hour. Ingham began to use these prayers hourly in March 1734, along with the hourly self-examination that was the basis of the newly begun "exacter" form of diary keeping. The Oxford Methodists also used a set of specific *collects* for nine o'clock, noon, and three o'clock, besides special collects for the beginning of each day of the week. Ingham copied many of these frequently used prayers into the front of his diary. Wesley had also developed a collection of prayers arranged according to the virtues for each day of the week. Thinking this useful for his friends, he published selections from this collection in 1733, incorporating questions for self-examination. The Oxford Methodists also used many other sources for the wide variety of forms of prayer noted in the diary, such as prayers of resignation, preparatory prayers for the Sacrament, and prayers to be used before reading at night. The methodical regularity of their practice of prayer seems to have drawn an occasional friendly protest, such as Anthony Natt's expressed desire at one point that they might pray "indifferent as to the days."

Bible reading was an essential part of the Methodists' devotional life, as well as a fundamental basis for their theological reflection; here again the spiritual and scholarly concerns overlap and fuse. Wesley later reflected that from "the very beginning" at Oxford, the Methodists were, "each of them, *homo unius libri*—a man of one book."[35] In view of the wide-ranging bibliography read by Wesley and his companions, this statement should be understood as corresponding to the definition of a Methodist provided by Wesley's *Complete English Dictionary* of 1753: "One that lives according to the method laid down in the Bible." The practical side of this guiding perspective is evident in Wesley's dictum, passed on to Ingham by John Gambold on the first day of April 1734, that one must "try all human writings [and actions] by the test of Scripture."[36] Wesley's diary during this period reveals an increasing amount of time spent reading the Bible (in English, Greek, and Hebrew), the study of Scripture providing the major, almost exclusive, focus of his study group during the fall and winter of 1734/35. Ingham also read and studied the Bible regularly, resolving in mid-November 1734 to read three chapters in the Greek New Testament every day, morning, noon, and night. In

35 Sermon 107, "On God's Vineyard," I.1.
36 Wesley's version in OD II reads "actions" in place of "human writings."

some instances, he shared the activity with a colleague. In the course of the one year recorded in this diary, Ingham read the Greek Testament through the Book of Acts twice, read Romans once, and Matthew four times. He abridged Daniel Whitby's *Paraphrase and Commentary on the New Testament* through Hebrews, studied the verses marked with an asterisk in Johannes Leusden's edition of the Greek Testament, and read August Hermann Francke's *Manuductio ad lectionem Scripturæ Sacræ*.[37] In addition to this, Ingham read the Bible frequently to children and "old people" at the workhouses.

These private aspects of the Methodists' personal lifestyle (meditation, self-examination, prayer, and Bible reading) were complemented by other activities that were also personal but, by their nature, could not be quite so private. Various acts of self-denial, such as fasting and early rising, were for the Methodists an important means of evoking and exhibiting humility, a necessary corollary to their basic principle of loving God and neighbor. The opening pages of Ingham's diary show him grappling with the question of fasting. Within a week he was persuaded by Wesley that the Stations (Wednesday and Friday fasts) should be observed, but only after subsequent readings in Wesley's treatise on the subject and Robert Nelson's comments on fasting did Ingham actually begin to abstain from eating until three o'clock on the Stationary days. Others at the university might not have noticed whether or not the Methodists were having their breakfast at three in the afternoon instead of eight in the morning since the latter was not a community meal. But the statutes required that students both reside and take their meals in the colleges and any Methodist's absence from the Hall at dinnertime on Wednesday or Friday would be noticed.[38] This attempt to follow the discipline practiced by the Early Church was not unique to the Wesleyans by any means. The Church of England in fact prescribed fasting but it was typically promoted and practiced by the high-church, nonjuring pietists whose religious zeal struck many observers as bordering on fastidious fanaticism. Wesley, who began his faithful observance of the Stations under the influence of John Clay-

---

[37]   The asterisked verses in Leusden contained all the words used by the sacred writers; see 10 July, note 32. Francke's handbook outlined a method for studying scripture both as respects the "letter" (grammatical, historical and analytic) and the "spirit" (expository, doctrinal, inferential, and practical) of the Word. See Appendix 3.

[38]   *Statutes*, III.1.

ton in 1732, was later told by one of his Methodist pupils, "I believe if I would go into the hall on fast days all my other activities would be less taken notice of."[39] Ingham seems to have felt the same pressures; from the very start of his observance of the Stationary fasts in October 1733 he changes the usual noon notation on Wednesdays and Fridays from "dinner" to "Hall."

As might be expected, the Methodists were not of one mind on all aspects of the fasting issue. Ingham's diary is dotted with disputes among his friends on the question, with mixed results. In one case, Robert Watson became convinced that observing the Stations was even more obligatory than observing Sunday. Ingham was not always ready to accept every aspect of fasting promoted by the Wesleys. Although he did adopt Charles's Lenten rule to have only one meal (at three o'clock) on fast days, he was "not fully determined" to accept Charles's suggestion to refrain from eating flesh at supper. John Wesley tried to impress upon Ingham both in person and through his writings the necessity of fasting, including even the rather obscure fast on the sixteenth day of the month. Even though Wesley was shortly to begin questioning the unequivocal position he held in 1733/34, he nevertheless encouraged fasting among the Methodists throughout his lifetime.

Among the Methodists, fasting was observed on specific days; temperance, however, was a constant rule. One of their Resolutions for Every Day asked, "Have I been temperate in the desire and in the use of sensual pleasure, and particularly have I been recollected and thankful in eating and drinking?" More specific injunctions were stipulated in the Resolutions for Lent, including the suggestion "to limit the quantity before sitting down" at every meal. Ingham recognized his weakness in this regard, and his diary discloses many occasions when he ate too much, to which he sometimes attributed subsequent headaches or "dullness." "Intemperance" in eating or sleeping is a frequent confession in Ingham's diary as in Wesley's, and "not intemperate" is the occasional note of joy for unexpected conquests over temptation. Ingham tried to follow Wesley's Rules for Eating and even made special lists of general and particular questions. His trials in this regard may be the reason he suggested to

---

[39] *Letters*, I, 433. This is reminiscent of Wesley's own comment to his brother Samuel that if he could have given up early rising, "not one man in ten of those that are offended at me as it is would ever open their mouth against any of the other particulars." *Letters*, I, 320 (17 November 1731).

Hervey, in a conversation about drawing up resolutions, "not to insert anything about eating."

If temperance was a trial for Ingham, early rising was a real battle, and the constant skirmishing presents some of the most amusing notations to be found in the diary. The basic principle of this part of one's fight against "the world, the flesh, and the devil" Ingham noted succinctly in shorthand: "From sufficient and sad experience I do consider that it is sinful to lie waking in bed, or to sleep longer than the health and strength of our bodies require." He tried to follow the Wesleyan pattern of rising at 4 a.m. but was frequently unsuccessful. On one occasion he lay in bed from four to five "to warm my shirt," as he confessed in his diary, followed by the warning, "No more such trivial excuses." Three days later one diary note, "I doubted whether I should rise or not," is juxtaposed with another which may explain the first: "Meditate no more on the bed." A stronger note of chagrin appears in the diary during July: "I was waking at 4.30 and would not rise; Oh! Shame!"

Ingham tried several methods to overcome his sloth in this area: sleeping without a mattress or sheets, "sconcing" himself a penny for going back to bed after once rising, doing without dinner or supper, "watching" at night a proportional amount of time, and even having a friend sit "century" (sentry) by his bed during the night. He tried Thomas Broughton's suggestion "to leap out of bed at the first ringing of the larum and, falling on [my] knees, pray for purity." At home in Ossett he arranged to have Molly Harrup (a neighbor or servant?) call him in the mornings. Resolutions, friends, fines, and prayer notwithstanding, he was unable to persevere and just at the point of success, disaster often struck. After boasting to James Walker one night that he never missed hearing his alarm, Ingham overslept the very next morning, which convinced him of his "inability to do anything" of himself. The moral (as he noted in his diary that morning): "Trust not to thine own strength, but be humble."

If Ingham had some problems of consistency with early rising, he certainly made up for it in his attendance at public church services. His attendance at morning and evening chapel service at Queen's was unfailing; the time of these services can be charted daily for nearly ten months from his diary entries.[40] In addition, he attended the 10 a.m. sermon on every saint's day and other festivals of the church. Moreover, Ingham had

[40] See, for example, 1 October, note 40, 2 October, note 43, et seq.

no difficulty adopting Wesley's suggestion to receive the Sacrament whenever possible.[41] At the beginning of every term (in this diary), Ingham
attended the statutory celebration of the Eucharist at St. Mary's, a record
better than Wesley's. He also joined other Methodists quite often on
Sunday mornings at Christ Church or at the Castle prison to receive the
Sacrament. He had read Wesley's sermon on the Sacrament which ad-
monished "constant communion" and, as time went on, found increasing
opportunities to commune. Not all of Ingham's friends shared his enthu-
siasm in this regard, however. When Ingham heard of a Sacrament to be
offered on Maundy Thursday for the servitors at Christ Church and dis-
covered that Wesley and other Methodists would be there, he tried to
convince some of his friends to go along. A heated debate ensued, John
Ford arguing that they were not duty-bound to receive the Sacrament "as
often as we have opportunity" because they would then be obliged to receive "four or five times a day" (perhaps a bit of hyperbole). In two
weeks' time, however, Ford began to relent and after an intense round of
debate, enticement, and prayer on the part of his Methodist companions,
he agreed to ask the president of his college for permission to attend the
Sunday morning celebrations of the Sacrament at Christ Church cathedral. This story is duplicated many times in both Ingham's and Wesley's
diaries as the Methodists gathered their forces for this public expression
of their religious commitment. This was more than just a nonchalant de-
cision whether or not to go to a church service. George Whitefield's comment about seeing the Methodists "go through a ridiculing crowd to receive the Holy Eucharist at St. Mary's"[42] is confirmed by Ingham's note
after the service at the beginning of Easter term: "I was very bold, and
not at all concerned at the crowds of gazers." Such trials did not deter
Ingham, Wesley, and some of the others, who had a touch of Madame
Guyon's tendency to think that hardship and persecution were the seal of
one's Christian calling.[43] Several Methodists even began participating as
often as possible in private administrations of the Sacrament in the city
of Oxford. Wesley began taking the Sacrament to sick persons as early as
March 1732, and occasionally some of the Methodists would attend as
well. Ingham first noted receiving the Sacrament with a sick woman on

---

41 See note 20.
42 George Whitefield, *A Short Account of God's Dealings with the Reverend
Mr. Whitefield* (London: W. Strahan, 1740), p. 26.
43 Wesley commented to his brother Samuel in February 1735, "No one is a
Christian till he is despised." *Letters,* I, 417.

8 April 1734 after receiving the celebrant's consent. On at least six occasions during the next two months he attended such private administrations of the Sacrament in homes and at the workhouses, at times with as
many as nine other Methodists present.[44]

SOCIAL OUTREACH   The activities of religious devotion just described
were only one manifestation of the Methodists' adherence to the *Country
Parson's Advice* "to lay open that piety which they practice in secret and
to let the world know, by actions suitable to a good profession, that there
are some that own the cause of real holiness."[45] Yet holy living, in the
centuries-old tradition the Wesleyans had adopted, also stressed the second half of the Great Commandment, "love thy neighbor," which meant
that their personal exercise of piety included a program of charitable activities directed toward their community. The Methodists at Oxford developed a program of social outreach aimed primarily toward the poor
and disadvantaged: the prisoners at the Castle prison and Bocardo jail,
the inmates at the workhouses, the children of the poor, and other individuals with special needs.

Visiting the prisoners had been suggested to the Wesleys in 1730 by
one of their earliest religious companions, William Morgan. John Wesley frequently preached and administered the Sacrament at the Castle
prison, and his friends helped read prayers, teach the prisoners to read,
and provide some of their financial and legal needs. They also developed,
at about the same time, a similar program at the Bocardo jail. After the
middle of 1732, their "method" in both places included a rotating schedule of visitation and a system for donating funds for the support of needy
prisoners. John Clayton, who joined the Wesleys about the time Morgan
left Oxford in 1732, extended this program to include one of the local
workhouses in St. Thomas's parish.[46]

Although Ingham and his friends from Queen's College did not become involved in the Methodists' work at the Castle (other than to attend the Sunday morning service and Sacrament frequently) and did not
visit the Bocardo at all, they did become active in the program at the
workhouses—even more so than Wesley himself. The workhouses presented an ideal opportunity for the Methodists to exercise their beneficent

---

[44]   The opening rubric for the Communion of the Sick stipulates that "at least
two" others should receive the Sacrament with the sick person. *B.C.P.*
[45]   *Country Parson's Advice*, p. 81.
[46]   *Letters*, I, 334 (Clayton to John Wesley, 1 August 1732).

intentions toward disadvantaged people. Ingham first visited St. Thomas's Workhouse, near the southwest corner of Little High Bridge, in January 1734. He immediately resolved to go there two or three times a week to teach and catechize the children, read family prayers, talk with the old people, and read the Bible or some devotional work such as *The Christian Monitor*. In March he and Robson decided to apply to the workhouse the "method" of scheduling used by Wesley at the Castle: everyone would choose a day and go morning and night to perform their mission of teaching, reading, and prayer. Ingham's day was Wednesday, but he often took Ford's turn on Mondays or Smith's on Fridays as well.

In mid-April, Ingham and two Queen's colleagues decided also to begin visiting the paupers at St. Bartholomew's Hospital (Bartlemas House), a medieval foundation near Cowley Road that had become, in effect, a city almshouse. Four visits in one week all proved fruitless as there were no almsmen to be found. Understandably, the group "resolved to go no more." Instead, Ingham began to visit the poor people in the Hamel in St. Thomas's parish, reading to them *The Christian Monitor*.[47] Before another week had passed, Ingham and Hervey decided to try visiting the workhouse at Whitefriars in Gloucester Green. They found many poor folk there also, and a master, James Piggot, who was amenable to reading family prayers morning and evening. During the six weeks prior to Ingham's receiving his bachelor's degree and his subsequent departure from Oxford, we find him and his friends filling a very busy schedule of charitable activities.

In addition to this general ministry to groups of poor persons, Ingham and the other Methodists also sought out individuals who had special needs, especially among the children and the aged. The sick and infirm were particular objects of their concern; Ingham and Wesley both note frequent visits to such. Some hungry poor folk were at times provided with food. Ingham's giving away his commons (college meal) now and then was more likely the result of his Methodist inclinations than the consequence of an old (and probably disregarded) Queen's College tradition.[48] Children received special attention, particularly in the workhouses, which, unlike the prisons, provided for children as a normal part

47   The Hamel is a street in west Oxford. See 24 April, note 48.
48   The founder's statutes at Queen's College stipulated that thirteen poor persons were to be fed in the Hall daily. John Richard Magrath, *The Queen's College* (Oxford: Clarendon Press, 1921), vol. 1, 58. There seems to be no evidence that this act of charity had persisted into the eighteenth century.

of their routine. Besides teaching and catechizing at the workhouses and prisons, the Methodists helped to support schools for the poor children. Wesley's financial accounts for this period included notes of gifts to the Grey-Coat School, a charity school in Oxford. Ingham visited two such schools at Oxford with Hervey, and shortly afterward convinced some of his friends to give sixpence a month "to maintain some poor children at the school." This may have been the school for which the Methodists had assumed responsibility, set up in the first instance by William Morgan and taken over by Wesley after the Irishman's departure.[49] Ingham's interest in the plight of such children and in teaching them, which begins to bud in this diary (particularly after he returned to his home in Ossett), came to full blossom later in Georgia and in his subsequent activities in Yorkshire.

The scope of the Methodists' good will seemed to be boundless at times. Many of their colleagues did not understand or appreciate the inward motivation that elicited their visible and public, much less their personal and private, program of activity. The outward manifestations of their religious perspective appeared fanatical to many in that age of spiritual lethargy, overshadowing anything that might have been said by way of theological rationale. Two hundred and fifty years after *Fog's Weekly Journal* published the first vitriolic description of these "sons of sorrow," we are compelled to do more than repeat the old criticisms or the time-worn apologies; to smirk at the Oxford Methodists as well-intentioned Pharisees who had not yet seen the light (or had not yet felt its warmth) is no better than to decry their "enthusiastick madness and superstitious scruples." The activities of the Oxford Methodists were of a piece with their theology, a relationship worth trying to understand since both the life and thought of Oxford Methodism had a positive and basic impact on the development and shape of Wesleyan theology and activity.

Theology

The extant diaries of the Oxford Methodists (Ingham, Wesley, and Whitefield) do not contain many explicitly theological entries. But the pattern of Christian living described in the diaries (including the diary

[49] *Letters*, I, 282. Ingham also attended a "charity sermon" at St. Mary's on the Thursday after Easter; these occasions provided the opportunity to extol the values of such schools and raise funds for their support.

keeping itself) does exhibit a theological perspective that is quite explicable when viewed in the light of the books they were reading. In fact, the lifestyle described in these diaries cannot be fully understood without a clear grasp of the theological impulses from which these activities sprang.

Part of the legend of the Wesleyans at Oxford is that the name Methodist was given them because of their methodical lifestyle. Historians have almost universally overlooked the fact that their theology could also be designated by the same term. The theology of holy living that provided the basic structure for Wesleyan theology in the early 1730s was essentially the same as that of the so-called New Methodists of the seventeenth century. The term derived from their opponent's point of view. Strict Calvinists of that day saw any tendency toward synergism, freedom of the will, a conditional covenant of grace, or any other concept that detracted from the sovereignty of God, as an attack on orthodoxy and as a "new method" of doing theology ("new" being of course a derogatory term in this case). Attacks against the New Methodists could be aimed in a number of directions—against the Pelagianism of the papists, the moralism of the Socinians, the active mysticism of the Bellarmines, or the Arminianism of some Anglicans and Dissenters.[50] The common denominator in the list of charges was that each of these "new methods" incorporated some degree of "works-righteousness" in its soteriology.[51] In England, the targets were persons such as John Goodwin and Richard Baxter whose emphasis on the continuing necessity and possibility of obedience to the "Law" even under the new covenant of grace seemed to challenge the two main pillars of Reformed Protestantism, *sola fide* and

50 For examples of this polemic see Pierre Daillé, *Faith Grounded upon the Holy Scriptures; against the New Methodists* (1675); Johannes Vlak, *Dissertationum trias: de Operum & pacis fœderibus, atque de justificatione* (1689); and an anonymous work, *A War Among the Angels of the Churches, Wherein is Shewed the Principles of the New Methodists on the Great Point of Justification* (1693). Wesley seems to have been unaware of the term "New Methodist" and its theological connotations even though he adopted the basic position they represent.

51 The anonymous "Country Professor of Jesus Christ" who wrote *A War Among the Angels* recognized that "the real design" of all these groups was "to promote holiness," to which he could not object, observing nevertheless that the point of disagreement was "at what door to bring in works and holiness" (p. 8).

sola gratia. Such ideas were seen to undermine the derivatives of these pillars most emphasized by the Calvinists—unconditional election, limited atonement, and irresistible grace (in a word, predestination).

The holy living tradition adopted by the Wesleyans at Oxford shared much of the theological heritage represented by the New Methodists and suffered (then and now) under the same common misrepresentation of having a doctrine of salvation by works-righteousness.[52] Although the Wesleyan brand of Methodism was not, strictly speaking, a doctrine of "salvation by faith" in the more radical evangelical Protestant understanding of that term (which to some implied the antinomian dangers inherent in the Solifidian position), it was definitely a doctrine of "salvation by grace" (not "by works"). And although this theological perspective did result in a disciplined lifestyle characterized by charitable and devotional activities, the emphasis was always on the interior aspects of holiness. Works were not seen as the *means* to any state; they were the manifestations of virtues, which had been carefully cultivated through various meditative practices.[53] Salvation, spiritual health, and freedom involved being restored to the original state of humanity as created—in the image of God.[54] This was the purpose of the redemptive act of God's grace in Jesus Christ, making possible the restoration of human beings to their intended relationship to God, as before the Fall.[55] This restoration

[52]   Studies of the Oxford Methodists have usually portrayed them in the same terms that Luke Tyerman used to describe Ingham at this point: "He was a conscientious, earnest Pharisee, seeking to be saved by works of righteousness rather than by penitential faith in Christ." *The Oxford Methodists* (London: Hodder and Stoughton, 1873), p. 59. Cf. Ingham's conversation with John Gambold concerning the Solifidians and "morality," 1 April.

[53]   In *Poetry of Meditation* (New Haven: Yale University Press, 1954), Louis Martz examines the definition of "meditation" among the writers of the seventeenth century, typified by Francis de Sales's view that "meditation is an attentive though iterated, or voluntarily intertained in the mynd, to excitate the will to holy affections and resolutions," to which might be added Richard Gibbons's comment ". . . from whence doth arise in our affectionate powers of good motions, inclinations, and purposes which stirre us up to the love and exercise of vertue and the hatred and avoiding of sinne" (pp. 14f.).

[54]   The best expression of Oxford Methodist theology is found in the early sermons of John Wesley, to be published in vol. 4 of *The Works of John Wesley* (Sermons 133–51), ed. Albert C. Outler (Nashville: Abingdon Press). See Sermon 146, "The One Thing Needful," which Wesley designates as "to be born again, to be formed anew after the likeness of our Creator" (I.5).

[55]   See Sermon 141 on Gen. 1:27, "So God created man in his own image."

is only effected when the believer has faith, a faith that works in love[56] and draws the person closer toward "having the mind of Christ, and walking as he walked."[57] Individuals are thereby enabled to fulfill the expectations of the Law, not through their own activity alone, but through the grace of God acting in them.[58] The concept of a universal atonement that this perspective assumes (theoretical as in Amyraldus, or actual as in Wesley) was protected from a Pelagian works-righteousness by an understanding of prevenient grace: no act that contributes to a person's salvation is self-initiated but is rather the result of God's grace, which "prevenes" (comes before) any human act.[59] Salvation is not a momentary event but involves a process of restoration and becoming holy, of cultivating the love of God in such a way as to draw closer to the goal of "having the mind of Christ." The emphasis of the Christian life then was on sanctification as one pressed on, with the assistance of God's grace, toward perfection in love and final justification.

The personal discipline evinced by such thinking had a dual focus represented by the *imitatio Christi* on the one side and the *pugna spiritualis* on the other. The goal was, in the end, Christian perfection, but this was not meant to imply having the ability to conform one's actions to every jot and tittle of the Law (as defined by any particular set of rules or standard of activity). Perfection must be understood in the context of a virtue-oriented ethic. The desired end is not perfect obedience to a standard of conduct; it is perfect conformity to a model of divine-oriented virtue. Being restored in the image of God is basic to the whole process. The goal is not to be able to act perfectly; the goal is to *be* perfect, to

---

[56] See Sermon 146, "The One Thing Needful," III.3: "Be it our one view . . . to regain the highest measure we can of that faith which works by love."

[57] This goal is first stated by Wesley in 1733 in Sermon 17, "The Circumcision of the Heart," and constantly repeated in his subsequent delineations of the doctrine of Christian perfection.

[58] See Sermon 144, "Love of God," in which Wesley states that "love is still the fulfilling of the Law," which includes the positive commandments of Christ; these "either enjoin the use of the means of grace, which are only so many means of love, or the practice of those particular virtues, which are the genuine fruits of love" (sec. 3).

[59] See Sermon 17, "The Circumcision of the Heart," I.3: "We are convinced that we are not sufficient of ourselves to help ourselves; . . . that it is he alone who worketh in us by his almighty power, either to will or to do that which is good; it being as impossible for us even to think a good thought, without the supernatural assistance of his Spirit, as to create ourselves, or to renew our whole souls in righteousness and true holiness."

achieve an inward perfection of intentions and attitudes, of will as well as of understanding. Truly good actions are the result of the inward dispositions of the soul (virtues)—thankfulness, meekness, humility, self-denial, mortification, chastity, love of neighbor, and (the ground of them all) love of God. The Christian life involves a life of devotion that will cultivate these virtues (the imitation of Christ) as well as contend with "the world, the flesh, and the devil" (the spiritual combat). The means by which this double-edged form of spirituality could be effected in the life of the believer was the practice of meditation.

Meditation for the Oxford Methodists, as for many of their spiritual forebears, was different from the contemplative mysticism of the Eastern Church.[60] Meditation was inextricably tied to the whole process of self-examination that lay at the heart of the discipline of holy living. By contemplating Christ and the many virtues exemplified in his life and death (his active and passive work respectively), one was made vividly aware of one's own sinful state and of particular faults that precluded achievement of the desired virtues. The one or two hours a day set aside for meditation were as apt to be filled with thoughts of "sins and infirmities" as they were of "God's perfections" or "Christ's sufferings." The list of virtues mentioned as topics for meditation in the diaries follows very closely the topics under which questions for self-examination were arranged.[61] Sin was not so much the commission or omission of a particular action but rather the absence of, or at least the failure to manifest, a particular virtue, thus a falling short of the glory of God as seen in Jesus Christ. Everything was to be done to the glory of God, as seen in one of the questions for general examination by which the Methodists daily tested their conscience: "Have I said or done anything without a present or past perception of its direct or remote tendency to the glory of God?"[62]

The Methodists used many books of meditation, but the method exhibited by most of those works displayed the "modern" form of a centuries-old tradition of meditative piety and "spiritual exercises" seen in

[60] Wesley and his companions used the exercise of meditation to lead them to a life of devotion and action rather than a state of mystical contemplation and union, although the two processes cannot always be completely distinguished or severed from each other. See Martz, *Poetry of Meditation,* p. 20.

[61] See pp. 19f.

[62] As this question indicates, the Wesleyan position at this point allowed for no "indifferent acts"—every action had either good or evil implications. *Letters,* I, 322, 325.

Thomas à Kempis, Ignatius of Loyola, Lorenzo Scupoli, Francis de Sales, Joseph Hall, Johann Gerhard, Richard Baxter, Jeremy Taylor, Henry Scougal, Madame Guyon, Anthony Horneck, and William Law—each one having a slightly different perspective, but most of them superimposing a practical Pelagianism upon a mysticism of *sola gratia*.[63] One interesting aspect of this strain of thought is the fascinating combination of people who make up this "family," including French Catholic mystics, Jesuits, English Puritans, nonjuring bishops, continental pietists, and Scottish Divines.[64] They are all, however, theological cousins, and several common features evident in their writings are significant not only for Oxford Methodism, but also for the subsequent shape of Wesleyan theology. In the face of theological bickering and divisions, many of these writers stress the need to return to a simple religion based on the love of God. On the basis of this common denominator, they call for an approach that emphasizes unity in the essentials of belief and toleration of differences in the more subtle theological distinctions. In this regard, the Early Church (its unity perhaps idealized by these writers) becomes an important

[63] Louis Bouyer notices this particularly in the way Hall and Baxter adapted the Ignatian system; see *A History of Christian Spirituality* (London: Burns & Oates, 1969), vol. 3, 159.

[64] In noting the similarities between Puritan exhortations and Jesuit practices, Martz tries to shift attention away from the question of influences in one direction or another by making the important observation that "all these practices arose from a central preoccupation of the entire age, shared by Christians of every creed." *Poetry of Meditation*, p. 123. Bouyer also acknowledges this ecumenical tendency when he explains how Anglican spirituality, in attempting to recuperate some of the tradition of the ancient Church, reconciled the positive elements of both Protestantism and modern humanism with Catholicism, "not by abandoning its principles but by sifting and renewing all that was most positive in their origins." *History of Christian Spirituality*, vol. 3, 62. See also C. F. Allison, *The Rise of Moralism* (New York: Seabury Press, 1966). Gordon Wakefield admits that the piety of the Puritans has much in common with the great devotional traditions of the past but is careful to distinguish some essential differences between Protestant and Catholic devotion he feels Martz overlooked; see *Puritan Devotion* (London: Epworth Press, 1957), pp. 5, 160. This same willingness to categorize has led many historians to view any tendency among Protestants to use meditative exercises as an *invasion* or *infiltration* of mysticism into the Protestant traditions, a rather parochial view that overlooks the deeply ecumenical nature of meditative piety. See, for example, F. Ernest Stoeffler, *The Rise of Evangelical Pietism* (Leiden: E. J. Brill, 1965), pp. 15, 81; R. Newton Flew, *The Idea of Perfection in Christian Theology* (Oxford: Oxford University Press, 1934), p. 277.

model and source for thought and action.[65] Religion is not seen as a matter for argument but for practice.[66] The Great Commandment is the bedrock of such a theology, the life of Christ its pristine manifestation, and the lives of the saints its further confirmation. Love of God manifests itself in a virtuous life—this theme even provides the organizing principle for the biographies of exemplary Christians.[67] The center of this religion is in the heart. The life of God in the soul of man redirects the affections, purifies the intentions, restores the virtues, and brings about a life of love. This "theology of the heart"[68] was not simply visceral emotionalism, but an attempt to understand God's saving activity in ways that were more biblical, apostolic, historical, and personally authentic than the antiseptic intellectualism (and divisiveness) of rationalistic or scholastic theology; more ethically responsible than the antinomianism of the quietist mystical theology; and more Christ-centered than the humanistic moralism that

[65] The theme of unity, grounded in a discernible "consensus," was not only basic to these writers' view of the Primitive Church but may also be seen in Wesley's often repeated (and also somewhat idealistic) reflections upon the Oxford Methodists as being "all precisely of one judgment," "all of one heart and of one mind," "exactly of the same mind," and other hyperbolic terms. Sermon 112, "On Laying the Foundation of the New Chapel," I.3; Wesley, *A Short History of the People Called Methodists* (1781), para. 3; letter from Wesley to Henry Brooke, 14 June 1786.

[66] Jean Orcibal, "The Theological Originality of John Wesley," in *A History of the Methodist Church in Great Britain* (London: Epworth Press, 1965), vol. 1, 88.

[67] See, for example, Jean Baptiste de Saint Jure, *The Holy Life of Monsr de Renty* (1658) (in Appendix 3); cf. John Wesley's *Extract of the Life of Mons. de Renty* (1741). William Cave, in the preface to his *Apostolici,* claims that the lives of these saints "acquaint us with the most remarkable occurrences of the Divine Providence, and present us with the most apt and proper rules and instances that may form us to a life of true Philosophy and Vertue; history (says Thucydides) being nothing else but 'Philosophy drawn from examples.'" Vol. I (1677), "To the Reader" (see Appendix 3). Wesley not only read many such biographies but included spiritual biographies in his fifty-volume *Christian Library* (1749–55) and, later in the century, incorporated many autobiographies as a regular feature in his *Arminian Magazine* (1778–), many being the lives of his preachers written by themselves.

[68] This term was used by Pierre Poiret, an indefatigable propagator of the Catholic mystics among the Protestants, who seems to have influenced some of the Oxford Methodists on the matter of the *ordo salutis.* John Byrom, *The Private Journal and Literary Remains of John Byrom* (Manchester: Chetham Society, 1856), II, 230. See also Orcibal, "Theological Originality of John Wesley," p. 111.

seemed to challenge biblical theology in every age. It is no surprise that the earliest of Wesley's sermons to ring forth this theme was "The Circumcision of the Heart" (1733), a clarion call to holy living that stressed the necessity of *inward* holiness ("that habitual disposition of the soul") and outlined its implications in terms of "being cleansed from sin" and "endued with those virtues which were also in Christ Jesus."

One problem that constantly accompanied such a theology was that of assurance. How does one know one is saved? How does one know when one is proceeding in the proper direction in an attempt to press on toward perfection? If the emphasis is more on the *process* of salvation than the *state* of salvation, how does one know he or she is doing the right things? The answer that permeates the perspective of the Oxford Methodists (as well as many of their theological forebears) is that one's hope rests in one's *sincerity*.[69] As long as one is doing the best one can, one must trust that God will not withhold his grace. In trying to deal with the tension between impatience on the one hand and want of zeal for improvement on the other (or between scrupulosity and self-indulgence), Wesley noted in the front of his diary in 1734 a quotation from Thomas à Kempis: "Fac quod in te est, et Deus aderit bonæ tuæ voluntati," which he translated in his edition of Kempis the following year, "Do what lieth in thy power, and God will assist thy good will."[70] This was entirely in keeping with Wesley's understanding of a theology of grace—while sincerely doing one's best, one must acknowledge that every effort springs from God's grace. Thus a person exercises the prevenient grace given to one by God, responding to the promptings of the Holy Spirit and cooperating with God's grace in the present moment to conform one's will and affections to God's will and intentions. Holy living is thus the exercise of grace[71] in the development of those virtues which make

---

69 "Our hope is sincerity, not perfection, not to do well, but to do our best." *Letters,* I, 318 (John Wesley to Anne Granville, 3 October 1731).

70 *De imitatione Christi,* I.vii.1 (with a footnote citing Augustine, *Sermones ad fratres in eremo,* 27); see Appendix 3. Wesley's edition was entitled *The Christian's Pattern* (1735). This perspective can also be seen in Wesley's contrast of the Old Covenant and its absolute demand, "Do this and live," with what he saw in 1732 as the tempered conditions of the New Covenant, "Try to do this, and live." John Wesley MS., Colman Collection XX, "The Duty of Receiving the Lord's Supper," fol. 18 verso, MA.

71 William Law, *A Practical Treatise Upon Christian Perfection* (1726), ch. IX, "Of the Necessity of Divine Grace and the several Duties to which it Calleth all Christians" (see Appendix 3).

one fully human (renewed after the image of God, seen in Christ) while at the same time continually struggling with the contrary vices. Grace is not given in opposition to the exercise of the will, but rather it directs (or redirects) the will. The saints are not those who had a more excellent nature, but rather those who had a more exact care over it, by the grace of God.[72]

But if the emphasis is on the process (tentatively allowing for the possibility of reaching a level of perfection), then the question of assurance persists as a nagging companion in the struggle. And resting one's hope in one's sincerity is little consolation to a person who is also struggling to develop a sense of humility that recognizes that his or her own efforts must be distrusted.[73] The closer and more intricate the process of self-examination becomes, the more one's failings become evident. The practices of meditation and self-examination that are supposed to assist the process of improving in holiness simply serve to point out just how feeble and worthless any efforts are, no matter how sincere. The methods used in this process often lead to the temptation (felt even by predestinarians) of becoming obsessed with good works which, though thought to be a secondary manifestation of an inner condition, are the primary measure of that condition and, therefore, the focus of attention.[74] This problem in part led some theologians to emphasize the necessity of passivity (passive obedience) which can result either in a rejection of any good works (and the sacraments) as means of grace (as in the quietism of Molinos, Molther, and others) or in a preoccupation with suffering as the mark of a true Christian (as in the mysticism of Guyon, Bourignon, and others). Some of the Oxford Methodists, notably Ingham, Gambold, and Wesley, were eventually attracted to Moravian Solifidianism, which helped solve the problem of assurance by relying solely on faith but which also bordered on a type of quietism that Wesley soon found necessary to refute. Although Wesley's adoption of an emphasis on *sola fide* finally helped him reorient his understanding of the order of salvation during the years 1736 to 1738 (particularly the crucial place of "justification by grace through faith" *preceding* sanctification), he never allowed it to supplant the necessity of holy living and pressing on toward perfection. The per-

---

72   Saint Jure, *The Holy Life of Monsr de Renty*, p. 356 (quoting St. Ambrose).
73   See Ingham's resolution dated 1 February 1733, followed by the comment, "therefore ever distrust thyself."
74   Bouyer, *History of Christian Spirituality*, vol. 3, 155; Wakefield, *Puritan Devotion*, p. 157.

vasive synergism of Wesley's mature theology, with its tension between "faith alone" and good works, testifies to the solid grounding he had at Oxford in the synergistic perspective of the holy living tradition.[75]

It might be said that the Oxford Methodist concept of true Christianity in 1734 was not so much patterned after any particular system or systems of theology as it was modeled upon the lives of persons the Methodists considered to have epitomized the Christlike life. The religion of Ingham, Wesley, and the others could not be defined simply by applying terms such as Arminianism, Puritanism, pietism, or mysticism. Rather, it was best described in terms of the holy lives of de Renty and Guyon, the "Christian gnostic" of Clement of Alexandria, August Hermann Francke's *Nicodemus,* and a long series of witnesses to the love of God in the lives of human beings, from Ephraem Syrus and Augustine to Ambrose Bonwicke and James Bonnell.

In summary, the Oxford Methodists shared a view of Christianity with a long-standing heritage in the holy living tradition. Their perspective embraced the simple essentials, which were grounded in the Great Commandment—to love God and to love neighbor—revealed in Scripture and epitomized in the life of Christ, which they hoped to imitate. The focus was upon nurturing the virtues basic to the Christian (Christlike) life and combating the vices that impede the development of inward holiness. This tradition, while based in Scripture, is confirmed and exemplified in Primitive Christianity; the Bible and the Early Fathers are the sources for the Oxford Methodists' thought and action. Their theology is irenic and ecumenical, with an emphasis on unity (consensus) and toleration and with an aversion to disputation and speculation. Theology was not unimportant in this whole enterprise, but theology was the handmaid of holy living, a practical theology devoted to Christian living.[76] Salvation, "the one thing needful," meant being renewed in the image of God, recovering that purity of love once lost, and nurturing the virtues so constantly as to purify (perfect) the heart of conscious sinful inclinations. The life

[75] Orcibal notes that Wesley claimed after 1770 to have remained "as tenacious a champion of inner holiness as any mystic and of outward holiness as any Pharisee." "Theological Originality of John Wesley," p. 102. See also Albert C. Outler, *John Wesley* (New York: Oxford University Press, 1964), pp. 119, 425.
[76] The spirituality of the holy living tradition shares some of the pietist aversion to theological disputation, their occasional lack of solid theological reinforcement deriving more from indisposition than inability. See Bouyer, *History of Christian Spirituality,* vol. 3, 58f.

of the faithful Christian is a grace-full life, one that cultivates the virtues through the practice of meditation, self-examination, and prayer, and manifests its inner reorientation in a disciplined life of devotion and charitable activities.

This basic outline describes a perceivable tradition that exists within many Christian bodies, a tradition that cuts across denominational and national lines. It is neither exclusively Catholic nor uniquely Protestant; it cannot be enclosed within simple terms such as puritan, pietist, or mystic.[77] It has authentic representatives within many different Christian traditions, differing perhaps on some points of theology or ecclesiology but sharing a common approach to the Christian life of meditative piety. One can see why Wesley, Ingham, and the other Oxford Methodists did not conceive of themselves as straying from their Church of England roots, even while developing a close kinship to other groups, for example, the Moravians. Most of the ideas found in the "puritan" Catholics, the "pietist" mystics, or the "spiritual" moralists they were reading (and with whom at times they were linked) were repeated and confirmed by many of their favorite English writers who also shared this perspective (Law, Deacon, Norris, Taylor, Nelson) and who considered themselves no less Church of England men for their interests in reform and renewal.

The eclectic methodology of the Oxford Methodist theology which Wesley continued to exemplify throughout his later theological development is very much in keeping with the tolerant, ecumenical orientation and methodology of the meditative pietists in the holy living tradition. The particular strain of active devotion that is obvious in de Renty, Guyon, Fénelon, Taylor, Law, Francis de Sales, Scupoli, the Country Parson, and Thomas à Kempis helps us understand how Ingham, Wesley, and their friends could combine the emphases on the apostolic Fathers and the Scriptures, acts of charity and devotional contemplation, ethical responsibility and a theology of grace, sincerity and faith to yield a special blend of disciplined devotion, methodical meditation, and practical piety that gave shape to their own pattern of Christian thought and life.

[77] Cell's familiar dictum that Wesley's teaching exhibited a synthesis of "the Protestant ethic of grace and the Catholic ethic of holiness" is based on the sort of categorizing tendencies that we have tried here to avoid, recognizing instead the more basic significance of the common elements that undergird the ecumenical nature of the holy living tradition. See George Croft Cell, *The Rediscovery of John Wesley* (New York: Henry Holt, 1935), p. 361.

THE OXFORD SCENE

Oxford University in the first half of the eighteenth century was the object of a great deal of criticism, some from within but most from without. The critics, though often agitated by political concerns, usually trained their attack upon the profligate state of spiritual and intellectual life in the university, their harsh portrayals apparently not without some cause, though at times exaggerated.[1] The Methodists, themselves the object of other sorts of criticism, might be seen as exempt from some of the typical attacks, but it would be as wrong to suggest that they were unique in their conscientiousness as it would be to suggest that they were representative students of the day. They were, it should be remembered, living within certain conditions, schedules, opportunities, and expectations that were common to all. If they were different from many of their colleagues, it was in one sense in the degree of their effort to live up to the best expectations of the Laudian Statutes as enforced by the university officers of that day.[2] While the Oxford Methodists may not have been typical Oxford students in many ways, any deviation from the norm would probably have been on the side of scrupulosity and conscientiousness, and in that sense, their daily lives (and their diaries) would reflect more fully the scholarly and spiritual opportunities present in the university at that time.

The diary of an Oxford Methodist, as noted earlier, was primarily a chart of his spiritual condition, a ledger of his soul. But the eye of self-examination peered into every corner of life, and no activity escaped its careful scrutiny. There were no "indifferent actions"—every thought, word, and action was of moral consequence to the Wesleyan at this time. The diaries are therefore quite exhaustive, and although the manner of diary notation is such that the diarist seldom adds comments or reflections upon events (be they routine or extraordinary) except in the way

[1] See W. R. Ward, *Georgian Oxford, University Politics in the Eighteenth Century* (Oxford: Clarendon Press, 1958), pp. 150ff.; V. H. H. Green, *John Wesley* (London: Nelson, 1964), pp. 12f.

[2] Charles Wesley, in his later years, remembered the earliest Methodists in terms of their attempt "to observe the *Method* of Study prescribed by the Statutes of the University." Letter to Dr. Chandler, 28 April 1785, quoted in Frank Baker, *Charles Wesley as Revealed by His Letters* (London: Epworth Press, 1948), p. 14.

of spiritual analysis, they do provide a rather complete picture of the daily lives of these particular students, and in turn, of university life at that time.

The daily routine of college life provides part of the framework for the disciplined Methodist routine displayed in Ingham's diary. Morning prayers in the chapel, breakfast, disputations, dinner, lectures, evening prayers, supper—all these can be charted from the regular entries from day to day. The morning prayer services at Queen's College chapel on the six weekdays usually began at six during the spring and summer months (seven on Thursdays) and at seven during the autumn and winter.[3] Evening prayers were read either at five or five-thirty, the fluctuating schedule seeming to follow neither the academic calendar nor the seasons. Sunday morning chapel services were held rather consistently at eight at Queen's, a half-hour to an hour later than the service at Christ Church on those days. Breakfast was not provided as part of the commons; those who wanted such could eat whenever they wished in their rooms. Dinner and supper were common meals in the Hall, the former regularly at noon,[4] the latter served immediately after evening prayers and thus fluctuating between five-thirty and six. Disputations were held in the Hall at eleven on Monday, Tuesday, Wednesday, and Friday mornings during term. Lectures were generally reserved for the afternoon hours, although Ingham occasionally notes a lecture at an odd hour such as Sunday morning at seven-thirty or Saturday evening at nine.

Ingham's academic life seems to have centered primarily around collegiate exercises. Although the diary entries make no distinction between college and university functions, the occasional entry that refers distinctly to university places or events leaves the impression that they were somewhat remote aspects of the life of an undergraduate, at least until the time came to stand for one's degree. Ingham's single explicit note that he "called at the Schools [and] walked in the Picture Gallery and the Library" in April implies that he was venturing into unfamiliar territory. The lectures, declamations, and disputations he attended also appear to have been mostly college exercises; none of the times correspond with the

---

3   Cf. *The Fothergills of Ravenstonedale,* ed. Catherine Thornton and Frances McLaughlin (London: William Heinemann, 1906), p. 83.
4   The dinner hour was changed by several colleges from 11 a.m. to noon about 1720, "that people might lye in bed the longer." Thomas Hearne, *Remarks and Collections of Thomas Hearne,* ed. H. E. Salter (Oxford: Clarendon Press, 1921), vol. 11, 140.

statutory hours for university exercises.[5] The exceptions, again noted explicitly by Ingham, are the Poetic Lectures which he attended at the beginning of Michaelmas and Hilary terms, and the Bodleian Lecture, given at the time of the directors' visitation in November. The disputations that would certainly have been university exercises are the Divinity Disputation on 13 December at which Wesley disputed, the Generals in early May at which Ingham "sat over" two of his friends, and Ingham's own disputation for his degree in June. Other university functions noted by Ingham include the collector's and proctor's speeches at the Theatre during Lent, and the Latin sermon and Holy Sacrament celebrated at St. Mary's at the beginning of every term, a service always attended by Ingham, whose punctiliousness in such matters exceeded even Wesley's.

Ingham received his bachelor's degree in June 1734, and his diary contains a good record of the exercises leading up to that occasion. Toward the end of April he began working on what he called "a speech for my degree," which he gave on 3 May. His monthly summary contains a note explaining that this speech permitted him "to be freed from exercises," possibly referring to the examinations that would have normally been required and that he seems not to have taken.[6] The day before he "spoke" his speech, he also thought about composing three lectures, these also for his degree, though not listed as a requirement for the B.A. degree in the Laudian Statutes.[7] He chose the tenth satire of Juvenal as the topic for his lectures, which he presented the first week in June on three successive days after dinner in the Hall at Queen's. The middle lecture came on Friday, a fast day, which Ingham undauntedly kept even in this instance. On 13 June, Ingham disputed for his degree, after which he immediately wrote an "epistle" requesting that he be excused from two terms of the residency requirement. This "Grace" was granted by the House of Congregation, as the records verify.[8] The following day, he returned to the Schools and, following the statutory stipulations, stood bareheaded in the

5 Cf. *Statutes,* IV.1.
6 The scandalous condition of the examining system at Oxford during this period has been noted by many commentators. See Nicholas Amhurst, *Terræ Filius; or, The Secret History of the University of Oxford* (London, 1726), no. XLII.
7 These were probably college exercises preparatory to the university requirement. Six lectures were required for the master of arts degree, and were most often read to the walls of nearly empty rooms, bringing upon them the name "wall lectures." *Statutes,* VI.2.2.
8 See 13–17 June (and notes) for additional details on these procedures.

Pig-Market (the proscholium of the Divinity School) most of the morning to "get his Grace" on the pro forma matter of not having attended
university lectures. This also was granted, leaving him only to collect his
"scios" and stand for his degree on the seventeenth of June. He celebrated
on that evening by "treating" the bachelors in the Taberdars' common
room at Queen's.

The protocol of college life glimmers through all of these records in
Ingham's diary. He is careful to use proper appellations, such as Boy
(Poor Boy), Dominus, and Master. He writes a polite Latin "epistle" on
New Year's Day, probably to the provost. He tries to keep his cap and
gown in good condition, mending them on several occasions. He makes
sure the servitors are paid toward the end of Hilary term, and checks his
own accounts with his tutor before leaving Oxford.

Beyond listing the events and activities, Ingham gives little descriptive
information in his diary about most aspects of college or university life.
He does mention going to the college buttery on Shrove Tuesday evening, but does not reveal the purpose of his half-hour visit. Christmas
Day finds him at the traditional Queen's College feast which includes the
procession with the boar's head; all he notes in the diary is "dinner" from
twelve-thirty to three, an uncommonly long eating period but that is all.
There is no mention of the "needle and thread" tradition on New Year's,
no comments on the "treat" for the senior scholars in June.[9] Somewhat
surprisingly, the diary contains only the slightest hints that his college was
in the midst of a major building program. The whole south end of
Queen's as it now stands was under construction during the period of
this diary, but Ingham's interest in the matter is reflected only by his
showing friends through the new chapel on several occasions. It had been
completed nearly two decades earlier as part of a previous stage of the
building program.[10] Although he tells us much about his friends, Ingham
does not indicate where his room was, who his roommate was (if he had
one), who his tutor was, or what his financial condition might have been.
These bits of information, now lost in missing college records, were not
central to Ingham's main purpose for keeping a diary and managed to es-
cape his otherwise detailed manner of diary notation.

9 See John Richard Magrath, *The Queen's College* (Oxford: Clarendon Press,
1921), vol. 2, 241ff., and John Pointer, *Oxoniensis academia* (London: S. Birt,
1749), pp. 38f., for many of these college customs.
10 See *The Present State of the New Buildings of Queens College in Oxford*,
dated at end, December 21, 1730 (cf. earlier edition dated February 20, 1718).

The city of Oxford does not receive a great deal of notice from Ingham; undergraduates did not have much contact with civic affairs, a situation entirely in keeping with the intentions of the university statutes. Occasional references to common locations in the city help us place his local visits: the workhouse and the Hamel to the west across the river in St. Thomas's parish, the workhouse on Gloucester Green outside the North Gate, Littlemore and St. Bartholomew's to the south and east of the city, the Crown Inn on Cornmarket Street and Peisley's bookshop at the East Gate. Other places mentioned are not so easily located, such as the Boar-Head (presumably a tavern), and the post office, operated by William Underwood (on "Bristol Road"?).

We could wish for more, but at the same time, we must recognize that, for a document as concentrated as it is on the interior aspects of life, Ingham's diary permits us a better view of life at Oxford than perhaps we should expect. The first three-quarters of his account display a great deal of information about himself, the Methodists, their lifestyle and attitudes, the college and university curriculum, charity work among the poor, and many other aspects of daily life. The diary continues to supply more names, places, and activities as Ingham leaves Oxford after receiving his bachelor's degree and heads north.

INGHAM AND THE NORTH COUNTRY

Benjamin Ingham was a Yorkshireman. This first volume of his diary, which extends through the summer of 1734, shows the beginnings of Ingham's life beyond Oxford as he tried to implement his educational and religious concerns among his relatives, friends, and neighbors in the North Country. Although Ingham returned to Oxford briefly in the spring of 1735 and then, after his ordination and a short stint in London, went to Georgia in America with the Wesleys for nearly two years, his home county of Yorkshire was to become the primary focus of his activities during the rest of his life.

Ingham's main influence was as a preacher and a teacher. These interests are implicit throughout much of this diary, and are quite explicit in several entries. Even though while he was at Oxford he made more than one resolution to refuse or to disregard the question of ecclesiastical preferment, Ingham had hardly set foot in his hometown in July before he began entertaining "thoughts of preferment": on one occasion he noted in his diary, "thought how I would act if a priest." Although he was not ordained a deacon in the Church of England until the following year, Ingham had written a sermon as early as May 1734 and mentions writing three more in the North before this diary ends in August. The topics are appropriate for an Oxford Methodist: self-denial, zeal, and keeping the commandments. Only after 1736 did his preaching develop a more evangelical ring which, under Moravian (and later Sandemanian) influence, sounded more exclusively the theme of "faith."

Although Ingham was not yet a priest or a preacher, he found it quite natural at Ossett to continue his role as spiritual leader for a small company of friends, who began gathering in his home at 7–9 Town End, just off the Wakefield–Dewsbury Road. His later friend and biographer, William Batty, noted this extension of the Oxford Methodist pattern into the North Country:

> [Ingham] began to keep religious meetings in his mother's house every night. He read and expounded the Scriptures and other good books, sang hymns and Psalms, and prayed. He first began with their own family only, next a poor man, and afterwards two poor widows who were neighbours desired to attend them; but within half a year a good number came.[1]

The initiation of these activities is reported in this diary on his very first day at home in July.

Another way Ingham could apply his interests and talents in his home setting was as a teacher. While at Oxford, he had spent a good deal of time teaching and catechizing the children at the workhouses. Back in Ossett, Ingham continued to work with the poor children, teaching the neighbors (as well as his own sister) how to read and write. Within a month of his return, the would-be schoolmaster noted in his diary, "thought how I could manage a school." Thomas Rhodes, Ingham's own teacher at Batley Grammar School, perhaps provided the model, having been both vicar and schoolmaster at the same time for over thirty years before his death in 1753.[2] By the end of August 1734, Ingham was teaching at least twelve persons how to read and/or write, all children save one—the poor rug-maker, William Wilby (who was also attending family prayers).

---

1   Eng. MSS. 1062, "An Account of Benjamin Ingham and His Work," The John Rylands University Library of Manchester, p. 3.
2   D. N. R. Lester, *The History of Batley Grammar School, 1612–1962* (Batley, Yorkshire: J. S. Newsome & Son, n.d.), pp. 46–50.

Teaching was one task that seems to have given Ingham a great deal of satisfaction and joy even when other aspects of country life weighed heavily on his soul. In early 1738, shortly after his second return to Yorkshire, Ingham appears to have been instrumental in making permanent arrangements for a charity school in Ossett, which by 1743 had forty scholars and listed Ingham as its "patron."[3]

Ingham soon rediscovered that life in Ossett was quite removed in many ways from life in Oxford. In his first letter back to Wesley he remarked, "I did not altogether know the advantage of living at Oxford so well before as I do now. Those that have it in their power to reside there are wise if they do so." He goes on to explain, in terms that Wesley would understand: "To act well in the country requires more knowledge and prudence, and a great deal more zeal. Tis scarce possible to imagine how wicked the world is."[4] Ingham's diary indicates that he was nevertheless trying his best to carry on the "spiritual combat" he had begun at Oxford, "methodizing" his time, examining his activities, meditating on his sins and infirmities, and making even more resolutions to implement the virtues upon which rested the holy life.

Everyday life in the country was very different from the routines of academic life. The disciplined framework of meditative piety which had become set in Ingham's life over the past months struggles to encompass a new round of daily activities reflecting many aspects of the agricultural society of the North: making hay, gleaning in the fields, hewing trees, loading corn, gathering apples, and picking plums. He notes going shooting and "a-setting" for partridges several times, although he had resolved "not to throw myself into the temptations of sports" and had meditated on the vanity of such activities. His interest in scientific topics results in two special notations in the diary: an hour of "learned talk" with his family on the subject of lightning on 14 August and an evening of observing a comet with the Wesley family at Epworth toward the end of the month. His interest in books takes him to Pontefract for a book sale, and while there, he visits the Castle, as any tourist might. At Dewsbury, he dines at the Crow Nest with the "Captain and Lady," no doubt the owners of that stately mansion. The diary records a new round of persons and places visited by Ingham in and around Ossett: Dame Whitaker at Low Laithes,

3   The lease was dated 2 February 1737/38, and two masters were licensed that year. John F. Goodchild, *The History of Ossett Church* (Ossett, Yorkshire: n.p., 1965), pp. 9f.
4   See 27 July, note 54.

the Wrights at Wakefield, the Dickinsons at Batley, Mr. Thomas at Dewsbury. Many of the trivial tasks of life in Yorkshire are fixed in the diary—making pens, mailing letters, getting a shave, paring his nails—activities that might have been seen only as "necessary business" amidst the busy schedule at Oxford.

The diary ends with Ingham at Epworth, visiting the Wesleys. John Wesley's diary indicates that Benjamin was at that time falling in love with Patty Wesley; Ingham's diary mentions all the Wesley girls by name except Patty.[5] This perhaps inadvertent lapse might be seen as yet another indication, subconscious though it might have been, of the extent to which Ingham was struggling to overcome "the world, the flesh, and the devil" in whatever guise he felt these might come. His success was already apparent enough to the Wesleys to give Ingham the nickname Nathanael, after the biblical figure Jesus described as "an Israelite indeed, in whom is no guile."[6]

The last entry in this diary is a fitting one for Ingham: "religious and useful talk with Charles Wesley." Charles had been one of his closest friends at Oxford; he would continue to be a devoted friend throughout his life. Charles was the main channel through which Ingham had learned what it meant to be a "Methodist"; Ingham later associated the beginnings of Methodism at Oxford primarily with Charles.[7] Ingham's subsequent associations with the Moravians were much closer than the Wesleys' and lasted for at least a decade beyond the date of the Wesleyan break with the Moravians (which had in part caused Ingham to renounce for a time his Methodist connections). Yet Charles supported his friend and in 1755 favored allowing Ingham to rejoin the Conference of Methodist preachers, even "vindicating his old friend" from the appearance of Moravianism, which Ingham had since renounced.[8]

This diary represents not much more than one chapter in the life of Benjamin Ingham; there are several other interesting chapters ahead:

[5] OD IV [Summaries], 24; OD V, 1–3. See August entries and note 120.

[6] Luke Tyerman, *The Life and Times of the Rev. Samuel Wesley* (London: Simpkin, Marshall & Co., 1866), p. 427 (letter from Samuel Wesley to Westley Hall, 11 July 1734); see also John 1:47.

[7] Eng. MSS. 1057, "Minutes of the Committee for finding out the first aim and intention of our Saviour by the Awakening in England going under the name Methodism," minutes of the First Committee, Synod of Herrnhaag, May 1747, The John Rylands University Library of Manchester.

[8] *The Journal of the Rev. Charles Wesley* (London: John Mason, 1849), II, 119: "It is hard a man should be hanged for his looks."

his trip to Georgia; his connection with the Cambridge Methodists in the late 1730s; his relationship to the Yorkshire riots in the early 1740s; his evangelistic work which established the societies known to posterity as the Inghamites; his marriage to Lady Margaret Hastings and their patronage of the Moravian work in the North; his association with Lady Huntingdon and her connection of preachers (she called him a "bishop"); and his part in the Hervey–Sandeman controversy over the nature of faith. The larger story of Ingham's life and work is a unique and fascinating part of the evangelical revival of the eighteenth century.[9]

This little diary is more than just a part of Ingham's biography. It is, as we have said, an important window into the first stages of Methodism, a significant representation of (as well as key to) the Wesley style of diary keeping, and yet another primary source that sheds light on the language, travel, attitudes, and customs of eighteenth-century England, a small sample of life from times gone by that contributes in its own way to our better understanding the past.

[9] No full-length biography of Ingham has ever been published. Luke Tyerman included a chapter "Rev. Benjamin Ingham, the Yorkshire Evangelist" in *The Oxford Methodists,* and Richard W. Thompson wrote "Benjamin Ingham (Yorkshire Evangelist) and the Inghamites" (Kendal, Cumbria: privately published, 1958). The only other available source of collected materials on Ingham's life is a short account written by a friend and contemporary, William Batty, containing a brief summary based on Ingham's diaries (including later ones apparently now lost). See Selected Bibliography for additional details on the works by Tyerman, Thompson, and Batty.

The Diary

Glossary

Argument: a set of syllogisms (in Latin) on a question in logic, comprising the two positions to be taken in a *Disputation;* often passed on from one student generation to another and referred to as "strings."

Breakfast: the first meal of the day, ending the fast; usually early in the morning, but on fast days at three or six o'clock in the afternoon.

Business and virtue: planned the business of the day and prayed for the virtue of the day. (See "Resolutions for Every Day," nos. 4 and 7.)

Called: awakened.

Came home: returned to the abode of the day; usually his room at college (in Oxford) or his mother's house (in Ossett).

Casting up: putting into order; writing a monthly summary of readings, compositions, letters, and acquaintances.

Chapter: read a chapter in the Greek New Testament (three times daily beginning 14 November).

Collect: a short prayer consisting of an invocation, petition, and conclusion; used daily, especially at nine, twelve, and three o'clock (see preliminary pages).

Commons: a meal supplied from the college buttery and kitchen at noon and night.

Corn: one of the cereal plants; in England, usually wheat.

Daily examination: self-examination based on lists of questions and resolutions; in some cases, a daily review of hourly self-examinations.

Declamation: a rhetorical exercise (in Latin) on set topics, recited from memory; usually presented in the college Hall in the presence of other scholars; served as practice for the disputations.

Dinner: the noon meal; at college, in the Hall.

Disputations: scholastic exercises (in Latin) which formed a large part of the requirements for degrees; a respondent and opponent developing syllogistic arguments in the presence of a moderator, in the Hall of a college or in the Schools of the university.

Dominus (Ds): title prefixed to the name of a bachelor to distinguish him from a master (Mr) and from an undergraduate (no prefix).

Dressed: changed clothes; put on academic gown, customary dress when walking in public within the university grounds.

Eat: usually means "ate," indicating a snack between meals.

Ejaculatory prayers (Ejaculations): short prayers of praise or petition often focusing on the main virtues; collected and used hourly by the Methodists in conjunction with their periods of recollection.

Ember days: Wednesday, Friday, and Saturday of the four Ember weeks (during Lent, after Whitsunday, in September, and in December), set apart as fast days in order to consecrate to God the seasons of the year and to prepare for the ordinations the following Sunday.

Family prayers: an adaptation of the morning or evening prayer service, designed for the use of families in the home.

Fasting: abstinence from eating and drinking certain or all foods; cf. *Stations.*

General examination: summary self-examination, usually reviewing the previous week.

Genesis: a scholarly composition that inquires into first principles; often focused upon a topic (*genesis thematica*) or a question (*genesis problematica*).

Good talk: a conversation that was "useful," the general tone or substance of which is usually described (religious, various, etc.).

Grace: a dispensation, granted by the Congregation or Faculty, from some statutable condition required for a degree.

Greek Testament: the New Testament in Greek.

Hall: a large assembly room in the college, used for dining, lectures, disputations, and other collegiate exercises.

Hamel: a street in west Oxford, midway between the Castle and St. Thomas's church.

Imposition: a literary exercise assigned as a punishment.

Laid with: stayed overnight with (perhaps, though not necessarily, sharing the same bed).

Larum: an alarm clock; sometimes may refer to a person (servitor) who awakens others.

Learned talk: a conversation about scholarly topics.

Lent rule: a reference to one of the Ten Resolutions for Lent.

Logic: read and studied one of the standard texts on logic (Aldrich, Sanderson, etc.).

Meditated: reflected closely upon particular subjects (often listed); frequently accompanied by self-examination.

Mistress (Mss): (1) used in place of Mrs.; (2) sweetheart or girlfriend, with nothing illicit implied.

N.B.: nota bene, note well.

Necessary business: some small chore, such as sorting books, preparing breakfast, setting up a shelf, being shaved, and so on.

Necessary talk: a conversation indispensable to the furtherance of some particular action (concerning exercises for degree, schedule, etc.).

Observe: please note; cf. N.B.

Opposition: the opponent's position in an argument for disputation; answered by the respondent's *Supposition.*

Preferment: advancement of position within the Church by means of an ecclesiastical appointment.

Private prayer: a period of prayer, read or spontaneous, by an individual either alone or in a group; distinguished from *Public Prayers* held in a church.

Public prayers: the office of Morning Prayers or Evening Prayers from the Book of Common Prayer, read in a church.

Read: may imply "read together" or "studied."

Read {aloud}: may also mean "heard read."

Recollected: (1) a state of spiritual composure, usually associated with "simplicity"; (2) an exercise of self-examination recalling and reviewing one's demeanor, usually at the end of each hour or day.

Religious talk: conversation characterized by spiritual concerns.

Resolution: a reference to the list of fifteen Resolutions for Every Day.

ri: (?) a notation in some way associated with the process of recollection.

Sacrament: the sacrament of the Lord's Supper.

Sermon: the university preaching service, Sundays at ten and two o'clock and other holy days at ten.

Setting: hunting partridges ("setting snares" or "shooting").

Simple: a state in which everything is done with a single view of pleasing God; the criterion for measuring "temper of devotion" (simplicity).

Stations (stationary fasts): abstinence from food and drink until three in the afternoon on the Stationary days (Wednesday and Friday) following the pattern of the Early Church.

Supper: the evening meal; at college, in the Hall.

Supposition: the respondent's position in an argument for disputation, answering the opponent.

Taberdar: member of the foundation at Queen's College, chosen from among the Poor Boys after becoming B.A.

Thanksgiving: a prayer of thanksgiving; often, the prayer after the Sacrament.

Theme: a written composition concerned with one topic.

Various talk: conversation that covers a number of topics, the prevailing tone or subject of which is often described (useful, religious, etc.).

Walked: often refers to a solitary perambulation for exercise or meditation; "walked with" might also be read "went with."

Watched: prepared for the coming of Sunday by reading and praying during the final hours of Saturday (devotional and meditative exercise).

Workhouse: a house established for the employment and care of the poor; in this diary, either in St. Thomas's parish or in Gloucester Green.

Wrote diary: transcribed notes of daily or hourly recollection into diary; "summary" refers to "casting up" the monthly record.

Preliminary Pages

Ingham began his diary on the fourth leaf of an empty notebook, leaving the opening pages blank. On the first three leaves, as well as on the endpapers, he eventually inscribed a variety of notations, many of them intended for constant and easy reference: a key to the symbols used in the diary, a key to the abbreviations, a list of collects for the hours of the day and for the days of the week, and other prayers for specific purposes and times. These pages of prayers he used as a devotional aid. In addition, he also made a few miscellaneous notes, filling one page with shorthand poetry, perhaps of his own composition.

Collect for every hour

Consider and hear me, O Lord my God; lighten mine eyes that I sleep not in death. O purge me, and I shall be clean; O wash me and I shall be whiter than snow; O knit my heart unto Thee, that I may love thy nation. Lo I come to do thy will, O God; let my sacrifice be acceptable in thy sight.

Into thy hands I commend my spirit, for Thou hast redeemed me, O Lord thou God of truth.[1]

---

1 This prayer, attributed to Bishop Thomas Ken, is a conflation of biblical quotations, including Psalms 13:3, 51:7, and 31:6. Ingham underlined "hear me" in the first line and noted in the margin an alternate reading, "heal me." John Wesley's copy of this prayer reads "help me." John Wesley MS., Colman Collection VIII, pp. ii, [22], MA. See plate 4.

For the day

Lord, teach me to know and cleave unto thee; let me be always present [to call with Thee].[2]

[Symbols] (see plate 4)

[Collects]

For the 9th [*hour*]. O God, who hast prepared for them that love Thee, such good things as pass man's understanding; pour into our hearts such love toward Thee, that we, loving Thee above all things, may obtain thy promises, which exceed all that we can desire, through Jesus Christ our Lord. Amen.[3]

At 12. Almighty god, unto whom all hearts be opened, all desires known, and from whom no secrets are hid; cleanse the thoughts of our hearts by the inspiration of thy Holy Spirit, that we may perfectly love Thee, and worthily magnify thy holy name, through Jesus Christ our Lord. Amen.[4]

At 3. Remember not, Lord, our offenses, nor the offenses of our forefathers, neither take Thou vengeance of our sins; spare us, good Lord, spare thy people, whom Thou hast redeemed with thy most precious blood, and be not angry with us forever.

    Spare us, good Lord.[5]

Quis, quid, ubi, quibus auxilius, cur, quomodo, quando?[6]

Quis? Quid? Quomodo? Att; God; Vertue.
Who? what? the manner?[7]

---

[2] The text and source of this prayer are not clear; the portion of the transliteration in brackets remains problematic.

[3] Collect for the sixth Sunday after Trinity, *B.C.P.* See p. 119, Resolution 2.

[4] Collect for Purity, the Communion, ibid.

[5] Collect, with response, from the Litany, ibid.

[6] In his *Address to the Clergy* (1756), John Wesley uses this same list of terms ("who, what, where, with what helps, why, how, when") in his definition of *prudence:* "an habitual consideration of all the circumstances of a thing, *quis, quid* . . ." (I.2). Cf. Francis de Sales, *Introduction to a Devout Life,* part 2, xi.2 (see Appendix 3).

[7] Cf. OD IV, [ix]: "As to Examination, I resolve (1) Every hour to consider the last, *Quis, quid, quomodo;* What right, what wrong in the manner?"

James Hervey at Hardingstone near Northampton.[8]

Collects for the days.

For Sunday. O Almighty God, who alone canst order the unruly wills and affections of sinful men; grant that I may <u>love</u> the things which Thou commandest, and desire that which Thou dost promise, that so among the sundry and manifold changes of this world, my heart may surely there be fixed, where true joys are to be found through <u>Jesus Christ</u> our Lord. Amen.[9]

For Monday. O Lord, who hast taught us that all our doings without charity are nothing worth; send thy Holy Ghost, and pour into my heart that most excellent gift of charity, the very bond of peace and of all vertues, without which whosoever liveth is counted dead before Thee. Grant this for thine only Son Jesus Christ's sake. Amen.[10]

or this—Lord, I beseech Thee, grant thy people grace to withstand the temptations of the world, the flesh, and the devil, and with pure hearts and minds to follow Thee the only true God, through <u>Jesus Christ</u> our Lord. Amen.[11]

For Tuesday. Lord, what am I, and what art Thou? O mortify my pride and convince me throughly that I am nothing, that I have nothing, that I can do nothing.[12]

For Wednesday and Friday. Almighty and everlasting God, who hatest nothing that Thou hast made, and dost forgive the sins of all them that are penitent; create and make in me a new and contrite heart, that I, worthily lamenting my sins and acknowledging my wretchedness, may obtain of Thee, the God of all Mercy, perfect remission and forgiveness, through <u>Jesus Christ</u> our Lord. Amen.[13]

For Thursday. Almighty God, who madest thy blessed Son to [be] cir-

---

8 This notation by Ingham of James Hervey's name and home address misled later owners of this volume, one of whom inscribed on the back page, "Diary of James Hervey."

9 Collect for fourth Sunday after Easter, *B.C.P.* Ingham transcribed these "particular collects" into his diary on 4 and 5 March 1733/34.

10 Collect for Quinquagesima Sunday, ibid.

11 Collect for eighteenth Sunday after Trinity, ibid.

12 Cf. John Wesley MS. Colman Collection VIII, p. [48], MA.

13 Collect for first Sunday in Lent, *B.C.P.*

cumcised, and obedient to the law for man; grant me the true circumcision of the Spirit, that my heart and all my members being mortified from all worldly and carnal lusts, I may in all things obey thy blessed will, through the same thy Son Jesus Christ our Lord. Amen.[14]

For Saturday. I will give thanks unto the Lord with my whole heart, his praise shall be ever in my mouth;[15] thy mercy, O Lord, reacheth unto the heavens, and thy faithfulness unto the clouds.[16] O taste and see how gracious the Lord is; blessed is the man that trusteth in Him.[17]

In time of temptation. O Lord, who never failest to help and govern them, whom Thou dost bring up in thy stedfast fear and love; keep me, I beseech Thee, under the protection of thy good providence,[18] increase and multiply upon me thy mercies,[19] O succor, defend, and deliver me in this and all other temptations; make me to have a perpetual fear and love of thy holy name, through Jesus Christ our Lord. Amen.[20]

Against evil thoughts. Keep me, O Lord, under thy perpetual mercy;[21] let thy grace always prevent and follow me;[22] and because without Thee I cannot but fall, defend me ever by thy help from all things hurtful;[23] grant me the inspiration of thy Holy Spirit, that I may think those things that be good, and by thy merciful guiding may perform the same, through Jesus Christ our Lord. Amen.[24]

O Thou who alone can order the unruly wills and affections of sinful men;[25] mercifully vouchsafe me by thy almighty grace[26] such a constant repression of my thoughts and careful government of my passions and appetites as may restrain me from running so after sensual pleasure, with such abstemiousness and thankfulness in the use of them as may deaden

---

14   Collect for New Year's Day or the Circumcision of Christ, ibid.
15   A conflation of Psalms 9:1 and 34:1, ibid.
16   Psalm 36:5, ibid.
17   Psalm 34:8, ibid.
18   Collect for second Sunday after Trinity, ibid.
19   Collect for fourth Sunday after Trinity, ibid.
20   "Make me . . . Amen," Collect for second Sunday after Trinity, ibid.
21   Cf. Collect for fifteenth Sunday after Trinity, ibid.
22   Collect for seventeenth Sunday after Trinity, ibid.
23   Collect for fifteenth Sunday after Trinity, ibid.
24   Collect for fifth Sunday after Easter, called Rogation Sunday, ibid.
25   Collect for fourth Sunday after Easter, ibid.
26   Cf. Collect for eleventh Sunday after Trinity, ibid.

me to the love and desire of them,[27] and despise me always and in all
things, to glorify thy name forever through Jesus Christ our Lord. Amen.[28]

Hear, Lord, thy fainting creature prop,[29]
    confound my pride, confirm my hope,
    a firm and saving faith impart;
Bring the strong curse of nature tied,
    control my will and safely guide
    by love divine my softened heart.
To Father, Son, and Holy Ghost,
    the God whom heaven's triumphant host
    and suffering saints on earth adore,
Be glory as in ages past
    is now and shall forever last
    when heaven and earth shall be no more.

When here

To God whose glory fills the sky,
    to his dear Son who deigned to die,
    our guilt and error to remove,
To that blest Spirit who grace imparts,
    who rules in all believing hearts,
    be endless glory, praise, and love.

O Thou whose presence fills these all,
    the earth, and air, and seas, and skies;
Still humbly may I wait thy call,
    still be thou present to my eyes.

2

On my dull soul all-cheering Dove,
    let heaven in all its glory shine,
And steadfast hope, and spotless love,
    seal my poor soul forever thine.
All glory to the sacred Three,
    co-equal, co-eternal Lord;

27 "Such a constant . . . of them," cf. John Wesley MS., Colman Collection
VIII, p. [108], MA.
28 This prayer is written on the inside back cover of Ingham's diary.
29 These poems may well be original composition; see 7 August. My appreciation to Esther and Douglas Lister, Leigh-on-Sea, Essex, for several helpful
suggestions on the transliteration of this page of shorthand.

As at the first still equal be,
    with hope believed, with love adored.

Charles Wesley, A.M., Student of Christ Church, Oxford, taught me the following method of keeping a diary. I became acquainted with him and his brother John Wesley, A.M. and Fellow of Lincoln College, Oxford, through Charles Burton.[30]

Abbreviations (see plates 5, 6, and 7)

[30] Ingham began transcribing this list into his diary on 4 March 1733/34. Charles Burton appears in this diary only as a correspondent of Ingham. He is mentioned several times in John Wesley's diary in July 1733, usually in the company of Ingham but without any clue to help identify him.

The diary opens with Ingham at Oxford in the middle of the long vacation between Trinity and Michaelmas terms. He has already settled into a pattern of meetings with some of his companions: a Wednesday–Saturday–Sunday schedule of reading with Smith, which will persist (with changes in personnel) throughout his stay at Oxford; a Monday–Tuesday–Thursday–Friday schedule with Natt and William Knail; and a regular Sunday afternoon study session with Christopher Atkinson, Washington, Smith, and James Richardson. Their reading list is typically Wesleyan at this point. Ingham is already observing the Stationary fasts to some extent, a practice he quickly adopts in strict fashion and begins to promote among his friends. His attendance at Public Prayers and the regular religious services of the university is from the first day a model of diligence. In addition, occasionally on Sunday mornings, he goes with the Wesleys to the Castle prison for the Sacrament. The method of diary keeping used here is the same as that which John Wesley had been using since 1729, heavily abbreviated entries in a paragraph-style format.

Through the fall and winter, the number and composition of Ingham's groups change so that by the end of February he is meeting with five clearly distinguishable groups, some daily, some weekly, others two or three times a week. The most notable additions are a Friday evening meeting starting in November and persisting through his departure in June and a breakfast group at Charles Wesley's on Wednesday and Friday afternoons beginning in October. He also begins to incorporate some shorthand entries into his format in October and to change from a weekly to a daily pattern of self-examination at the end of December. In January he begins visiting St. Thomas's Workhouse and in February begins attending regularly the Sacrament at Christ Church. By the end of this period, he is noticeably associated with the methods, schedules, practices, and theology of the Wesleyans and discloses this association to his friends at Queen's. The resolve to dedicate himself to God, first made in early October, is renewed toward the end of February with a prayer for perseverence.

SATURDAY, SEPTEMBER 1.   5 Necessary business in attending sick Watson. 5.30 Private prayer; abridged Nelson.[1] 6 Public Prayers. 7 Breakfast at Charles Wesley's, religious talk, Law's *Christian Perfection,* read [aloud].[2] 8 Came home; necessary business for Watson. 8.30 Began sixth chapter, second book, Brown on the Understanding.[3] 9.30 Translated and read Aldrich's Logic. 11.30 Finished abridgement of Nelson's *Devotion;* private prayer; wrote diary. 12 Dinner. 1 Logic at Charles Wesley's.[4] 2.30 Came home; read Welchman. 3 Began to transcribe *Christian Prudence.*[5] 5 Wrote diary; private prayer. 5.30 Public Prayers. 6 Supper. 7 At Smith's, began to read *The Life of James Bonnell, Esq.*[6] 9 Came home; thoughts. 10.15.

SUNDAY, SEPTEMBER 2.   5 Wrote diary; private prayer; transcribed *Christian Prudence.* 8 Public Prayers. 9 Read Secker's sermon.[7] 10 Ser-

[1] See entry for eleven-thirty. Abridging or "collecting" an extract of a work was a common academic exercise, used among the Methodists and by John Wesley throughout his life.

[2] To indicate that he read a certain work, Ingham used the abbreviation "r" *before* a title or author. In entries such as this one, however, he used the abbreviation "r^d" *after* the name of the work, perhaps indicating that the book was read aloud in the presence of others. Cf. 30 August where he "heard" the *Minute Philosopher.*

[3] The chapter title is "Of the different kinds of knowledge and evidence." Ingham was abridging this work also. See Peter Browne in Appendix 3 and monthly summary for September 1733.

[4] Ingham's almost daily sessions studying logic with Charles Wesley continue through September and most of October, two weeks into Michaelmas term.

[5] See John Norris in Appendix 3. John Wesley had abridged this work in June 1731 and would publish it in 1734. Ingham very well could have been making a copy of Wesley's work for himself, a common practice among the Methodists (which in part seems to have encouraged Wesley to begin publishing some of these materials in late 1733).

[6] MS. reads "Bonnel." See William Hamilton in Appendix 3.

[7] Thomas Secker wrote many sermons, of course, but his sermon on "right

mon. 11 Walked with Atkinson, religious talk. 11.15 Transcribed *Christian Prudence;* private prayer. 12 Dinner. 1 With Watson. 2 Sermon.[8] 2.45 With Atkinson, etc,[9] read Wake's *Catechism.* 5 Wrote diary; private prayer. 5.30 Public Prayers. 6 Supper. 7 At Smith's, read Bonnell. 9 Came home; meditated. 10.

MONDAY, SEPTEMBER 3. 5.30 Read Nelson; private prayer. 6 Public Prayers. 7 Read Brown. 8 Breakfast with Natt, good talk. 9.30 With Watson; dressed. 10 Read and translated Aldrich. 11.45 Private prayer; wrote diary. 12 Dinner. 1 Logic at Charles Wesley's. 2.30 Came home; began Virgil's fifth *Æneid.*[10] 5 Wrote diary; private prayer; read Nelson. 5.30 Public Prayers. 6 Supper. 7 Walked.[11] 7.30 With Natt and Knail, read Brown on the Understanding. 10.30.

TUESDAY, SEPTEMBER 4. 4.45 Private prayer; read Nelson; transcribed *Christian Prudence.* 6 Public Prayers. 7 Walked. 7.30 Read Brown. 9 Breakfast with Natt, good talk. 9.30 Translated Aldrich. 11.45 Private prayer; wrote diary. 12 Dinner. 1 Logic at Charles Wesley's. 2 Came home; read Logic. 5 Wrote diary; private prayer. 5.30 Public Prayers. 6 Supper. 7 With Natt and Knail, read Brown's Preface to the Understanding, various and useful talk. 10.30.

WEDNESDAY, SEPTEMBER 5. 5.15 Private prayer; read Nelson; transcribed *Christian Prudence.* 6 Public Prayers; walked. 6.30 Translated Aldrich. 9 Read Brown. 11.30 Wrote diary; private prayer; transcribed *Christian Prudence.* 12 Dinner. 1 Logic at Charles Wesley's. 2.30 Came home; read Brown. 5 Wrote diary; private prayer. 5.30 Public Prayers.

---

learning," preached at the Public Act in Oxford just two months earlier, was enjoying wide circulation at this time; see Appendix 3. John Wesley had read it on August 13. Cf. Thomas Hearne, *Remarks and Collections of Thomas Hearne,* ed. H. E. Salter (Oxford: Clarendon Press, 1914–21), vol. 11, 231, 241, 243.

8 The university statutes required that an English sermon be preached on Sundays in the forenoon and evening at St. Mary's (*Statutes,* XVI.1–2). These sermons "before the University" were at 10 a.m. and 2 p.m., usually lasting about half an hour. Cf. Thomas Salmon, *The Present State of the Universities* (London: J. Roberts, 1744), pp. 34f.

9 See 16 September, note 27.

10 In Latin (see Appendix 3 and monthly summary for September 1733).

11 Walking was, of course, Ingham's normal manner of getting around in Oxford; these frequent notations ("walked") seem to indicate periods of intentional exercise, usually lasting thirty to forty-five minutes.

6 Supper. 7 At Smith's, read Bonnell, religious and useful talk. 9.15 Came home; thought on fasting. 10.

THURSDAY, SEPTEMBER 6.   5 Wrote diary; private prayer; read Nelson; transcribed *Christian Prudence.* 7 Public Prayers. 8 Breakfast at John Wesley's, religious and useful talk.[12] 9 Came home; read Brown. 10.30 Translated Aldrich. 11.30 Wrote diary; private prayer. 12 Dinner. 1 Walked with Smith, religious talk; read Logic. 2 Came home; read Virgil. 5 Wrote diary; private prayer; transcribed *Christian Prudence.* 5.30 Public Prayers. 6 Supper. 7 With Natt and Knail, read Plutarch's life,[13] various and useful talk. 11.

FRIDAY, SEPTEMBER 7.   6 Public Prayers. 7 Wrote diary; read Nelson; private prayer; transcribed *Christian Prudence.* 8.30 With Atkinson, learned talk. 9 Translated Aldrich. 10.30 Read Brown. 11.30 Private prayer. 12.30 Dinner. 1 Logic at Charles Wesley's. 2 Came home; read Brown. 5 Wrote diary; private prayer; read Nelson. 5.30 Public Prayers. 6 Read Nelson on the Fasts;[14] General Examination;[15] private prayer. 7

---

[12]   Wesley noted in his diary summary for this day, "Ingham convinced of Stations" (OD III, 105), that is, observing Wednesdays and Fridays as fast days. Ingham had already begun omitting morning breakfasts on Stationary days (see 5 September), but continued eating dinner at the usual time through the remainder of September, during which time he read Nelson on fasting or Wesley's treatise on the Stations every Friday evening. The following week he began observing the Stations more properly, fasting every Wednesday and Friday until three in the afternoon (see 3 October).

[13]   After 1603 the English editions of Plutarch's *Lives* (first published in English in 1579) usually contained several additional biographies, including one of Plutarch himself. See note 16.

[14]   Robert Nelson's *Companion for the Festivals and Fasts of the Church of England* (hereinafter cited as *Fasts* or *Festivals;* see Appendix 3) begins with "Preliminary Instructions concerning Fasts," which includes a section on the Primitive Church's practice of observing the Stations, Wednesdays and Fridays, "till after three in the afternoon." Ingham chose reading and self-examination rather than eating on this Friday evening, a pattern that persisted throughout the remainder of his Oxford days.

[15]   A weekly review based on a list of resolutions or questions for self-examination, usually done by Ingham on Fridays in the place of supper. At the end of December, these periods of self-examination became daily late afternoon exercises (daily examination, "x"), but the weekly review each Friday continued (denoted "Ex," and after 15 March often accompanied by a list of his sins for the week).

With Natt and Knail, read the life of Theseus and Romulus.[16] 10.

SATURDAY, SEPTEMBER 8. 5 Private prayer; wrote diary; transcribed *Christian Prudence.* 6 Public Prayers. 7 Read Brown. 8.30 Breakfast with Natt and Atkinson, various and useful talk. 9.30 Dressed; translated Aldrich. 11 With Watson, religious talk. 11.45 Wrote diary; private prayer. 12 Dinner. 1 Logic at Charles Wesley's. 2 Religious talk. 2.30 Came home; with Watson, religious talk. 3 At Lecture, 35th Article.[17] 3.45 Read Virgil. 5 Wrote diary; private prayer; read Nelson. 5.30 Pubblic Prayers. 6 Supper, learned talk. 7 At Smith's, read Bonnell. 9.15 Came home; meditated. 10.

SUNDAY, SEPTEMBER 9. 5 Wrote diary; private prayer; read Nelson. 6 Transcribed *Christian Prudence;* dressed. 8 Public Prayers. 9 Read *Christian Prudence.* 10 Sermon. 11 Read *Christian Prudence.* 11.45 Wrote diary; private prayer. 12 Dinner. 1 Read *Christian Prudence* with Watson. 2 Sermon. 3 With Atkinson, etc, read Wake. 5 Wrote diary; private prayer; read Nelson. 5.30 Public Prayers. 6 Supper. 7 At Smith's, read Bonnell. 9 Came home; meditated. 10.

MONDAY, SEPTEMBER 10. 5 Wrote diary; private prayer; read Nelson; transcribed *Christian Prudence.* 6 Public Prayers. 7 Finished Brown. 8.30 Breakfast. 9 Read and translated Logic. 11 Walked. 11.45 Wrote diary; private prayer. 12 Dinner. 1 Logic at Charles Wesley's. 2.30 Came home; read Virgil. 5 Wrote diary; private prayer; read Nelson. 5.30 Public Prayers. 6 Supper. 7 At Johnson's, etc, various and useful talk. 10.

TUESDAY, SEPTEMBER 11. 5 Wrote diary; private prayer; read Nelson; transcribed *Christian Prudence.* 6 Public Prayers. 7 Read Logic. 8 Walked. 8.30 Breakfast. 9 Translated Aldrich. 11 Walked. 11.30 Wrote diary; private prayer. 12 Dinner. 1 Walked. 1.30 Came home;

---

[16] See Plutarch, Appendix 3. That they were reading an English edition is evident from the monthly summary for September 1733.

[17] The Thirty-fifth Article is "Of the Homilies." These lectures on the Articles of Faith were apparently concluding. Beginning in October and continuing through April, the afternoon lectures on Saturday and Monday turn to Robert Sanderson's *De obligatione conscientiæ.* Note that Ingham had been reading Edward Welchman on the Articles instead of attending a lecture the previous Saturday afternoon (1 September). See Appendix 3.

read Virgil. 5 Wrote diary; private prayer; read Nelson. 5.30 Public Prayers. 6 Supper. 7 At Shepard's,[18] etc, various and useful talk. 10.

WEDNESDAY, SEPTEMBER 12.   5 Wrote diary; private prayer; read Nelson; transcribed *Christian Prudence*. 6 Public Prayers. 7 Began Grotius' *de Veritas*. 8 Finished *Christian Prudence;* dressed. 10 Read Bennet's Letter on the Study of Divinity. 11 Walked. 11.45 Private prayer. 12 Dinner. 1 Logic at Charles Wesley's, religious talk. 2.15 Came home; read Virgil. 5 Wrote diary; Public Prayers.[19] 5.30 Supper. 6.30 At Smith's, finished Bonnell. 9 Came home; private prayer. 10.

THURSDAY, SEPTEMBER 13.   5 Wrote diary; private prayer; read Nelson. 6 Read Logic. 7 Public Prayers. 8 Breakfast with Natt and Yates, good talk (various). 9 Washington, religious talk; home, translated Aldrich. 11.45 Wrote diary; private prayer. 12 Dinner. 1 Logic at Charles Wesley's. 2 Drank tea; Law, read [aloud]; religious talk. 3 Came home; read Virgil. 4.30 Wrote diary; General Examination; began the *Country Parson's Advice*.[20] 5 Public Prayers. 5.30 Supper. 6.30 With Natt and Knail, began Brown's *Divine Analogy*,[21] religious and useful talk. 10 Private prayer; meditated.

FRIDAY, SEPTEMBER 14.   5 Wrote diary; private prayer; read Nelson; read Country Parson. 6 Public Prayers. 7 Read Grotius. 8 Read Nelson; private prayer. 9 Grotius. 10 Translated Aldrich. 11 Walked. 11.45

18   Will Johnson (B.A. 1733, seven o'clock entry, September 10) and John Shepard (B.A. 1733; MS. reads "Shepherd"), both of University College (just across High Street from Queen's), were from Wakefield, near Ingham's home in Yorkshire.

19   Evening prayers and supper were a half hour earlier than usual, a schedule that remained in effect until 2 October (see also 11 February through 26 March).

20   In a letter to the *London Magazine* on 12 December 1760 explaining the rise of Methodism, John Wesley quoted from *The Country Parson's Advice to His Parishioners* (1680; see Appendix 3) and noted its importance in the promotion of their design. See p. 17 and note 25. Wesley first read this book in June 1733, just three months before Ingham began it for the first time (OD III, 83).

21   Peter Browne's *Things Divine and Supernatural Conceived by Analogy* (1733) is in answer to George Berkeley's *Alciphron* (1732), which had claimed that the position held by some "Minute Philosophers" (such as Browne's argument in his *Procedure, Extent, and Limits of Human Understanding* that our knowledge of the attributes of the divine nature is based only on analogical knowledge through revelation) often leads to atheism. See *Alciphron*, the Fourth Dialogue, XVI–XXI, and Browne's works in Appendix 3.

Wrote diary; private prayer. 12 Dinner. 1 Logic at Charles Wesley's. 2 Came home; read Virgil. 4.30 Wrote diary; read Nelson and Country Parson. 5 Public Prayers. 5.45 Private prayer; read 'Stationary Fasts'.[22] 7 Walked. 7.30 With Natt and Knail, read Brown. 10.

SATURDAY, SEPTEMBER 15. 5 Wrote diary; private prayer; read Nelson and Country Parson. 6 Public Prayers. 7 Breakfast at John Wesley's, learned and useful talk.[23] 8 Came home; translated Aldrich. 10 Read Virgil. 11.45 Wrote diary; private prayer. 12 Dinner. 1 Logic at Charles Wesley's, religious talk. 2 Came home; Lecture in Articles. 3.45 Wrote to my mother.[24] 4.30 Wrote diary; read Nelson. 5 Public Prayers. 5.30 Supper. 6.30 Private prayer. 7 At Smith's, began 'Stationary Fasts'. 9 Came home; General Examination. 10.

SUNDAY, SEPTEMBER 16. 5 Wrote diary; private prayer; read Nelson on the Sacrament[25] and Country Parson. 8 Public Prayers. 9 Breakfast at Mr Smith's, religious talk. 10 At the Castle.[26] 12 Dinner. 1 Read Country Parson. 1.30 Walked with Natt, religious talk. 2 Sermon. 3.15 Read Wake.[27] 4.30 Wrote diary; private prayer; read Nelson. 5 Public Prayers.

[22] John Wesley had just written a *"genesis* on the Stations" in July 1733, which he later corrected and revised (OD III [Summaries], 46). Two remnants from his pen at this time (perhaps drafts of the *genesis*) provide us with the general line of his thinking: "Of the Weekly Fasts," in John Wesley MS., Colman Collection XII, p. 4, MA, and "Essay upon the Stationary Fasts," in Thomas Deacon, *A Compleat Collection of Devotions* (1734), Appendix, pp. 72–74 (see Appendix 3). See 27 March, and note 111.
[23] Wesley's diary entry reports "Ingham, religious talk (learned)." OD III, 108.
[24] Ingham's mother, Susannah (nee Casselhouse), was a widow, her husband William having died the previous decade.
[25] See Robert Nelson, *The Great Duty of Frequenting the Christian Sacrifice* (1707), in Appendix 3; cf. Nelson's *Fasts,* ch. IX.
[26] The Castle was an ancient relic even in Ingham's day. From the time of Henry III, some part of the Castle had been used as the jail for the county. By the eighteenth century the remains of the tower of St. George's church served that purpose for both the county and the university, the city jail being at the North Gate (Bocardo). Wesley and his friends had begun reading the Morning Prayer service there in November 1730 and administering the Sacrament in January 1731. Wesley's diary indicates that he was also there on this occasion, and that the Sacrament as administered (OD III, 108). See plate 8.
[27] Ingham does not always note complete details of recurrent events. In this case, he was reading William Wake's *Principles of the Christian Religion Explained* (see Appendix 3) every Sunday afternoon with Atkinson, Washington,

5.30 Supper. 6.30 Went to Smith's, finished 'Stationary Fasts.' 9 Came home; read Country Parson. 10.

MONDAY, SEPTEMBER 17.   5 Wrote diary; private prayer; read Nelson and Country Parson. 6 Public Prayers. 7 Read Logic. 8.30 Breakfast. 9 Translated Aldrich. 10.30 Read Brown. 11 Walked. 11.45 Wrote diary; private prayer. 12.15 Dinner. 1 Logic at Charles Wesley's. 2 Came home; at Lecture. 3.30 Read Virgil. 4.30 Wrote diary; private prayer; read Nelson and Country Parson. 5 Public Prayers. 5.30 Supper. 6.15 With Natt and Knail, read Brown. 10.

TUESDAY, SEPTEMBER 18.   4.45 Private prayer. 5 Wrote diary; read Nelson and Country Parson. 6 Public Prayers. 7 Read Logic. 8 Breakfast at Ford's,[28] learned talk. 9 At Charles Wesley's, Logic and religious talk. 10.15 Came home; mended my gown.[29] 11 Walked. 11.45 Wrote diary; private prayer. 12 Dinner. 1 Read Virgil. 3 At Lecture. 3.30 Read Virgil. 4.30 Wrote diary; private prayer; read Nelson. 5 Public Prayers. 6 Supper. 6.30 Walked with Washington, religious talk. 7 With Natt, read Virgil. 10.

WEDNESDAY, SEPTEMBER 19.   5 Wrote diary; private prayer; read Nelson and Country Parson. 6 Public Prayers. 7 Translated Aldrich. 11.30 Dressed. 11.45 Wrote diary; private prayer. 12 Dinner. 1 Walked. 1.30 Logic at Charles Wesley's. 2.30 Read Virgil. 4.30 Wrote diary; private prayer; read Nelson on the Ember Days.[30] 5 Public Prayers. 5.30 Sup-

---

Smith, and Richardson, which becomes apparent when the weekly entries from 2 September through 30 September are compared.

[28]   Ingham spelled the name here with an "e," as does Joseph Foster in *Alumni Oxonienses* (London: Joseph Foster, 1887). Throughout the remainder of the diary the "e" is dropped, which is the spelling found in the Queen's College Entrance Book. Ford is the youngest of Ingham's Oxford friends at this time, being fourteen years old (Washington is next youngest at sixteen; James Walker, also fourteen years old, matriculated during Hilary term, 1733/34).

[29]   A long black gown and round hat were the proper academic dress of an undergraduate when abroad within the university (see *Statutes,* XIV.3). Ingham usually made his own repairs when the need arose (see 6 December, 26 January, 12 March; cf. 1 April).

[30]   Nelson, *Fasts,* ch. VIII, "Ember Days in September." Ember Days are defined by Nelson as "certain days set apart for consecrating to God the four seasons of the year, and for the imploring of his blessing by fasting and prayer upon the ordinations performed in the Church at such times" (ch. III). The Wednesday, Friday, and Saturday following the first Sunday in Lent, Whitsun-

per. 6.30 At Smith's, began the Country Parson. 9 Came home; translated Aldrich. 10.

THURSDAY, SEPTEMBER 20. 5 Wrote diary; private prayer; read Nelson. 6 Logic. 7 Public Prayers. 8 Breakfast with Natt, religious and useful talk. 9 Translated Aldrich. 10 With Atkinson, dissected a cat. 12 Dinner. 1 Logic at Charles Wesley's, religious talk. 2.15 Came home; read Virgil. 4.30 Read Nelson on the Vigils.[31] 5 Public Prayers. 5.30 Supper. 6.30 With Natt and Knail, read Brown. 10 Wrote diary; private prayer.

FRIDAY, SEPTEMBER 21. 5 Wrote diary; private prayer; read Nelson and Country Parson. 8 Public Prayer. 9 Began 'Stationary Fasts'. 10 Sermon.[32] 11 Wrote to Rhodes.[33] 12 Dinner. 1 Logic at Charles Wesley's. 2 Came home; wrote to brother Will.[34] 3 Tea at Johnson's, various and useful talk. 4 Read Grotius. 4.30 Wrote diary; private prayer; read Nelson. 5 Public Prayers. 5.30 Finished 'Stationary Fasts' with Washington, read Nelson and Country Parson, religious talk. 10.

SATURDAY, SEPTEMBER 22. 5 Wrote diary; private prayer; read Nelson and Country Parson. 6 Public Prayers. 7 Read Logic. 8 Breakfast with Natt, learned talk. 9 Atkinson, religious talk. 10 Translated Aldrich; dressed. 11.30 Walked with Natt, learned talk. 12 Dinner. 1 Logic at Charles Wesley's. 2.30 Came home; Lecture. 3.30 Read Virgil. 4.30 Wrote diary; private prayer; read Nelson. 5 Public Prayers. 5.30 Supper. 6 With Watson, religious talk. 6.45 At Smith's, read Country Parson. 9 With Natt, learned talk. 10.

---

day, the fourteenth of September and the thirteenth of December are designated as Ember Days, with the ordination of ministers taking place on the Sundays immediately following these fasts.

31 Nelson, *Fasts,* ch. IX, "The Vigils." These were originally "night watches" preceding most festival days (such as 21 September) outside of Christmastide and Eastertide, later changed to fasts but preserving the former name.

32 The statutes required an English sermon to be preached in St. Mary's on every holiday through the year (*Statutes,* XVI.2). This day was the festival of St. Matthew. See Nelson, *Festivals,* ch. xxx. The holiday service was held at 10 a.m., with the morning prayers at Queen's College chapel adjusted on such occasion to a later-than-usual hour of eight.

33 Thomas Rhodes was schoolmaster at Batley School (1723–1754), which Ingham had attended. Rhodes was also vicar of Batley. See 13 and 25 July.

34 William Ingham, Benjamin's older brother (b. 1698), named after their father.

SUNDAY, SEPTEMBER 23.   5 Wrote diary; private prayer; read Nelson and Country Parson; dressed. 8 Public Prayers. 9 Read Grotius. 10 Sermon. 11 Walked with Natt, religious talk. 11.30 Meditated; wrote diary; private prayer. 12 Dinner. 1 Read Country Parson. 2 Sermon. 3 Read Wake. 4.30 Wrote diary; private prayer. 5 Public Prayers. 5.30 Supper. 6.30 At Smith's. 9 With Watson, religious talk. 10.

MONDAY, SEPTEMBER 24.   5 Wrote diary; private prayer; finished Country Parson. 6 Public Prayers. 7 Logic. 8.30 At Smith's, read Logic. 9 At Charles Wesley's, Law, read [aloud]. 10.15 Came home; translated Aldrich. 11.30 Walked. 12 Dinner. 1 Read Virgil. 4.30 Wrote diary; private prayer; Nelson. 5 Public Prayers. 5.30 Supper. 6.30 Walked. 7 With Natt and Knail. 10.

TUESDAY, SEPTEMBER 25.   5 Wrote diary; read Nelson and meditated; private prayer; began Country Parson the second time.[35] 6 Public Prayers. 7 Read Logic. 8.30 Breakfast with Natt, good talk. 9 Translated Aldrich. 11 Walked with Natt, learned talk. 11.45 Wrote diary; private prayer. 12 Dinner. 1 Logic at Charles Wesley's, religious talk. 2.30 Read Virgil. 4.30 Wrote diary; private prayer. 5 Public Prayers. 5.30 Supper; walked with Knail, learned talk. 7 With Natt and Knail, read Brown. 10.

WEDNESDAY, SEPTEMBER 26.   5 Wrote diary; meditated; Nelson; private prayer; Country Parson. 6 Public Prayers. 7 Translated Aldrich. 8 Read *Christian Prudence.* 10 Wrote Rules for Spending Time.[36] 11 Dressed; walked with Atkinson, religious talk. 11.45 Meditated; private prayer. 12 Dinner. 1 Logic at Charles Wesley's. 2 Read Virgil. 4.30 Wrote diary; private prayer. 5 Public Prayers. 5.30 Supper. 6.15 Read Virgil. 7 At Smith's, read Country Parson. 9 Came home; read Virgil. 10.

THURSDAY, SEPTEMBER 27.   5 Wrote diary; meditated; Nelson; private prayer; read Country Parson. 6.15 Logic. 7 Public Prayers. 8 Breakfast with Watson, Atkinson, religious talk. 9 Began translating Sanderson's

---

[35]   See 13 September and note 20. Ingham read this book through a number of times, alone as well as with friends.

[36]   This typical Wesleyan concern (see OD I, viii, "General Rules for Employing Time") is found throughout Ingham's diary (see especially 31 December and 28 February). On 6 July he "methodized" his time, the results of which can be seen in part on 17 July, below, and more fully outlined in his letter to John Wesley on 27 July 1734 (see note 54 on that date).

'Use of Logic'.[37] 12 Dinner. 1 Logic at Charles Wesley's. 2 Lecture. 3 Read Virgil. 4.30 Wrote diary; private prayer; Nelson. 5 Public Prayers. 5.30 Supper. 6.30 Finished Virgil's *Æneid* with Natt. 10.

FRIDAY, SEPTEMBER 28. 5 Wrote diary; Nelson; meditated; private prayer; read Country Parson. 6 Public Prayers. 7 Read Grotius. 10 Translated Sanderson. 11.45 Wrote diary; private prayer. 12.15 Dinner. 1 Logic at Charles Wesley's, religious talk. 2.30 Came home; with Natt, religious talk. 4.30 Wrote diary; private prayer; Nelson. 5 Public Prayers. 5.30 Walked with Natt, good talk (various). 6.30 With Watson, read Nelson on Fasts, religious talk. 9 General Examination. 10.

SATURDAY, SEPTEMBER 29. 5 Wrote diary; Nelson;[38] meditated; private prayer; read Country Parson; dressed. 8 Public Prayers. 9 Breakfast with Natt, Yates, good talk (various). 10 Sermon.[39] 11 Read Country Parson and walked with Natt, religious talk. 4.30 Wrote diary; private prayer; Nelson. 5 Public Prayers. 5.30 Supper; walked. 7 Smith's, read Country Parson. 9 Logic. 10.

SUNDAY, SEPTEMBER 30. 5 Wrote diary; Nelson; meditated; private prayer; read Country Parson; dressed. 8 Public Prayers. 9 Read Country Parson. 10 Sermon. 11 Read Country Parson. 11.45 Wrote diary; private prayer. 12 Dinner. 1 Read Country Parson; walked with Natt, religious talk. 2 Sermon. 3 Finished Wake's *Catechism* with Atkinson, Washington, Smith, Richardson. 4.30 Wrote diary; private prayer. 5 Public Prayers. 5.30 Supper. [6]:30 Read Country Parson. 7:00 At Smith's, finished Country Parson. 9 Read Country Parson. 10.

MONDAY, OCTOBER 1. 5 Wrote diary; private prayer; read Nelson and meditated with Natt. 7 Public Prayers.[40] 8 Breakfast at Charles Wes-

---

37 *De usu logicæ* was *Appendix prima* of Robert Sanderson's *Logicæ artis compendium* (1615; see Appendix 3); cf. 4 April and 13 May. John Wesley published an abridged English translation of this ("Of the Manner of Using Logic") as an appendix to the second edition of his translation, *A Compendium of Logic* (1756), of Henry Aldrich's similar textbook, *Logicæ artis compendium* (1691; see Appendix 3).

38 This day was the festival of St. Michael and All Angels (see Nelson, *Festivals,* ch. XXXI).

39 Ibid.

40 The time for weekday morning prayers in the Queen's College chapel now moves to seven and remains so quite regularly throughout the short daylight hours of the winter months until after Easter (when it reverts to the earlier hour).

ley's, religious talk. 9.30 Came home; translated Sanderson. 11.30 Walked with Natt, religious talk (various). 12 Dinner. 1 Translated Sanderson. 2 Began Longinus with Natt. 4.30 Wrote diary; private prayer; wrote diary [summary].[41] 5 Public Prayers. 5.30 Supper. 6.30 With Natt and Knail, read Brown's *Divine Analogy*. 10.

TUESDAY, OCTOBER 2. 5.30 Wrote diary; private prayer; read Nelson and meditated with Natt. 7 Public Prayers; read Aldrich; breakfast. 9.30 Translated Sanderson. 11 Walked. 11.45 Wrote diary; private prayer. 12 Dinner. 1 Logic; Charles Wesley's, wrote diary [summary], religious talk. 3 Wrote questions to be asked of our friends.[42] 5 Wrote diary; private prayer. 5.30 Public Prayers.[43] 6 Supper. 7 With Natt and Knail, read Brown. 10.

WEDNESDAY, OCTOBER 3. 4.45 Wrote diary; private prayer; began Country Parson with Watson. 6 Read Nelson and meditated. 7 Public Prayers. 8 Read Nelson on Fasting and Fridays[44] with Natt. 10 Wrote Theme.[45] 11 Walked. 11.45 Wrote diary; private prayer. 12 Hall. 1 Logic at Charles Wesley's. 2 Translated Sanderson. 3 Private prayer; breakfast;[46] Law, read [aloud]. 4 Came home; read Longinus. 5 Wrote diary; private prayer. 5.30 Public Prayers. 6 Hall. 7 At Smith's, began Barrow on Industry. 9 Translated Sanderson. 10.

THURSDAY, OCTOBER 4. 5.30 Wrote diary; private prayer; read Country Parson; read Nelson and meditated. 7 Public Prayers. 8 Breakfast with Natt, good talk. 9 Read Logic. 10 Translated Sanderson. 11 Walked

---

[41] Following the Wesleyan pattern, Ingham reviewed his activities monthly and wrote a summary of readings, compositions, letters, and acquaintances in the back of his diary (in dos-à-dos fashion, turning the book over and upside down to begin as at the front). This he later calls "casting up" his diary, but for several months indicates this process by some simple extension of his usual abbreviation for "wrote diary" ("d"), such as "wr d," or "ddd." See plate 16.

[42] See *Letters*, I, 339–40.

[43] Evening chapel here reverts to five-thirty as the regular time, until 11 February (supper changing likewise to a new time).

[44] Nelson, *Fasts*, ch. XI, "All the Fridays in the Year, except Christmas Day."

[45] An exercise or essay generally written for a tutor as a part of the weekly course of collegiate studies (s.v. "Genesis," in Glossary).

[46] This was Ingham's first full observance of the Stations, not breaking the fast until 3 p.m. Note that he also fasted at suppertime, going to the Hall (as also at noon, as required by the college statutes; see *Statutes*, III.1) but not eating (cf. *Letters*, I, 434f.). See plate 9.

with Washington, religious and useful talk. 11.45 Wrote diary; private prayer. 12 Dinner. 1 Logic at Charles Wesley's. 2.30 Came home; Lecture. 3.45 Wrote to Charles Burton. 5 Wrote diary; private prayer. 5.30 Public Prayers. 6 Supper. 7 With Natt and Knail, read Brown. 10.

FRIDAY, OCTOBER 5. 4.30 Wrote diary; private prayer; read Country Parson; read Nelson; meditated. 7 Public Prayers. 8 Read Grotius. 9 Translated Sanderson and wrote *genesis* [*thematica*]. 11 Walked with Natt, learned and useful talk. 12 Hall. 12.30 Wrote diary; private prayer. 1 Logic at Charles Wesley's. 2 Read Barrow. 3 Private prayer; breakfast; Law, read [aloud]. 4 Came home; finished Longinus. 5 Wrote diary; private prayer. 5.30 Public Prayers. 6 General Examination. 7 With Natt, [read] Grotius. 10.

SATURDAY, OCTOBER 6. 4.45 Wrote diary; private prayer; read Country Parson; read Nelson and meditated. 7 Public Prayers. 8 Breakfast with Natt and Knail, various and useful talk. 9 Translated Sanderson. 11 Walked with Washington. 11.45 Wrote diary; private prayer. 12 Dinner. 1 Logic at Charles Wesley's, religious talk. 2.30 Came home; Lecture. 3.30 Translated Sanderson. 5 Wrote diary; private prayer. 5.30 Public Prayers. 6 Supper. 7 At Smith's, read Barrow. 9 Came home; read Nelson with Watson, religious talk. 10.

SUNDAY, OCTOBER 7. 4.30 Wrote diary; private prayer; read Country Parson. 6.30 Dressed. 7 At Christ Church, Public Prayers, Sacrament;[47] with Charles Wesley, religious talk. 9 Read Ellis. 10 Sermon. 11 Walked with Natt, religious talk. 11.45 Wrote diary; private prayer. 12 Dinner. 1 Began *genesis* [*thematica*] on the Sacrament. 2 Sermon. 3 Finished *genesis* on the Sacrament with Natt. 5 Wrote diary; private prayer. 5.30 Public Prayers. 6 Supper. 7 At Smith's, finished Barrow on Industry. 9.15 Came home; with Watson, religious talk. 10. I dedicated myself to God.[48]

47 When they were in town, the Wesleys regularly received the Sacrament early Sunday mornings at Christ Church. Except for this one occasion, Ingham attended early Sunday morning chapel (at eight) at Queen's College every week until February, when he began joining the Wesleys quite regularly for the Sacrament. At this diary entry, in the margin, Ingham drew a cross, a mark used throughout the rest of the diary to indicate "contrition" and frequently associated with the Sacrament (see key to symbols, plate 4; cf. 17 October, 3 and 4 April, and 17 July for use of this symbol in other contexts).

48 This entry, the first in shorthand in the diary, is the first of several notices of personal resignation and dedication (see especially 22 February and 12 April). See 3 December, note 116.

MONDAY, OCTOBER 8.   5 Wrote diary; private prayer; read Nelson; read Country Parson. 7 Public Prayers. 8 Breakfast with Natt and Atkinson, good talk. 9 Read Logic. 10 Translated Sanderson. 11 Walked with Washington, good talk (various). 11.45 Wrote diary; private prayer. 12 Dinner. 1 Logic at Charles Wesley's. 2 Came home; Lecture; began Sanderson *De obligatione conscientiæ.*[49] 5 Wrote diary; private prayer. 5.30 Public Prayers. 6 Supper. 7 With Natt and Atkinson, read Ellis on the Sacrament. 10.

TUESDAY, OCTOBER 9.   5 Wrote diary; private prayer; read Nelson and Country Parson. 6 At Charles Wesley's. 7 Public Prayers. 8 Breakfast at Charles Wesley's, religious talk. 9 Public Prayers, Sermon, and Sacrament.[50] 12 Dinner. 1 Walked with Natt, religious and useful talk. 1.30 Came home; began Greek Testament with Natt. 5 Wrote diary; private prayer. 5.30 Public Prayers. 6 Supper. 7 With Natt, read Greek Testament, religious talk. 10.

WEDNESDAY, OCTOBER 10.   5.30 Wrote diary; private prayer; read Nelson; meditated and Country Parson. 7 Public Prayers. 8 Read Logic. 10 Disputations.[51] 12 Wrote diary; private prayer. 1 Logic at Charles Wesley's, private prayer; breakfast; Law, read [aloud]. 4.15 Came home; with Natt, religious talk. 5 Wrote diary; private prayer; read Nelson. 5.30 Public Prayers. 6 Hall. 7 At Smith's, and Robson, began Lucas'[52] *Practical Christianity.* 9 Read Logic. 10.

THURSDAY, OCTOBER 11.   6 Wrote diary; private prayer; read Country Parson. 7 Public Prayers. 8 At the Sale. 9 Breakfast with Natt, good talk (various). 10 Sale. 11.45 Wrote diary; private prayer. 12 Dinner. 1

---

[49]   The Saturday afternoon lectures here turn to ethics, focusing on this popular textbook; see Appendix 3.

[50]   This is the service required by the statutes at the beginning of term—"after public prayers according to the Church of England Liturgy have been read in St. Mary's Church, a Latin sermon to the clergy shall be preached . . . ; the sermon ended, they shall with all decency and reverence commence the celebration of the holy sacrament." *Statutes,* I.2. Wesley noted that there were "10 Masters of Arts at St Mary's Sacrament" on this occasion, a larger crowd than on most previous occasions (OD IV, 2; cf. 12 January, 23 April, and 10 June).

[51]   This is the first day of Michaelmas term. Ingham's attendance at disputations is quite regular on Mondays, Tuesdays, Wednesdays, and Fridays at 11 a.m. As there are no statutory provisions for disputations in the university at that hour, these appear to be collegiate exercises at Queen's (cf. *Statutes,* VI.2).

[52]   MS. reads "Leucas."

Logic at Charles Wesley's. 2 Read Greek Testament. 5 Wrote diary; private prayer; read Nelson. 5.30 Public Prayers. 6 Supper. 7 With the Servitors, learned talk (various). 10.

FRIDAY, OCTOBER 12. 5 Wrote diary; private prayer; read Nelson and Country Parson. 7 Public Prayers. 8 Composed Opposition; and [at] Disputations. 12 Wrote diary; private prayer; Hall. 1 Logic at Charles Wesley's, private prayer; breakfast; Law, read [aloud]. 4 Read Logic. 5 Wrote diary; private prayer. 5.30 Public Prayers. 6 Supper.[53] 6.30 With Natt and Knail. 10.

SATURDAY, OCTOBER 13. 5 Wrote diary; private prayer; read Nelson; meditated. 7 Public Prayers. 8 Breakfast with Natt. 9 Composed Theme. 10 Translated Sanderson. 12 Wrote diary; private prayer; dinner. 1 Logic at Charles Wesley's, religious talk. 2 Read Greek Testament, and at Lecture. 5 Wrote diary; private prayer. 5.30 Public Prayers. 6 Supper. 7 With Smith and Robson, read Lucas. 9 Read Logic. 10.

SUNDAY, OCTOBER 14. 6 Wrote diary; private prayer; read Nelson; meditated; read Country Parson. 8 Public Prayers. 9 Dressed. 10 Sermon. 11 Began *The Whole Duty of Man* with Natt. 11.45 Wrote diary; private prayer. 12 Dinner. 1 Read *Whole Duty*. 2 Sermon. 3 Read *Whole Duty*. 5 Wrote diary; private prayer. 5.30 Public Prayers. 6 Supper. 7 [At][54] Smith's, and Robson, read Lucas. 9 Meditated. 10.

MONDAY, OCTOBER 15. 4.30 Wrote diary; private prayer; read Nelson; meditated; finished the Country Parson with Watson. 7 Public Prayers. 8 Translated. 9 Logic at Charles Wesley's. 10 Disputations. 12 Wrote diary; private prayer; dinner. 1 Walked. 1.30 Read Greek Testament. 5 Wrote Diary; private prayer. 5.30 Public Prayers. 6 Supper. 7 With Natt and Knail, read Brown. 10.

TUESDAY, OCTOBER 16. 5 Wrote diary; private prayer; read Nelson and meditated. 7 Public Prayers. 8 Breakfast. 8.30 Translated Sanderson. 11 Disputations. 12 Wrote diary; private prayer; dinner. 1 Logic at Charles

---

[53] This is the only exception in this diary before 21 December to Ingham's fasting at suppertime on Fridays, a practice he again implements during Lent (see Lent Rule 8, p. 119).

[54] MS. reads "with," which would imply they had met in Ingham's room; the normal pattern up to this point, however, had been to meet Sunday evenings at Christ Church in Smith's room, as the possessive ending in this entry also indicates.

Wesley's. 2 Read Greek Testament. 3 At the Poetic Lecture.[55] 4 Read Greek Testament. 5 Wrote diary; private prayer; read Nelson. 5.30 Public Prayers. 6 Supper. 7 With Knail and Natt. 10.

WEDNESDAY, OCTOBER 17.   5 Wrote diary; private prayer; read Nelson. 6 Composed *genesis thematica* on Humility. 7 Public Prayers. 8 Read Grotius. 10 Wrote *genesis thematica*. 11 Disputations. 12 Wrote diary; private prayer; Hall. 1 At Smith's, began Rodriguez on Humility. 3 Breakfast at Charles Wesley's. 4 Walked. 5 Wrote diary; private prayer; read Ken's *Meditations*.[56] 5.30 Public Prayers. 6 Hall. 7 With Smith and Robson, read Lucas. 9.15 Came home; thought. 10.

THURSDAY, OCTOBER 18.   4.30 Wrote diary; private prayer; read Nelson.[57] 7 Read Grotius. 8 Public Prayers. 9 Breakfast; read Norris on Singularity.[58] 10 Sermon.[59] 11 Walked with Brownsword, religious and useful talk. 11.45 Wrote diary; meditated; private prayer. 12 Dinner. 1 At Charles Wesley's. 2 Read Greek Testament. 5 Wrote diary; private prayer. 5.30 Public Prayers. 6 Supper. 7 With Natt and Knail, learned and useful talk. 10.30.

FRIDAY, OCTOBER 19.   5.30 Wrote diary; private prayer; read Nelson. 7 Public Prayers. 8 Read Logic. 9 At Charles Wesley's. 10 Wrote letter

---

[55]   The professor of poetry from 1728 to 1738 was Joseph Spence who, under the conditions establishing the poetical lectureship by Henry Birkhead, was "to lecture in the Natural Philosophy school on every first Tuesday in full term at three o'clock in the afternoon," and during the period of the Act. *Statutes*, Appendix, p. 299. It appears, however, that Spence held the position as an academic sinecure and apparently did not deliver any lectures (*D.N.B.*, vol. 18, 745). He does seem to have arranged for substitute readers on some occasions, as here and on 22 January. At the Act in July 1733 Spence was concluding a thirty-month tour of Europe, and the Poetic Lecture was given by Mr. Roller, Fellow of New College. *The Oxford Act, 1733; being a Particular and Exact Account of that Solemnity* (London: J. Wilford, 1735), p. 6.

[56]   See Thomas Ken, *The Retired Christian Exercised in Divine Thoughts and Heavenly Meditations for the Closet* (1737), in Appendix 3.

[57]   This day was the festival of St. Luke the Evangelist (see Nelson, *Festivals*, ch. XXXII).

[58]   "Religious Singularity," a sermon on Rom. 12:2, in John Norris's *Practical Discourses Upon the Beatitudes of Our Lord* (1728), vol. II; also published separately as *Religious Singularity Displayed* (9th ed., London, 1725); see Appendix 3.

[59]   Festival of St. Luke the Evangelist.

to my mother.[60] 11 Disputations. 12 Wrote diary; meditated; private prayer; Hall. 1 Greek Lecture.[61] 2.30 Breakfast with Natt, religious talk, read Country Parson. 5 Wrote diary; General Examination; private prayer. 5.30 Public Prayers. 6 With Natt, read Greek Testament. 8 Knail, various talk. 10.

SATURDAY, OCTOBER 20. 4.30 Wrote diary; private prayer; read Nelson. 6 Composed a Theme. 7 Public Prayers. 8 Breakfast with Natt, various and useful talk. 9 Wrote Supposition. 11.45 Wrote diary; private prayer. 12 Dinner. 1 Read Logic. 2 Lecture. 4 Walked with Natt, learned talk. 5 Wrote diary; private prayer. 5.30 Public Prayers. 6 Supper. 7 At Robson's, and Smith, read sermon [of] Atterbury. 9 With Natt, learned talk. 10.

SUNDAY, OCTOBER 21. 6 Wrote diary; private prayer. 6.30 Breakfast at John Wesley's, religious talk. 7.30 Meditated. 8 Public Prayers. 9 Read Nelson on the Sacrament. 9.30 At the Castle.[62] 11.45 Wrote diary; meditated; private prayer. 12 Dinner. 1 With Natt, read *Whole Duty*. 2 Sermon. 3 Walked with Knail, religious and useful talk. 4 Abridged sermon. 5 Wrote diary; private prayer; meditated. 5.30 Public Prayers. 6 Supper. 7 At Robson's, and Smith, read Lucas. 9.30 With Natt, good talk. 10.

MONDAY, OCTOBER 22. 4.30 Private prayer; read Nelson; meditated; read Country Parson and a sermon on Indifferency[63] with Watson. 5 Wrote diary; wrote a Supposition for Yates. 7 Public Prayers. 8 Break-

[60] This letter is not extant; the curious might wonder if Ingham would have mentioned that this day the builders began tearing down the eastern portion of the south side of Queen's College in order to begin building a new quadrangle. See Hearne, *Collections*, vol. 11, 270.

[61] This may have been a collegiate rather than a university lecture. Beginning 23 October, Ingham attended Greek lectures regularly at 3 p.m. on Tuesdays and Fridays, quite a different hour from that specified in the statutory regulations for the Regius Professor of the Greek Language (see *Statutes*, III.12). Henry VIII had appointed Greek lectures in Queen's College and Merton College (Salmon, *Present State*, p. 131).

[62] There is a cross in the margin at this entry ("contrition"), although there is no indication here or in Wesley's diary that the Sacrament was administered (the usual occasion for such a notation); see 7 October and plate 10.

[63] Though no author is here noted, Ingham does read Edward Young's sermon, "The Danger of Indifferency," on 24 March. See Appendix 3.

fast with Yates, learned talk. 9 Wrote a Supposition. 11 Disputations.
12 Dinner. 1 Logic at Charles Wesley's. 2 Read Greek Testament. 5
Wrote diary; private prayer. 5.30 Public Prayers. 6 Supper. 7 At Atkinson's, read Country Parson, religious talk. 9.

TUESDAY, OCTOBER 23.   5 Wrote diary; private prayer; read Nelson
and Country Parson. 6.30 Began a *genesis thematica* on Patience. 7 Public Prayers. 8 Breakfast. 8.30 Read Logic. 11 Disputations. 12 Wrote
diary; meditated; private prayer. 12.15 Dinner. 1 At Charles Wesley's.
2 Read Greek Testament. 3 Greek Lecture. 4 Read Logic. 5 Wrote
diary; private prayer; meditated. 5.30 Public Prayers. 6 Supper. 7 With
Whitaker, religious and useful talk. 9 Came home; wrote letter to brother
William. 10.

WEDNESDAY, OCTOBER 24.   5 Wrote diary; private prayer; read Nelson
and Country Parson. 6.30 Wrote a letter [to] mother. 7 Public Prayers.
8 Finished letter. 9 Read Logic. 10 Wrote a Supposition. 11 Disputations. 12 Wrote diary; private prayer. 12.30 Hall. 1 At Charles Wesley's. 2 Read Rodriguez. 3 Private prayer; breakfast at Charles Wesley's;
Law, read [aloud]. 4 Read Greek Testament. 5 Wrote diary; private
prayer. 5.30 Public Prayers. 6 Supper. 7 At Smith's, and Robson, read
Lucas. 9 Came home. 10.

THURSDAY, OCTOBER 25.   Wrote diary; private prayer; meditated. 6
Finished *genesis thematica.* 7 Public Prayers. 8 Breakfast. 8.30 Translated Kennet.[64] 10 Read Logic. 11 Walked. 11.45 Wrote diary; meditated; private prayer. 12 Dinner. 1 Logic at Charles Wesley's. 2 Read
Greek Testament. 5 Wrote diary; private prayer. 5.30 Public Prayers.
6 Supper. 7 With Natt and Knail. 9.30 Began to read a chapter in the
Greek Testament; design to continue.[65] 10.

[64] This exercise translating Basil Kennet's *Romæ Antiquiæ Notitia* (1696)
invariably occurs on Thursday mornings (see Appendix 3).
[65] Ingham had begun reading the Greek Testament with Natt two weeks
earlier but here regularized the exercise to a chapter a day. During October, he
and Natt read Matthew and Mark (see monthly summary for October 1733). On
20 November he extended this plan to Atkinson as well, having by then settled
on a personal schedule of three chapters a day, morning, noon, and night (see
14 November). Marginal checks ("xxx") here and at selected subsequent entries
apparently indicate the implementation of special actions or good resolutions
(usually entered in shorthand) until just before the new format begins in
March, whereupon the symbol for good resolutions becomes "o" (see key to
symbols, plate 4; also see plate 10 and 14 February, note 203).

FRIDAY, OCTOBER 26. 5.45 Private prayer; read Nelson and Country Parson. 7 Public Prayers. 8 Read Nelson. 8.30 Composed Opposition; Disputations. 12 Wrote diary; private prayer; Hall. 1 At Charles Wesley's. 2 Greek Lecture. 4 Breakfast at Charles Wesley's, religious talk. 4.30 Read John Wesley's letter to Morgan.[66] 5 Wrote diary; private prayer. 5.30 Public Prayers. 6 General Examination. 6.30 With Natt and Knail, read Brown. 10.

SATURDAY, OCTOBER 27. 5 Wrote diary; private prayer; read Nelson and Country Parson; meditated. 7 Public Prayers. 8 Breakfast with Ford, religious talk, read Nelson and Country Parson. 9.30 Came home; read Logic. 11.45 Wrote diary; meditated; private prayer. 12 Dinner. 1 At Charles Wesley's, religious talk. 1.30 Came home; read Greek Testament. 3 Lecture. 4 Walked. 5 Wrote diary; private prayer. 5.30 Public Prayers. 6 Hall. 7 At Robson's, and Smith. 9 Came home; read Nelson [on] Vigils. 10.

SUNDAY, OCTOBER 28. 6 Wrote diary; private prayer; read Nelson,[67] and Norris' _Advice to his Children._[68] 8 Public Prayers. 9 Breakfast with Natt and Ford, religious and useful talk. 10 Sermon.[69] 11 Began Ellis' _Christianity in Short_ with Natt. 11.45 Wrote diary; meditated; private prayer. 12 Dinner. 1 Read Ellis. 2 Sermon. 3 With Ford, religious talk. 5 Wrote diary; private prayer; read Nelson. 5.30 Public Prayers. 6 Supper. 7 At Robson's, and Smith, read Lucas. 9 Finished Ellis. 10.

MONDAY, OCTOBER 29. 6 Wrote diary; private prayer; read Nelson and Country Parson. 7 Public Prayers. 8 Breakfast with Atkinson; read Country Parson, religious talk. 9 Read Greek Testament. 11.45 Wrote diary; private prayer. 12 Dinner. 1 At Smith's. 1.30 Came home; read Greek

[66] This was probably the letter of 19 October 1732 outlining for William Morgan's father the rationale and development of the first Wesleyan group at Oxford. The letter provided the substance for an anonymous publication, _The Oxford Methodists,_ in 1733, and Wesley later prefixed his own text of the letter ("as it was wrote, without any addition, diminution, or amendment") to his published _Journal._

[67] This day was the festival of St. Simon and St. Jude (see Nelson, _Festivals,_ ch. XXXIII).

[68] See John Norris, _Spiritual Counsel_ (1694), in Appendix 3.

[69] Festival of St. Simon and St. Jude. The statutes specified that this sermon be delivered in the church of St. Peter in the East (just across the lane from Queen's College) by some member of University College (_Statutes,_ XVI.5).

Testament. 5 Wrote diary; private prayer. 5.30 Public Prayers. 6 Supper. 7 With Yates. 9 <u>Made an Argument for him.</u>[70] 10.

TUESDAY, OCTOBER 30.   4 Wrote diary; private prayer; meditated; read Nelson and Taylor on the Sacrament.[71] 7 Public Prayers. 8 Walked with Ford and Atkinson, and breakfast, religious talk. 9.30 Read Greek Testament. 11.45 Wrote diary; meditated; private prayer. 12 Dinner. 1 At Charles Wesley's. 2 Read Greek Testament. 4.30 Walked. 5 Wrote diary; private prayer; read Nelson. 5.30 Public Prayers. 6 Supper. 7 With Natt, read *Whole Duty* on the Sacrament. 10.

WEDNESDAY, OCTOBER 31.   5.30 Wrote diary; read Nelson; private prayer; Country Parson. 7 Public Prayers. 8 Read *genesis problematica* on the Stations[72] with Atkinson and Ford. 10 Read Greek Testament. 11.45 Wrote diary; private prayer; meditated. 12 Hall. 12.45 At Smith's, transcribed Stationary prayers.[73] 3 Breakfast at Charles Wesley's. 4 Walked with Natt, religious talk. 5 Wrote diary; meditated; private prayer. 5.30 Public Prayers. 6 Hall. 7 With Smith and Robson, finished Lucas on Happiness.[74] 9 At Lecture.[75] 9.30 With Natt, religious talk. 10.

THURSDAY, NOVEMBER 1.   4 Meditated. 4.30 Wrote diary; private prayer; read Brevint. 7 Breakfast at Ford's, etc, read Country Parson and Nelson, religious talk. 9 Dressed. 9.30 Public Prayers, Sermon and Sacrament.[76] 11.30 Read Country Parson; private prayer. 12 Wrote

[70]   A set of syllogisms (in Latin) on a question in logic, to be used in a disputation (see Glossary, s.v. "Supposition," "Disputation," and "Opposition"). Standard forms of these were frequently passed on from one student generation to another, as in this instance, and often referred to as "strings." See Nicholas Amhurst, *Terrae Filius; or, The Secret History of the University of Oxford* (London, 1726), no. XX, XXI. "Argument" was the more common term at Cambridge University. *Gentleman's Magazine* 50 (July 1780), p. 277.

[71]   See Jeremy Taylor, *The Rule and Exercises of Holy Living* (1650), ch. IV, sec. 10, "Of preparation to, and the manner how to receive the sacrament of the Lord's Supper" (see Appendix 3).

[72]   See 14 September, note 22.

[73]   Ingham gives no clue as to the source of these prayers (cf. 12 June).

[74]   This would appear to be Richard Lucas's *An Enquiry after Happiness* (1685), but the monthly summary mentions only Lucas's *Practical Christianity* (1700), which they had begun to read thrice weekly on 10 October. (See Appendix 3).

[75]   An unusual time for a lecture (see also 3, 4, and 10 November).

[76]   This day is the festival of All Saints (cf. Nelson, *Festivals,* ch. XXXIV).

diary. 12.15 Dinner. 1.30 Read *Christian Prudence*[77] with Ford and Washington. 4.30 Tea at Natt's, good talk (various). 5 Wrote diary; private prayer. 5.30 Public Prayers. 6 Supper. 7 With Natt and Knail, religious and useful talk. 10.30. Observe, this day I taught Ford, Atkinson, and Washington to write a diary.[78] I was with Natt and them the first part of the day. I had good conversation, and I received a great deal of attention and pleasure. At night I had a dispute with Knail, whom I had obliged to observe the fast; he held that the Church did not [have] power to institute such things, neither are we obliged to keep them.[79]

FRIDAY, NOVEMBER 2. 6 Wrote diary; private prayer; read Nelson. 7 Public Prayers. 8 Read Grotius. 12 Wrote diary; Hall. 1 At Smith's, read Rodriguez. 3 Breakfast at Charles Wesley's, Law and Norris, read [aloud], religious talk. 5 Wrote diary; private prayer. 5.30 Public Prayers. 6 With Ford, read Country Parson. 7 With Natt and Knail, finished Brown. 10.

SATURDAY, NOVEMBER 3. 2.30 Private prayer; wrote diary. 3 Read Norris and Country Parson. 4 Read Norris on religious conversation.[80] 5.30 Thought and meditated. 6.30 Private prayer; read Country Parson. 7 Public Prayers. 8 Breakfast; dressed. 9 Read a sermon on Meditation with Atkinson and walked with him, religious talk. 11.45 Wrote diary; private prayer. 12 Dinner. 1 Charles Wesley's. 2 Lecture. 4 Read a sermon of Norris. 5 Meditated; private prayer; wrote diary. 5.30 Public Prayers. 6 Supper. 7 At Robson and Smith's, began Goodman's *Penitent*

[77] See John Norris in Appendix 3. Ingham had transcribed this work in September.

[78] Diary keeping was a common but not universal practice among the Oxford Methodists. There is evidence that fifteen of them did keep a diary. Ingham taught at least six of his friends the method (Hervey and Watson in addition to those mentioned here), but some others, such as Greives, refused to adopt the practice (see 30 April). He also kept his friends up to date with revisions in the method, passed on from John Wesley through Charles, which apparently became burdensome for some, such as Watson and Smith (see 19 and 25 April). Ingham occasionally helped his friends by writing out their diaries for them (see 15 November, 1 January, 4 May).

[79] Fasting (observing the Stations) was another characteristic, though not universally practiced, discipline exercised by many early Methodists. This is only the first of several major disputes that Ingham notes on this topic (see 27 March, 4, 15, 16, 17 April, 25 May, and 6 June).

[80] See Norris, "Religious Discourse in Common Conversation," a sermon on Psalm 37:30, in *Practical Discourses,* vol. IV. Note the early hour of rising on this day.

Pardoned. 9 At Lecture. 9.30 With Natt, religious talk about fasting, he would we pray indifferent as to the days.[81] 10.30.

SUNDAY, NOVEMBER 4.   5 Private prayer; wrote diary; meditated; read Nelson. 6 Began Thomas à Kempis. 7 Dressed. 7.30 With Ford, religious talk. 8 Public Prayers. 9 Breakfast at John Wesley's, religious talk.[82] 10 Sermon. 11 With Ford, read sermon. 12 Dinner. 1 Wrote diary; at Ford's, read Norris. 2 Sermon. 3 Walked with Ford, Atkinson, and Washington, religious talk; read Norris. 5 Wrote diary; private prayer. 5.30 Public Prayers. 6 Supper. 7 At Smith's, and Robson, read Goodman. 9 Lecture. 9 .30 With Natt, good talk. 10.

MONDAY, NOVEMBER 5.   5 Read Nelson; private prayer. 6 General Examination; read Thomas à Kempis; private prayer; with Ford, religious talk. 8 Public Prayers. 9 Breakfast with Ford, etc, religious talk, read Nelson. 10 Public Prayers, Sermon, Sacrament.[83] 12.30 Dinner. 2 Walked with Smith, good talk. 3 Wrote diary; read Grotius. 5 Wrote diary; private prayer. 5.30 Public Prayers. 6 Supper. 7 With Natt and Knail, read Collier. 10. Observe: this day I was overjoyed.

TUESDAY, NOVEMBER 6.   5 Private prayer; meditated; read Thomas à Kempis. 6 Wrote diary [summary].[84] 7 Public Prayers. 8 Began Aldrich's Logic with Ford, Atkinson, and Washington. 8.30 Breakfast with Natt and Knail, various and useful talk. 9.30 Disputations. 12 Private prayer; wrote diary. 12.15 Dinner. 1 Walked. 1.30 Read Grotius. 3 Greek Lecture. 4 Began Sanderson *De obligatione conscientiæ.* 5 Private prayer; wrote diary. 5.30 Public Prayers. 6 Supper. 7 With Ford, Atkinson, and Washington, read *Spectator.* 10.

[81]   A reference to the practice of using particular prayers for each day of the week. See 20 January, note 168.

[82]   Wesley's diary entry reads: "9 Ingham, tea, religious talk, he resolved to attend Sacrament at St. Mary's" (OD IV, 10). See also 5 November.

[83]   This day commemorated the "happy deliverance" in 1605 from the "Papist Conspiracy" or "Gunpowder Treason," popularly known as Guy Fawkes Day. See "A Form of Prayer with Thanksgiving to be used Yearly upon the Fifth of November . . ." (*B.C.P.*). The statutes provide for an "extraordinary" sermon (distinguished from a "routine" sermon) to be delivered at St. Mary's, preceded by public prayers and followed by Holy Communion (*Statutes,* XVI.4). The sermon on this occasion was preached by Mr. Walwin (Francis Walwyn?), Fellow of University College. Hearne, *Collections,* vol. 11, 274.

[84]   See monthly summary for October 1733.

WEDNESDAY, NOVEMBER 7. 6 Wrote diary; read Nelson; private prayer; meditated; read Thomas à Kempis. 7 Public Prayers. 8 Read Logic. 8.30 Private prayer. 9 Read Sanderson. 11 Disputations. 12 Wrote diary; private prayer. 12.15 Hall. 1 Read Sanderson. 3 Breakfast at Charles Wesley's, Law, read [aloud]. 4 Walked with Natt, learned talk (various). 5 Private prayer; read Nelson; wrote diary. 5.30 Public Prayers. 6 Supper. 7 Walked. 7.30 With me, Atkinson and Washington, read Thomas à Kempis, religious talk. 9 Meditated.[85] 10.

THURSDAY, NOVEMBER 8. 5 Meditated; private prayer; meditated; read Thomas à Kempis. 6.30 Read Sanderson. 7 Public Prayers and Sermon.[86] 8.30 Breakfast. 9. Translated Kennet. 10 Ford came, religious and useful talk. 11 Read Logic. 12 Dinner. 1 Walked with Knail, learned talk (various). 3 At the Bodleian Speech.[87] 4 Read Grotius. 5 Wrote diary; private prayer. 5.30 Public Prayers. 6 Supper. 7 With Natt, read *Spectator*. 10.

FRIDAY, NOVEMBER 9. 6 Wrote diary; read Nelson; private prayer; read Thomas à Kempis. 7 Public Prayers. 8 Read Aldrich. 8.30 Country Parson. 9 Read Sanderson. 11 Disputations. 12 Wrote diary; private prayer; Hall. 1 Walked. 1.30 Read Homer. 2.45 Private prayer and breakfast with Ford. 3 Greek Lecture. 4 Transcribed copy of verses.[88]

[85] Ingham's previous abbreviations for "meditated" had been "Med," until 26 September, and then "m" until this day. Here he adds a hooked stem to the beginning of the letter m, apparently to indicate some detail. For the next two or three months, he appears to be using this last variation, as well as the regular uppercase M and lowercase m, to indicate some particular distinctions relative to meditation. A possible reading incorporating Weston's shorthand might be: M—read meditations; m—meditated; m with hooked stem—I meditated. For lack of a clear distinction, I have transcribed all these entries as "meditated."

[86] Only twice does Ingham note a sermon at these early chapel services (see 22 November).

[87] This was the day of the annual visitation of the Bodleian Library by its curators (board of governors, see *Statutes*, Appendix, p. 257). The oration given yearly by an M.A. of Christ Church was a set form recording in Latin the praises of Sir Thomas Bodley and lauding the study of Hebrew, although other material was sometimes included (appreciation to Miss R. F. Vyse, University of Oxford Archives, for this information). Fifield Allen, Student of Christ Church (B.A. 1722, M.A. 1725, B.D. 1733) and recently appointed chaplain (7 May 1733) to Bishop Gibson of London, was the speaker on this occasion (Hearne, *Collections*, vol. 11, 275). See 2 April, note 140.

[88] Ingham reveals his interest in poetry several times in this diary, including a whole page of verse in shorthand in the preliminary pages (see p. 59) and the

5 Wrote diary; private prayer. 5.30 Public Prayers. 6 General Examination. 6.30 Supper at Ford's. 7 Began Law's *Christian Perfection* with Ford, Atkinson, and Washington. We appointed to meet every Friday night for the future, to read and encourage one another in virtues and religion.[89] 9.30.

SATURDAY, NOVEMBER 10.   5 Private prayer; meditated; read Nelson and Thomas à Kempis. 6.30 Breakfast at John Wesley's, religious talk.[90] 7.30 Public Prayer. 8 Read Sanderson. 11.45 Wrote diary; private prayer. 12 Dinner. 1 Read Aldrich. 1.30 Read Sanderson. 3 Lecture. 4 Walked with Natt, various and useful talk. 5 Wrote diary; private prayer. 5.30 Public Prayers. 6 Supper. 7 At Smith's, and Robson, read Goodman. 9 Lecture. 9.30 Walked. 10.

SUNDAY, NOVEMBER 11.   6 Wrote diary; read Nelson and meditated; private prayer; read Thomas à Kempis with Atkinson. 7.30 Dressed. 8 Public Prayers. 9 Breakfast and read Goodman. 10 Sermon. 11 Read Thomas à Kempis. 11.45 Wrote diary. 12 Dinner. 1 Read Thomas à Kempis with Natt. 2 Sermon. 3 At Charles Wesley's, read sermon of Norris. 4 Read John Wesley's sermon on the Sacrament with Ford.[91] 5 Wrote diary; private prayer. 5.30 Public Prayers. 6 Supper. 7 At Selby's[92] with Robson and Smith, disputed and [read] Goodman. 9 Read Thomas à Kempis. 10.

MONDAY, NOVEMBER 12.   5.30 Meditated; private prayer; read Thomas à Kempis. 7 Public Prayers. 8 Breakfast at Ford's with Broughton, religious talk. 9 At Charles Wesley's, began the Statutes.[93] 10 Read Sanderson. 11 Walked. 11.45 Wrote diary; private prayer. 12 Dinner. 1 Read

confession on 8 August, "indulged vain thoughts of being a fine poet." One of the two works he later published was *A Collection of Hymns for Societies* (Leeds: Printed by James Lister, 1748). See 15 November.

89   This weekly meeting, with some change in personnel, was maintained regularly throughout the remainder of Ingham's stay at Oxford.

90   Wesley's diary entry reads: "6.30 Smith of Christ Church, Ingham, Selby, tea, ri, religious talk." OD IV, 13.

91   See 8 April, note 168.

92   Ingham had just met Prideaux Selby (Lincoln College, matric. 17 December 1731) at John Wesley's the previous morning (see 10 November, note 90).

93   See *Parecbolae sive excerpta & corpore statutorum Universitatis Oxoniensis* (1729) in Appendix 3.

Aldrich. 1.30 Read Sanderson. 3 With Natt.[94] 4 Read Norris. 5 Wrote diary; private prayer. 5.30 Public Prayers. 6 Supper. 7 With Natt, various talk. 10 Laid with Natt.[95]

TUESDAY, NOVEMBER 13. 2.45 Private prayer; with Natt, various talk; he set forward to London.[96] 4 Went to bed again. 7 Public Prayers. 8 Breakfast. 9 Read Sanderson. 11 Disputations. 12 Dinner. 1 Read Sanderson. 2 At Charles Wesley's. 3 Greek Lecture. 4 Necessary business about ordering the room. 5 Wrote diary; private prayer. 5.30 Public Prayers. 6 Supper. 7 With Ford, etc, read *Guardian*, good talk. 10.

WEDNESDAY, NOVEMBER 14. 6 Private prayer, read Nelson and Thomas à Kempis. 7 Public Prayers. 8 Read Aldrich. 8.30 Read Country Parson, and private prayer with Ford. 9 Read Sanderson. 11 Disputations. 11.45 Wrote diary; private prayer. 12 Hall. 12.30 Began St Luke. 2 At Charles Wesley's. 3 Private prayer and breakfast, Law, read [aloud]. 4 Read Greek Testament. 5 Private prayer. 5.30 Public Prayers. 6 Supper. 7 At Robson's, and Smith. 9 Read Greek Testament. 10. This day I started to read three chapters in the Greek Testament, one at morn, another at noon, and another at night before going to bed.[97]

THURSDAY, NOVEMBER 15. 5 Read Greek Testament; private prayer;

94 This afternoon the "foundation stone" was laid for the new building begun at the southeast end of Queen's College. Hearne, *Collections,* vol. 11, 277.

95 Most of the rooms at Queen's College were suited to double occupancy, and the college statutes expected as a rule "at least two in each chamber." *Queen's College Statutes,* p. 19; cf. John Richard Magrath, *The Flemings in Oxford* (Oxford: Oxford Historical Society, 1904), vol. 1, 3, 257. The housing records for this period are missing, but it appears that Ingham did not at this point have a roommate, though he occasionally stayed with ("laid with") a friend, possibly (though not necessarily) sharing the same bed. When Henry Fothergill came to Queen's in 1730, his older brother George (already a student there) offered to have him "lay with me" though he felt he had enough influence to obtain a "convenient room" if his brother should desire it. *The Fothergills of Ravenstonedale,* ed. Catherine Thornton and Frances McLaughlin (London: William Heinemann, 1906) p. 130.

96 Natt appears to have gone home to Stepney (just east of London) for three months, during which Ingham may have used his room to some extent (see 4 p.m. this day, and 21 February, when Ingham removed his books from Natt's room after his return).

97 For two weeks Ingham will note this as "Greek Testament," or "read Greek Testament." After 27 November the entry becomes simply "chapter."

Thomas à Kempis. 6 Read Sanderson. 7 Public Prayers. 8 Breakfast at Broughton's with Ford, religious talk. 9 Translated Kennet. 10 Began to compose a copy of verses on the marriage of the Prince of Orange.[98] 11 Walked with Ford, learned talk. 11.45 Wrote diary; Greek Testament; private prayer. 12 Dinner. 1 Read Aldrich. 12.30 Wrote Ford's diary. 2 At Charles Wesley's. 3 Verses. 5 Private prayer. 5.30 Public Prayers. 6 Supper. 7 Finished the verses. 9 Greek Testament. 10.

FRIDAY, NOVEMBER 16.   5 Read Greek Testament; private prayer; read Nelson and Thomas à Kempis. 7 Public Prayer. 8 Read Aldrich. 8.30 Began Ellis on the Sacrament with Ford. 9 Read Sanderson. 11 Disputations. 12 Wrote diary; private prayer; Hall. 1 Read Greek Testament. 2 At Charles Wesley's. 2.45 Private prayer, and breakfast with Ford and Atkinson. 3 Greek Lecture. 4 Read Greek Testament. 5 Private prayer. 5.30 Public Prayers. 6 General Examination. 6.30 At Ford's with Atkinson and Washington, read Law. 9 Read Greek Testament; wrote diary. 10.

SATURDAY, NOVEMBER 17.   5 Read Greek Testament and Nelson; private prayer; read Thomas à Kempis. 7 Public Prayers. 8 Breakfast with Ford, religious talk. 9 Composed a Theme. 11 Read Sanderson. 11.45 Wrote diary; private prayer. 12 Dinner. 1 Read Aldrich. 2 Walked with Smith, religious talk. 3 Lecture. 4 Read Greek Testament. 5 Private prayer. 5.30 Public Prayers. 6 Supper. 7 With me, Smith and Robson and Ford, read Goodman. 9 Ford with me, read Bible, religious talk. 10.

SUNDAY, NOVEMBER 18.   6 Meditated. 7 Private prayer; read Nelson. 8 Public Prayers. 9 Breakfast with Ford, religious talk. 10 Public Prayers, Sermon, and Sacrament at the Castle.[99] 11.45 Private prayer. 12 Dinner. 1 Began Norris' *Advice to his Children.* 2 Sermon. 3 Walked with Ford, Atkinson, and Washington, religious talk. 4 Finished Norris. 5

---

[98] William IV, Prince of Orange, had arrived in England on 7 November, intending shortly to marry Princess Anne, eldest daughter of George II. He fell ill, however, and was confined at Bath until late February, the marriage finally taking place on 25 March 1734. The impending nuptials inspired a flood of poetry, including a book of Oxford Verses (by William Harte?) that William Holmes, Vice-Chancellor of the university, took to London "upon account of the marriage" (Hearne, *Collections,* vol. 11, 277, 304, 319f., 331. See 28 February and 1 March).

[99] John Wesley was also at the Castle on this occasion: "read prayers, Sacrament." OD IV, 17.

Private prayer. 5.30 Public Prayers. 6 Supper. 7 At Robson's, and Smith and Ford. 9 Read Bible. I spent this day all together with Ford; read, prayed with him and laid with him.

MONDAY, NOVEMBER 19. 6 Meditated; private prayer; read Nelson. 7 Public Prayers. 8 Read Aldrich. 8.30 Breakfast with Ford and Atkinson. 9 Read Sanderson. 11 Disputations. 12 Wrote diary; private prayer; dinner. 1 Greek Testament. 2 Walked with Smith, good talk. 3 Read Greek Testament. 4.30 Wrote Ford's diary. 5 Private prayer. 5.30 Public Prayers. 6 Supper. 7 With Ford, began 'The Great Importance of a Religious Life'.[100] 9 Read Greek Testament. 10.

TUESDAY, NOVEMBER 20. 6 Private prayer; meditated; finished Thomas à Kempis. 7 Public Prayers. 8 Read Aldrich. 8.30 Breakfast. 9 Read Sanderson. 11 Walked with Ford, learned talk. 11.45 Wrote diary; private prayer. 12 Dinner. 1 Greek Testament. 1.45 Walked with Smith, good talk. 2.15 at Charles Wesley's. 3 Greek Lecture. 4 Greek Testament. 4.30 Began to read chapter in the Greek Testament with Atkinson, promised to continue, began in Romans.[101] 5 Private prayer. 5.30 Public Prayers. 6 Supper. 7 With Knail, read sermon of South's, good talk. 10.

WEDNESDAY, NOVEMBER 21. 6 Private prayer; read Nelson and Greek Testament. 7 Public Prayers. 8 Read Aldrich. 8.30 Wrote Supposition; and Disputations. 12 Hall. 1 Greek Testament. 2 At Charles Wesley's, private prayer, breakfast, Law, read [aloud]. 4 Greek Testament. 4.30 Atkinson. 5 Private prayer. 5.30 Public Prayers. 6 Supper. 7 At Smith's, Robson and Ford, read Goodman. 9 Greek Testament. 10. This day I hired a larum for two shillings a year; Atkinson was to pay one-half and I to call him.[102]

100 "The Importance of a Religious Life, Considered from the Happy Conclusion of It," a sermon on Psalm 37:38 in Norris, *Practical Discourses,* vol. II.

101 Ingham had already agreed to read the Greek Testament regularly with Natt (see 25 October) and was reading it three times a day on his own (see 14 November). His reading with Atkinson, weekdays at four-thirty (entered simply "Atkinson"), continued quite regularly through 20 December when they finished the Book of Romans.

102 Though it was a common practice to pay a servitor to act as an alarm, Ingham seems to have rented an alarm clock, as all references to "larum" in the diary imply a mechanical device ("removed," "set," "stopped," etc.). The alarm was an important part of Ingham's continuing battle against "intemperance in sleep," a typical Wesleyan concern. He not only woke Atkinson regularly, according to their agreement, but during the coming spring also began awakening several other friends to promote their rising early.

THURSDAY, NOVEMBER 22.   4 Private prayer; meditated. 4.30 Greek Testament. 7 Public Prayers and Sermon.[103] 8.15 Read Aldrich. 8.45 Breakfast with Ford, read second part of 'The Great Importance of a Religious Life'. 9.30 Read News.[104] 10 Translated Kennet. 11 Walked. 11.45 Wrote diary; private prayer; meditated. 12 Dinner. 1 Composed Greek Theme. 3 Read Greek Testament. 4.30 Atkinson. 5 Private prayer. 5.30 Public Prayers. 6 Supper. 7 Composed Opposition and Argument. 9 Greek Testament. 9.30.

FRIDAY, NOVEMBER 23.   4 Private prayer; meditated; meditated.[105] 5 Read Greek Testament; private prayer. 7 Public Prayers. 8 Read Aldrich; private prayer. 9 Transcribed Opposition. 9.30 Read Sanderson. 11 Disputations. 12 Wrote diary; private prayer; Hall. 12.45 Private prayer. 1 Greek Testament. 2.45 Private prayer and breakfast at Ford's with Atkinson and Washington, read Taylor on Fasting,[106] religious talk. 4.30 Atkinson. 5 Wrote diary; private prayer. 5.30 Public Prayers. 6 General Examination. 6.30 At Ford's, and Atkinson, Washington, read Law, religious talk. 9.30.

SATURDAY, NOVEMBER 24.   4 Read Greek Testament; private prayer; read Nelson and began the Country Parson. 6 Greek Testament. 7 Public Prayers. 8 Breakfast. 8.30 Composed Theme; dressed. 10 Read Sanderson. 11 Walked. 11.45 Wrote diary; private prayer. 12 Dinner. 1 Greek Testament. 3 Lecture. 4 Walked. 4.30 Atkinson. 5 Private prayer. 5.30 Public Prayers. 6 Supper. 7 At Ford's, Smith, Robson, read Goodman. 9.30.

SUNDAY, NOVEMBER 25.   5.30 Dressed. 6 Private prayer; read Nelson and Country Parson and meditated. 8 Public Prayers. 9 Breakfast with Ford, finished 'The Great Importance of a Religious Life'. 10 Sermon. 11 Walked with Ford, religious talk. 11.45 Wrote diary; private prayer. 12 Dinner. 1 Read sermon with Ford. 2 Sermon. 3 Walked with Ford, religious talk. 4 Read Country Parson and meditated with Ford. 5 Pri-

---

[103] One of two instances where Ingham notes a sermon at the early chapel service (cf. 11 November).

[104] Except for a brief period in the mid-seventeenth century, Oxford had no local newspaper until 1746. The 'News" probably refers to any one of a number of London news sheets which circulated in the country.

[105] The diary reads "M, m," the intended distinction is unclear (see 7 November, note 85).

[106] Taylor, *Holy Living,* ch. IV, "Of Christian Religion," sec. 5, "Of Fasting."

vate prayer. 5.30 Public Prayers. 6 Supper. 7 At Robson's, and Ford, read sermon, religious and useful talk. 9.15 Read Greek Testament. Observe: to rise [at] 4.30 for the full week, to repeat the morning hymn, then dress, then use the prayer of oblation; afterwards wash, then read Greek Testament, private prayer, Country Parson, etc.[107]

MONDAY, NOVEMBER 26.   4.30 Hymn; prayer; read Nelson and Greek Testament; private prayer; read Country Parson. 6 Read Greek Testament. 7 Public Prayers. 8 Read Aldrich. 8.30 Breakfast and composed Argument for Ford. 10 Read Sanderson. 11 Disputations. 12 Wrote diary; private prayer; dinner. 1 Walked with Ford, good talk. 2 Read Greek Testament. 4.30 Atkinson. 5 Private prayer. 5.30 Public Prayers. 6 Supper. 7 Knail with me, began Gravesand's *Philosophy*.[108] 10 Wrote diary.

TUESDAY, NOVEMBER 27.   4.30 Hymn; prayer; read Nelson; dressed; Greek Testament; private prayer; read Country Parson. 6 Read Sanderson. 7 Public Prayers. 8 Breakfast with me, Ford and Smyth, religious talk. 9 Composed Argument for Ford. 10 Read Sanderson. 11 Disputations. 12 Wrote diary; private prayer; dinner. 1 At Smith's, various talk. 2 Read Sanderson. 3 Greek Lecture. 4 Sanderson. 4.30 Atkinson. 5 Read Greek Testament; private prayer. 5.30 Public Prayers. 6 Supper. 7 Knail with me, read Gravesande. 9.45.

WEDNESDAY, NOVEMBER 28.   4.30[109] Read Nelson and meditated. 5 Chapter;[110] private prayer; read Country Parson. 6 Sanderson. 7 Public Prayers. 8 Aldrich. 8.30 Composed Argument for Ford. 9 Meditated and meditated. 11 Disputations. 12 Hall. 12.30 Wrote diary; read Country Parson, and private prayer. 1 Read Sanderson. 3 Breakfast with me, Ford

107   This shorthand entry provides a fuller description of his early morning routine than the usual diary entries. The morning hymn and prayer of oblation may have been from Robert Nelson's *Practice of True Devotion* (ch. I, sec. 1, and "Hymns [and] Devotions" after ch. XX) or collected from a similar source. See Appendix 3; cf. 17 May, note 131.

108   See Willem Jacob van 's Gravesande, *Mathematical Elements of Natural Philosophy* (1720, 1721) in Appendix 3. Ingham often refers to this work as "Experimental Philosophy."

109   A hyphen after the time entry here and the following two mornings may indicate "hymn, prayer," in keeping with his resolution on the previous Sunday evening.

110   Ingham here begins using "chapter" to indicate "read chapter in Greek Testament" three times a day (see resolution, 14 November).

and Atkinson, good talk. 3.30 Walked with Ford. 4.30 Atkinson. 5 Chapter; private prayer. 5.30 Public Prayers. 6 Supper. 7 With me, Smith, Robson, Ford, read Goodman. 9 Chapter.

THURSDAY, NOVEMBER 29.   4.30 Read Nelson and meditated; chapter; private prayer; read Country Parson. 6 Sanderson. 7 Public Prayers. 8 Breakfast at Ford's with Smyth, religious talk. 9 Translated Kennet. 10 Sanderson. 11 Walked. 11.45 Wrote diary; chapter; private prayer. 12 Dinner. 1 Walked. 2 Read Sanderson. 4.30 Read Nelson and chapter; private prayer. 5.30 Public Prayers. 6 Hall. 7 At Ford's, Washington, Smyth, Richardson, read Sherlock on Death. 9.45 Chapter. 10.

FRIDAY, NOVEMBER 30.   4.30 Read Nelson for the day;[111] private prayer; finished Country Parson. 6 Read Ken with Ford. 7 Meditated. 8 Public Prayers. 9 Read Country Parson with Ford. 10 Sermon.[112] 11 Wrote Ford's diary. 11.45 Wrote diary; private prayer. 12 Hall. 12.45 Private prayer. 1 Wrote diary [summary]. 2 At Ford's with Atkinson, Washington, and Smyth, read *genesis problematica* on the Stations.[113] 3 Private prayer and breakfast. 5 Private prayer; meditated. 5.30 Public Prayers. 6 General Examination. 6.30 At Ford's, and Washington, read Law's *Christian Perfection,* religious talk. 9.

SATURDAY, DECEMBER 1.   4.30 Meditated. 5 Chapter; private prayer; began Taylor's *Holy Living.* 7 Public Prayers. 8 Breakfast at Ford's with Washington; composed verses. 9.30 Transcribed verses. 11 Walked. 11.45 Chapter; private prayer. 12 Dinner. 1 Wrote Ford's diary. 2 Began the Acts. 4.30 Atkinson. 5 Chapter; private prayer. 5.30 Public Prayer. 6 Supper. 7 At Ford's with Smith, read Nelson, religious and useful talk. 9 Began *The Whole Duty of Man.* 10.

SUNDAY, DECEMBER 2.   4.30 Read Nelson;[114] chapter; private prayer. 5 Read Taylor. 6 Began to abridge Whitby on the New Testament.[115]

---

[111]   This day was the festival of St. Andrew (see Nelson, *Festivals,* ch. III).

[112]   Ibid.

[113]   See diary summary for November 1733. For two o'clock entry, see 14 September, note 22.

[114]   This day was the first Sunday in Advent (see Nelson, *Festivals,* ch. II).

[115]   During December, Ingham abridged the two prefaces and the first five chapters of Matthew in Daniel Whitby's *Paraphrase and Commentary on the New Testament* (see Appendix 3). The "General Preface" is entitled "Concerning the Divine Authority of the Scriptures of the New Testament and the Truth of the Christian Faith." See monthly summary for December 1733.

8 Public Prayers. 9 Breakfast at Washington's with Ford, good talk. 10
Sermon. 11 Walked with Ford, good talk. 11.45 Chapter; private prayer;
wrote diary. 12 Dinner. 1 At Ford's, and Washington, read Nelson. 2
Sermon. 3 Walked with Ford, Washington, good talk. 4 Read Nelson.
4.30 Meditated. 5 Chapter; private prayer. 5.30 Public Prayers. 6 Supper. 7 At Smith's, Robson, Ford, read Goodman. 9.30.

MONDAY, DECEMBER 3. 4.30 Meditated; chapter. 5 Private prayer;
read Taylor. 6 Whitby. 7 Public Prayers. 8 Breakfast with me, Ford,
Smith, good talk (various). 9 Began Gravesande's Experimental Philosophy. 11 Walked with Ford, learned talk. 11.45 Wrote diary; chapter;
private prayer. 12 Dinner. 1 Aldrich. 1.30 Began Shorthand.[116] 2 Read
Greek Testament. 4 Walked. 4.30 Atkinson. 5 Chapter; private prayer.
5.30 Public Prayers. 6 Supper. 7 At Robson's with Smith and Ford. 9.30.

TUESDAY, DECEMBER 4. 4.30 Meditated; chapter; private prayer. 5
Read Taylor. 6 Whitby. 7 Public Prayers. 8 Breakfast at Broughton's
with Ford, religious talk. 9.30 Read Gravesande. 11 Walked with Ford,
learned talk. 11.45 Wrote diary; chapter; private prayer. 12 Dinner.
1 Aldrich. 1.30 Shorthand. 2 Greek Testament. 3 Greek Lecture. 4
Walked. 4.30 Atkinson. 5 Chapter; private prayer. 5.30 Public Prayers.
6 Supper. 7 With Watson, read Norris' sermon on 'Religious Singularity',
religious talk. 10.

WEDNESDAY, DECEMBER 5. 4.30 Meditated; chapter; private prayer;
read Taylor. 6 Whitby. 7 Public Prayers. 8 Began Ken's *Meditations*
with Ford; private prayer. 9 Began composing Declamation.[117] 11 Disputation. 11.45 Wrote diary; chapter; private prayer. 12 Hall. 12.30
Meditated; private prayer. 1 Aldrich. 2 Read News. 2.45 Private prayer.
3 Breakfast at Ford's with Atkinson and Washington, read Ken. 4 Walked.

---

116 See James Weston's *Stenography Compleated* in Appendix 3. Ingham had
begun using this system of shorthand in this diary as early as 7 October. John
Wesley had begun studying Weston's shorthand in 1732 but did not use it in
his diary until 1735 (and then only sporadically), changing to John Byrom's
system the following year at his brother's suggestion. Cf. 8 July and 29 August.
117 A rhetorical exercise (in Latin) on set topics, usually performed in the
college Hall (often at dinner or suppertime in the presence of other scholars),
which served as practice for the disputations (John Magrath, *Queen's College*
[Oxford: Clarendon Press, 1921], vol. 1, 253). Ingham seems to have not completed the exercise at this time (see 15–19 January).

4.30 Read Greek Testament.[118] 5 Meditated; private prayer. 5.30 Public Prayers. 6 Supper. 7 With me, Ford, Smith, Robson, read Goodman. 9.30.

THURSDAY, DECEMBER 6.   4.30 <u>Laid, meditated in bed.</u>[119] 6.30 Chapter; private prayer; read Taylor. 7.30 Public Prayers. 8 Breakfast with Ford, read Ken. 9 <u>Mended my cap.</u> 11.45 Chapter; private prayer. 12 Dinner. 1 <u>Mended my cap.</u>[120] 4.30 Walked. 5 Wrote diary; chapter; private prayer. 5.30 Public Prayers. 6 Supper. 7 With Knail, read Gravesande. 10.15.

FRIDAY, DECEMBER 7.   4.00 Chapter; private prayer. 5 Read Taylor. 6 Whitby. 7 Public Prayers. 8 Aldrich. 8.45 Read Ken; private prayer. 9.30 Read Sanderson. 11 Walked. 11.45 Wrote diary; chapter; private prayer. 12 Hall. 1 At Smith's, various talk. 1.30 Read Greek Testament. 2.45 Private prayer and breakfast at Charles Wesley's, Law, read [aloud]. 4.30 Atkinson. 5 Chapter; private prayer. 5.30 Public Prayers. 6 General Examination. 6.45 At Ford's with Atkinson and Washington, read Law. 9.30.

SATURDAY, DECEMBER 8.   6 Chapter; private prayer; read Taylor. 7 Public Prayers. [8] Walked with Atkinson, religious talk. 8.30 Breakfast at Ford's with Broughton, religious talk. 9.30 Read Sanderson. 11.45 Wrote diary; chapter; private prayer. 12 Dinner. 1 Walked with Ford, religious talk. 2 Lecture. 4 Greek Testament. 4.30 Atkinson. 5 Chapter; private prayer. 5.30 Public Prayers. 6 Supper. 7 At Ford's, Smith and Robson, read Goodman, mostly religious talk. 9.45.

SUNDAY, DECEMBER 9.   4 Nelson; chapter; private prayer. 5 Read Taylor. 6 Bible. 7 Dressed; read Ken with Ford. 8 Public Prayers. 9 Breakfast at Ford's with Smith, religious talk. 10 Sermon. 11 Walked with Ford, religious talk. 11.45 Wrote diary; chapter; private prayer. 12 Dinner. 1 With Ford, read Thomas à Kempis, religious talk. 2 Sermon. 3

[118] Probably with Atkinson; see 20 November and four-thirty on most weekdays since.

[119] This is the first indication of a long struggle that Ingham will have with early rising (see especially 10 and 13 March, 23 April, 3 May, 3 June, 27 and 29 July, 23 August, and long shorthand note after 31 January).

[120] A round black cap was the proper headdress of an undergraduate when walking about the university (see *Statutes,* XIV.3). Ingham's cap must have been in a sad state of repair to require over six hours' mending this day, unless this is a euphemism or colloquialism for some other activity. See p. 6, note 8.

Visited Smyth with Ford, read Nelson, and religious talk. 5 Chapter; private prayer. 5.30 Public Prayers. 6 Supper. 7 At Smith's with Robson and Ford, read Goodman. 9.30.

MONDAY, DECEMBER 10.   4.30 Meditated; wrote diary; chapter; private prayer; read Taylor; Whitby. 6.30 At John Wesley's, religious talk.[121] 7 Public Prayers. 8 Breakfast at John Wesley's with Ford, religious talk. 9 Read Gravesande. 11 Walked. 11.45 Chapter; private prayer. 12 Dinner. 1 Aldrich. 1.30 Shorthand. 2 Greek Testament. 4 Tea with Ford, wrote his diary. 5 Chapter; private prayer. 5.30 Public Prayers. 6 Supper. 7 At Ford's with Atkinson and Washington, read Law. 8.30 Read *Whole Duty.* 9.30.

TUESDAY, DECEMBER 11.   4.30 Hymn; meditated; wrote diary; chapter; private prayer. 5 Read Taylor. 6 Read Greek Testament. 7 Public Prayers. 8 Breakfast with me, Ford, Atkinson, good talk. 9 Read Gravesande. 11 Walked with Ford, learned talk. 11.45 Wrote diary; chapter; private prayer. 12 Dinner. 1 Aldrich. 1.30 Shorthand. 2 Greek Testament. 3 Greek Lecture. 4 Greek Testament. 4.30 Atkinson. 5 Chapter; private prayer. 5.30 Public Prayers. 6 Supper. 7 With me, Knail, read Gravesande. 9.30.

WEDNESDAY, DECEMBER 12.   4.30 Chapter; private prayer. 5 Read Taylor. 6 Whitby. 7 Public Prayers. 8 Read Sanderson; private prayers. 9 Wrote Supposition. 11 Private prayer. 11.15 Disputations. 12 Chapter; private prayer. 12.15 Hall. 1 Aldrich. 2 Read Greek Testament. 2.45 Charles Wesley's; private prayer and breakfast; Law, read [aloud]; religious talk. 4 Meditated. 4.30 Atkinson. 5 Chapter; private prayer. 5.30 Public Prayers. 6 Supper. 7 At Robson's, and Smith and Ford, read Goodman, religious talk. 9.30.

THURSDAY, DECEMBER 13.   4.30 Chapter; private prayer. 5 Read Charles Burton's letter. 5.45 Taylor. 6.15 Whitby. 7 Public Prayers. 8 Breakfast at Smith's with Ford, read the *Court Convert.* 9 Translated Kennet. 10 Read Gravesande. 11 Walked. 11.45 Wrote diary; chapter; private prayer. 12 Dinner. 1 Aldrich. 1.30 Shorthand. 2 At the Divinity Disputations.[122] 3 Read Greek Testament. 4.30 Atkinson. 5 Chapter,

---

121   Wesley diary entry reads: "6.50 Ingham, religious talk. 7 Morgan, necessary talk. . . . 8.15 Ingham and Ford, religious talk, tea. 9.15. . . ." OD IV, 27.
122   The university statutes stipulated that "ordinary disputations in divinity" be held in the Divinity School on the first and last Thursday of every full term

and private prayer with Ford and Atkinson. 5.30 Public Prayers. 6 Supper. 7 With me, Knail. 8 Gravesande. 8.30 *Whole Duty.* 9.30.

FRIDAY, DECEMBER 14.   4.30 Chapter; private prayer; read Taylor. 6 Ford came, religious talk. 7 Public Prayers. 8 Composed Opposition; and Disputations.[123] 12 Wrote diary; chapter; private prayer. 12.15 Hall. 12.30 Meditated. 1 Aldrich. 2 Religious talk with Ford and Atkinson. 2.45 Private prayer and breakfast. 3 Greek Lecture. 4 Greek Testament. 4.30 Atkinson. 5 With Atkinson and Ford, read Nelson, and private prayer. 5.30 Public Prayers. 6 General Examination. 6.45 At Ford's with Washington and Atkinson, read ninth chapter, Law's *Christian Perfection,*[124] religious talk. 9.30.

SATURDAY, DECEMBER 15.   4.30 Chapter; private prayer; read Taylor. 6 Whitby. 7 Public Prayers. 8 Breakfast. 8.30 Composed a Theme. 11 Walked. 11.45 Wrote diary; chapter; private prayer. 12 Dinner. 1 Aldrich. 2 Walked. 3 Lecture. 4 Read Ellis on the Sacrament. 5 Chapter; private prayer. 5.30 Public Prayers. 6 Supper. 7 With me, Ford, Smith, and Robson, finished Goodman's *Penitent Pardoned.* 9 *Whole Duty.* 10.

SUNDAY, DECEMBER 16.   4.30 Private prayer; chapter; private prayer; read Taylor. 6 Meditated. 7 With Ford, began *Companion to the Altar.*[125] 7.30 Lecture.[126] 8 Public Prayers. 9 Breakfast with Ford, religious talk. 10 Castle, Public Prayers, Sermon, and Sacrament.[127] 12 Dinner. 1 Private prayer, with Ford, finished *Companion to the Altar.* 2 Sermon. 3 Walked with Ford, religious talk. 3.30 Finished Ken's *Medita-*

---

from one to three in the afternoon (*Statutes,* VIII.1). Undergraduates were not required to attend, but in this instance, Ingham apparently went to hear John Wesley dispute. Wesley noted in his diary (for one to three in the afternoon), "responded in Divinity School" (OD IV, 29).

[123] These were the last disputations for the Michaelmas term; they resumed again on 14 January (Hilary or Nativity term).

[124] William Law, *A Practical Treatise upon Christian Perfection,* ch. IX, "Of the Necessity of Divine Grace, and the Several Duties to which it Calleth all Christians"; see Appendix 3.

[125] See William Vickers in Appendix 3.

[126] An unusual time and day for a lecture (see also 20 January).

[127] John Wesley was also present; his diary entry reads: "9.30 Castle, Sacrament. 11.45 . . ." (OD IV, 30). Ingham noted that he was "fervent" during Public Prayers and the Sacrament and put a cross in the margin of the diary at this point.

tions. 4.30 Meditated. 5 Private prayer and read Nelson with Ford. 5.30 Public Prayers. 6 Supper. 7 With Ford and Robson, read Country Parson. 9.30.

MONDAY, DECEMBER 17.   4.30 Chapter; wrote diary; private prayer; read Taylor. 6 Whitby. 7 Public Prayers. 8 Breakfast. 8.30 Read Sanderson. 10.30 Composed an Opposition for Ford. 11 Walked with Ford. 11.45 Chapter; private prayer. 12 Dinner. 1 Aldrich. 2 Began first volume of Blackwall's *Sacred Classics.* 5 Wrote diary; chapter; private prayer. 5.30 Public Prayers. 6 Supper. 7 With Knail, read Gravesande. 9.30.

TUESDAY, DECEMBER 18.   4.30 Wrote diary; chapter; private prayer; read Taylor. 6 Whitby. 7 Public Prayer. 8 Breakfast. 8.30 Read Sanderson. 11 Walked with Ford, religious talk. 11.45 Wrote diary; chapter; private prayer. 12 Dinner. 1 Finished the first book of Aldrich's Logic with Ford, Washington, and Atkinson. 2 Read Blackwell. 4.30 Walked. 5 Wrote diary; chapter; private prayer. 5.30 Public Prayers. 6 Supper. 7 At Ford's, etc,[128] read *Guardian.* 9.30.

WEDNESDAY, DECEMBER 19.   4.30 Meditated; chapter; private prayer; read Taylor. 6 Whitby. 7 Public Prayers. 8 Read Nelson on the Ember Days[129] with Ford, private prayer. 9 Wrote letter to Natt. 11.45 Chapter; private prayer. 12 Hall. 12.30 With Atkinson and Ford, religious talk. 1 Read News. 1.30 Finished letter. 2.45 Private prayer and breakfast at Charles Wesley's, religious talk; Law, read [aloud]. 4 Blackwall. 5 Wrote diary; chapter and private prayer with Atkinson. 5.30 Public Prayers. 6 Supper. 7 At Robson's, and Smith, began Goodman's *Winter Evening Conference.* 9.30.

THURSDAY, DECEMBER 20.   4 Laid waking and meditated in bed till 5.30; chapter; private prayer. 6 Whitby. 7 Public Prayers. 8 Walked. 8.30 Breakfast with Ford. 9 With Atkinson and Watson. 10 Various business. 11 Walked with Ford, religious talk. 11.45 Wrote diary; chapter; private prayer. 12 Dinner. 1 Parted with Ford. 2 Finished first volume of Blackwall. 4.30 Finished Romans with Atkinson. 5 Wrote diary;

---

128   "Etc" here probably means Atkinson, Washington, and Smith (see monthly summary for December 1733).
129   Nelson, *Fasts,* ch. X, "Ember Days in December" (see 19 September, note 30).

chapter; private prayer. 5.30 Public Prayers. 6 Supper. 7 At the Boar-Head.[130] 9.30.

FRIDAY, DECEMBER 21.   4.30 <u>Hymn</u>; religious talk <u>in bed</u> with Atkinson. 5 Read Nelson and private prayer with him. 6 Read Taylor. 7 Meditated. 8 Public Prayers. 9 Began letter to Charles Burton. 10 Sermon.[131] 11 At Prichard's.[132] 11.30 Finished letter. 12 Hall. 12.45 Wrote diary; chapter; private prayer. 1 With Atkinson, religious and useful talk. 2.30 Private prayer and breakfast. 3 Watson came, various and useful talk. 4.45 General Examination and private prayer with Atkinson. 5.30 Public Prayers. 6 Supper. 6.30 With me, Atkinson, Washington, Watson, Smyth, good talk (various). 9 Atkinson <u>laid</u> with me.

SATURDAY, DECEMBER 22.   2.30 Meditated and private prayer and breakfast with Atkinson. 3.45 <u>He set forward for</u> London. 4 <u>Went to bed again.</u> 6 Read Taylor and meditated. 7 Public Prayers. 8 Breakfast with me, Smyth, religious talk. 9.30 Dressed. 10 Began the second volume of Blackwall. 11 Walked. 11.45 Wrote diary; chapter; private prayer. 12 Dinner. 1 Read Dr. Horneck's life.[133] 2 Read Blackwall. 3 Lecture; finished the second *Prælection.*[134] 4 Read Blackwall. 4.45 Wrote diary; chapter; private prayer. 5.30 Public Prayers. 6 Supper. 7 With Smith, religious and useful talk. 9.30.

SUNDAY, DECEMBER 23.   4.30 Wrote diary; chapter; private prayer. 5.30 Read Taylor. 7 Meditated. 8 Public Prayers. 9 Breakfast. 9.30

130   This may have been a local tavern, although no reference to one of that name for this period has come to my attention. In the fifteenth century, a Boar Head ("Borehede") was operating at 111 High Street across from All Hallows, and in the nineteenth century an alehouse of that name was located on Queen's Lane. In the late seventeenth century, Anthony Wood reports there were over 370 alehouses in Oxford, but the university statutes warned that students were not to "haunt" such places. See Anthony Wood, *The Life and Times of Anthony Wood, Antiquary, at Oxford 1632–1695, Described by Himself,* ed. Andrew Clark (Oxford: Oxford Historical Society, 1891), vol. 2, 404; and *Statutes,* XV.5. This entry could possibly refer to preparations for the Christmas dinner at Queen's (see 25 December, note 138), but that seems unlikely.

131   This day was the festival of St. Thomas the Apostle (see Nelson, *Festivals,* ch. IV).

132   This might be the barber mentioned on 25 March; cf. 9 March, note 36.

133   See Richard Kidder in Appendix 3.

134   See Robert Sanderson, *De obligatione conscientiæ prælectiones decem . . .* (1660, 1661) in Appendix 3. These lectures on Sanderson began on 6 November and resume again on 18 March.

Dressed. 10 Sermon. 11 With Watson, religious talk. 11.45 Wrote diary; chapter; private prayer. 12 Dinner. 1 Walked. 1.30 Meditated. 2 Sermon. 3 Finished Taylor's *Holy Living.* 5 Wrote diary; chapter; private prayer. 5.30 Public Prayers. 6 Supper. 7 With me, Smith, religious talk. 9.30.

MONDAY, DECEMBER 24. 4.30 Chapter; private prayer; read *Whole Duty of Man* and meditated. 7 Public Prayers. 8 Began Ellis on the Sacrament. 10 Religious talk with Mother Harris. 10.30 Removed Ford's larum to Smyth's. 11 General Examination. 11.45 Chapter; private prayer. 12 Hall.[135] 12.30 Meditated and private prayer. 1 General Examination and private prayer. 2.45 At Charles Wesley's, breakfast, Law read [aloud]. 4 Read Ellis. 5 Wrote diary; chapter; private prayer. 5.30 Public Prayer. 6 Supper. 7 With Smyth and Washington, read Ellis, religious talk. 9.30.

TUESDAY, DECEMBER 25. 4 Hymn; meditated; chapter; private prayer; read *Whole Duty;* meditated. 7 Washington and Smyth came, and breakfast, read Nelson[136] and finished Ellis, religious talk. 9 Meditated. 9.30 Public Prayers, Sermon, and Sacrament. [137] 11.45 Private prayer. 12 Chapter; private prayer. 12.30 Dinner.[138] 3 Walked with Watson, religious talk. 4 Began the *Life of Bonwicke*[139] with Watson, Washington, and Smyth. 5 Wrote diary; private prayer and meditated. 5.30 Public Prayers. 6 Supper. 7 With me, Watson, Smyth, and Washington, finished Bonwicke, religious talk. 9.15 With Watson, religious talk. 10.

WEDNESDAY, DECEMBER 26. 4.30 Hymn; meditated; wrote diary; chap-

---

135 24 December is a fast day.

136 Nelson, *Festivals,* ch. V, "The Nativity of Our Lord, or the Birth Day of Christ, commonly called Christmas Day."

137 The university statutes specified that this service be held at Christ Church cathedral (*Statutes,* XVI.5).

138 This is the boar's head ceremony at Queen's, a feast commemorating the "ancient" tradition of a Taberdar who slew a wild boar that had plagued Shotover Forest just east of Oxford by stuffing a copy of Aristotle down his throat. See John Magrath, *The Flemings in Oxford* (Oxford: Oxford Historical Society, 1904–24), vol. 3, 348f., for notes on the tradition and the text of the song sung by the Taberdars as they bring the boar's head into the Hall. The feast provided an ample and festive holiday repast for the students, most of whom were from the North Country and may have had difficulty reaching home for Christmas.

139 See Ambrose Bonwicke, *A Pattern for Young Students in the University* (1729), in Appendix 3.

ter; private prayer; read *Whole Duty* and meditated. 8 Public Prayers. 9 Walked with Watson, Washington, and Smyth, read News. 10 Sermon.[140] 11 With Watson, Washington, and Smyth, began the *Lives of the Fathers.*[141] 11.45 Wrote diary; chapter; private prayer. 12 Dinner. 1 Walked with Watson, religious talk. 1.30 Read *Lives.* 4.30 Walked with Watson, religious talk. 5 Wrote diary; chapter; private prayer. 5.30 Public Prayers. 6 Supper. 7 With Smith, religious talk. 9.30.

THURSDAY, DECEMBER 27.   7 Read Nelson; private prayer; chapter. 8 Public Prayers. 9 Breakfast with me, Smith, various and useful talk. 10 Sermon.[142] 11 Read *Lives.* 12 Wrote diary; private prayer; dinner. 1 At Prichard's,[143] religious talk. 3 Came home; taught Smyth and Watson to write diary.[144] 3.45 Read *Lives.* 5 Chapter, finished Acts. 5.15 Wrote diary; private prayer. 5.30 Public Prayers. 6 Supper. 7 With me, Washington, Smyth, and Watson, read *Lives,* religious talk. 9.30.

FRIDAY, DECEMBER 28.   4.30 Meditated; wrote diary; read Nelson; private prayer. 5.30 Read *Whole Duty* and meditated. 8 Public Prayers. 9 Read *Lives.* 10 Sermon.[145] 11 Read *Lives.* 11.45 Wrote diary; private prayer. 12 Hall. 12.45 At Washington's, read *Lives.* 2.45 With Smith, various talk. 3 Breakfast at Charles Wesley's with Smith and M̲r̲. Colley,[146] learned and useful talk. 4 Read *Lives.* 5 Wrote diary; General Examination; private prayer. 5.30 Public Prayers. 6 Supper. 6.30 At Washington's, e̲t̲c̲, read *Lives,* religious and useful talk. 9.30.

SATURDAY, DECEMBER 29.   4.30 Necessary business and dressed. 5 Wrote diary; private prayer; read Nelson and *Whole Duty,* and meditated. 7.30 Public Prayers. 8 Breakfast with Watson, read Nelson, and religious talk. 10.15 Meditated. 11 Read Bible. 11.45 Wrote diary; pri-

---

[140] This day was the festival of St. Stephen ("the first martyr"). See Nelson, *Festivals,* ch. VI.

[141] See William Cave in Appendix 3.

[142] This day was the festival of St. John the Evangelist (see Nelson, *Festivals,* ch. VII).

[143] This might be the barber mentioned on 25 March; cf. 9 March, note 36.

[144] Both Smyth and Watson later had second thoughts on keeping a diary (see 19 and 25 April).

[145] This day was the festival of the Holy Innocents (those infants slain in Bethlehem at Herod's command). See Nelson, *Festivals,* ch. VIII.

[146] Jonathan Colley, Brasenose College, B.A. 1697; at this time vicar of Cassington and a chantor or precentor at Christ Church (Hearne refers to him as "chaplain"; *Collections,* vol. 11, 254).

vate prayer. 12 Dinner. 1 Walked with Watson. 2 Composed verses.
4 Walked with Watson, good talk. 5 Wrote diary; General Examination; private prayer. 5.30 Public Prayers. 6 Supper. 7 Read Goodman's
Conference. 9.

SUNDAY, DECEMBER 30. 7 Dressed; read *Whole Duty*. 7.45 Wrote
diary; private prayer. 8 Public Prayers. 9 Wrote letter to Brownsword.
10 Sermon. 11 Walked with Watson, religious talk. 11.45 Wrote diary;
private prayer. 12 Dinner. 1 Read Bible. 2 Sermon. 3 Walked with
Broughton, religious talk. 4 Meditated. 5 Wrote diary; General Examination; private prayer. 5.30 Public Prayers. 6 Supper. 7 At Smith's, and
Robson, religious and useful talk. 9.30.

MONDAY, DECEMBER 31. 4.45 Dressed. 5 Private prayer; wrote diary;
read *Whole Duty*. 7 Public Prayers. 8 Considered how to spend my
time, and made resolutions thereupon.[147] 10 Private prayer. 10.30 Finished *The Whole Duty of Man*. 11.45 Wrote diary; private prayer. 12
Dinner. 1 Finished Sanderson's *De obligatione conscientiæ*. 2 Transcribed Opposition and verses for Christmas. 4 Walked with Watson and
Richardson, good talk (various). 4.45 Chapter. 5 General Examination;
private prayer. 5.30 Public Prayers. 6 Supper. 7 At Smyth's with Washington and Watson, religious and useful talk. 10.

TUESDAY, JANUARY 1. 4 Meditated; hymn;[148] private prayer; read Nelson.[149] 5 Chapter, began St Matthew. 5.30 Began Taylor's *Holy Dying*.
6 Abridged Whitby.[150] 7.30 Dressed. 8 Public Prayers. 9 Delivered
epistle.[151] 9.15 Breakfast. 9.30 Walked with Smyth and Washington,
religious and useful talk. 10 Sermon.[152] 11 Read *Lives*. 11.45 Wrote

---

[147] Ingham frequently reviewed and revised his rules concerning the use of
time (see especially 26 September, 28 February, 6 and 17 July).
[148] See resolution of 25 November.
[149] This day was the festival of the Circumcision of Our Lord (see Nelson,
Festivals, ch. IX).
[150] During January, Ingham abridged Daniel Whitby's *Paraphrase and Commentary* through Luke 17; see monthly summary for January 1733/34.
[151] Polite Latin epistles to the provost or other senior dignitaries were expected
of undergraduates on many occasions: for leave to "go down," graces for degrees,
permission for exercises, or simply the wishing of "health and happiness" or a
"happy New Year." See Magrath, *Queen's College,* vol. 1, 272, and *Flemings,*
vol. 3, 309, for examples; cf. Robert Howard Hodgkin, *Six Centuries of an
Oxford College* (Oxford: Basil Blackwell, 1949), p. 125. See also 13 June.
[152] This day was the festival of the Circumcision of Our Lord.

diary; chapter; private prayer. 12 Dinner. 1 Walked with Watson, reli-
gious and useful talk. 2 Finished the *Lives of the Fathers* at Smyth's with
Washington and Watson. 4 Walked with Watson, religious talk. 4.45
Wrote Watson's diary. 5 Chapter; wrote diary; daily examination;[153] pri-
vate prayer. 5.30 Public Prayers. 6 Supper. 7 With me, Knail, read
Gravesande, learned talk. 9.30.

WEDNESDAY, JANUARY 2.   4.30 Meditated; hymn; private prayer; wrote
diary. 5 Chapter. 5.30 Read Taylor. 6.30 Whitby. 7 Public Prayers. 8
Began Sanderson's Logic with Watson, promised to continue. 8.45 Private prayer. 9 Whitby. 11.45 Wrote diary; chapter; private prayer. 12
Hall. 12.30 Meditated and private prayer. 1.30 Read Blackwall. 2.45
Private prayer and breakfast at Charles Wesley's with Smith; Law, read
[aloud]. 4 Walked. 4.45 Chapter. 5 Wrote diary; daily examination;
private prayer. 5.30 Public Prayers. 6 Supper. 7 With Watson, religious
and useful talk. 10.

THURSDAY, JANUARY 3.   4.30 Hymn; meditated; private prayer. 5
Chapter. 5.30 Read Taylor. 6 Wrote diary; Whitby. 6.30 Breakfast at
John Wesley's, religious talk. 7.30 Public Prayers. 8 Walked. 8.30 Read
News. 9 Read Logic with Watson, and various and useful talk. 10
Dressed. 10.30 Read Gravesande. 11.45 Wrote diary; chapter; private
prayer. 12 Dinner. 1 Walked. 1.30 Shorthand. 2 Read Blackwall. 4.30
With Watson, religious talk. 5 Chapter. 5.15 Wrote diary; daily exam-
ination. 5.30 Public Prayers. 6 Supper. 7 With me, Knail, read Grave-
sande. 9 Private prayer; meditated. 9.45.

FRIDAY, JANUARY 4.   4.30 Meditated; hymn; private prayer. 5.15
Wrote diary; chapter. 5.45 Read Taylor and meditated. 7 Public Prayers.
8 Read Logic. 9 Abridged Whitby. 11 Began *The History of Charles XII
of Sweden.* 12 Hall. 12.30 Wrote diary; chapter; private prayer. 1 Read
Charles [XII] with Watson. 2.45 Private prayer and breakfast at Charles
Wesley's, Law, read [aloud]. 4 Meditated. 5 Chapter; private prayer.

---

153 Ingham's "General examination" had been, up to this week, a regular Friday evening exercise, but starting on 29 December he began examining himself
every evening. On this day he recognized the daily nature of the practice by
means of a new symbol ("x"), reserving the previous denotation of General
Examination ("Ex") for the weekly review, still held on Fridays (after 11
January).

5.30 Public Prayers. 6 Supper.[154] 6.30 At Watson's with Smyth and Washington, read Norris' sermon on Singularity. 9.45.

SATURDAY, JANUARY 5. 4.30 Meditated; hymn; wrote diary. 5 Private prayer. 5.15 General Examination. 6.15 Chapter. 6.30 Read Taylor. 7 Public Prayers. 8 Read Logic. 8.30 Breakfast at Smith's with Evans, religious talk. 9.15 Abridged Whitby. 11 Read *Charles* [*XII*]. 12 Dinner. 1 Read *Charles* [*XII*]. 4.45 Chapter. 5 Wrote diary; daily examination; private prayer. 5.30 Public Prayers. 6 Supper. 7 At Robson's with Smith, various and useful talk.[155]

SUNDAY, JANUARY 6. 4.30 Meditated; hymn; wrote diary. 5 Private prayer; chapter; read Nelson and meditated. 7 Taylor. 8 Public Prayers. 9 Breakfast. 9.30 Taylor. 10 Sermon.[156] 11 Walked. 11.30 Taylor. 11.45 Chapter; private prayer. 12 Dinner. 1 Read Greek Testament. 2 Sermon. 3 With me, Washington and Smyth, religious talk, read Country Parson. 4.45 Chapter. 5 Wrote diary; daily examination; private prayer. 5.30 Public Prayers. 6 Supper. 7 With me, Smith, religious talk. 9.45 Private prayer.

MONDAY, JANUARY 7. 6 Meditated and meditated. 7 Private prayer; chapter. 7.30 Public Prayers. 8 Breakfast at Charles Wesley's with Smith and Evans, religious talk. 9.30 Whitby. 10.30 Religious talk with Watson. 11 Walked. 11.45 Wrote diary; chapter; private prayer. 12 Dinner. 1 Walked. 2 Finished second volume of Blackwall's *Sacred Classics*. 4.45 Chapter. 5 Wrote diary; daily examination; private prayer. 5.30 Public Prayers. 6 Supper. 7 With Knail, read Gravesande, good talk (various). 9.45.

TUESDAY, JANUARY 8. 4.30 Hymn; private prayer; wrote diary. 5 Chapter; read Taylor. 6 Whitby. 7 Public Prayers. 8 Breakfast with me, Smith and Evans, and walked, religious talk. 10.45 Read Gravesande. 11.45 Chapter; private prayer. 12 Wrote diary; dinner. 1 Finished *The History of Charles XII* with Watson, religious talk. 5 Wrote diary; daily examination; private prayer. 5.30 Public Prayers. 6 Supper. 7 With Knail, read Gravesande, various and useful talk. 9.30.

---

154 Ingham omitted the usual General Examination this week.
155 No bedtime noted.
156 This day was the festival of the Epiphany (see Nelson, *Festivals,* ch. X).

WEDNESDAY, JANUARY 9.   4.30 Private prayer. 5 Chapter; Taylor. 6 Meditated in bed. 7 Public Prayers. 8 Read Logic. 8.45 Private prayer. 9 Whitby. 11.45 Chapter. 12 Hall. 12.30 Read Country Parson and private prayer. 1 Whitby. 2.45 At Charles Wesley's. 3 Breakfast with Smith and Evans; Law, read [aloud]. 4 With Watson, religious talk. 4.45 Chapter. 5 Wrote diary; daily examination; private prayer. 5.30 Public Prayers. 6 Supper. 7 At Smith's with Evans, began Goodman's *Conference.* 8.15 At Alsop's with the Servitors, idle talk. 10.45.

THURSDAY, JANUARY 10.   7 Private prayer and chapter. 7.30 Public Prayers. 8 Breakfast at Smith's with Evans, good talk (various). 9 Whitby. 11 Read Logic. 11.45 Chapter; private prayer. 12 Dinner. 1 Walked. 1.45 Watson came, religious talk. 2.30 Whitby. 4.30 With Watson, learned talk. 5 Wrote diary; daily examination; private prayer; Public Prayers. 6 Supper. 7 With Knail, read Gravesande, began the Hydrostatics.[157] 9.30.

FRIDAY, JANUARY 11.   4.30 Hymn; private prayer. 5 Read chapter. 5.30 Taylor. 6 Wrote diary; Whitby. 7 Public Prayers. 8 Read Logic; private prayer. 9 Whitby. 11.45 Chapter; private prayer. 12 Hall. 12.30 Meditated. 1 Began Ellis on the Sacrament; and General Examination. 3 At Charles Wesley's, breakfast, read Lucas' sermon on Company.[158] 4 Finished Ellis. 5 Chapter; private prayer; Public Prayers. 6 Supper. 6.30 At Watson's with Smith and Washington, read sermon of Lucas, religious talk. 9.30.

SATURDAY, JANUARY 12.   6 Hymn; private prayer; walked to Charles Wesley's twice; chapter. 7 Public Prayers. 8 Breakfast with me, Smyth and Washington, religious talk, read Ellis. 9.30 At Sermon and Sacrament.[159] 11.45 Walked with Watson, religious talk. 12 Dinner. 1 Walked. 1.30 With Watson, religious talk. 3.30 Atkinson came, religious and useful talk. 5 Wrote diary; daily examination; private prayer;

---

157   See Gravesande's *Mathematical Elements of Natural Philosophy,* book II, part I, "Of the Gravity, Pressure, and Resistance of Fluids."

158   Richard Lucas, *The Influence of Conversation With the Regulation Thereof* (1707); see Appendix 3. The heading of the first section is "That men generally become such as the company they keep."

159   This is the service, with Latin sermon, prescribed by the university statutes to be held at St. Mary's at the beginning of each full term, this being Hilary (or Nativity) term (see 9 October, note 50). The Wesleys missed this Sacrament, not returning from a five-day visit to the Cotswolds until late Saturday evening.

Public Prayers. 6 Supper. 7 With me, Smith and Evans, read Goodman, religious talk. 9 With Watson, religious talk. 9.30.

SUNDAY, JANUARY 13. 7.45 Dressed. 8 Public Prayers. 9 Breakfast with me, Smith and Evans, good talk. 10 Sermon. 11 Walked with Atkinson, religious talk. 11.30 Chapter; private prayer. 12 Dinner. 1 Read Bull's life[160] with Watson, Washington, and Atkinson. 2 Sermon. 3 At Charles Wesley's with Smith, sermon, read [aloud]. 4 With Watson, Washington, and Atkinson, religious and useful talk. 5 Chapter; daily examination; private prayer; Public Prayers. 6 Supper. 7 With Watson, religious talk. 9.45.

MONDAY, JANUARY 14. 5 Hymn; private prayer. 5.30 Chapter. 6 Whitby. 7 Public Prayers. 8 Read Logic and breakfast. 9 Whitby. 11 Disputations. 12 Private prayer; dinner. 1 Walked. 2 Whitby. 4 Walked. 4.30 With Watson and Atkinson, various talk. 5 Wrote diary; daily examination; private prayer; Public Prayers. 6 Supper. 7 With Watson, read Country Parson. 9.30.

TUESDAY, JANUARY 15. 6 Meditated in bed. 7 Private prayer. 7.30 Public Prayers. 8 Breakfast and Logic. 9 Began composing a Declamation.[161] 11 Disputations. 12 Dinner. 1 With Ford, various and useful talk. 4 Walked. 4.45 Chapter. 5 Wrote diary; daily examination; private prayer; Public Prayers. 6 Supper. 7 With me, Knail, read Gravesande, learned talk. 9.45.

WEDNESDAY, JANUARY 16. 4 Could not strike a light,[162] went to bed and meditated till 7; private prayer. 7.30 Public Prayers. 8 Logic. 8.30 Read Country Parson and private prayer. 9.15 Transcribed Declamation. 11.30 Dressed. 12 Wrote diary; Hall. 12.45 At Ford's, read Country Parson, and religious and useful talk. 2 Declamation. 2.45 Private prayer and, [at] 3, breakfast with Smith and Evans, religious talk. 4 With Watson, good talk (various). 5 Wrote diary; daily examination; private prayer; Public Prayers. 6 Supper. 7 With Ford, read Goodman's *Conference,* religious talk. 10.

160 See Robert Nelson, *Life of Dr. George Bull* (1714), in Appendix 3.
161 See 5 December. Ingham worked on this exercise daily until he presented it in the Hall at dinner on 19 January.
162 Unable to start a fire, Ingham had come up with yet another excuse for not rising early.

THURSDAY, JANUARY 17.   5.30 <u>Hymn</u>, and meditated with Ford. 6 Dressed; read Nelson; private prayer; read Thomas à Kempis. 7 Public Prayers. 8 Breakfast at Evans' with Smith, various and useful talk. 9.15 Translated Kennet. 11.15 Walked with Ford, religious talk. 11.45 Private prayer. 12 Dinner. 1 Walked with Watson, various and useful talk. 2 Whitby. 4.45 Chapter. 5 Wrote diary; daily examination; private prayer. 5.30 Public Prayers. 6 Supper. 7 With Watson, read the News, and Secker's sermon.[163] 10.

FRIDAY, JANUARY 18.   4.30 <u>Hymn</u>, and meditated. 6 Private prayer; read Nelson; chapter; Taylor. 7 Public Prayers. 8 Read Logic. 9 Religious talk with Watson. 10 Private prayer; meditated, and began *genesis problematica* on the Stations.[164] 11.45 Wrote diary; chapter; private prayer. 12 Hall. 12.30 With Ford, read Thomas à Kempis and private prayer. 1.30 Finished *genesis problematica* on the Stations. 3 Breakfast at Charles Wesley's with Smith and Evans, began *Nicodemus*. 4 Transcribed Declamation. 5 Chapter; private prayer; Public Prayers. 6 General Examination. 6.30 At Ford's with Smyth and Washington, read Law's *Christian Perfection,* religious talk. 10 <u>Laid</u> with Ford.

SATURDAY, JANUARY 19.   5.30 Meditated and <u>hymn</u>. 6.15 Dressed. 6.30 Read Nelson and private prayer and chapter with Ford. 7 Public Prayers. 8 Read Logic and breakfast. 9 Whitby. 11 Walked. 11.45 Wrote diary; chapter; private prayer. 12 Dinner and Declamation.[165] 1.15 Began Ellis' *Communicant's Guide*. 3 Lecture. 4 Read Ellis. 5 Chapter; daily examination; private prayer; Public Prayers. 6 Supper. 7 With me, Ford, Smith, and Evans, read Goodman's <u>*Conference,*</u> religious talk. 10.

SUNDAY, JANUARY 20.   5 Meditated, <u>hymn</u>, and <u>sang</u> with Ford. 7 Dressed and private prayer. 7.30 Lecture.[166] 8 Public Prayers. 9 Breakfast with Ford. 9.45 Castle, Public Prayers, Sermon, Sacrament. 12 Private prayer. 12.15 Dinner. 1 At Ford's with Map,[167] various talk. 2

---

[163]   See 2 September, note 7.

[164]   Ingham was reading here rather than composing; see monthly summary for January 1733/34. See also 14 September, note 22.

[165]   Ingham here presents his declamation in the Hall before his colleagues.

[166]   An unusual hour and day for a lecture (see also 16 December).

[167]   From the form of this entry, "Map" would seem to be a person, but no such name appears in Foster's *Alumni,* the Wesley diaries, or other standard sources. If the reference is to a map, the significance is unclear.

Sermon. 3 At Charles Wesley's with Smith, began *Prayers for Every Day in the Week.*[168] 4 Walked and meditated. 5 Chapter; wrote diary; daily examination; private prayer; Public Prayers. 6 Supper. 7 At Ford's with Smith and Evans, read Goodman, religious talk. 9 With Ford, laid with him. 10.

MONDAY, JANUARY 21. 6 Meditated. 6.30 Dressed. 6.45 Read Nelson and private prayers. 7.30 Public Prayers. 8 Read Logic. 9.30 With Ford, regulated his time for business and devotion. 10 Began Brown's *Divine Analogy.* 11 Walked with Ford, good talk (various). 11.45 Wrote diary; chapter; private prayer. 12 Dinner. 1 Logic with Ford and Watson. 2 At Charles Wesley's, read *Prayers.* 3 Whitby. 4.30 At Ford's, religious talk, read Nelson. 5 Daily examination; private prayer; Public Prayers. 6 Supper. 7 At Camplin's,[169] read Pope's *Satire,* various talk. 10.

TUESDAY, JANUARY 22. 7 Dressed; private prayer. 7.30 Public Prayers. 8 Breakfast at Smith's, good talk. 9 Transcribed prayers. 11.15 Walked. 11.45 Chapter; private prayer. 12 Dinner. 1 Began to read Aldrich's Logic with Ford, Watson, Washington, Atkinson, and Smyth. 2 At Charles Wesley's, read *Prayers,* religious talk. 3 At the Poetic Lecture.[170] 3.30 With Ford, religious talk. 4.45 Chapter. 5 Wrote diary; daily examination; private prayer; Public Prayers. 6 Supper. 7 At Ford's with Washington, Atkinson, Smyth, and Richardson, read *Tatler,* learned talk. 9 With Ford, religious talk. 9.45 Private prayer. 10.

WEDNESDAY, JANUARY 23. 5 Dressed. 5.15 Hymn; wrote diary; private prayer; chapter; read Taylor. 6.15 Transcribed *Prayers.* 7.30 Public Prayers. 8 Meditated and private prayer. 9 Ford came, religious talk and read *The Oxford Methodists.*[171] 11.15 Disputations. 11.45 Wrote diary; chapter; private prayer. 12 Hall. 12.30 Transcribed *Prayers.* 1 Aldrich.

---

[168] See John Wesley, *A Collection of Forms of Prayer for Every Day in the Week* (1733), in Appendix 3. This was Wesley's first publication, copies of which had arrived from London the previous Thursday, 17 January (OD IV, 46). The prayers, along with questions for self-examination, are arranged according to the virtues to be considered on each day of the week (cf. p. 20).

[169] Thomas Camplin, Queen's College, B.A. 1735/36.

[170] See 16 October, note 55.

[171] An anonymous pamphlet describing the movement, using Wesley's letter of 19 October 1732 to Richard Morgan, Sr., as a basis. See Richard P. Heitzenrater, *John Wesley and the Oxford Methodists, 1725-1735* (Ph.D. diss., Duke University; Ann Arbor, Mich.: University Microfilms, 1972), pp. 205-10.

2 Went to the Workhouse in St Thomas',[172] taught the children and catechized and read Bible. 3 Breakfast at Charles Wesley's with Smith and Evans, read *Nicodemus.* 4 With Ford, religious talk. 4.45 Meditated. 5 Daily examination; private prayer; Public Prayers. 6 Supper. 7 At Smith's with Ford and Evans, began *Nicodemus or the Fear of Man.* 9 Came home with Watson, read News, and religious talk. 10 Wrote diary; private prayer. I went to the Workhouse by the advice of Charles Wesley; Hall[173] said he was going with me the first time but I disappointed him; I promised to continue and go two or three times a week to teach the children and read to the old people.

THURSDAY, JANUARY 24.   5.30 Meditated and meditated.[174] 7 Private prayer and chapter. 7.30 Public Prayers. 8 Breakfast at Ford's with Broughton, religious talk. 9.15 Translated Kennet. 10 Transcribed directions for reading religious books.[175] 11 Shorthand; translated. 11.15 Walked. 11.45 Chapter; private prayer. 12 Dinner. 1 Read Aldrich. 1.45 To Charles Wesley's, finished the *Prayers.* 2.45 Came home. 3 Wrote diary; Whitby. 4.45 With Ford, daily examination, and private

---

172   John Clayton appears to have initiated the Methodists' interest and involvement in the workhouse in St. Thomas's parish (see *Letters,* I, 334). John Wesley resolved to go there "the first Monday or Tuesday in every month" (OD IV, 8). While in this instance Ingham's involvement came at Charles Wesley's suggestion, he and Hervey later initiated the Methodists' endeavors at the Gloucester Green Workhouse (see 25 April). The workhouse system was designed to ease the tax burden ("poor rates") within a parish by providing useful employment for the poor. Idealists of the time saw them as "nurseries of religion, virtue, and industry," and provided a biblical rationale: "Idleness and sloth are immoralities as well as publick nusances; and as the Apostle commands, They who are guilty of them ought not to eat, if they will not work." *An Account of Several Workhouses for Employing and Maintaining the Poor* (London: J. Downing, 1732), pp. i, iii.

173   Westley Hall, student of John Wesley; see Appendix 2. Although Ingham uses only surnames in this diary, the dozen or so references to this person (mostly in May and June) are quite unambiguous and clearly distinct from references to the college hall.

174   See 23 November, note 105.

175   See "Directions How to Read This and Other Religious Books with Benefit and Improvement" appended to John Wesley's published extract of John Norris, *A Treatise on Christian Prudence* (1734); cf. the Preface to Wesley's *The Christian Pattern* (1735). Wesley translated these directions from a Latin preface by Jacobus Merlo Horstius to a German edition of the *Imitatione Christi* (Cologne: Friessem, 1682); my appreciation to Professor Frank Baker for this information.

prayer. 5.30 Public Prayers. 6 Supper. 7 With Knail, read *The Provoked Husband.*[176] 10.

FRIDAY, JANUARY 25. 7 Meditated. 8 Public Prayers. 9 Wrote diary; private prayer; read Taylor. 10 Sermon.[177] 11 Read Nelson. 11.45 Private prayer and meditated. 12 Hall. 12.30 Wrote diary; private prayer. 1 Read Country Parson with Atkinson, Watson, Washington, Smyth, and Ford. 1.45 Walked with Hall to St Thomas' Workhouse, good talk; taught the children and read to the old women. 2.45 Private prayer and breakfast at Charles Wesley's with Smith and Evans, read *Nicodemus.* 4 With Ford, religious talk. 4.30 Read Nelson. 5 Daily examination; private prayer; Public Prayers. 6 General Examination and private prayer. 6.45 At Ford's with Watson, Washington, Atkinson, and Smyth, read Law and good talk. 10.

SATURDAY, JANUARY 26. 7 Private prayer. 7.30 Public Prayers. 8 Breakfast at Evans' with Smith, good talk. 9 Composed Theme. 11 Walked. 11.45 Wrote diary; chapter; private prayer. 12 Dinner. 12.45 Theme. 1.15 Aldrich. 2 Mended my cap.[178] 4.30 Read Nelson; General Examination and private prayer with Ford. 5.30 Public Prayers. 6 Supper. 7 With me, Smith, Evans, Ford, read *Nicodemus.* 9.30.

SUNDAY, JANUARY 27. 3.30 Meditated; hymn. 3.45 Private prayer. 4.15 Read Greek Testament. 4.45 Meditated. 5.30 Wrote diary; read Taylor. 7.45 Wrote diary. 8 Public Prayers. 9 Breakfast with me, Smith, Evans, and Ford, religious talk. 10 Sermon. 11 Walked with Ford, good talk. 11.45 Wrote diary; chapter, private prayer. 12 Dinner. 1 Finished Ellis with Ford. 2 Sermon. 3 At Charles Wesley's with Smith and Evans, read *Nicodemus.* 4 Meditated. 4.45 Read Nelson, daily examination, and private prayer with Ford. 5.30 Public Prayers. 6 Supper. 7 At Ford's with Smith and Evans, read *Nicodemus.* 9 With Ford, laid with him. 10.

MONDAY, JANUARY 28. 4.45 Meditated. 5 Chapter; read Nelson and private prayer. 6 Read Taylor. 7.30 Public Prayers. 8 Breakfast with me, Broughton and Ford, religious talk. 9.30 Ford, religious talk. 10 Wrote diary; read Brown. 11 Walked with Ford, began *Tully's Offices.*[179] 11.45

---

176 See John Vanbrugh in Appendix 3.
177 This day was the festival of the Conversion of St. Paul (see Nelson, *Festivals,* ch. XI).
178 Cf. 6 December, note 120.
179 See Marcus Tullius Cicero in Appendix 3.

Chapter; private prayer. 12 Dinner. 1 Aldrich. 2 Walked with Watson, read the questions of examination,[180] religious talk. 3 Whitby. 5 Daily examination; wrote diary; private prayer; Public Prayers. 6 Supper. 7 With Ford, composed an Opposition and Argument for him; Smith came, desired me to go to Gambold's. 9.45.

TUESDAY, JANUARY 29.   5.45 Dressed. 6 Wrote diary; private prayer. 6.30 Breakfast at John Wesley's, religious talk.[181] 7.30 Walked with Smith and Evans to Stanton Harcourt to visit Gambold,[182] religious and useful talk. 5.15 Came home; private prayer. 5.30 Public Prayers. 6 Supper. 7 At Evans' with Smith, read Ellis on the Sacrament. 9 Came home; private prayer. 9.30 Laid with Ford.

WEDNESDAY, JANUARY 30.   6 Read Nelson and private prayer; dressed. 7 Meditated. 7.30 Public Prayers. 8.45 General Examination and private prayer. 10 Public Prayers and Sermon.[183] 12.30 With Charles Wesley, religious talk. 1 Walked with Smith to Workhouse. 1.45 Read *Gerard's Meditations*.[184] 2.30 Private prayer and breakfast at Charles Wesley's with Smith and Evans, read *Nicodemus*. 3.30 Wrote diary; Public Prayers.

180   Several lists of questions for self-examination used by the Oxford Methodists can be found in printed and manuscript sources in addition to the lists found in this diary (see pp. 119f.). John Wesley's Oxford diaries contain several such lists, as does his *Collection of Forms of Prayer,* his letter to William Morgan's father (prefaced to published editions of his *Journal*), and the June 1781 issue of the *Arminian Magazine* 4, pp. 319–22. See pp. 19f. above.

181   Wesley's diary entry reads: "6 . . . Ingham, of pleasing ourselves, Stations (he convinced before). 7 Tea . . ." (OD IV, 53). Cf. 6 September above. This day is the only instance in this diary that Ingham was absent from the morning chapel service. Cf. 20 June, note 236.

182   Stanton Harcourt (MS. reads "Hartcourt"), a small village ten kilometers west of Oxford, was the seat of the Harcourts. Harcourt House, adjacent to the parish church of St. Michael, was dominated by a tower containing rooms in which, in 1718, Alexander Pope studied and wrote, finishing his fifth volume of Homer; see *Gentleman's Magazine* 89 (May 1819), p. 393f. Gambold, a friend of Charles Wesley since March 1730, and of John since April 1731, and active with the Methodists since April 1732, had been ordained in September 1733, shortly thereafter becoming the vicar of St. Michael's, Stanton Harcourt.

183   This day was the commemoration of the Martyrdom of King Charles I in 1649. Cf. *B.C.P.,* and George Smalridge's sermons in Appendix 3. Dr. Theophilus Lee [Leigh], Master of Balliol College, preached the sermon at St. Mary's on this occasion. Hearne, *Collections,* vol. 11, 300.

184   See Johann Gerhard in Appendix 3.

4 Hall.[185] 5 Read News. 5.30 Read Nelson; daily examination; private prayer; finished Taylor's *Holy Dying*. 6.30 At Smith's with Ford and Evans, read two sermons of Smalridge on the day.[186] 9.30.

THURSDAY, JANUARY 31. 7 Public Prayers. 8 Breakfast at Ford's with Smith and Evans, read Nelson and religious talk. 9.15 Got a *Narrare*.[187] 11.15 Walked. 11.45 Wrote diary; private prayer. 12 Dinner. 1 Aldrich. 1.30 Shorthand. 2 Whitby. 4 Walked. 4.45 Chapter. 5 Wrote diary; daily examination; private prayer. 5.30 Public Prayers. 6 Supper. 7 With Watson, religious talk, read Country Parson. 10. I started to drink tea without sugar, and eat bread without butter on Wednesday and Friday, and hope I shall be enabled to do it at other times. From sufficient and sad experience I do consider that it is sinful to lie waking in bed, or to sleep longer than the health and strength of our bodies require. I find it also necessary for a true soldier of Jesus Christ to be improving at all times and in all things and to deny himself of even those pleasures as he has sought only for the sake of pleasure. I trust that by God's mercy and grace I shall be enabled to inure myself to hardship and to fight manfully against the world, the flesh, and the devil;[188] and am resolved, God's grace assisting me, to make the salvation of my soul my chief and only concern, but never to depend upon my own strength because I can do nothing without God's assistance; therefore ever distrust thyself.[189] February 1, 1733/34. Amen.

FRIDAY, FEBRUARY 1. 4.30 Meditated, hymn, and private prayer, and chapter. 5.30 Whitby. 7.30 Public Prayers. 8 Meditated and private prayer. 9 Whitby. 11.15 Disputations. 11.45 Wrote diary; chapter; private prayer. 12 Hall. 12.30 Wrote diary [summary].[190] 1 Aldrich. 1.45

---

[185] "Public Prayers" and "Hall" in mid-afternoon on Wednesday are strange entries. Notice there are no prayers at five o'clock. Cf. note 183 above.

[186] See Smalridge's sermons in Appendix 3.

[187] This seems to have been a literary exercise which involved the translation of narrative themes (see MS. Top. Oxon. d. 314 [Bodleian Library, Oxford], fol. 146, for a list of "Narranda" collected by Falconer Madan; see also 9 May.

[188] Typical way of denominating evil as a triumvirate; cf. collect for the eighteenth Sunday after Trinity (*B.C.P.*) and *The Country Parson's Advice*, part II ch. 3, sec. 1, para. 5 (see Appendix 3).

[189] A typical perspective of an Oxford Methodist, based on a theology of grace that is both actively synergistic and thoroughly self-deprecating.

[190] Ingham seems to have fallen behind in his "casting up" the diary sum-

Walked with Smith to the Workhouse. 2.45 Private prayer and breakfast at Charles Wesley's with Smith and Evans, read *Nicodemus.* 4 Walked. 4.45 Chapter. 5 Wrote diary; daily examination; private prayer. 5.30 Public Prayers. 6 General Examination. 6.45 At Ford's, etc, read Law. 9.30.

SATURDAY, FEBRUARY 2.   4.30 Meditated. 5 Private prayer and chapter. 6 Meditated. 7 Whitby. 8 Public Prayers. 9 Breakfast with Ford, read Nelson. 10 Sermon.[191] 11 Walked. 11.45 Meditated; private prayer. 12 Dinner. 1 Shorthand. 2 Whitby. 4 Walked. 4.45 Chapter. 5 Wrote diary; daily examination; private prayer; Public Prayers. 6 Supper. 7 With me, Ford, Smith, and Evans, read *Nicodemus.* 9 Private prayer. 9.45.

SUNDAY, FEBRUARY 3.   4.30 Hymn; meditated: called Smyth and At- kinson.[192] 5 Private prayer. 5.30 Chapter. 6 Read Meditations with me, Smyth and Atkinson. 7.15 Walked with them to Christ Church; Public Prayers and Sacrament.[193] 8.30 Walked with them, religious talk. 9 Breakfast. 9.15 Meditated and private prayer. 10 Sermon. 11 Walked with Ford, good talk. 11.45 Wrote diary; chapter; private prayer. 12 Dinner. 1 Walked with Smith; Workhouse, began *The Christian Moni- tor,*[194] religious talk. 2 Sermon. 3 At Charles Wesley's with Smith and Evans, finished *Nicodemus.* 4 Walked. 4.45 Chapter. 5 Wrote diary; daily examination; private prayer; Public Prayers. 6 Supper. 7 At Smith's with Ford and Evans, read *Nicodemus.* 9.15 Private prayer. 9.30.

MONDAY, FEBRUARY 4.   4.30 Hymn; wrote diary; meditated; private prayer. 5 Chapter; meditated. 5.30 Whitby. 7 Public Prayers. 8 Read Brown. 10 Disputations. 12 Wrote diary; chapter; private prayer. 12.15 Dinner. 1 Aldrich. 1.30 Walked. 2 Whitby. 4.15 Visited Bolton, reli- gious talk. 5 Wrote diary; daily examination; private prayer; Public

---

maries, not yet having done so for December (see monthly summary for De- cember 1733). Cf. 27 July, where he was also nearly two months behind.

[191]   This day was the festival of the Purification of the Blessed Virgin (see Nelson, *Festivals,* ch. XII).

[192]   See 21 November, note 102.

[193]   Ingham and some of his friends attended the early morning Sacrament at Christ Church quite regularly on Sundays through February and March, follow- ing the long-standing practice of the Wesleys and some other Methodists.

[194]   See John Rawlet in Appendix 3.

Prayers. 6 Supper. 7 With Ford, religious talk. 8.45 Walked with Atkinson and Smyth, religious talk. 9.15 Private prayer. 9.45.

TUESDAY, FEBRUARY 5. 4.30 Hymn; meditated. 5 Private prayer; chapter. 5.30 Read *The Way of Living by Method*. 6 Whitby. 7 Public Prayers. 8 Meditated and private prayer. 9 Composed Opposition; and Disputations. 12 Wrote diary; chapter; private prayer. 12.15 Dinner. 1 Aldrich. 1.45 Walked with Atkinson and Watson, religious talk. 2.45 Greek Lecture. 3.45 Whitby. 5 Wrote diary; daily examination; private prayer. 5.30 Public Prayers. 6 Supper. 7 Sat with Bolton,[195] together with Knail and Alsop, various and useful talk. 12.45 Private prayer. 1.15.

WEDNESDAY, FEBRUARY 6. 7 Public Prayers. 8 With Bolton. 10.30 Wrote diary; private prayer. 11 Disputations. 12 Chapter and private prayer; Hall. 12.45 At Bolton's, religious talk, received the Holy Sacrament with Bolton, Watson, Dixon, and Brown.[196] 2 With Smith, religious talk. 2.45 At Charles Wesley's with Smith, private prayer. 3 Breakfast, religious talk. 4 At Bolton's. 5 Wrote diary; daily examination; private prayer; Public Prayers. 6 Supper. 7 With me, Ford and Smith, read *Nicodemus*. 9.

THURSDAY, FEBRUARY 7. 7 Private prayer. 7.30 Public Prayers. 8 Breakfast. 8.30 At Bolton's. 9.45 Translated Kennet. 10.30 Read sermon on Method.[197] 11 Walked and read News. 11.45 Wrote diary; chapter; private prayer. 12 Dinner. 1 Aldrich. 1.45 Walked with Watson, Atkinson, and Ford, religious talk. 2.30 Whitby. 4.45 Wrote diary; chapter. 5 Daily examination; private prayer; Public Prayers. 6 Supper. 7 At Bolton's, religious talk. 11.30 Private prayer. 11.45.

195 See monthly summary for February 1733/34: "Sat with Bolton, Sr, in his sickness." This was Richard Bolton, older brother of Thomas, both of Queen's (cf. 22 March).

196 Either Joseph Brown, B.A. 1721 (Fellow 1731), or Philip Brown, B.A. 1728, both of Queen's College. This private administration of the Sacrament for the ill Richard Bolton was the first that Ingham had attended; beginning on 8 April he attended many such administrations of "The Communion of the Sick" for persons in the workhouses of Oxford. There is no indication of who administered the Sacrament on this occasion (cf. 8 April and 14 May). John Wesley had been administering communion privately to individuals at Oxford since March 1732 (OD II, 123).

197 Most likely the tract by "A Presbyter of the Church of England," *The Way of Living in a Method* (1722), noted on 5 February (see Appendix 3).

FRIDAY, FEBRUARY 8.   5.45 <u>Hymn</u>. 6 Wrote diary; read Nelson; meditated; private prayer; chapter; meditated. 7.15 Public Prayers. 8 Meditated; private prayer. 9 Composed Argument. 11 Disputations. 11.45
Wrote diary; chapter; private prayer. 12 Hall. 12.30 Meditated and private prayer. 1 Aldrich. 1.30 Walked with Smith; Workhouse. 2.45 Greek
Lecture. 3.45 Private prayer and breakfast. 4 Whitby. 5 Wrote diary;
daily examination; private prayer; Public Prayers. 6 General Examination. 6.30 At Ford's with Atkinson, Watson, Washington, Smyth, read
Law. 9 Walked with Atkinson, religious talk. 9.45 Private prayer. 10.

SATURDAY, FEBRUARY 9.   7 Public Prayers. 8 Walked with Atkinson,
religious talk; breakfast. 8.45 Wrote diary; private prayer. 9 Whitby.
11 Walked. 11.45 Wrote diary; chapter; private prayer. 12 Dinner. 1
Aldrich. 1.30 Walked with Watson, religious talk. 2 Whitby. 3 Lecture.
3.45 Wrote letter to Brownsword. 4.15 Began Patrick's *Christian Sacrifice* with Ford. 5 Wrote diary; daily examination; private prayer; Public
Prayers. 6 Supper. 7 At Ford's with Smith, read Goodman. 9 Private
prayer. 9.30.

SUNDAY, FEBRUARY 10.   4.45 Dressed. 5 Meditated and private prayer.
5.30 Read Patrick with Ford. 6.45 Wrote diary; dressed and private
prayer. 7.15 Walked with Ford to Christ Church; Public Prayers and
Sacrament. 9 Breakfast with Ford, good talk. 10 Sermon.[198] 11 Walked
with Washington, Watson, and Ford, religious talk. 11.45 Wrote diary;
chapter; private prayer. 12 Dinner. 1 Walked with Smith; Workhouse,
read *Christian Monitor*. 2 Sermon. 3 At Charles Wesley's with Smith, began <u>treatise on Self-Denial</u>. 4 Wrote letter to Charles Burton. 5 Wrote
diary; daily examination; private prayer; Public Prayers. 6 Supper. 7
With me, Ford, Watson, Washington, Atkinson, Smyth, and Richardson,
read the sermon which John Wesley <u>preached</u> in the forenoon on the

---

198   John Wesley preached at St. Mary's, his topic ("The Love of God") perhaps inspired by the remembrance of the riots that began on this day (St. Scho-
lastica's Day) in 1354/55 when townsmen "knocked sixty-two innocent scholars
on the head" (John Pointer's euphemistic way of referring to the killings, beat-
ings, and other violence that took place; see *Oxoniensis academia* [London:
S. Birt, 1749], p. 38f.). The settlement that followed required the mayor of
Oxford and sixty-two townsmen to attend St. Mary's annually on the anniversary
of that event in order to do penance, an annual occurrence not abolished until
1825. Charles Edward Mallet, *A History of the University of Oxford* (New
York: Longmans, Green and Co., 1924), vol. 1, 160ff.

Love of God;[199] religious talk; <u>discovered to them my acquaintance with the Wesleys.[200]</u> 9.15 Watson, religious talk. 10.

MONDAY, FEBRUARY 11. 4.30 Dressed and <u>hymn</u>. 5 Wrote diary; meditated; private prayer. 5.30 Chapter. 6 Whitby. 7.15 Public Prayers. 8 Breakfast. 8.15 Meditated and private prayer. 9 Whitby. 11 Disputations. 11.45 Chapter and private prayer. 12 Dinner. 12.45 Aldrich. 1.30 Walked with Watson, religious talk. 2 Wrote diary; <u>slept</u>.[201] 4 Whitby. 4.45 Chapter. 5 Wrote diary; Public Prayers. 5.30 <u>Daily</u> examination and private prayer. 6 Supper. 6.30 Walked with Fothergil, religious talk. 7.15 At Bolton's with Dixon, religious talk, read Nelson and Country Parson. 1.30 Private prayer.

TUESDAY, FEBRUARY 12. 7.15 Public Prayers. 8 Meditated and private prayer. 8.45 Breakfast. 9 Whitby. 11 Walked. 11.45 Chapter; private prayer. 12 Dinner. 1 Aldrich. 1.45 Read Nelson. 3 Greek Lecture. 4 Wrote diary; chapter; daily examination; private prayer. 5 Public Prayers. 5.30 Supper.[202] 6.30 Read Bible. 7 With me, Robson, religious and useful talk. 9.15 Private prayer. 9.30.

WEDNESDAY, FEBRUARY 13. 4.30 <u>Hymn</u>; meditated; private prayer; chapter. 5.30 Meditated. 7 Public <u>Prayers</u>. 8 Meditated and private prayer. 9 Whitby. 11 Disputations. 12 Wrote diary; chapter; private prayer; Hall. 12.30 Meditated and private prayer. 1 Aldrich. 1.45 Walked; Workhouse. 2.45 Private prayer and breakfast at Charles Wesley's with Ford, religious talk. 3.45 Walked with Ford, religious talk. 4.15 Chapter; daily examination; private prayer. 5 Public Prayers. 5.30

---

199 Charles Wesley's transcript of this sermon is found in Charles Wesley MS. Sermonbook (MA), pp. 1–33. This collection of sermons was long thought to have been composed by Charles Wesley and was published by his widow, Sarah, in *Sermons by the Late Rev. Charles Wesley, A.M.* (London: Baldwin, 1816). Charles noted in shorthand on the manuscript, however, that most of them were "transcribed from my brother's copy." See R. P. Heitzenrater, "John Wesley's Early Sermons," in *Proceedings of the Wesley Historical Society* 37 (February 1970), pp. 110–28.

200 A fascinating comment, considering that he had been encouraging them in the Wesleyan "method" of thought and action for nearly half a year.

201 This entry, in shorthand, comes at an unusual hour but is yet another indication of Ingham's ongoing struggle with the "weakness" of the flesh.

202 Evening prayers and supper move back a half-hour, effective through 26 March.

Supper. 6.15 At Ford's with Atkinson, Watson, Washington, Smyth, finished Law's *Christian Perfection.* 9.30.

THURSDAY, FEBRUARY 14.[203]   7 Public Prayers and Lecture.[204] 8.30 Wrote diary; meditated and private prayer. 9 Breakfast with Ford, religious talk. 10.30 Translated Kennet. 11.15 Walked. 11.45 Wrote diary; chapter; private prayer. 12 Dinner. 12.45 Aldrich. 1.15 Walked with Atkinson, religious talk. 2 Whitby. 4.15 Chapter. 4.30 Daily examination and private prayer. 5 Public Prayers. 5.30 Supper. 6.30 At Ford's with Atkinson, Washington, Smyth, and Richardson, read Brown. 9 Tea. 9.30.

FRIDAY, FEBRUARY 15. 6 Meditated and private prayer. 7 Public Prayers. 8 Composed Argument for Ford. 8.30 Meditated and private prayer and religious talk with Ford. 10 At Bolton's. 10.15 At Watson's. 10.45 Began General Examination of my whole life. 11.45 Private prayer and chapter. 12 Hall. 12.30 Meditated. 1 Aldrich. 1.30 Walked; Workhouse. 2.15 Transcribed Epigrams[205] at Charles Wesley's. 3 Greek Lecture. 3.45 Private prayer and breakfast. 4.15 Wrote diary; daily examination; private prayer. 5 Public Prayers. 5.30 Supper. 6 Finished General Examination. 7 At Ford's with Atkinson, Watson, Washington, Smyth, read Law. 9 Tea. 9.30.

SATURDAY, FEBRUARY 16. 7 Public Prayers. 8 Meditated and private prayer and breakfast. 9 At Bolton's. 9.30 Whitby. 11.15 Walked. 11.45 Chapter; private prayer. 12 Dinner. 1 Aldrich. 2 Whitby. 3 Lecture. 4.15 Chapter; daily examination; private prayer. 5 Public Prayers. 5.30 Supper. 6.30 At Bolton's. 7 At Ford's with Atkinson, Watson, Washington, Smyth, began Law's *Serious Call,* religious talk. 9.15 Private prayer. 10.

SUNDAY, FEBRUARY 17. 4.45 Hymn and thanksgiving. 5 Wrote diary; meditated. 5.30 Private prayer. 5.45 Chapter. 6 Meditated and private

[203]   Ingham here alters the diary format slightly, adding a ruled column at the left-hand margin specifically for symbols indicating important entries (see key to symbols, plate 4; see also plate 11).

[204]   The statutes stipulated that university lectures in rhetoric (for first-year students) and logic (for students beyond the first year but not yet presented for the B.A.) should be given on Mondays and Thursdays respectively at 8 a.m. (*Statutes,* IV.1). The only other occasion in this diary that Ingham notes attending a lecture on this schedule is 16 May.

[205]   MS. reads "Epgr"; see also 11 April.

prayer for the Sacrament. 7 Walked with Ford and Atkinson to Christ Church. 7.30 Public Prayers and Sacrament. 9 Breakfast with them. 10 Sermon. 10.45 Walked with Washington and Smyth, good talk. 10.30 Wrote diary; meditated; chapter; private prayer. 12 Dinner. 1 Walked; Workhouse, read *Christian Monitor*. 2 Sermon. 3 Read sermon with Watson, religious talk. 4.15 Chapter. 4.30 Wrote diary; daily examination; private prayer. 5 Public Prayers. 5.30 Supper. 6.30 With Watson and Ford, religious and useful talk. 10.

MONDAY, FEBRUARY 18. 5 Hymn; meditated; private prayer; chapter. 6 Meditated. 6.30 Whitby. 7.15 Public Prayers. 8 Began *Nicodemus*. 8.45 Breakfast. 9 Whitby. 11 Walked with Ford, religious talk. 11.45 Wrote diary; chapter; private prayer. 12 Dinner. 1 At Ford's, meditated. 2 Whitby. 4 Meditated. 4.15 Chapter. 4.30 Wrote diary; daily examination; private prayer. 5 Public Prayers. 5.30 Supper. 6.30 Read Blackmore on the Creation. 8 Private prayer.

TUESDAY, FEBRUARY 19. 2 Sat with Bolton, meditated and private prayer. 6 Wrote diary; meditated and private prayer. 7 Public Prayers. 8 Read *Nicodemus* and private prayer and breakfast. 9 Finished Whitby on the Acts.[206] 11 Walked. 11.45 Chapter and private prayer. 12 Dinner. 1 Aldrich. 1.45 Walked; read *Nicodemus* and meditated. 4.30 Wrote diary; daily examination; private prayer. 5 Public Prayers. 5.30 Supper. 6.30 At Bolton's. 9.

WEDNESDAY, FEBRUARY 20. 6.15 Dressed. 6.30 Wrote diary; meditated and private prayer. 7.15 Public Prayers. 8 Read *Nicodemus* and private prayer. 9 Whitby. 11.30 Chapter and private prayer. 12 Hall. 1 Aldrich. 1.45 Walked to Workhouse. 2.45 Walked. 3.15 Private prayer. 3.30 Whitby. 4 Meditated; chapter; daily examination; private prayer. 5 Wrote diary; Public Prayers. 5.30 Supper. 6.30 Read News. 7.30 Transcribed Opposition for Watson. 9 Natt came; various talk. 9.45 Private prayer. 10 Laid with him.

THURSDAY, FEBRUARY 21. 5.45 Meditated; private prayer; chapter; read *Nicodemus*. 7.30 Public Prayers. 8.15 Removed my books, etc, out of Natt's room.[207] 9 Breakfast. 9.30 Wrote diary; necessary business.

---

[206] This completed his abridgment of the first volume of the *Paraphrase and Commentary;* see 30 March, note 124.

[207] Natt had returned to Oxford the previous day after a three-month absence; see 13 November, note 96.

11 Walked. 11.45 Chapter; private prayer. 12 Dinner. 1 Aldrich. 1.45 With Natt, good talk (various). 3 Read Greek Testament. 4 Chapter. 4.15 Daily examination; private prayer. 5 Public Prayers. 5.30 Supper. 6.30 With Natt, good talk (various). 9 With Ford, private prayer, laid with him. 10.

FRIDAY, FEBRUARY 22.   6 Dressed; meditated; private prayer; chapter. 7 Public Prayers. 8 With Watson, religious talk. 9 Private prayer. 9.30 Washington came, religious talk. 10 Whitby. 11.30 Chapter; meditated, and private prayer. 12 Hall. 12.30 Meditated and private prayer with Ford. 1 Aldrich. 1.45 With Smith, good talk (various). 3 With Watson, good talk. 3.15 Private prayer and meditated. Observe: I am giving myself to God and am resolved to please him only; the Lord be Master to me and give me humility and grace and strength and courage to persevere on to the end of my days. Amen.[208] 4.30 Wrote diary; daily examination and private prayer. 5 Public Prayers. 5.45 Supper and General Examination. 7 At Ford's with Watson, Washington, Atkinson, and Smyth, read Law's *Serious Call.* 9.15 Came home, private prayer. 9.30.

SATURDAY, FEBRUARY 23.   4.45 Dressed. 5 Meditated; private prayer; chapter. 6 With John Wesley, religious and useful talk.[209] 6.30 Meditated. 7.15 Public Prayers. 8 Breakfast at Ford's, religious talk. 9 Meditated. 11 Walked with Atkinson, good talk. 11.45 Dressed and private prayer. 12 Dinner. 1 Aldrich. 2 Meditated. 4 Chapter; daily examination; private prayer. 5 Public Prayers. 5.30 Supper. 6.45 At Smith's with Ford, religious and useful talk. 9.15 Came home; private prayer. 9.30.

SUNDAY, FEBRUARY 24.[210]   4.30 Wrote diary; meditated. 5 Private prayer and chapter. 5.45 Meditated and private prayer. 6.45 Dressed. 7 Walked to Charles Wesley's; private prayer with John Wesley.[211] 7.30 Christ Church, Public Prayers and Sacrament. 8.45 Walked with Broughton. 9 Private prayer. 9.30 At Ford's with Broughton, breakfast, religious talk. 10 Walked with Ford to the Castle; Public Prayers and

---

208   Cf. 7 October, note 48. In the margin of this entry, Ingham drew a stick figure in cruciform position; see plate 11.

209   There is no record of this visit in Wesley's diary, which notes only "transcribed sermon" during this half-hour (OD IV, 78).

210   This day was the festival of St. Matthias the Apostle (see Nelson, *Festivals,* ch. XIII).

211   John Wesley's diary entry reads: "7 At Charles', Carter etc, private prayer," followed by the service at the cathedral (OD IV, 79).

Sermon, Clayton ministered.[212] 12 Walked with Clayton, Smith, and Ford; at the Castle, religious talk. 2.30 Public Prayers and Sermon. 3.30 Walked with Smith to Charles Wesley's, religious talk with them. 4 Came home; abridged Clayton's sermons. 4.30 Wrote diary; daily examination; private prayer. 5 Public Prayers. 5.30 Supper. 6.45 At Ford's with Smith, began Goodman's second Conference. 9.15 Read Nelson; private prayer. 9.45.

MONDAY, FEBRUARY 25. 5 Meditated; private prayer; chapter. 6.15 Whitby. 7.15 Public Prayers. 8 With Natt, religious talk. 8.15 With Watson, religious talk. 9 Meditated and private prayer; read Whitby. 11.30 Necessary business. 11.45 Wrote diary; chapter; private prayer. 12 Dinner. 1 Aldrich. 1.45 With Ford, read Nelson, tea, religious talk. 4.15 Daily examination. 4.45 Necessary business. 5 Public Prayers. 5.30 Private prayer. 5.45 Supper. 6.30 With Watson, religious talk and read Country Parson. 9.30 Private prayer.

TUESDAY, FEBRUARY 26. 6 Meditated; private prayer; chapter. 7.15 Public Prayers. 8 Breakfast at Ford's with Natt, religious talk. 9 Necessary business. 9.30 Natt came, good talk (various). 10 Whitby. 11 Walked with Ford, religious talk. 11.45 Wrote diary; chapter; private prayer. 12 Dinner. 1.15 Aldrich. 1.30 Walked with Ford, etc, religious talk. 2.30 Walked with Gambold, religious talk. 4 Meditated. 4.15 Chapter. 4.30 Daily examination; private prayer. 5 Public Prayers. 5.30 Supper. 6.15 Walked. 6.45 With Natt, began Alleine's *Sure Guide to Heaven.* 8.30 In the Buttery.[213] 9 Read the News. 9.30 Private prayer.

[ASH] WEDNESDAY, FEBRUARY 27. 4 Private prayer; meditated. 5 Private prayer. 5.15 Read Nelson and wrote Rules for Lent.[214] 7 Private prayer. 7.15 Public Prayers. 8.15 Meditated and private prayer. 10 Ser-

212 John Clayton, Brasenose College, B.A. 1729, M.A. 1732; at this time he had the cure of Sacred Trinity Chapel at Salford, near Manchester (*D.N.B.,* vol. 4, 469). John Wesley did not go to the Castle this morning but attended the sermon at St. Mary's. In the evening, Clayton attended a meeting of Wesley's group in Salmon's room (Clayton's former student), where he "read his sermon," presumably the one preached that morning and perhaps abridged by Ingham in the afternoon (OD IV, 79).
213 The storeroom, near the college kitchen, where bread, ale, butter, and other provisions were kept (perhaps not an unusual gathering place on Shrove Tuesday).
214 See the "Resolutions for Lent" listed below. This day was Ash Wednesday (see Nelson, *Fasts,* ch. II).

mon.[215] 10.45 Walked with Smith, good talk. 11 Transcribed a prayer.
11.45 Chapter and private prayer. 12 Wrote diary; Hall. 12.45 Private
prayer. 1 Walked with Smith to Workhouse. 2 Walked with Smith, good
talk (various). 2.45 At Charles Wesley's, private prayer. 3 Breakfast;
began Patrick on Repentance.[216] 4 With Ford, religious talk. 4.30 Daily
examination; private prayer. 5 Public Prayers. 5.30 Hall. 6.15 With
Ford and Atkinson, religious talk. 7 At Smith's with Ford, read Goodman. 9 Came home; private prayer; meditated. 9.30.

THURSDAY, FEBRUARY 28.   6 Dressed; meditated; private prayer; chapter. 7.15 Public Prayers. 8 Breakfast at Charles Wesley's with Smith,
religious talk. 9.45 See the Prince of Orange.[217] 10 Came home. 10.15
Necessary business. 10.30 Whitby. 11 Walked with Washington, religious talk. 11.45 Chapter; private prayer. 12 Wrote diary; dinner. 12.45
Walked with Ford, good talk. 1.15 Wrote resolutions for improving my
time.[218] 2 Whitby. 3 Walked with Natt, religious talk. 4 Chapter. 4.30
Daily examination; private prayer. 5 Public Prayers. 5.30 Supper. 6.30
With Natt, read Alleine's *Sure Guide.* 9.15 With Watson, various talk.
9.30 Wrote diary; private prayer.

With all humility and diffidence I desire, O God, of thy goodness,
strengthen and enable me to rise at 4, and that before the larum ceases
ringing, and O may my mind be always filled with most solemn thoughts
of thee and a serious consideration of the important business of life.

10 Resolutions for Lent[219]

1. If I be not up before the larum ceases, to miss one meal that day or
   at least to sconce myself one pence to be given to the poor, if on a
   Stationary Day.

---

[215] A Latin sermon on Ash Wednesday at St. Mary's, "to be preached before
the determining bachelors, who are to wear their hoods with the rheno, or lamb's
wool exposed, and sit according to custom on the master's benches." *Statutes,*
XVI.4; cf. John Ayliffe, *The Antient and Present State of the University of
Oxford* (London: E. Curll, 1714), II, 122.

[216] Simon Patrick, *A Treatise of Repentance* (1686); see Appendix 3.

[217] William IV, Prince of Orange, had arrived in Oxford the previous evening
and lodged at Christ Church (Richard Smith's and Charles Wesley's college),
where this morning he attended Public Prayers at ten (Hearne, *Collections,* vol.
11, 309).

[218] See 26 September, note 36.

[219] Ingham also refers to this list as "Rules for Lent" (see 27 February).

2. To set apart from 4 to 5 morning and afternoon for Devotion.

3. To set apart from 8 to 9 in the morning for Devotion on Monday, Tuesday, Wednesday, and Friday.

4. To meditate from 5 to 6 on my knees [and] 11 to 12 on Wednesday and Friday; from 5 to 7 on Sunday.[220]

5. To set apart Saturday afternoon to prepare for the Sabbath, besides Lecture.

6. To eat no butter all Lent, unless with strangers.

7. To fast or abstain on Monday and Tuesday, at least breakfast.[221]

8. To make only one meal at 3 on Wednesday and Friday, if possible.

9. To eat no baked pudding on Sunday.

10. Every meal to limit the quantity before sitting down.

X To use a Collect before and after reading the Holy Scripture.

X To begin an exacter diary according to Charles Wesley's direction and to observe his 16 resolutions.

Transcribed into diary, March 4, 1733/34

MARCH 9.   Set apart from 5 to 6 on Saturday morning to thank God for the blessings of the past week.

Resolutions for Every Day[222]

1. Have I prayed with fervor by myself and at Church?

2. Have I used 'O God, who hast prepared' at 9; 'Almighty God unto whom' at 12; 'Remember not, Lord, the offenses' at 3?[223]

3. Have I used the Ejaculations[224] once an hour?

---

220   After the 6, Ingham placed =, which in some contexts seems to mean "on my knees" (see 23 April, note 39).

221   "Breakfast" here used in the sense of "early morning meal."

222   This list, which Ingham received from Charles Wesley (see 1 and 2 March), follows very closely the lists of "General Questions," which John Wesley developed and revised continually during this period and which George Whitefield also transcribed into the front of his 1736 diary. See p. 19 above.

223   Ingham transcribed these three collects into the front of his diary (see p. 56).

224   Gambold describes the nature and use of ejaculatory prayers among the Wesley circle: "They had a book of Ejaculations relating to the chief virtues, which lying by them as they stood at their studies, they at intervals snatched a short petition out of it. But at last, instead of that variety, they contented themselves with the following aspirations . . . 'Consider and hear me, etc'" ("Collect for every hour," see p. 55 above). John Gambold, "The Character of Mr. John Wesley," *Methodist Magazine* 21 (March 1798), p. 170. See also 2 May and 23 August.

4. Have I at ingress or egress[225] prayed for the virtue of the day?
5. Have I said or done anything without a present or previous perception of its remote or immediate tendency to the glory of God?
6. Have I after every pleasure immediately given thanks? After every commendation?
7. Did I in the morning plan the business of the day?[226]
8. Have I been simple and recollected in every thing?[227]
9. Have I been zealous in undertaking, and active in doing what good I could?
10. Have I before visiting or being visited, considered what end, what means?
11. Has good will been and appeared the spring of all my actions toward others?
12. Have I been or seemed angry?
13. Have I thought or spoke unkindly of or to any one?
14. Have I felt or entertained any proud, vain, unchaste, or discontented thoughts?
15. Have I been temperate in the desire and in the use of sensual pleasure, and particularly have I been recollected and thankful in eating and drinking?

---

[225] "Coming in or going out." Ingham began noting his consideration of "virtue" of the day along with the "business" of the day (question 7 below) on 4 March with the entry "B-V".

[226] George Whitefield viewed this practice as giving rise to the term Methodist: "The world (and not themselves) gave them the title of Methodists, I suppose from their custom of regulating their time and planning the business of the day every morning." *A Short Account of God's Dealings with the Reverend Mr. Whitefield* (London: W. Strahan, 1740), p. 31.

[227] Ingham uses the term "recollected" in two distinct ways: (1) to indicate an hourly exercise of self-examination reviewing one's demeanor (see 23 August: "Resolve to recollect and use ejaculations at the beginning of each hour"), and (2) as here, to indicate a state of spiritual composure, usually associated with the virtue of simplicity.

PLATE 1. The Chapel, Queen's College (T. Malton, 1810). By permission of the British Library.

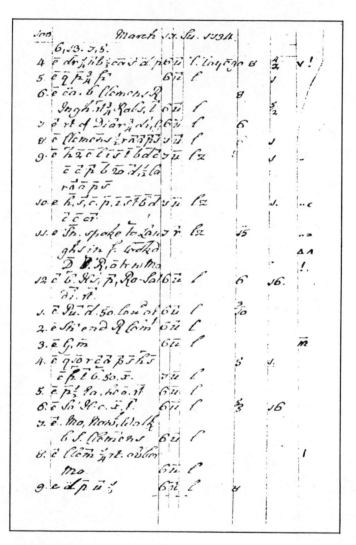

PLATE 2. Wesley diary page, 17 March 1733/34. Courtesy of The Methodist Archives, Manchester.

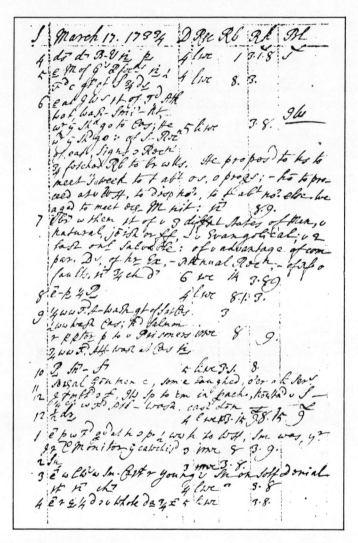

PLATE 3. Ingham diary page, 17 March 1733/34. Courtesy of The Methodist Archives, Manchester.

Charles Wesley A.M. Student of
Ch Ch Oxford taught me ye following
Method of keeping a Diary. I
became acquainted wth him, & his
Brother John Wesley A.M & Fellow
of Lincoln College Oxon through
Charles Burton :—

Abbreviations.

nb	necessary business.	Cw	Charles Wesley
br	breakfast,	Jw	John Wesley
Dr	Dinner,	Sm	Rd Smith of CC:
sp	Supper,	Atk	Atkinson of Q
b	began,	wat	Watson
r	read.	Wash	Washington —
tra	translate.	Smi'	Smith of Queens
tr	transcribe,	F	Ford —
ch	came Home,	nt	Natt —
ww	walk with	Kn	Knail —
w	walk or went.	Br	Brownswood —
tht	thought	Rb	Robson of Linc
Sn	Sermon,	Hv	Hervey —
nel	Nelson	Bro	Broughton of Ex
gt	good talk	Gam	Gambold of
rt	religious —		Stanton Harcourt
lt	learned —	Ev	Evans of CC
vt	various —	talk	walker of B.N
gr	mostly religious	Grieg	of Linc
rtg	religious & useful	WH	work-House in
it	idle talk		St: Tho.s Oxford
iti	vitious —	GWH	Gloset Green
			work House.

PLATE 5. Key to abbreviations and symbols. Courtesy of The Methodist
Archives, Manchester. *Smi'* = [*Thomas*] *Smith of Queens:* the spelling in the
Entrance Book of Queen's College is "Smyth," the form we have used
throughout this diary to distinguish him from Richard Smith of Christ
Church.

Abbreviation for "my mother's family at Ossett": Ingham's father, William, had died in 1723 when Benjamin was eleven. The entries in this part of the list, and thus those that follow, must have been written after Ingham returned to Ossett in July 1734, indicating the late date of the transcription of part of the "key" into the diary.

The dot symbol for "cold in prayer" (and the next three combinations of dots symbolizing "indifferent," "attentive," or "fervent") could be used after an entry, indicating Ingham's degree of attention during the activity noted, such as "Public prayers [attentive]."

The five modifications to the letter "p" shown above indicate various "degrees of attention." A sixth variant indicating "zealous" appears in the Diary but is not shown here.

The special S symbol indicating "simplicity" was used beginning on 9 May as the heading for the column of numbers down the middle of the page in the "exacter" diary format, a column formerly headed D (temper of devotion). See Appendix 1.

'f	m Mother & family at Opret.	H.	sister Hannah
ppap	william wilby	Lr	Letter
mm	my mother	Lt	Latin
w'	at Bro' williams	GrT	Greek Testam'
J	Joseph	Acq	Acquaintance
J	John	R	Religious
J'	Isaacs	ds	dress
ta'	taught y' child-ren y' come 3d a day —	Cas	Castle at Oxon
		dis	disipated
at wilbs	ta' his children	Fnd	Friend
Dec	Declamation	ɔ	for, — and
Th	Theme	v	the, ō not
C	Compose	c	came, y they
Disp	Disputation	y	there, yr their
S	Sacrament	wk	walk; fr. from
Ch	Church	h	him or his
P	Public Prayers	d	wr Diary
p	private —	Sl	Simplicity
x	daily Examinatio	R//	Recollection
Gx	General Ex	Bol	Bolton S'.—
M	Meditate	Dix	Dixon of 2
:	cold in praer	uc	uncollected
:	indifferent —	mc	uncollected
:	attentive —	·ing	at v end of a word
:	fervent —	Tks	Thanksgiving
f	dead in praer	f-	family
f	cold —	wr	write
f	indifferent —	unc	unchast —
f	attentive	v Tht	vain thought
f	fervent		

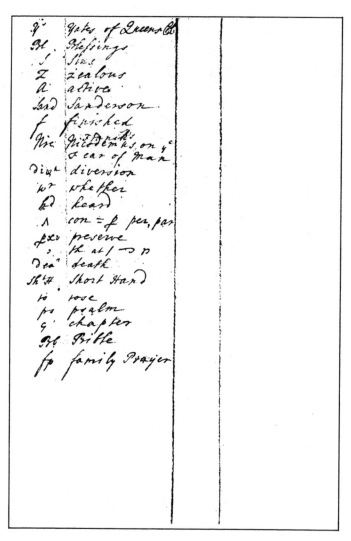

PLATE 7. Key to abbreviations and symbols. Courtesy of The Methodist Archives, Manchester.

PLATE 8. Oxford Castle, north prospect (S. & N. Buck, 1729). By permission of the British Library.

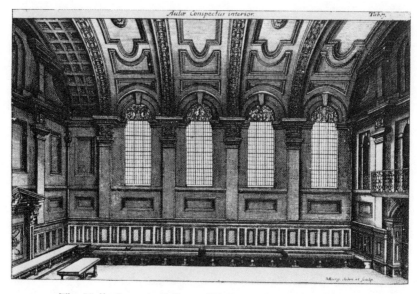

PLATE 9. The Hall, Queen's College (N. Burghers, 1730). By permission of
the British Library.

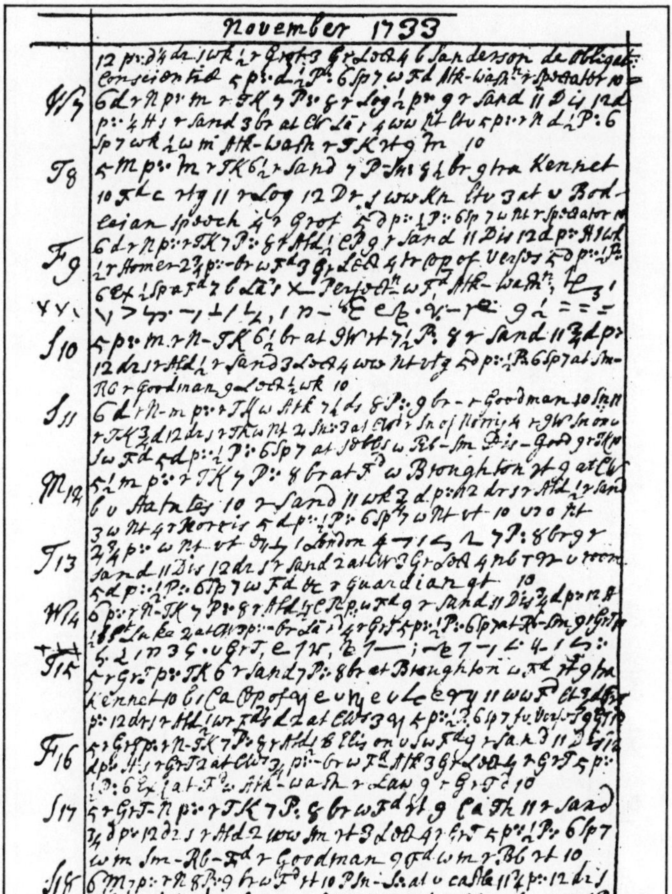

PLATE 10. Paragraph diary format, November 1733. Courtesy of The Methodist Archives, Manchester.

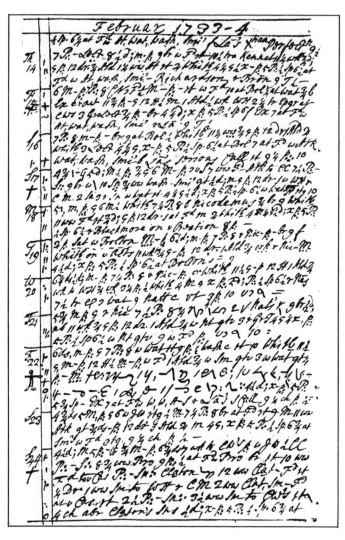

PLATE II. Paragraph diary format, February 1733/34. Courtesy of The Methodist Archives, Manchester.

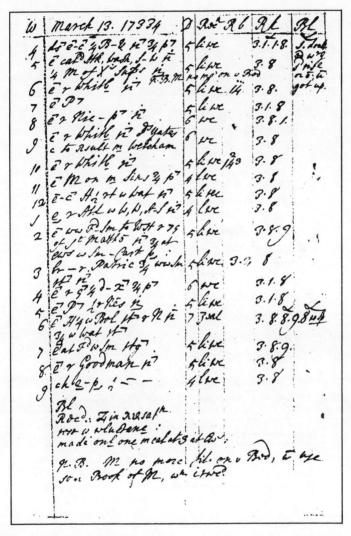

PLATE 12. "Exacter" diary format (A), 13 March 1733/34. Courtesy of The Methodist Archives, Manchester.

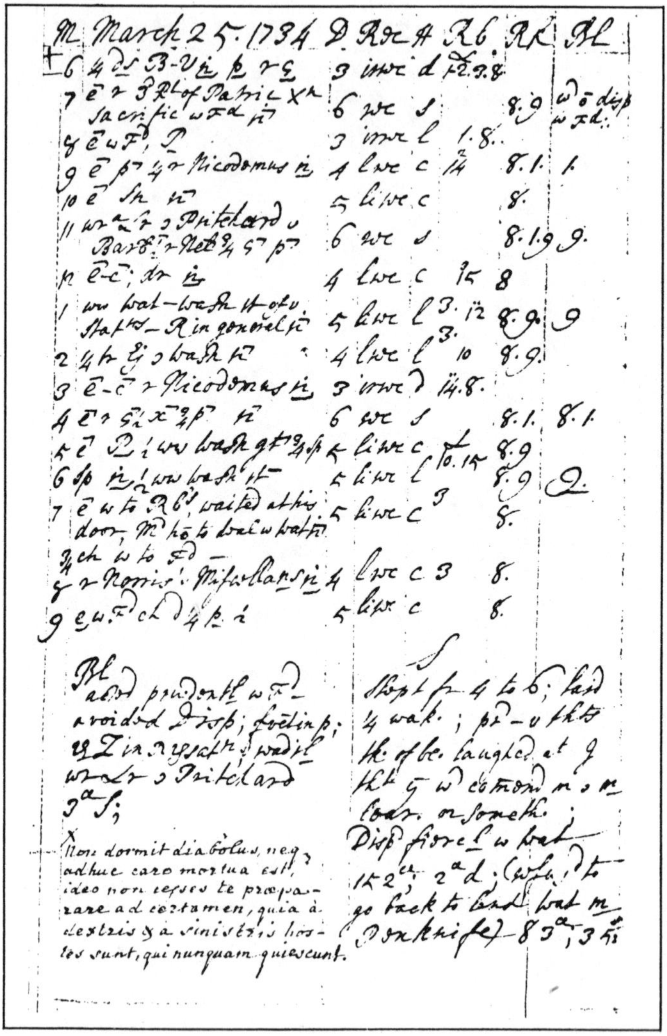

PLATE 13. "Exacter" diary format (B), 25 March 1734. Courtesy of The Methodist Archives, Manchester.

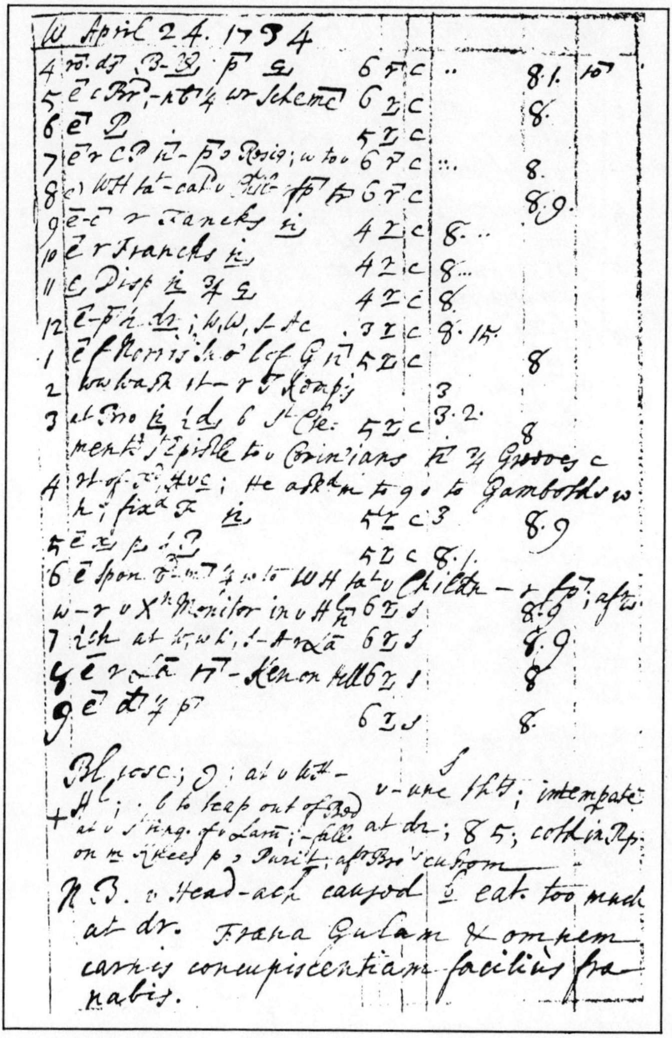

PLATE 14. "Exacter" diary format (C), 24 April 1734. Courtesy of The Methodist Archives, Manchester.

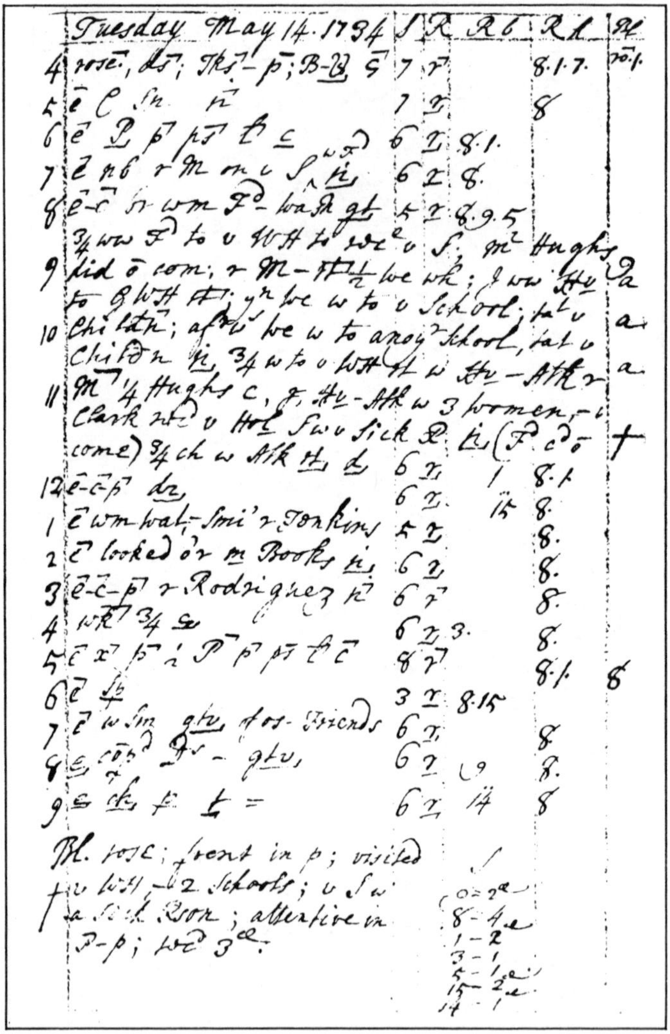

PLATE 15. "Exacter" diary format (D), 14 May 1734. Courtesy of The Methodist Archives, Manchester.

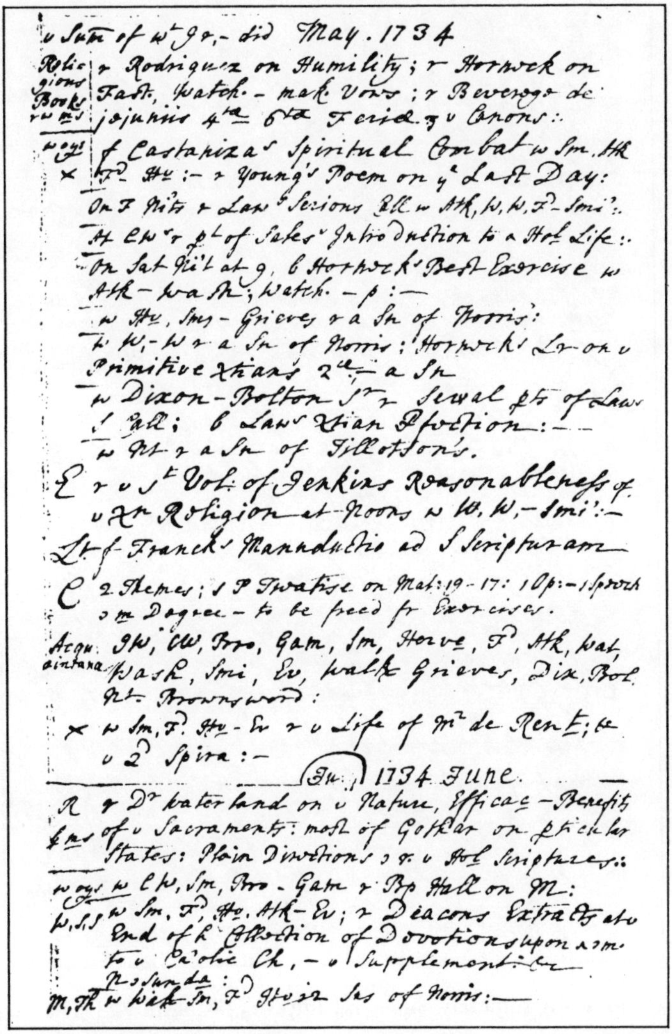

PLATE 16. Monthly summary, May and June 1734. Courtesy of The Methodist Archives, Manchester.

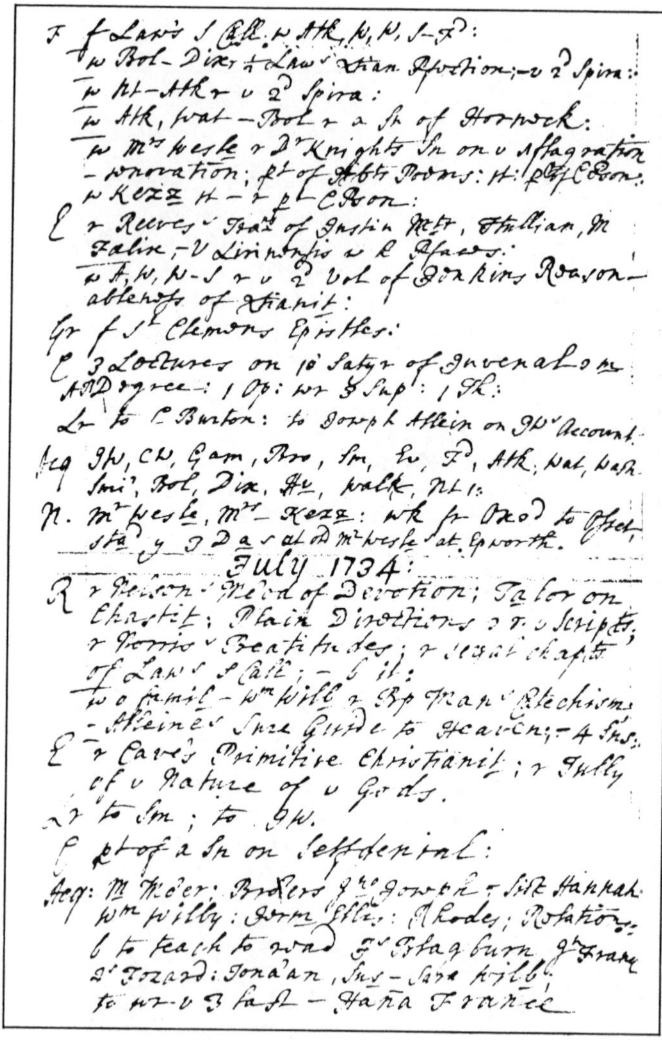

PLATE 17. Monthly summary, June and July 1734. Courtesy of The Methodist Archives, Manchester.

PLATE 18. Map of area around Leeds, 1724. By permission of the British Library.

The striking change in format that marks the beginning of this section of Ingham's diary is coincident with other noticeable changes in the manner and intensity of his "Methodist" lifestyle during this Lenten season. Charles Wesley not only teaches him John's "exacter" method of diary keeping, but also passes on to him the General Questions ("Resolutions") for daily self-examination, a sign that Ingham is becoming more closely associated with the intricacies of the Wesleyan system, such as hourly ejaculatory prayer, collects at the stated hours, and systematic recollection of "temper of devotion." His Resolutions for Lent, copied from the Wesleys, are supplemented by an additional list of Resolutions for Observing the Passion Week. This personal aspect of Ingham's meditative piety builds toward an important climax with his formal "resignation" of himself to God, patterned after Charles Wesley's, and in the words of the *Country Parson's Advice,* and confirmed with his own blood on Good Friday. The resulting resolutions and resignations take up several pages in this middle portion of his diary.

Ingham's schedule of group meetings continues to expand to include additional persons and places beyond the walls of Queen's College, notably at Lincoln College. He becomes more directly involved with the Wesleys, calling on John frequently for advice and visiting Charles's room for study and counsel. He begins to develop a close relationship with John Gambold at Stanton Harcourt, a fellow Methodist who shared many of Ingham's sentiments. On Wesley's advice, Ingham begins in mid-March to "compare diaries" with other Methodists, a means of confession and mutual encouragement. By Easter, Ingham has become totally involved in the lifestyle, organization, and thought patterns of Oxford

Methodism, although not participating directly in the activities of John Wesley's own personal group.

FRIDAY, MARCH 1.   4 Dressed; meditated; private prayer; chapter. 5 Meditated. 6 Read Whitby; ri.[1] 7.15 Public Prayers. 8.15 Ejaculatory prayers.[2] 8.30 Watson and Dominus Dalton[3] importuned me to oppose them. 8.45 Prepared. 9 Walked with Watson, various talk, opposed his answering under Bachelor;[4] see the Prince of Orange walk to take his degree;[5] ri. 11 Opposed Dalton. 11.30 E; chapter; private prayer; meditated. 12.30 Hall. 1 Walked with Smith; Workhouse; ri. 2.15 With Smith at Charles Wesley's, he taught us to keep an exacter diary;[6] ri. 3

---

1   The precise meaning of the abbreviation "ri" is unclear, although it appears to be associated in some way with "recollection" and is usually accompanied by one of the symbols indicating a degree of attention; see list of symbols in plate 4.

2   See p. 119, note 224; ejaculatory prayers hereinafter cited as E.

3   John Dalton, Queen's College, B.A. 1730. The title Dominus (Ds) was prefixed to the name of a bachelor (of arts, in this case) to distinguish him from a master (Mr) and from an undergraduate (no prefix). John Richard Magrath, *The Queen's College* (Oxford: Clarendon Press, 1921), vol. 1, 229. Cf. *O.E.D.,* s.v. "Don" (from the Latin *dominus*). In this diary, persons such as Alsop and Yates are listed only by surname until they received their B.A. degree, after which Ds is prefixed (see 12 and 18 March).

4   MS. reads "Batchelor." "Answering under Bachelor" was an exercise required for the B.A. degree, being respondent twice at the Lent disputations ("Determinations") under a bachelor of arts and on the same questions which the bachelor had defended; four terms of study in logic were prerequisite, and the disputation was expected to last for one hour and a half on each occasion (*Statutes,* VI.1.6–7); cf. John Richard Magrath, *The Flemings in Oxford* (Oxford: Oxford Historical Society, 1904–24), vol. 2, 7, note 15; and Robert Howard Hodgkin, *Six Centuries of an Oxford College* (Oxford: Basil Blackwell, 1949), p. 115.

5   William IV, Prince of Orange, was created a doctor of civil law in a convocation at 10 a.m. in the Theatre. Thomas Hearne (who, with Tory pride, says, "I never wagged out all the while he was here to see him") explains that Vice-Chancellor William Holmes "thinks of getting great favour at Court by inviting the Prince thither, and by shewing such profound reverence to him." *Remarks and Collections of Thomas Hearne,* ed. H. E. Salter (Oxford: Clarendon Press, 1914–21), vol. 11, 309f.

6   The "exacter diary" is a new format, in columns, begun by John Wesley on 27 January 1734, apparently taught to his brother Charles on 1 February ("talk of diary," OD IV, 56), the new method here being passed on to Ingham and Smith. See descriptive analysis in Appendix 1; see also plate 12.

Private prayer, breakfast, ri, religious talk, read Patrick. 4 Walked with Ford and Atkinson, religious talk. 4.15 Chapter; daily examination; private prayer. 5 Public Prayers. 5.30 Wrote diary [summary];[7] ri. 6 General Examination; private prayer; meditated. 7 At Ford's with Watson, Washington, Smyth, and Atkinson, read Law's *Serious Call,* disputed. 9 Private prayer; meditated. 9.45.

[Blessings:] Charles Wesley taught Smith and myself to keep an exacter diary, to use examination and ejaculatory prayer every hour; he gave us the 16 resolutions for every day;[8] he advised us to show one another our diaries every time we meet.

SATURDAY, MARCH 2. 4 Dressed; meditated; private prayer. 5 E; chapter. 5.15 Read Whitby; ri. 6 E; read Whitby; ri. 7.15 Public Prayers. 7.45 Read *Nicodemus;* ri; private prayer. 8.15 E; breakfast at Natt's with Ford and Knail, various talk; ri. 8.45 At the Theatre,[9] heard the Collector's Speech;[10] ri. 9.30 E; read Whitby; ri. 10 E; read Whitby; ri. 11 E; walked with Watson, religious talk. 11.45 Chapter; private prayer. 12 Wrote diary; E; dinner; ri. 1 Read Aldrich; ri. 1.45 Religious talk with Ford, walked with him; Natt came, read Norris on Seriousness;[11] ri. 2.30 With Gambold at Broughton's Shop,[12] good talk. 3 E; at Lecture in Greek Testament.[13] 4 E; dressed. 4.15 Chapter. 4.30 Daily examination;

---

[7] See 1 February, note 190; see monthly summary for January 1733/34.

[8] See p. 119f.

[9] The Sheldonian Theatre, built in 1668 to the design of Sir Christopher Wren. Many regular university gatherings such as this speech and the proctor's speech (6 April) were formerly held at St. Mary's church, but moved to the Theatre to preserve the sanctity of the church from the rowdiness of the students on these occasions.

[10] Two collectors were responsible for assigning participants in the Lent disputations and maintaining an orderly schedule (presumably the topic of this speech). *Statutes,* VI.2.5; cf. Nicholas Amhurst, *Terrae Filius or, The Secret History of the University of Oxford* (London, 1726), no. XLII.

[11] See "Solitude, Courage, Seriousness" in John Norris, *A Collection of Miscellanies* (1687), in Appendix 3.

[12] Edward Broughton, bookbinder with *"privilegiatus"* of the university (1727), owned a shop at 46–47 High Street, midway between Queen's College and the East Gate. See Herbert Edward Salter, *A Cartulary of the Hospital of St John the Baptist* (Oxford: Oxford Historical Society, 1914), vol. 1, 318, and plate VII; see also Hearne, *Collections,* vol. 11, 328.

[13] This is the only instance in this diary when Ingham appears to have attended the university lecture in Greek, the statutes requiring the Regius Professor

private prayer. 5 E; Public Prayers. 5.30 Supper; ri. 6.45 At Ford's with Smith, transcribed Charles Wesley's 16 resolutions, and good talk; ri; began to say grace before and after drinking. 9.15 Came home; private prayer; ri. 9.30.

[Blessings:] I, Smith, and Ford began to use Grace before and after drinking or eating at night.

SUNDAY, MARCH 3.   4 Dressed; E; meditated. 5 E; private prayer; chapter; meditated. 6 E; meditated. 6.30 Private prayer; ri. 7 E; transcribed Resolutions for Lent; ri. 7.45 Dressed. 8 E; at Ford's, breakfast and read Patrick's *Christian Sacrifice;* ri. 9 E; Public Prayers, Sermon, and Sacrament.[14] 11.15 E; walked; ri. 11.45 Private prayers. 12 Wrote diary; E; dinner; ri. 1 With Ford and Smith at Workhouse, read *Christian Monitor;* ri. 2 E; Sermon.[15] 2.45 Necessary business. 3 At Charles Wesley's with Smith, he gave us further directions for keeping diary; ri. 4 E; chapter; daily examination; private prayer. 5 Wrote diary; E; Public Prayers. 5.30 Supper; ri. 6.30 E. 6.45 At Ford's with Smith, read the Resolutions for Lent, and Law upon particular examination for every day.[16] 9 With Ford, various and useful talk; ri. 9.15 Private prayer; ri. 9.30.

[Blessings:] began comparing diaries with Smith. *Juvat non parum ad profectum Spiritualem, devota rerum Spiritualium collatio.* Kempis.[17]

MONDAY, MARCH 4.   3.45 Dressed. 4 E. 4.15 Business and virtue;[18] ri. 4.30 Private prayer. 4.45 Read chapter. 5 E; read Whitby; ri. 6 E; read Whitby; ri. 7 E; Public Prayers. 7.45 Transcribed Rules for Lent into

---

of the Greek Language to lecture on Wednesday and Saturday afternoons (see *Statutes,* III.12; the hour stipulated is from one to two).

14   This day was the first Sunday in Lent.

15   The statutes designated St. Peter's in the East as the location for the sermons on Sunday afternoons during Lent (*Statutes,* XVI.2–3).

16   William Law, *A Serious Call to a Devout and Holy Life* (1729), ch. XXIII, "Of the nature and necessity of examination. How we are to be particular in the confession of all our sins" (see Appendix 3).

17   *De imitatione Christi,* I.x.2 (see Appendix 3), translated by Wesley as, "Devout conversation upon spiritual subjects doth greatly further our spiritual growth." *The Christian's Pattern* (London: Rivington, 1735), p. 18.

18   The diary entry "B-V" indicates that Ingham planned the *business* of the day and prayed for the *virtue* of the day, following resolutions 7 and 5 for every day (see p. 120).

my diary; ri. 8.15 At Ford's, taught him the method of casting up the diary at the month's end.[19] 9.45 Began transcribing the 16 resolutions; ri. 10 E; finished resolutions; ri. 11 The smith came to mend my door; ri. 11.45 Private prayer. 12 E; dinner; ri. 12.45 Read Aldrich at Ford's, etc.[20] 1.15 Wrote diary [summary].[21] 1.45 With Smith, religious talk of diary. 2.15 With Charles Wesley, religious talk of diary. 2.45 E; transcribed abbreviations into diary;[22] ri. 3 E; Collect; transcribed particular Collects;[23] ri. 4 E; read chapter; daily examination; private prayer; wrote diary. 5 E; Public Prayers. 5.30 Supper; ri. 6.15 With Watson, religious talk. 7.15 With Natt, read Alleine's *Sure Guide,* religious talk upon the Sacrament at Christ Church. 9.30 Private prayer on my knees; meditated of the unsearchable ways of God's providence.

Blessings: recollected for an hour; enabled to observe the 15 resolutions at dinner and supper; very good talk with Natt about resolutions and going to the Sacrament at Christ Church; fervent in private prayer.

TUESDAY, MARCH 5. 4 Dressed; E and Collect. 4.15 Business and virtue; ri. 4.45 Private prayer. 5 E; read chapter. 5.45 Transcribed Collects. 6 E; transcribed Collects. 6.30 Read Whitby; ri. 7 E. 7.15 Public Prayers. 8 E; breakfast at Natt's with Jourd,[24] Ford, Dixon, various talk; ri. 9 E and Collect. 9.30 Came home; Collect; read Whitby; ri. 10 E; read Whitby; ri. 11 E; walked; ri. 11.45 Read chapter. 12 E and private prayer. 12.15 Wrote diary; dinner; ri. 1 E; at Broughton's Shop; ri; exchanged some books. 2.30 Came home; thoughts of my books. 3 E; Collect; read Whitby; ri. 4 Read chapter. 4.30 Daily examination and wrote diary; ri. 4.45 Private prayer. 5 E; Public Prayers. 5.30 Supper. 6.15 Walked with Watson, religious talk; ri. 7 With Watson, religious talk; ri. 9 E; private prayer. 9.30.

---

19 "Casting up" is Ingham's term for writing a monthly summary (see 1 October).

20 "Etc" is still Washington, Watson, Atkinson (see 6 November), and Smyth (see 22 January and monthly summaries for February 1733/34 and March 1734).

21 Ingham was trying to bring his diary summaries up to date, probably working on the January 1733/34 and February 1733/34 summaries at this point (cf. 1 February, note 190).

22 See key to abbreviations in plates 5, 6, and 7.

23 See his transcription, pp. 57f. On 5 March he begins noting his use of the collects for nine, noon, and three.

24 William Jourd, Queen's College, B.A. 1736.

WEDNESDAY, MARCH 6.   4.30 Dressed, and business and virtue; ri. 5 E
and private prayer. 5.20 Meditated on Christ's sufferings;[25] ri. 6 E; read
Whitby; ri. 7 E. 7.15 Public Prayers; ri. 8 E with Ford, transcribed the
Ejaculations for him, and religious talk of managing Natt. 8.15 Read
Nelson on the Ember Days;[26] ri. 8.45 Private prayer. 9 E and Collect;
dressed; read Whitby; ri. 10 E; read Whitby; ri. 11 E; meditated of my
own sins; ri; read chapter; ri. 12 E and private prayer; ri. 12.15 Hall;
ri. 12.30 At Ford's read Ken's *Meditations,* and private prayer with him.
1 Read Aldrich's Logic; ri. 1.45 Walked with Ford and Smith to the
Workhouse, good talk; ri; read 5[th chapter] of St Matthew; ri. 2.45
With Smith at Charles Wesley's, private prayer. 3 E; breakfast; ri; religious talk; read prayer of Gother for a wavering friend,[27] etc; ri. 4 Came
home; E; read Chapter. 4.30 Wrote diary; daily examination; private
prayer. 5 E; Public Prayers. 5.30 Hall; ri. 6 E; Hall. 6.15 Came home;
Collect and private prayer. 6.45 Walked with Ford to Smith's, good talk;
ri. 7 At Smith's with Ford, E, religious talk of diaries, of fasting, of going
to the Sacrament at Christ Church, of the beginning of our acquaintance;
ri. 9.15 Came home with Ford; E; good talk of the Sacrament; private
prayer.

Blessings: wept for Christ's suffering;[28] fervent in Public and private
prayer; made only one meal; refused dainties, gave away my commons;
kept Lent Rule 8.[29]

---

[25]   See Johann Gerhard, *Gerhard's Meditations and Prayers* (1695), ch. 5, "An
Exercise of Faith, from the Love of Christ in the Agony of Death"; and Thomas
Ken, *The Retired Christian Exercised in Divine Thoughts and Heavenly Meditations for the Closet* (1737), ch. [IX], "A consolatory penitential Meditation upon
the Merits of Christ's Sufferings (translated from the Latin of St Gerard's)"
(see Appendix 3).

[26]   See Robert Nelson, *A Companion for the Festivals and Fasts of the Church
of England* (1704), ch. III, "Ember Days in Lent." (Hereinafter cited as *Fasts*
or *Festivals.*)

[27]   John Gother, *Instructions and Devotions for the Afflicted and Sick* (1697),
"Prayers in time of Affliction," ch. XII: "Upon a child, friend, etc. taking evil
ways" (see Appendix 3).

[28]   Marginal symbol indicates this was between 5 and 6 a.m.

[29]   Having only one meal, giving away his commons (see Glossary, s.v. "Commons," and cf. 11 and 23 May), and the marginal note "no supper" at six, are
all a part of his observing Lent Rule 8—"to make only one meal at 3 on Wednesdays and Fridays" (see pp. 118f., Resolutions for Lent, hereinafter cited by number as Lent Rule 8, as distinguished from the fifteen Resolutions listed on
pp. 119f.).

THURSDAY, MARCH 7.[30]   4 Dressed; business and virtue. . . . 5 E and read chapter. 5.15 Read. . . . 6 E; read Whitby. . . . 7 E; Public Prayers. . . . 8 E; read *Nicodemus* and. . . . 9 E and private prayer. 9.15 Read. . . . 10 E; read Whitby. . . . 11 E; read Law upon. . . . 11.45 Chapter and private prayer. 12 E and transcribed diary. . . . 1 Walked with Ford, religious talk . . . States of. . . . 2.15 E and private prayer; read Whitby. . . . 3 E and Collect; read Whitby. . . . 4 E; chapter. 4.15 Daily examination and [private prayer]. . . . 5 E and Public Prayers. 5.30 Supper. 6.30 With Watson, religious talk. . . . 7 With Natt, read Alleine's [*Sure*] *Guide,* religious [talk]. . . . 9 Religious talk of the Sacrament. . . .

Blessings: recollected 8 times; zealous . . . observed the 15 [resolutions] . . . ; convinced of . . . hearing Ford's . . . ; she commend . . . expected to . . . ; our fears are . . . danger.

[FRIDAY, MARCH 8.   Only "resolutions kept" and "blessings" visible, the latter including the notation, "Lenten Rule 8, No supper."]

SATURDAY, MARCH 9.   4 Dressed; E and private prayer. 4.15 Business and virtue. 4.30 Wrote diary. 4.45 Private prayer; ri. 5 E; began to compose a Theme; ri. 6 E; finished Theme; ri. 7 E; Public Prayers; ri. 8 Walked with Watson, religious talk. 8.15 Breakfast; ri. 8.30 Meditated on the vanity of the world; ri. 9 E; read Whitby; ri. 10 E; translated Imposition[31] for Ward; ri. 11.15 Walked with Brownsword and Watson, various talk. 11.45 Wrote diary [summary].[32] 12 E and private prayer, at dinner; ri. 1 At Ford's, read Aldrich. 1.30 Ford fell into a passion, said he would read Logic no more with us.[33] 1.45 Came home; meditated thereon. 2 E; translated for Ward; ri. 3 E and Collect, at Lecture; ri. 4.15 Wrote diary. 4.30 Daily examination. 4.45 Dressed; ri. 5 E; Public Prayers. 5.30 Supper; ri. 6.30 Meditated of Passion, and private prayer; ri. 7 E; at Ford's with Smith, read Law of rising,[34] disputed about

---

30 Almost all of the page containing 7 and 8 March has been cut out of the diary; only a narrow strip (25–29 mm wide) remains. Cf. 1–4 August.

31 A literary exercise imposed as a punishment. The recipient of this favor was Matthias Ward who seems never to have received a degree; see also 3 April.

32 See monthly summary for February 1733/34. See also resolution dated this day on p. 119.

33 Ford did not read any more of Aldrich with the group; on 11 March the others continue at Atkinson's, finishing the book on 29 March.

34 Law's *Serious Call,* ch. XIV, "Concerning that part of Devotion which relates to times and hours of Prayer. Of daily early prayer in the morning."

going to the Sacrament; ri.[35] N.B. Avoid disputing in religious conversation. 9.15 Private prayer; ri. 9.30.

Blessings: preserved from quarreling with Ford; kept resolution 8, recollected 13 times.

Sins: anger; neglected private prayer at the set hours, and the chapter; broke Lent Rule 5; interrupted by the barber at 4.45.[36]

SUNDAY, MARCH 10.   5 Dressed; business and virtue; ri. 5.30 Private prayer. 6 E and private prayer. 6.15 Meditated of the Sacrament;[37] ri. 7 E; with Charles Wesley, read meditation on the Sacrament;[38] ri. 7.30 Christ Church, Public Prayers; ri. 8 Sacrament; ri. 8.45 Walked with Watson and Ford, religious talk and read meditation of the Sacrament; ri. 9.15 Breakfast; ri. 9.30 Came home; private prayer and meditated; ri. 10 E; Sermon;[39] ri. 11.15 Walked; ri. 11.30 Read chapter and private prayer. 12 E and wrote diary. 12.15 Dinner; ri. 1 E; walked with Ford and Smith; Workhouse, read *Christian Monitor;* ri. 2 E; at Sermon;[40] ri. 3 E; at Charles Wesley's with Smith and Carter, read Patrick; ri. 3.45 Walked with Smith, religious talk. 4 Came home; E; read chapter; ri. 4.15 Wrote diary; daily examination. 4.45 Private prayer; ri. 5 E and

[35] A marginal note ("8 E") indicates that Ingham paused at the hour for ejaculatory prayer.

[36] The college statutes provided for servants, including a barber who was also to be the porter (*Queen's College Statutes,* p. 33; cf. Magrath, *Queen's College,* vol. 1, 49). We do not know if this diary entry and/or that of 25 March, mentioning Pritchard the barber, refers to the college servant. Cf. 21 and 27 December.

[37] In the column listing the results of his hourly "recollection," Ingham here wrote "zealous," the first instance of this superlative "degree of attention" in this "exacter" format.

[38] This might have been any one of several such meditations by Ken, Gerhard, or other authors he read frequently, although the selections he read this day seem to be designed specifically for the use before and after the service (see 8:45 a.m.), such as those found in Anthony Horneck, *The Fire of the Altar* (1684), Simon Patrick, *The Christian Sacrifice* (1671), and others. (See Appendix 3.)

[39] The preacher at St. Mary's on this occasion was Edward Wilson of Balliol College, who was to have preached the Assize sermon the following day but changed to the Sunday at the request of the judges. Hearne, *Collections,* vol. 11, 314.

[40] The preacher at St. Peter's in the East on this occasion was Dr. De Blossiers Tovey, Principal of New Inn Hall. Hearne, *Collections,* vol. 11, 314.

Public Prayers. 5.30 Supper; ri. 6.45 With Ford at Smith's, read Goodman, religious talk; ri. 9 E; came home. 9.15.

Blessings: Sacrament; fervent in private prayer;[41] recollected; abstained from eating pudding; zealous in conversation; temperate and recollected.

Sins: passionate thoughts in Public Prayers; laid in bed from 4 to 5 to warm my shirt;[42] N.B. No more such trivial excuses.

MONDAY, MARCH 11. 4 Dressed; E and Collect. 4.15 Business and virtue; ri. 4.30 Private prayer. 4.45 Chapter. 5 E; read Whitby; ri. 6 E; read Whitby; ri. 7 E; Public Prayers. 8 E; Watson came, good talk. 8.15 Read *Nicodemus,* and private prayer; ri. 9 E; thought of sleeping, and rising; ri. 10 E; read Whitby; ri. 11 E; read Whitby; ri. 11.30 Chapter, and private prayer, and wrote diary. 12 E and Collect; dinner; ri. 1 Read Aldrich at Atkinson's with Watson and Washington. 1.30 At Broughton's Shop; ri. 2 E; read Whitby; ri. 3 E and Collect; read Whitby; ri. 4 E; read chapter. 4.15 Wrote diary; daily examination. 4.45 Private prayer. 5 E; Public Prayers. 5.30 Supper; ri; walked; ri. 6.45 With Bolton, religious talk; ri. 7.15 At Bird's with Watson, Thompson, Harrison, Fothergill, Potter, Lowther, Wilson the Commoner, Thomas, Backhouse, Bewsher, Hodgson,[43] various talk; ri. 9.15 Came home with Watson; wrote diary; private prayer.

Blessings: recollected 6 times; zealous in private prayer and conversation;[44] left Bird's company in good time; refused to [have] tea with Natt at 4.[45]

Sins: avoid set companies.

TUESDAY, MARCH 12. 4 Dressed; E and Collect. 4.15 Business and virtue; ri. 4.30 Private prayer. 4.45 Chapter. 5 E; meditated on my infirmi-

---

[41] Recollection at ten and five, for the previous hour, "zealous."

[42] See resolution on p. 166, "My bed shall be left winter so soon as my body is refreshed with sufficient sleep."

[43] Information on Watson, Thompson, Fothergill, and Bewsher is given in Appendix 2. The other persons listed here are all of Queen's College: James Bird (he had just entered on 6 March), B.A. 1737; Francis Harrison, B.A. 1736; Emmanuel Potter, no degree (matric. 5 July 1733); John Lowther, B.A. 1736/37; Roger Wilson (had just entered on 25 February), B.A. 1737/38; John Thomas, B.C.L. 1741/42(?); George Backhouse, B.A. 1735; and Hugh Hodgson, no degree (matric. 23 February 1729/30).

[44] Recollection for 6–7 p.m., "zealous."

[45] Marginal symbol indicates "conquest over lawful things."

ties, sins, and follies; ri. 6 E; read Whitby; ri. 7 E; Public Prayers. 7.45 Walked with Atkinson, good talk; ri. 8 E and private prayer. 8.15 Breakfast with Yates, good talk; ri. 9 E and Collect; thoughts of regulating conversation. 9.30 Read Whitby; ri. 10 E; read Whitby; ri. 11 E; walked with Watson, religious talk. 11.45 At Broughton's Shop, bought Taylor's *Holy Living and Dying,* one shilling; ri. 12 E; dinner; ri. 1 E; read Aldrich at Atkinson's with Watson, Washington, and Smyth. 1.30 Walked; ri. 1.45 With Natt, good talk; ri. 2 E. 2.15 Mended my gowns.[46] 3 E; thoughts of various things; ri. 4.15 Wrote diary, and daily examination; ri. 4.45 Private prayer. 5 E; Public Prayers. 5.30 With Bolton, religious talk; lent him Taylor's *Holy Dying.* 5.45 Supper; ri. 6.15 Went with Atkinson, Watson, Smyth, and Richardson, good talk. 7 E; with me, Atkinson and Watson, read *The History of Charles XII;*[47] ri. 9.45 Private prayer. 10.

Blessings: lent Law's *Serious Call* to Dominus Yates;[48] Bolton consented to use private prayer night and morning; Watson owned the obligation of the Stations; zealous in conversation;[49] recollected 13 times; forbore eating rice and milk at the first thoughts of self-denial.[50]

Sins: neglected noon private prayers by loitering at Broughton's Shop; missed reading chapter twice; irrecollected thrice.

WEDNESDAY, MARCH 13.   4 Dressed; E and Collect. 4.15 Business and virtue; ri. 4.45 Private prayer. 5 E; called Atkinson, Washington, Smyth, and Watson;[51] ri. 5.15 Meditated of Christ's sufferings; ri. N.B. Meditate no more on the bed. 6 E; read Whitby; ri. 7 E; Public Prayers. 8 E; read *Nicodemus,* and private prayer; ri. 9 E; read Whitby; ri; Dominus Yates came to consult my Welchman.[52] 10 E; read Whitby; ri. 11 E; meditated on my sins. 11.45 Private prayer. 12 E and Collect; Hall. 12.30 Religious talk with Watson; ri. 1 E; read Aldrich with Washington, Watson, Atkinson, and Smyth; ri. 2 E; walked with Ford and Smith to Work-

---

[46]   This is Ingham's only reference to "gowns" in the plural, and may refer to both academic and studying gowns; see Magrath, *Flemings,* vol. 1, 241, note 3.
[47]   See Voltaire in Appendix 3.
[48]   The prefix to Yates's name was omitted in the entry at 8:15, the first mention of him since becoming a B.A. on 16 November (see 1 March, note 3).
[49]   With Yates between eight and nine in the morning.
[50]   A marginal symbol (··) indicates that this "conquest over lawful things" occurred at suppertime.
[51]   See 21 November, note 102.
[52]   See Edward Welchman, Appendix 3.

house, read seventh chapter of St. Matthew; ri. 2.45 At Charles Wesley's with Smith and Carter, private prayer. 3 Breakfast and read Patrick. 3.45 Walked with Smith, religious talk; ri. 4 E; read chapter. 4.15 Wrote diary and daily examination. 4.45 Private prayer. 5 E; Public Prayers. 5.30 Read Nelson; ri. 6 E; Hall. 6.15 With Bolton, religious talk, read Nelson; ri. 6.45 With Watson, religious talk. 7 E; at Ford's with Smith, religious and useful talk. 8 E; read Goodman; ri. 9 Came home; E and private prayer. 9.30.

Blessings: recollected thrice; zealous in conversation; rose with reluctancy;[53] made only one meal, at 3 at Charles Wesley's.[54] N.B. Meditate no more sitting on the bed, but use some book of meditations when irrecollected.

THURSDAY, MARCH 14. 4 Dressed; E and Collect. 4.15 Business and virtue; ri. 4.30 Private prayer. 4.45 Chapter. 5 E; read Whitby; ri. 6 E; read Whitby; ri. 7 E; Public Prayers. 8 E; read *Nicodemus.* 8.15 Breakfast at Ford's with Broughton, religious talk.[55] 9 E; read Whitby; ri. 10 E; translated Kennet's *Antiquities;* ri. 11 E; Hall. 11.15 Walked with Ford, good talk; ri. 11.45 Chapter and private prayer. 12 E; dinner; ri. 1 E; read Aldrich with Watson, Washington, Smyth, and Atkinson; ri. 1.30 Walked. 2 E; vain thoughts; ri. 3 E and Collect; read Whitby; ri; resolutions; ri.[56] 4 E; read chapter. 4.15 Wrote diary. 4.30 Daily examination. 4.45 Private prayer. 5 E; Public Prayers. 5.30 Supper; ri. 6 Supper; ri. 6.30 Walked with Smyth and Richardson, various talk. 7 At Ford's with Washington, Watson, Atkinson, Smyth, and Richardson. 8 Washington's birthday, he treated, good talk (various); ri. 9 Came home; private prayer.

Blessings: resolved never to regard preferment;[57] grieved at my past life;[58] Broughton good success with Ford; fervent in private and Public Prayers; recollected 4 times; kept Lent Rules 6 and 1.

---

53 In the margin at 4 a.m. Ingham wrote, "I doubted whether I should rise or not, but got up." See plate 12.
54 Marginal note at 6 p.m., "kept Lent Rule 8, no supper."
55 Marginal note at 8–9 a.m., "Good conversation with Broughton."
56 Recollection from 3–5 p.m. is "zealous," after being "irrecollected" from 2–3 p.m.
57 Symbol for "good resolutions" in margin at 3–4 p.m. Cf. 23 July, summary of sins.
58 "Contrition" indicated by the cross symbol here and at 3–4 p.m.

Sins: broke resolution 14 once; indifferent in Public Prayers; broke resolution 3 three times, 8 once.

FRIDAY, MARCH 15.   4 Dressed; E and Collect. 4.15 Wrote diary. 4.30 Business and virtue; ri. 4.45 Private prayer. 5 E; private prayer and meditated of Christ's sufferings; ri. 6 E; read Whitby; ri. 7 E; read Whitby; ri. 7.30 Public Prayers. 8.15 E; read *Nicodemus;* ri; private prayer. 9 E; private prayer; read Whitby; ri. 10 E; read Whitby; ri. 11 E; meditated of my sins; ri. 11.30 Chapter. 11.45 Private prayer. 12 E; wrote diary. 12.15 Hall; ri. 12.45 Read Nelson on watchfulness,[59] at Ford's; ri. 1 E; read Law on fasting.[60] 1.15 Read Aldrich with Watson etc; ri. 1.45 Walked with Ford and Smith to the Workhouse. 2 E; read *Christian Monitor;* ri. 2.30 Walked with Smith, good talk. 2.45 At Charles Wesley's with Smith and Carter, private prayer. 3 E; breakfast, read Patrick; ri; came home. 4 E; read chapter. 4.15 Wrote diary. 4.30 Daily examination, private prayer. 5 E; Public Prayers. 5.30 Declamation. 5.45 Read Stearne *Of Visiting the Sick;* ri. 6 E; General Examination for the past week; ri; anger, unkind thoughts of friends, unchaste thoughts; confession and private prayer.[61] 7 E; at Ford's with Atkinson, Smyth, Watson, and Washington, read Law's *Serious Call;* ri; religious talk; walked with Atkinson, religious talk of the Sacrament at Castle.[62] 9 E; came home; private prayer; ri.

Blessings: kept resolution 8, recollected; fervent in Public and private prayers; grieved for my sins; at Charles Wesley's; kept resolution 9, zealous in conversation at Ford's, no disputing; Atkinson consented to receive the Sacrament at Castle.

SATURDAY, MARCH 16.   4.45 Dressed. 5 E; private prayer. 5.15 Read chapter. 5.30 Wrote diary; thanksgiving for Blair; ri. 6 E; read Whitby; ri. 7 E; Whitby. 7.15 Public Prayers. 8 E; read *Nicodemus;* ri; breakfast; ri; private prayer. 9 E; read Whitby; ri. 10 E; read Whitby; ri. 11

[59] See Nelson, *Festivals,* ch. XIII (St. Matthias the Apostle), on "the duty of Watchfulness."
[60] See William Law, *A Practical Treatise upon Christian Perfection* (1726), ch. VII, "Some farther Considerations upon the Reasonableness of Self-denial," where Law argues that fasting is the "common duty" of all Christians; see Appendix 3.
[61] Marginal note, "no supper." This begins Ingham's practice of listing, as a result of his General Examination, his sins for the week.
[62] Accompanied by marginal symbol for "conversation blessed with success"; see daily summary of blessings.

E; walked; ri. 11.45 Private prayer. 12 E; wrote diary. 12.15 Dinner; ri. 1 Thought. 1.15 Read Aldrich; ri. 1.45 Walked with Atkinson, Smyth, and Washington, religious talk of Sacrament at Castle. 2 Came home; religious talk with Watson of Sacrament at Castle and fear of man, read Bible and *Nicodemus;* ri. 3 Watson consulted me whether he should go into the North, whether he should marry or not; ri. 4.15 Wrote diary; daily examination; private prayer. 5 E; Public Prayers. 5.30 Supper; ri. 6.30 With Watson, good talk. 7 E; at Smith's with Ford, religious talk. 8 E; read Goodman. 9 E; came home. 9.15 Private prayer.

Blessings: refused to breakfast with Blair the Commoner;[63] zealous in conversation; good success with Watson, Atkinson, and Washington; heard of being reproached for going to the Castle.

Sins: neglected ejaculatory prayers 6 times; broke resolution 14 thrice, 2 once, 13 once.

SUNDAY, MARCH 17.   4 Dressed; wrote diary; business and virtue; ri; private prayer. 5 E; meditated of God's perfections; ri. 5.30 Ford came, good talk of Sacrament. 5.45 Dressed. 6 E; at John Wesley's, religious talk of Ford, Atkinson, Watson, Washington, Smyth, and Natt, whether they should go to Castle; he would they should go; [religious talk] of simplicity and recollection, of eating, signs for recollection.[64] 6.45 Fetched Robson to breakfast with us; he [John Wesley] proposed to us to meet once a week to talk about ourselves, our progress, and how to proceed at the Workhouse; to dispute nothing, to talk about nothing else;[65] we agreed to meet every Monday night; ri. 7 E; breakfast with them, reli-

---

63   Accompanied by marginal symbol for "conquest over lawful things." John Blair, commoner, entered Queen's College in September 1732, and apparently received no degree; he was to be distinguished from John Blair, batteler, who had entered in March 1730/31.

64   The "signs" discussed here may have included the abbreviations to be used by Ingham in a new column that will be added the following day (see 19 March, note 77). Wesley's diary entry for this hour reads: "Ingham, religious talk. 6.45 Robson, tea. 7 Religious talk of diary. 7.45 . . ." (OD IV, 100).

65   This is a good indication of the sort of agenda that might be typical of the small Methodist groups at this point (see Monday evenings below, 1 April, et seq.). In the Wesleyan scheme at this time, these meetings were often followed by a study session, sometimes including a larger group; see Richard Morgan's letter to his father (*Letters,* I, 365); cf. Wesley's entry for the evening of 17 March: "6 Salmon's, Hall, etc. [including Charles Wesley, Broughton], daily examination, tea. 7 Morgan, Nowell, Walker [came], began St Clemens . . ." (OD IV, 100). The next evening they talked of the work at the Castle, the following evening "of Diary." See plates 2 and 3.

gious talk of the three different states of men, the natural, [the] Jewish or fearful, and the evangelical, the two last only salvable;[66] of the advantage of comparing diaries, of hourly examination, continual recollection, and of confessing our faults; ri. 7.45 Came home; wrote diary. 8 E; private prayer. 8.15 Public Prayers. 9.15 Walked with Ford, Atkinson, and Washington, good talk of Sacrament at Castle. 9.30 Walked with Washington; Castle, heard Salmon read preparatory prayer to the prisoners. 9.45 Walked with Ford, Atkinson, Washington, at Castle; ri. 10 Public Prayers, Sermon, and Sacrament; several gown men came, some laughed, other[s] a little serious; I trembled for fear; John Wesley spoke to them in preaching; none stayed the Sacrament.[67] 12.15 Came home with Ford, Atkinson, and Washington; cast down. 12.30 Dinner. 1 E; private prayer with Ford, grieved at him for praying. 1.30 Walked with him to Workhouse, Smith was there; I read *Christian Monitor,* they catechized. 2 Sermon. 3 E; [at] Charles Wesley's with Smith and Carter, read Young's sermon on Self-Denial, religious talk; ri; came home. 4 E; read chapter. 4.15 Wrote diary for the whole day. 4.45 Daily examination. 5 E; Public Prayers. 5.30 Private prayer. 5.45 Supper. 6.30 Walked; ri. 7 E; at Ford's with Smith, good talk (various); ri. 8 E; read Goodman; ri. 9 Came home; religious talk with Atkinson of exacter diary; read Charles Burton's letter of John Wesley;[68] ri; private prayer. 9.45

Blessings: the Sacrament at Castle; religious talk and breakfast with John Wesley; with Charles Wesley; zealous in conversation.

Sins: very much dissipated[69] at Public Prayers and most of the day; vexed at my sins.

[66] Wesley had been discussing this topic with Westley Hall the preceding week (OD IV, 96). Cf. John Wesley, Sermon 9, "The Spirit of Bondage and of Adoption," in which he describes these states in progression, natural man coming to an awareness of the law (being then under the spirit of fear and bondage), and from thence being received by grace into the "state of love" through the spirit of adoption.

[67] Wesley's diary entry reads: "11.00 Sermon, spoke to laughers in faith, looked, Sacrament" (OD IV, 100; cf. p. 27, "Spoke in faith to the felons"). Wesley's sermon, on Eph. 4:30 ("Grieve not the Holy Spirit"), was an extract from William Tilly; see John Wesley MS. Sermonbook, Colman Collection XIX, pp. 103–14, MA. "Gown men" are university students.

[68] Apparently now lost.

[69] "Distracted" or "the soul uncentred from God"; see Wesley's sermon "On Dissipation," where he defines the concept in the light of the Oxford Methodist question, "Have I been simple and recollected in all I said or did?" Sermon 79, sec. 20.

MONDAY, MARCH 18. 1.45 Dominus Alsop[70] called me up to go sit with Bolton, Sr; dressed and private prayer; went and sat with him. 2 E; read Nelson of conquering vice.[71] 3 E; meditated of pride and other vices. 4 Dull and heavy, meditated and slumbered. 5.15 Read Nelson of acquiring any virtue.[72] 6 E and private prayer. 6.15 Atkinson came, we read Nelson on meditation,[73] and religious talk with Bolton; he consented that I should remind him of his resolutions; he consented to use private prayer, meditation, and Nelson, to shake off his company; I pressed daily examination, he scarcely consented. 7.15 E; Public Prayers. 7.45 Dressed. 8 E; with Smith, religious talk of my conversation with John Wesley, and Bolton. 8.15 Went to Charles Wesley's, religious talk of ourselves, and of comparing diaries; breakfast; he proposed that Smith and I should meet twice per week purely to compare our diaries; Tuesday and Thursday appointed; ri. 9.15 Came home; wrote diary. 9.30 Transcribed John Wesley's resolutions for eating;[74] ri. 10 E; read Whitby; ri. 11 Slept. 12.15 Dinner; ri. 1 Read Aldrich; ri. 1.30 Walked with Washington, religious talk. 2 E; translated Imposition. 3 E and Collect; at Lecture in Sanderson's De [obligatione] conscientiæ. 4 E; Lecture. 4.15 Daily examination; private prayer; ri. 5 E; Public Prayers. 5.30 With Watson, good talk of his condition.[75] 5.45 Supper. 6.30 Walked with Washington and Smith, good talk. 7 E; at Robson's, religious talk of Workhouse, to read family prayers, everyone to choose a day and to go nights and

---

70 Alsop received his bachelor's degree on 22 February 1733/34. See 1 March, note 3.

71 See Robert Nelson, The Practice of True Devotion (1698), ch. XI, "Reflections relating to the conquering of any vice," in Appendix 3.

72 Ibid., ch. III, "Some considerations in relation to the practice of Christian virtues, which is the great end of religion."

73 Ibid., ch. XVI, "For Tuesday. Meditation."

74 See OD IV, [viii]: "As to Temperance, I Resolve in Eating,
   1. Taste only of two flesh dishes.
   2. Only one slice of each.
   3. At each [meal], fix your quantity before you taste.
   4. If possible, help yourself last.
   5. When I have port, only port and water.
   6. Before you sit at full table, pray for help.
   7. In C[ompany], only a Cheese and Roots.
   8. After any excess, abridge the next meal.
   9. Only three dishes of tea in the afternoon, never but six.
   10. When sugar or cream in afternoon, no bread and butter."

75 See 16 and 21 March.

mornings to teach the children, read family prayers,[76] and talk to old people. 8 Religious talk of ourselves; ri. 9 E; came home with Ford and Watson, religious talk. 9.30 Wrote diary; private prayer.

TUESDAY, MARCH [19].[77]   5 Dressed; E; business and virtue; private prayer; read chapter. 6 E; meditated of my infirmities and follies; ri. 7 E; private prayer. 7.15 Public Prayers. 8 E; read *Nicodemus;* ri. 8.45 Private prayer. 9 E and Collect; read Whitby; ri. 10 E; read Whitby; ri. 11 E; dressed; Disputations; ri. 12 E and private prayer. 12.15 Dinner; ri. 1 E; read Aldrich. 1.30 Walked with Watson, various and useful talk. 2 E. 2.15 Read Whitby; ri. 3.15 E and Collect; read Whitby; ri. 4 E; read chapter. 4.15 Daily examination. 4.45 Private prayer.

Blessings:[78] grieved that I have been so impatient with my friends; feared disputing, and zealous with Robson; recollected 6 times; fervent in prayer.

Sins: broke Lent Rules 1, 2; wandering thoughts and proud; eat too much at dinner; an hour sleepy; irrecollected 5 times; vain at Disputations. 5 E; Public Prayer. 5.30 Walked; ri. 5.45 Supper. 6 E; supper. 6.30 Walked; ri. 7 E; at Smith's, good talk of Robson, Ford, and Watson, compared our diaries; ri.[79] 8 E; with Smith, religious talk of unchaste dreams and thoughts; ri. 9 E with Smith; came home. 9.15 Private prayer; ri.

Juvat non parum ad profectum Spiritualem, devota rerum Spiritualium collatio.[80]

---

[76] Several forms of prayer for families would have been available at that time, such as *Morning and Evening Prayers for Families* in the S.P.C.K. list of books "For the Use of the Poor," Appendix II of *An Account of the Origin and Designs of the Society for Promoting Christian Knowledge* ([London]: 1734), p. 29.

[77] Ingham introduces a new column to his format at this point, adjacent to the Recollection column and headed "H" (Heart?); see Appendix 1(B) and plate 13. From subsequent daily summaries, we discover the possible meaning of the abbreviated entries: d–dull; h–heavy; c–cheerful; s–serious; l–lively; z–zealous.

[78] This insertion of the summary of blessings and sins in the middle of a daily entry is unusual.

[79] Marginal note in Blessings column: "with Smith, compared diaries and confessed our faults."

[80] *De imitatione Christi,* I.x.2 (see 3 March and Appendix 3). This is a footnote to his comparing diaries with Smith at 7.

Διὸ παρακαλεῖτε ἀλλήλους, καὶ οἰκοδομεῖτε εἰς τὸν ἕνα, καθὼς καὶ ποιεῖτε. I Thess. 5:11.[81]

WEDNESDAY, MARCH 20.   4 Dressed; E. 4.15 Wrote diary; business and virtue. 4.30 Private prayer and chapter. 5 E; meditated of my sins; ri. 6 E; read Whitby; ri. 7 E; wrote index for the prayers in Taylor's *Holy Living.* 7.15 Public Prayers. 8 E; read *Nicodemus;* ri; private prayer. 9 E and Collect; read Whitby; ri. 10 E; read Whitby; ri. 11 E; meditated of Christ's sufferings; confessed my sins, and private prayer; ri. 12 E and Collect; dressed. 12.15 Hall; ri. 12.30 Private prayer. 12.45 Read chapter. 1 E; read Aldrich. 1.30 Walked with Ford and Smith to Workhouse. 2 E; finished *Christian Monitor.* 2.30 Walked with Smith, good talk. 2.45 At Charles Wesley's with Smith. 3 E; private prayer with Gambold and Carter. 3.15 Breakfast; read Patrick; came home; ri. 4 E; read chapter. 4.15 Daily examination; private prayer. 5 E; Public Prayer. 5.30 At Bolton's. 5.45 Hall; ri. 6 E; thanksgiving. 6.15 Read *Nicodemus.* 6.45 Walked with Ford to Smith's. 7 E with them, read Goodman; ri. 8 E and finished Goodman's second Conference, read Letter to a Young Lady upon Education by Samuel Wesley,[82] good talk; ri. 9 E with them; came home with Ford; ri. 9.15 Private prayer; wrote diary. 9.30.

Blessings: rose; attentive in Public and private prayer; thrice recollected; grieved for my sins; kept Lent Rules 4 and 8; breakfast at Charles Wesley's; zealous and active in conversation; serious, lively, and cheerful, 3, 8, and 6 times [respectively];[83] only one meal.

Sins: neglected ejaculatory prayer once; irrecollected once; three vain and one proud thoughts; once dull.

THURSDAY, MARCH 21.   4.15 Dressed; business and virtue; ri; private prayer; read chapter. 5 E; called Atkinson, Washington, and Smyth; read Whitby; ri. 6 E; read Whitby; ri. 7 E; read Whitby; ri; Public Prayers. 8 E; breakfast with Smith; ri; talk of love and the danger of it, the bad effects, etc; compared diaries, various talk; ri. 9 E and Collect with him; came home. 9.15 Read Whitby; ri. 10 E; translated Kennet; ri. 11 E; Hall. 11.15 Walked with Watson, good talk. 11.45 Chapter and private

81 "Wherefore comfort yourselves together, and edify one another, even as also ye do." This also is a footnote to the 7 p.m. entry. See also 29 March.
82 See Samuel Wesley, *A Letter from a Country Divine to His Friend in London* (1703), in Appendix 3.
83 Refers to entries in the new H column see 19 March and note 77.

prayer. 12 E and Collect; dinner; ri. 1 Read Aldrich at Atkinson's, etc. 1.30 Walked with Washington, Watson, and Smyth, read News. 2 E; Watson came, talk about his love affairs. 3 E and Collect; Lecture. 3.15 Tea with Watson; ri. 4 E; read chapter; daily examination; private prayer. 5 E; Public Prayers. 5.30 At Bolton's. 5.45 Supper; ri. 6.30 Walked with Watson, good talk. 7 E; at Robson's with Smith, religious talk of the Workhouse, of Country Parson, Wesleys, Hall,[84] etc; ri. 8 E; good talk (various); ri. 9 Came home. 9.15 Wrote diary and private prayer. 9.30.

Blessings: lively 8 times, cheerful 6, serious twice; recollected 14 times; zealous 5 times; refused to eat butter with Smith; kept resolution 15; attentive in private prayer; liberal to Mother Harris; avoided disputing with Robson; assisted Watson in conquering his loving passion.

Sins: broke Lent Rule 1; vain and unchaste thoughts; neglected ejaculatory prayers twice; irrecollected twice; dull twice.

FRIDAY, MARCH 22.   4 Dressed; business and virtue; ri. 4.30 Private prayer. 4.45 Read chapter. 5 E; called Smyth and Washington; necessary business; ri. 5.15 Meditated of my sins; ri; drowsy. 6 Slept.[85] 7 E; Public Prayers. 8 E; wrote diary. 8.15 Read *Nicodemus;* ri and private prayer. 9 E and Collect; read Whitby; ri. 10 E; read Whitby; ri. 11 E; meditated of Christ's sufferings, and confession; ri. 12 E; Hall. 12.30 Used Taylor's prayer for fasting days,[86] and Christ's Passion;[87] ri. 1 E; read Aldrich at Atkinson's with Watson, Washington, and Smyth. 1.45 Walked with Ford and Smith to Workhouse; ri. 2 E; began Trapp's sermon on Public Prayers,[88] private prayer, and family prayers; ri. 2.30 Walked with Smith, good talk. 2.45 At Charles Wesley's with Smith and Carter, private prayer. 3 E; breakfast; ri; read Patrick; ri; came home. 4 E; read chapter. 4.15 Daily examination. 4.45 Private prayer. 5 E;

---

[84]   This probably refers to Westley Hall, colleague of Robson's at Lincoln College. Cf. 1 April at 8 p.m. and note 139.

[85]   In the Devotion column this hour, Ingham rated his temper of devotion a very low 1; cf. 31 May, note 172.

[86]   Jeremy Taylor, *The Rule and Exercises for Holy Living* (1650), ch. IV, *ad* sec. 5, "Prayers for several occasions" (see Appendix 3).

[87]   Ibid., ch. IV, *ad* sec. 6, "A form of prayer recording all the parts and mysteries of Christ's passion, being a short history of it: to be used especially in the week of Passion, and before receiving the blessed Sacrament."

[88]   Joseph Trapp, *The Duties of Private, Domestic, and Public Devotion* (1717); see Appendix 3.

Public Prayers. 5.30 Heard Declamation. 5.45 Wrote diary; ri. 6 E; sup-per;[89] ri. 6.15 General Examination [for] the past week; ri; proud, vain, and unchaste thoughts, worse than the last (endeavor to attend to one thing), wandering thoughts of God.[90] 6.45 With Bolton, good talk. 7 E; at Atkinson's with Watson, Washington, Smyth, and Ford, religious talk of the Sacrament at Christ Church; disputed with Watson, he said that by asking the Fellows we might deprive ourselves of a great many opportunities, which we should lament; we held God would accept the will, when we cannot perform the deed.[91] 8 Read Law's *Serious Call;* ri. 9 Went to Bolton, Jr,[92] various talk; ri. 10 E; read Law's character of Miranda and the following chapter;[93] ri. 11 E; read Law. 11.30 Drowsy; ri. 12 E; read Law of Intercession. 1 E; read Law; ri. 1.45 Mother Ship-ton came;[94] I came home; wrote diary; ri. 2 Private prayer.

SATURDAY, MARCH 23. 7 Dressed; E. 7.15 Public Prayers. 8 Watson came, religious talk and disputed of the Sacrament at Christ Church; ri. 8.30 Breakfast; ri. 8.45 Private prayer. 9 E and Collect; read Whitby; ri. 10 E; read Whitby; ri. 11 E; walked; thanksgiving and resolutions; ri. 11.45 Read chapter. 12 E and private prayer. 12.15 Dinner; ri. 1 Read Aldrich at Atkinson's, etc; ri; good talk; ri. 2 E; read Patrick's *Christian Sacrifice* with Ford; ri. 3 E and Collect; Lecture in Sanderson;

89 Under "Resolutions broken" for this hour, Ingham noted Lent Rule 8 which stipulated only one meal (at three) on Wednesdays and Fridays.

90 See John Wesley's later sermon, "Wandering Thoughts" (Sermon 41, first published in 1762), where he distinguishes between thoughts that "wander from God" and thoughts that simply "wander from the particular point we have in hand" (I.1).

91 An expression of the typical Oxford Methodist theology of sincerely doing the best one can, trusting that God will honor one's good intentions; see p. 35.

92 Thomas Bolton, younger brother of Richard, had matriculated in October 1733, age sixteen. See monthly summary for March 1734: "Sat up once with Bolton, Jr."

93 Law, *Serious Call,* ch. VIII, "How the wise and pious use of an estate nat-urally carrieth us to great perfection in all the virtues of the Christian life; represented in the character of Miranda"; and ch. IX, "Containing some reflec-tions upon the life of Miranda and shewing how it may, and ought to be imi-tated by all her sex."

94 Ibid., ch. XXI, "Of the necessity and benefit of intercession, considered as an exercise of universal love. How all orders of men are to pray and intercede with God for one another. How naturally such intercession amends and reforms the hearts of those that use it." Mother Shipton may have been a laundress or seamstress; see 6:45 a.m., 1 April.

ri. 3.45 Walked with Knail, good talk of morality; ri. 4.15 Read chapter; daily examination, thanksgiving and private prayer; ri. 5 E; Public Prayers. 5.30 At Broughton's; ri. 5.45 Supper; ri. 6.30 Walked; ri. 7 E; at Ford's with Smith, read a Letter to a Religious Society;[95] ri; good talk. 8 E; read Goodman's third Conference; ri. 9 E; came home; private prayer. 9.30.

Blessings: resolved to persevere; zealous with Watson.

Sins: broke Lent Rule 10; irrecollected 7 times; neglected ejaculatory prayer thrice; wandering thoughts.

SUNDAY, MARCH 24.   4 Dressed; E and thanksgiving. 4.15 Business and virtue; ri. 4.30 Private prayer. 4.45 Read chapter; called Atkinson, Smyth, and Washington. 5 E; meditated on God's perfections and mercies, etc; ri. 6 E; preparation for the Sacrament;[96] private prayer; ri. 6.45 Dressed; Washington came and read *Meditations;* ri. 7 E. 7.15 Walked with Washington to Christ Church. 7.30 Public Prayers and Sacrament. 8.45 Thanksgiving with Smith; ri. 9 E and Collect and breakfast with Smith. 9.30 Read Horneck's thanksgiving after the Sacrament;[97] ri. 10 E with Smith; Sermon. 10.45 Walked. 11 E; walked; ri. 11.30 Read chapter; private prayer and thanksgiving. 12 E and Collect; dinner; ri. 1 E; with Smith at Workhouse, finished Trapp's sermon on Public Prayers; ri. 1.45 Walked with him, good talk. 2 E; Sermon. 2.45 Walked with Carter, good talk; ri. 3 E; at Charles Wesley's with Smith, Carter, and Newton,[98] read Young's sermon on Indifferency. 4 E; read chapter. 4.15 Daily examination. 4.45 Private prayer. 5 E; Public Prayers. 5.30 With Bolton, Sr, good talk; ri. 6 Supper. 6.30 Walked with Ford, good talk; ri. 7 E; at Smith's with Ford, read Goodman; ri. 8 Read Goodman; ri. 9 E; came home with Ford; ri. 9.15 Private prayer. 9.30.

[95]   See Samuel Wesley in Appendix 3.

[96]   This may refer to exercises contained in any one of a number of books that Ingham used for this purpose, such as in Jeremy Taylor's *Holy Living,* ch. IV, sec. 10: "14 Rules for preparation and worthy communicating"; cf. Nelson, *Fasts,* ch. IX.

[97]   Horneck, *Fire of the Altar* [part II], "Prayers and devotion to be used before and after receiving the holy Sacrament of the Lord's Supper," ch. VI: "A Thanksgiving after the receiving of the Lord's Supper, to be said either at church or at home." This prayer contains an image especially familiar to later Methodists: "I feel the Fire of God within me: My heart grows hot within me." (See Appendix 3.)

[98]   Probably James Newton, Christ Church (matric. 13 February 1732/33), M.A. 1736 (Corpus Christi College).

Blessings: the Sacrament; fervent in Public Prayers; and attentive in private prayer; breakfast with Smith; at Charles Wesley's.

Sins: irrecollected 5 times; unchaste thoughts; proud thoughts; intemperate twice; spoke unkindly of Natt; broke Lent Rule 9, eat pudding of a different sort.

MONDAY, MARCH 25.[99]   6.15 Dressed;[100] business and virtue; ri; private prayer; read chapter. 7 E; read third part of Patrick's *Christian Sacrifice* with Ford;[101] ri. 8 E with Ford; Public Prayers. 9 E; private prayer. 9.15 Read *Nicodemus;* ri. 10 E; Sermon;[102] ri. 11 Wrote a letter for Pritchard the barber.[103] 11.30 Read Nelson.[104] 11.45 Chapter; private prayer. 12 E and Collect; dinner; ri. 1 Walked with Watson and Washington, religious talk of the Stations and religion in general; ri. 2.15 Transcribed ejaculatory prayers for Washington; ri. 3 E and Collect; read *Nicodemus;* ri. 4 E; read chapter. 4.30 Daily examination. 4.45 Private prayer; ri. 5 E; Public Prayers. 5.30 Walked with Washington, good talk. 5.45 Supper; ri. 6.30 Walked with Washington, religious talk. 7 E; went to Robson's, waited at his door; meditated how to deal with Watson; ri. 7.45 Came home; went to Ford's. 8 Read Norris' *Miscellanies;* ri. 9 E with Ford; came home; wrote diary. 9.15 Private prayer. 9.30.

[99] This was "Lady Day," the first day of the new year in the Julian (Old Style) calendar, which Great Britain used until 1752. Since much of Europe had already adopted the "new" Gregorian calendar, with 1 January as the first day of a new year, many English letters and other documents written in January, February, or March were dated either in the New Style or in such a manner as to indicate both options, e.g., 1733/34. When just one year was indicated (during those three months), today's reader at times has difficulty knowing which year was actually intended. See plate 13.

[100] A footnote to this late hour of rising is entered at the bottom of the page, not in Ingham's handwriting: *"Non dormit diabolus, neque adhuc caro mortua est, ideo non cesses te præparare ad certamen, quia à dextris et à sinistris hostes sunt, qui nunquam quiescunt* (The devil does not sleep, nor is the flesh yet dead; therefore, do not cease to prepare yourself for battle, for the enemy are on the right and on the left, since they never rest). This entry may have been made by Smith the following evening when they compared diaries (see 26 March).

[101] "How to dispose ourselves to receive [the Sacrament] with profit and pleasure."

[102] This day was the festival of the Annunciation of Mary (see Nelson, *Festivals,* ch. XIV), popularly known as Lady Day; the service was normally held at New College (*Statutes,* XVI.5).

[103] See 9 March, above, note 36.

[104] See Nelson, *Festivals,* ch. XIV.

Blessings: acted prudently with Ford and avoided disputing; fervent in private prayer; very zealous in conversation; readily wrote letter for Pritchard; thrice serious.

Sins: slept from 4 to 6; laid ¼ waking; proud and vain thoughts; talking of being laughed at,[105] I thought they would commend me for my learning[106] or something; disputed fiercely with Watson; broke resolution 15 twice; twice dull; (refused to go back to lend Watson my penknife); broke resolution 8 thrice, 3 five times.

TUESDAY, MARCH 26.   4 Dressed; E. 4.15 Business and virtue; ri. 4.30 Private prayer. 4.45 Read chapter. 5 E; read Whitby; ri. 6 E; read Whitby; ri. 7 E; read Whitby; ri. 7.15 Public Prayers. 8 Watson came and read me the letter he was writing to Mss Gashwaithe.[107] 8.15 Read *Nicodemus;* ri. 9 E and Collect; read Whitby; ri. 10 E; read Whitby; ri. 11 E; walked; ri; at Broughton's; ri. 11.45 Read chapter; private prayer. 12 E and Collect; dinner; ri. 1 At Washington's with Smyth and Atkinson, read Aldrich. 1.30 Religious talk. 2 E; read Whitby; ri. 3 E and Collect; read Whitby; ri. 4 E; read chapter. 4.15 Daily examination; private prayer. 5 E; Public Prayers. 5.30 With Bolton, Sr, religious talk. 5.45 Supper; ri. 6.30 Meditated. 7 At Smith's, religious talk of ourselves and friends, compared diaries; ri. 8 E; confessed our infirmities and follies, drank a bottle of ale, good talk; ri. 9 E; came home. 9.15 Private prayer.

Blessings: rose; refused to breakfast at Natt's with Knail and Dixon; temperate; zealous in conversation with Atkinson, Washington, and Smyth; compared diaries with Smith and confessed; recollected twice; supper on milk and bread.

Sins: vain and wandering, unchaste and discontented thoughts; thought unkindly of Natt; very dull and irrecollected; neglected ejaculatory prayer 4 times.

Ἐξομολογεῖσθε ἀλλήλοις τὰ παραπτώματα. James 5:16.[108]

WEDNESDAY, MARCH 27.   4 Dressed; E and Collect. 4.15 Business and virtue; ri. 4.45 Private prayer. 5 E; wrote diary. 5.15 Read chapter. 5.45

---

105 Cf. 17 March, note 67.
106 MS. reads "learing"; cf. *O.E.D.*, s.v. "Learning."
107 This quite likely was in connection with Watson's love affair (see 21 March, 27 May, and 13 June).
108 "Confess your faults to one another." This is a footnote to Ingham's meeting with Smith from seven to nine.

Meditated. 6 E; read *Nicodemus;* ri; Public Prayers. 7 Heard Lecture.[109]
7.15 Lent Washington the 15 resolutions to transcribe; he consented to
begin exacter diary. 7.30 Private prayer. 7.45 Went to Workhouse,
taught the children first and then read the family prayers in Mrs Grey's
chamber because she was sick; added two prayers for the sick person to
Trapp's morning family prayer; I promised to go every Wednesday, morning and evening at 8 and 6, to teach the children and read family prayers.
8.30 Came home; called at John Wesley's, he was not at leisure;[110] to
go next morning at 5.30 to ask a few questions; called at Ford's, he would
not speak to me; vexed thereat and angry. 8.45 Private prayer. 9 E and
Collect; Watson came, began to read John Wesley's treatise on the Stations; Ford came, began again; they disputed warmly, I was moderate;
they owned the obligation after hearing the Fathers for their universality,
entirely convinced by the last quotation from Epiphanius,[111] read no further; they confessed we were under equal if not greater obligation to observe the Stations than Sunday; religious talk how to spend those days.
11.15 Ford told me how the Winchester men had deluded him, telling
him Charles Wesley wanted to speak with him; good talk of ourselves,
and how to order at the Workhouse; ri. 12 E with Ford; read chapter.
12.15 Hall. 12.30 Wrote diary. 12.45 Private prayer. 1 E; read Aldrich,
at Washington's, Watson, Atkinson, and Smyth; ri. 2 E; walked; ri; met
with Carter, good talk. 2.45 At Charles Wesley's with him [Carter] and
Smith, private prayer; E. 3 Breakfast, dry bread and tea without sugar;
ri; read Patrick on the Lent Fast;[112] ri. 4 E; read chapter. 4.15 Daily ex-

109 An unusual hour for a lecture in the Hall (see the next three days).
110 Wesley's diary indicates he was with a pupil, reading August Hermann
Francke's *Manuductio ad lectionem Scripturæ Sacræ* (1706); see Appendix 3.
111 Wesley's MS. treatise, "Of the Weekly Fasts of the Church," develops the
argument of "universality" and closes with a reference to Epiphanius using that
argument "against all hereticks" (John Wesley MS., Colman Collection XII,
p. 4, MA. The same argument was the topic of his "Essay upon the Stationary
Fasts" extracted by Thomas Deacon in *A Compleat Collection of Devotions*
(1734), though no reference is made to Epiphanius in the published portion
(see Appendix 3).
112 Part III (ch. XV–XX) of Simon Patrick's *A Treatise of Repentance* (see
Appendix 3). Beginning on Ash Wednesday, Charles Wesley's group continued
studying this book throughout Lent at their afternoon breakfast on Stationary
fast days. "Winchester men" refers to graduates of St. Mary College of Winchester (Hamps.), commonly called Winchester College and, along with Eton,
Westminster, and Charterhouse, one of the leading public schools (preparatory
schools) in England at the time.

amination. 4.45 Private prayer. 5 E; finished Francke's *Nicodemus, or Of the Fear of Man.* 5.30 Public Prayers. 6 E; went to Workhouse, read 25th chapter of St Matthew and family prayers in Grey's chamber; ri.[113] 7 E at Ford's, good talk how to improve them at Workhouse. 7.30 Smith came, various talk. 8 E; read Law's character of Miranda.[114] 9 E; came home; wrote diary. 9.15 Private prayer.

Blessings: began going twice on Wednesday to Workhouse; good success with Washington; convinced Watson of the Stations; breakfast at Charles Wesley's; no supper; Ford asked my pardon for affronting me; I prayed for reconciliation, God granted it.

Sins: irrecollected and dull; calling at Ford's, he would not give me admittance, whereon I rashly said I would not come in his room that week; after he asked my pardon, I went immediately.

THURSDAY, MARCH 28.   4 Dressed; business and virtue; ri; private prayer and chapter. 5 E; read Whitby. 5.30 With John Wesley, religious talk of the Prayer for the Dead[115] in answer to Atkinson; of disputing, always grant as much as you can;[116] of Ford, etc; called at Robson's, he was engaged the last Monday night. 6.30 Religious talk with Atkinson, satisfied his question; ri. 7.15 Public Prayers. 7.45 Lecture in the Hall. 8 Walked with Watson, about necessary business. 8.30 Breakfast. 8.45 Wrote diary. 9 E and Collect; read Whitby; ri. 10 E; read Whitby; ri. 11 Read Whitby; ri. 11.45 Read chapter. 12 E and Collect; dinner; ri. 1 E; at Washington's, etc, read Aldrich; ri. 1.30 Walked with Washington, good talk. 2 E; came home. 2.15 Washington came, taught him exacter diary; ri. 3 E and Collect with Washington; read Whitby; ri. 4 E; read chapter. 4.15 Daily examination. 4.45 Private prayer. 5 E; read Nelson; ri. 5.30 Public Prayers. 6 E; supper; ri. 6.45 Went to Smith's; ri.

---

113   Marginal note: "no supper."

114   Law, *Serious Call,* ch. VIII.

115   John Wesley's *Collection of Forms of Prayer,* beginning with the fifth edition (1740), contains prayers for the dead from St. Mary's liturgy; see also Thomas Lathbury, *A History of the Nonjurors* (London: W. Pickering, 1845), pp. 492–96.

116   Wesley noted some guidelines for this in the front of his diary for this period: "In disputing, let him 1. Define the terms of his question. 2. Limit the question, what grant, what he denys. 3. Seem to have no opinion; put him to explain and prove his, and then insinuate and press objections" (OD IV, vi). This follows the method "of treating on a problem" outlined in Robert Sanderson's *De usu logicæ* (translated and extracted by Wesley); see 27 September, note 37.

7 E; good talk of our friends and ourselves; ri. 8 E; compared diaries and religious talk; ri. 9 E; came home; wrote diary. 9.30 Private prayer.

Blessings: with John Wesley; satisfied Atkinson; taught Washington exacter diary; compared diaries with Smith.

Sins: dissipated and irrecollected; proud, vain, and unchaste thoughts; greedy in eating; impatient with Watson; hardly rose.

FRIDAY, MARCH 29. 4 Dressed; E. 4.15 Private prayer; business and virtue; ri; read chapter. 5 E; meditated of my sins; ri. 5.45 Private prayer. 6 E; confession; ri. 6.30 Public Prayers. 7 E; Hall.[117] 7.15 Read Whitby; ri. 7.45 Walked with Smith to the Workhouse, taught children, read family prayer and chapter; ri. 8.30 Came home; ri. 8.45 Necessary business; ri. 9 E and Collect; read Whitby; ri. 10 E; read Whitby; ri. 11 E; meditated on Christ's Passion; ri. 11.45 Private prayer. 12 E and Collect; Hall; ri. 12.30 Private prayer. 12.45 Meditated of levity; ri. 1 E; read, finished Aldrich's Logic with Atkinson, Washington, Smyth, and Watson (Ford left off at the second book);[118] Watson began disputing, I would not dispute with him. 1.45 Walked with Atkinson, religious talk of Watson; ri. 2 E; walked with Smith, good talk of the hanged man,[119] of Watson, Atkinson, and Washington; ri. 2.45 Private prayer at Charles Wesley's with Smith and Carter; ri. 3 E; breakfast; ri; read Patrick; ri. 3.45 Walked with Smith, good talk; ri; came home. 4 E and wrote diary. 4.15 Read chapter; daily examination. 4.45 Private prayer. 5 E; meditated to prevent disputes; ri. 5.30 Public Prayers. 6 E; General Examination [for] the past week, and confession; ri.[120] 7 E at Ford's, etc, read texts of Scripture against disputes, agreed to have no more disputes; read Law's *Serious Call;* ri. 8 E; read Law, edifying discourse; ri. 9 E; read Law; parted lovingly. 9.15 Private prayer and thanksgiving.

Blessings: rose; recollected 8 times; fervent in private prayer; cheerful

---

[117] Apparently a lecture, although an unusual hour (see 28 March, 7:45 a.m.).
[118] See 9 March.
[119] Edward Pope, "a lusty tall handsome young man," had been hanged at noon at the Castle for "stealing two colts." John Wesley had been with the condemned man for over two hours that morning, noting in his diary that there was "no confession," and that he himself, after the execution, was "but little affected" by the hanging. OD IV, 112; see also Hearne, *Collections,* vol. 11, 321; and Richard P. Heitzenrater, *John Wesley and the Oxford Methodists, 1725–1735* (Ph.D. diss., Duke University; Ann Arbor, Mich.: University Microfilms, 1972), pp. 394f.
[120] Marginal note: "no supper."

and serious; with Smith at the Workhouse; made only one meal, at 3 at Charles Wesley's, ½ bread without butter and tea without sugar; avoided disputes with Watson etc; prevented disputes at Ford's; no supper; would not eat ¼ dry bread at 9.

Sins: censured Watson for disputing.

Διὸ παρακαλεῖτε ἀλλήλους, καὶ οἰκοδομεῖτε εἰς τὸν ἕνα καθὼς καὶ ποιεῖτε.[121]

SATURDAY, MARCH 30.   4 Dressed; business and virtue; ri. 4.15 Wrote diary. 4.30 Private prayer. 4.45 Chapter. 5 E; thanksgiving for the blessings of the past week.[122] 6 E and wrote diary. 6.15 Public Prayers. 6.45 Hall;[123] ri. 7 E; necessary business. 7.15 Began composing a Theme; ri. 8 E; breakfast with Smith, good talk; read News; ri. 9 E; came home; wrote diary. 9.15 Finished Theme; ri. 10 E; read Whitby;[124] ri. 10.45 Dressed. 11 E; walked with Watson, disputed about the Sacrament at Christ Church; ri. 11.45 Read chapter; private prayer. 12 E and Collect; dinner; ri. 1 Hall. 1.30 Walked with Washington, religious talk; ri. 2.30 Lecture in Sanderson. 3 E and Collect; Lecture; ri. 4 E; read chapter. 4.15 Daily examination. 4.45 Private prayer. 5 E; read Patrick; ri. 5.30 Public Prayers. 6 Walked with Dominus Black, good talk of studying divinity; ri. 6.15 Supper; ri. 7 E; went to Smith's, various talk with him and Ford; ri. 8 E; read Goodman; ri. 9 E; came home; private prayer.

Blessings: rose; good resolutions; thrice recollected; twice zealous; fervent in Public Prayers; temperate.

Sins: disputed fiercely with Watson;[125] inactive with Smith and Ford; unchaste thoughts.

SUNDAY, MARCH 31.   5 Dressed. 5.30 Wrote diary; business and virtue; ri. 5.45 Private prayer. 6 E; meditated of the Sacrament and private

---

[121]   "Wherefore comfort yourselves together, and edify one another, even as also ye do" (1 Thess. 5:11). This is a footnote to the entry for eight to nine o'clock. See also 19 March.

[122]   Marginal note: "Resolved to persevere."

[123]   See 28 March, 7:45 a.m.

[124]   The monthly summary for March 1734 indicates Ingham had at this point completed "to the Hebrews" in his abridgment of Whitby. It appears that he continued working on the project only until 5 April and probably did not complete it during the time span of this diary, if ever.

[125]   The question at issue here and on several other occasions seems to have been simply whether or not they should attend the Eucharist at Christ Church, for which it appears they would need to obtain leave from the head of their college; see 9 May and 8 June, and OD III, 21, 40.

prayer; ri. 7 E with Atkinson; walked with him, Smyth, Ford, Watson, and Washington to Christ Church. 7.30 Public Prayers and Sacrament; ri. 9 Thanksgiving and read *Meditations* with Washington. 9.15 Breakfast at Ford's with Watson, religious talk; ri. 10 E; Sermon;[126] ri. 10.30 Walked with Washington, religious and useful talk; ri. 11.45 Wrote diary; thanksgiving and private prayer. 12 E and Collect; dinner; ri. 1 E; went to the Workhouse, read 6th chapter of Luke. 2 E; Sermon. 2.45 At Charles Wesley's with Carter and Smith, read Young's sermon of Nature and Grace; ri. 4 Walked; ri. 4.15 Read chapter. 4.30 Daily examination. 4.45 Private prayer. 5 E; meditated on God's mercies: 5.30 Public Prayers. 6 E; visited Bolton's, and supper; ri. 7 E; at Ford's with Smith, various and useful talk; ri. 8 Various and useful talk; ri; Smith taught Ford the degrees of attention;[127] came home; private prayer.[128]

Blessings: Ford, Atkinson, Smyth, Watson, and Washington went to Christ Church with me; the Sacrament; attentive at the Sermons; zealous in conversation with Washington; at the Workhouse; at Charles Wesley's.

Sins: slept an hour; dissipated[129] at Public Prayers and Sacrament; neglected the Ejaculations 4 times; spoke unkindly of Natt; indolent at night and inactive with Smith and Ford.

MONDAY, APRIL 1. 4 Rose; dressed. 4.15 Business and virtue; ri. 4.30 Wrote diary. 4.45 Private prayer. 5 E; began the Country Parson; ri. 6 E; necessary business. 6.15 Public Prayers. 6.45 Left my gown and cap at Mother Shipton's and went to Smith's at Christ Church. 7 E; we called at Charles Wesley's, he gave us directions for our journey, and conversation by the way and with Gambold. 7.20[130] Set forward to Stanton Harcourt, religious talk of Ford, etc. 7.45 Began a treatise on the 16th day of the month (as we walked);[131] ri. 8 E with Smith, read the treatise and religious talk; ri. 9 E; finished the treatise and resolved both of us

---

126 This day was the fifth Sunday in Lent, later to be called Passion Sunday but not listed as such in the *B.C.P.* until 1928.
127 See p. 276; see also plates 4 and 6.
128 Three of the last five entries in the H column for this day are "d"—"dull." The column is then discontinued until 21 April.
129 See 17 March, note 69.
130 Ingham here begins noting the time in finer distinctions than quarter hours (1/4, 1/2, etc.) by using the fraction to indicate minutes (20/60). Cf. 9 August.
131 See 16 May, note 128.

to observe it, σὺν Θεῷ;[132] ri. 9.45 Reached Stanton and saluted Gambold, and afterward wrote our diaries; ri. 10 E; tea with Gambold, Newton, and Smith, religious talk of faith, humility, and unlearning ourselves; ri. 10.30 Walked with Gambold in the garden, religious talk of morality, the great dangerousness thereof, subversive of religion; no religion without faith; pride the foundation of morality, they practise such duties because they are pleased with them, because their schemes flatter their pride and appear beautiful to the fancy; ri.[133] 11 Walked with Gambold alone, religious talk of the Solifidians and their writings, unhappy in their expressions, good men;[134] Scot, Barrow, and Tillotson triumphed over them by applying to reason and eloquence, and thereby got applause;[135] self-denial, chiefly of the understanding, the great means to learn humility and acquire true faith; ri. 12 E with Smith in the Chapel;[136] private prayer with Gambold and Smith in Gambold's study; Gambold gave me directions for reading the Scriptures, and recommended some books; ri. 12.45 Wrote diary. 1 E with Smith; dinner with Smith and Gambold, religious talk of temperance and faith; to meditate of God's omnipresence

[132]   "With God's help."

[133]   Marginal note, "good conversation."

[134]   The Solifidians were those who emphasized the Reformation doctrine of "justification by grace through *faith alone* (*sola fide*)" and argued that any attempt to give value to human effort or "good works" in the process of salvation (as the "moralists" would) contradicted the essential Christian truth that salvation was the gracious gift of a sovereign God. The Solifidian position, however, was often branded as "antinomian," having total disregard for the moral law. The faith-works controversy was of vital concern to the Oxford Methodists; Wesley's recognition of the danger of either position when taken to the extreme led him to take a mediating view (see pp. 30, 36f.); see also Basil Willey, *The English Moralists* (London: Chatto & Windus, 1964), and C. F. Allison, *The Rise of Moralism* (New York: Seabury Press, 1966), pp. 168ff., 194ff. Ingham and Gambold both eventually became associated with the Moravians, one of the more radically Solifidian denominations.

[135]   John Scot[t] (1639–1695), Isaac Barrow (1630–1677), and John Tillotson (1630–1694) were representative rationalists of the sort often called Latitudinarian in the seventeenth century, whose sympathies generally lay with the Arminian theology that the Solifidians attacked.

[136]   The Harcourt chapel (fifteenth century) of the parish church of St. Michael is filled with monuments to the Harcourt family including, for instance, the tomb of Sir Robert Harcourt, Standard Bearer to Henry VII at the battle of Bosworth Field (1485), with the remains of the standard itself hanging over the tomb. T. J. Goddard-Fenwick, *A Guide to St Michael's Church* (Oxford: Parchment, 1972), pp. 8f.

and peculiar care of us; to settle these things in our minds highly useful and the best means to acquire all the virtues; we should depend entirely upon God, as little children hang upon their mothers; the Scriptures recommended to be read constantly; the Holy Ghost delights chiefly to reveal to us our duty from those writings; we ought to try all human writings by the test of Scripture and only to approve of them so far as they agree with Scripture, but by no means to interpret Scripture by them;[137] the Holy Scripture is our Master, and if like new born babes we desire the sincere milk thereof, we shall undoubtedly be nourished up to eternal life; for the Holy Ghost opens to us our duty as we are fitted to practise it, and we at different times shall understand the same chapters in different meanings; ri. 2 Walked with Smith, religious talk of Gambold's discourse. 2.30 Walked with Gambold and Newton to see the Church,[138] good talk. 2.45 Smith and I set forward for Oxford, Gambold and Newton accompanied, good talk of the works of the Creation, superior to art; Adam's pleasure in Paradise; everything reveals us a lesson; the frailty of these beauties a motive to seek for more lasting enjoyment. 3 Parted with Newton and Gambold. 3.15 E and Collect with Smith, religious talk of Gambold and his discourse; ri. 4 E with Smith; questioned ourselves in Logic, and religious and useful talk. 5 E; religious talk of our journey; ri; parted with Smith; got to College just at 5.30, Public Prayers; ri. 6 E; walked with Ford, religious talk of Broughton's conversation with him. 6.15 Supper; ri. 7 E; private prayer. 7.15 At Robson's, religious talk of the Workhouse, appointed to meet altogether at Ford's to consult how to proceed in the best manner for the good of the children; ri. 8 Religious talk of ourselves, John Wesley, Hall,[139] Gambold, etc; ri. 9 E; came home; private prayer.

Blessings: recollected and cheerful; Charles Wesley's directions; walk with Smith; Gambold; health, safety, pleasure, profit; zealous and active with Robson, no disputes.

Sins: dissipated in Public Prayer.

---

137 Cf. Wesley's dictum: "Try all doubtful actions by the Test[ament]" (OD IV, ix; see also his *Address to the Clergy* [1756], I.2.2).

138 The church of St. Michael was built in the twelfth century and remained relatively unspoiled through the reformations and revolutions of the sixteenth and seventeenth centuries. The chancel is still divided from the nave by the oldest surviving wooden rood screen in England, dating from the thirteenth century. Goddard-Fenwick, *Guide to St Michael's,* pp. 2ff.

139 This would seem to be a list of persons, thus "Hall" would refer to Westley Hall; cf. 21 March.

TUESDAY, APRIL 2.   4 Dressed; E. 4.15 Business and virtue; ri. 4.30 Private prayer; read chapter. 5 E; read Country Parson; ri; Ford came. 6 E; transcribed diary for yesterday; Smith came to invite me to breakfast with him. 6.15 Public Prayers. 7 E; finished writing diary; ri. 8 E; breakfast at Smith's, compared diaries and religious talk; ri. 9 E and Collect with Smith; came home; wrote diary. 9.15 Read Whitby; ri. 10 E; read Whitby; ri. 11 E; walked with Ford, good talk. 11.45 Read chapter. 12 E and private prayer. 12.15 Dinner; ri. 1 E; walked with Washington, Watson, and Smyth, religious talk of reading the Scriptures, and the love of God; ri; called at the Schools, walked in the Picture Gallery and the Library with Ford and Washington.[140] 2 Came home and wrote diary. 2.30 Washington came, looked over his diary. 3 E and Collect with Washington; began writing diary [summary];[141] Ward came to fetch me to the Lecture.[142] 3.30 Wrote diary. 3.45 Washington came, taught him exacter diary; ri. 4 E with Washington. 4.30 Daily examination and private prayer. 5 E; Yates came, religious talk of Law. 5.15 Wrote diary; Public Prayers. 6 E; finished diary. 6.30 Supper. 6.45 Considered how to spend this month, and what books to read; ri. 7 E; went to the Crown Inn,[143] with John Whitaker and his son, religious and useful talk; spent sixpence. 9 Came home; wrote diary; E and private prayer. 9.15 Wrote letter to my mother; ri. 10.

Blessings: rose; recollected 12 times; breakfast with Smith; zealous and active to do good; disengaged from Black the moment John Whitaker sent for me, good talk with him.

Sins: dull in Public Prayers; walked in the Schools without consideration.

---

[140]   The Public Schools of the university (that is, faculties or departments, such as natural philosophy, music, divinity, etc.) were located in a quadrangle north of St. Mary's church. The Bodleian Library, built by Duke Humphrey in the fifteenth century, was located over the Divinity School at the west side of the quadrangle. Thomas Salmon indicates that the library was difficult to use by students, it being open only three hours, morning and afternoon, the books being chained in place in the cold rooms (*The Present State of the Universities* [London: J. Roberts, 1744], p. 37). The Picture Gallery, containing portraits and statues of famous persons, filled three sides of the upper story of the Schools.

[141]   He apparently finished it on 4 May. See monthly summary for March 1734.

[142]   Ingham appears to have been giving special help to Matthias Ward in his studies. See also 9 March and 3 April.

[143]   The Crown Inn was on the west side of Cornmarket Street, north of Carfax.

WEDNESDAY, APRIL 3. 4 E; dressed. 4.15 Business and virtue. 4.30 Private prayer. 4.45 Read chapter. 5 E; meditated of my sins; ri. 5.45 Confession; ri. 6 E; confession; ri. 6.15 Public Prayers. 7 Interrupted by Watson; E. 7.15 Transcribed Imposition for Ward;[144] ri. 8 E; went to the Workhouse, taught the children and read family prayers; came home; ri. 9 E and private prayer; read Whitby; ri. 10 Dressed and mended my clothes; ri. 11 E; meditated on Christ's sufferings; ri. 12 E and private prayer; Hall. 12.30 Read Country Parson. 12.45 Confession. 1 E; at Washington's with Smyth and Watson, read the Country Parson on resolutions;[145] ri. 2 E with them, read Country Parson. 2.30 With Smith, read the letter he wrote his sister of the Sacrament. 2.45 At Charles Wesley's with Smith and Carter, private prayer. 3 E; breakfast; read Patrick; ri. 4 E; walked, meditated of faith. 4.45 Wrote diary; daily examination. 5 Private prayer. 5.15 Read chapter. 5.30 Public Prayers. 6 E; good talk with Watson. 6.15 Hall.[146] 6.30 Went to Workhouse, taught the children, read family prayers and chapter. 7 E; at Smith's with Ford and Evans, read Goodman; ri. 9 Came home with Ford, good talk. 9.15 Wrote diary; private prayer.

Blessings: rose; recollected 5 times; zealous twice; fervent in private prayer; contrite in confession; zealous in conversation, and active at Workhouse; Charles Wesley's; religious talk with Washington, Watson, and Smyth.

Sins: irrecollected 4 times; neglected ejaculatory prayer thrice; vain thoughts; indolent twice.

THURSDAY, APRIL 4. 4 E; dressed. 4.15 Business and virtue; ri. 4.30 Private prayer. 4.45 Chapter. 5 E; thoughts of rising. 5.15 Read Country Parson; ri. 6 E; read Whitby; ri. 7 E; necessary business. 7.15 Public Prayers; went to Smith's. 8 E; breakfast; good talk of Evans, and compared diaries. 9 E and Collect with Smith; came home; wrote diary. 9.15 Read Whitby; ri. 10 E; translated Kennet; ri. 11 E; Hall. 11.15 Walked with Ford, Atkinson, and Watson, religious talk of fasting and Lent. 11.45 Read chapter. 12 E and private prayer, dinner, 1 E; at Washington's with Smyth, Watson, and Atkinson, began Sanderson's appendix *De*

---

144 See also 9 March.
145 *The Country Parson's Advice to His Parishioners* (1680), part II, ch. 1 (see Appendix 3).
146 Marginal note: "no supper." Ingham had first entered "supper," then erased it and noted "Hall" instead.

usu logicæ;[147] ri. 1.45 At Broughton's;[148] ri. 2.30 Came home; Atkinson came, began to teach him the exacter diary; ri. 3 E and Collect with Atkinson, taught him exacter diary; ri. 4 E with Atkinson, taught him diary. 4.30 Daily examination; private prayer. 5 E; read Country Parson; ri. 5.30 Public Prayers. 6 E; with Bolton, Sr, recommended private prayer at 5 and daily examination, he said he would begin in a week's time. 6.15 Supper. 7 E; at Smith's, good talk of Evans,[149] etc, of Watson, and various talk of Smith's going to London.[150] 8 E with Smith, compared diaries and various talk; ri. 9 E; came home. 9.15 Ford came and told me that we were to go to Robson's room on Monday night; a hot dispute, whether Ford had not broken the Station by promising to breakfast with Mr Jackson;[151] he disputed rashly against the hours, that it was indifferent whether we fasted till 3, or only at night; and urged the prayer of the colleges[152] on Friday night; after a rash dispute, he owned his fault; I showed him that it was a greater sin to defend an error than to fall unwarily into it; religious talk of friendship. 10 Private prayer with Ford, went lovingly to bed together; ri.

Blessings: rose; recollected thrice; contrite by reading the Country Parson; breakfast and compared diaries with Smith; taught Atkinson the exacter diary; religious talk with Bolton, Sr; convinced Ford of his error; zealous and active to do good; began Sanderson with Washington, etc; kept resolution 11.

Sins: dead in Public Prayers; many wandering thoughts; irrecollected thrice; trifling at Smith's.

FRIDAY, APRIL 5. 4 E; dressed. 4.15 Business and virtue; ri. 4.30 Private prayer. 4.45 Chapter. 5 E; called Smyth, Atkinson, Washington, and Watson; ri; wrote diary. 6 E; read Country Parson; ri. 6.15 Public Prayers. 7 E; read Whitby; ri. 7.30 Necessary business. 8 E; at Broughton's Shop; ri. 8.30 Wandering thoughts; ri. 9 E and private prayer; read

[147]   Cf. 27 September, note 37.
[148]   Probably Broughton's bookshop; see 5 April and summary of sins.
[149]   Evans, apparently a friend as well as colleague of Smith's at Christ Church, had been absent from any reading group for two months prior to 3 April. He also disappears from notice in this diary for a month after 8 April.
[150]   See 19 April.
[151]   Mr denotes master (of arts); see 1 March, note 3. Lancelot Jackson (Queen's College, B.A. 1728) had proceeded M.A. in 1731.
[152]   The bidding prayer?

Whitby; ri. 10 E; with Ford, good talk about the election at Corpus Christi College;[153] ri; vain thoughts. 11 E; at Broughton's, exchanged books; ri. 12 E and collect; Hall; ri. 12.30 Read Country Parson; ri. 1 E; at Washington's, etc, read Sanderson, and religious talk. 2 E with them; went to Smith's, good talk. 2.30 Went to Ford's, and Atkinson, read Bible and religious talk; ri. 3 Private prayer and breakfast; read Nelson and Bible; ri. 4 E with them; came home; wrote diary. 4.15 Read chapter. 4.30 Daily examination. 4.45 Private prayer. 5 E; General Examination for the past week (indolent; dead in Public Prayers; irrecollected; wandering thoughts; greedy in eating). 5.30 Public Prayers. 6 E; went to the Workhouse for Smith, taught the children, read family prayers and a chapter, and afterwards went with Mrs Grey to visit a sick woman; read prayers for the sick,[154] and religious talk of examination, repentance, and receiving the Sacrament; exhorted the hearers to begin private prayer and daily examination that very night, to receive the Sacrament and go to church, etc; ri. 7.30 At Ford's with Atkinson, Washington, Watson, and Smyth, religious talk of repentance and the seriousness of dying persons; ri. 8 E with them; read Law; ri. 8.45 Reproved Ford for locking us out; he became more angry, and said he would not meet any more with us; I told him lovingly, I hoped he would change his mind before tomorrow night. 9 E and private prayer and thanksgiving. 9.15 Wrote diary. 9.45.

Blessings: rose; recollected 8 times; zealous and active in doing good and in conversation; gentle with Ford; no disputes.

Sins: irrecollected 6 times, and quite dissipated about exchanging books; neglected meditation and confession and private prayer.

[SATURDAY, APRIL 6.] 4 E; dressed. 4.15 Business and virtue; ri. 4.30 Private prayer. 4.45 Chapter. 5 E; meditated of the blessings of the past week, and thanksgiving. 6 E; read Country Parson; ri. 6.15 Public Prayers. 7 E; went to Smith's, good talk of Ford, etc; ri. 7.15 Came home and private prayer for brotherly love; ri. 8 E; breakfast at Natt's, read third chapter of Law's *Serious Call*,[155] and religious talk; ri. 9 E and Collect; went to the Theatre, heard the Collector's and the Proctor's Speech

---

153 Ford was hoping to be elected a scholar of Corpus Christi (see 20 April).
154 See *B.C.P.*, the Order for the Visitation of the Sick.
155 Ch. III, "Of the great danger and folly of not intending to be as eminent and exemplary as we can, in the practice of all Christian virtues."

of the vices of the University;[156] ri; came home. 10 Ford came, good talk of Broughton's conversation with him at breakfast, and how he should observe the Passion Week, to eat no flesh at supper, and none at all on Good Friday and Saturday; ri. 10.30 Necessary business. 10.45 Read Country Parson. 11 E; walked and read Country Parson; ri. 11.45 Private prayer. 12 E; dinner; ri; Ford asked me if I would receive the Sacrament at St Peter's on Good Friday;[157] I promised to consider of it. 1 With Washington and Watson at Smyth's, religious talk of the Sacrament, and the different lives of most Christians; ri. 2 E with them; came home and read Patrick's *Christian Sacrifice.* 2.45 Dressed; ri. 3 E and Collect; at Lecture in Sanderson. 4 E; read chapter. 4.15 Daily examination and wrote diary; ri; Ward came. 5 Private prayer. 5.15 Wrote resolutions for the Passion Week.[158] 5.30 Public Prayers. 6 Supper; ri. 7 E; Ford and Smith came, good talk (various); ri. 8 E; read Goodman; ri. 9 E; wrote diary. 9.15.

Blessings: rose; recollected twice; easily reconciled with Ford; zealous with Smyth, Washington, and Watson; N.B. Ward brought me some money[159] just when I was beginning to despair of fulfilling my promises to pay what I had borrowed.

---

[156]   Among the proctors' statutory duties was the responsibility to "hunt out night-walkers" and "to make diligent inquiry as to the several persons who may break the statutes, customs, and privileges of the University, and to set a severe mark upon them, by rebuking, chastising, fining, and imprisoning the younger sort [and] by the exaction of mulcts from the rest" (*Statutes,* XVII.4.3). The junior proctor (in this case James Edgecombe of Exeter College) was specifically charged with making a speech after Public Prayers on the eve of Palm Sunday, in which he should "inveigh with severity both on the errors in doctrine which have been allowed entrance during Lent and the offences against morals" as well as "praise, as they deserve, all those who have shown themselves subtle and acute in debate, and generally well-behaved and peaceable." *Statutes,* VI.2.7; see also John Ayliffe, *The Antient and Present State of the University of Oxford* (London: E. Curll, 1714), II, 123. One might expect the speech to be poorly received, as Thomas Wilson reported in 1732: "A dry one much hissed and clapt. Very unfit behaviour for a theatre of Scholars and Gentlemen." *The Diaries of Thomas Wilson D.D., 1731–37 and 1750,* ed. by C.L.S. Linnell (London: S.P.C.K., 1964), p. 50. See also 2 March, note 10.

[157]   Cf. 11 April, note 182. Ingham seems not to have attended the suggested Sacrament at St. Peter's in the East (see 12 April).

[158]   See below, following the entry for this day.

[159]   Perhaps in payment for translating an Imposition (see 3 April).

Sins: vain thoughts; neglected ejaculatory prayers twice; irrecollected thrice; indolent with Smith and Ford.

Σὺν Θεῷ[160]

APRIL 6.   Resolutions for observing the Passion Week.

1. Monday, Tuesday, and Thursday to eat no bread; one flesh meal at dinner; and to [have] supper on bread and milk.
2. Wednesday, Friday, and Saturday to make one meal on dry diet.
3. To spend at least seven hours a day in Public and private prayer, religious meditation and reading, and works of mercy.
4. To watch[161] on Easter Eve at least to 12.
5. To read the Country Parson, and by God's assistance to practise his directions.

SUNDAY, APRIL 7.   4 Rose; dressed; E and thanksgiving; private prayer; called Smyth, Washington, Atkinson, and Watson; business and virtue. 5 E; meditated and private prayer for the Sacrament; ri. 6 E; preparation for the Sacrament;[162] ri. 7 E; went with Ford, Smyth, and Washington to Christ Church, good talk. 7.30 Public Prayers and Sacrament; ri. 9 E and thanksgiving for the Sacrament with Smith; breakfast with him, good talk (various). 10 E; Sermon.[163] 10.45 Walked with Washington, religious talk of the advantage of religious friends, and of God's blessings; ri. 11.45 Read chapter. 12 E and private prayer. 12.15 Dinner; ri. 1 E; at Smith's with Evans, good talk. 1.15 Walked with Smith to the Workhouse; he stayed and read there; I went to visit a sick woman; read prayers for the sick, religious talk with her, etc, of receiving the Sacrament and preparation requisite;[164] gave her sixpence; ri. 2 At Sermon; ri. 2.45 Walked with Smith and Evans. 3 E; good talk (various); ri. 4 E; read chapter; wrote diary. 4.30 Daily examination. 4.45 Private prayer. 5 E; read Country Parson; slept. 5.45 Public Prayers. 6 Supper; ri. 7 E; with Ford, Smith, and Evans in the Chapel.[165] 7.30 Read Goodman's *Winter*

---

160   "With God's help." This list, dated 6 April, was written on a page between entries for 31 March and 1 April.
161   See Glossary, s.v. "Watch," and 13 April.
162   See 24 March, note 96.
163   This day, often called Palm Sunday, has never been listed in the *B.C.P.*
164   See 24 March, note 96.
165   Queen's College chapel had just been built in 1714. Although some observers felt the new building to be inferior to the medieval chapel it replaced,

Evening Conference;[166] ri. 9 Came home. 9.15 Private prayer.

Blessings: rose; Sacrament at Christ Church; fervent in Sacrament; zealous in conversation with Washington, and with the sick woman; recollected thrice.

Sins: vain and unchaste thoughts; inattentive at Sermon twice; broke Lent Rule 10; irrecollected twice; inactive with Smith and Evans.

MONDAY, APRIL 8.   5 Dressed. 5.15 Private prayer. 5.30 Wrote diary. 5.45 Read chapter. 6 E; showed Smith and Evans the Chapel. 6.30 Read Country Parson. 7 E; read Country Parson. 7.15 Public Prayers. 8.15 Went to visit the sick woman; she had sent for the person to administer the Sacrament; she desired that I would receive with her, the person was willing; I then readily consented; prayers for the sick and the Holy Sacrament;[167] ri. 9 Called at the Workhouse for Ford, family prayers. 9.30 Came home; thanksgiving and prayer after the Sacrament; ri. 10 E; read Country Parson; ri. 11 E; walked; ri. 11.45 Meditated; ri. 12 E and private prayer. 12.15 Dressed; ri. 1 E with me, Washington, Watson, Smyth, and Atkinson, began John Wesley's treatise on the Sacrament;[168] ri. 2 E with them; read Country Parson; ri. 3 E and Collect; at Lecture in the Greek Testament; ri. 4 E; read Country Parson; ri. 4.30 Wrote diary, and daily examination. 4.45 Private prayer. 5 E; thanksgiving. 5.15 Read Country Parson. 5.30 Public Prayers. 6 E; supper; ri; no flesh. 7 E; at Robson's with Hervey, Greives,[169] and Ford, religious talk of resigna-

---

Salmon remarked appreciatively that "the windows are admirably painted, and cast such a venerable shade, that it must inspire every one with devotion that enters this elegant oratory" (*Present State,* p. 52). The windows had been transferred from the old medieval chapel, most of them painted by Van Linge in 1635, with three dating to the sixteenth century. See plate 1.

[166]   A marginal note ("8 E") indicates that Ingham paused at the hour for ejaculatory prayer.

[167]   See *B.C.P.*

[168]   A discourse consisting primarily of extracts from Robert Nelson's *The Great Duty of Frequenting the Christian Sacrifice,* and William Beveridge's *The Great Necessity and Advantage of Publick Prayer and Frequent Communion* (John Wesley MS. Colman Collection XX [MA]). Wesley later condensed this work and published it as a sermon, "The Duty of Constant Communion" (Sermon 101).

[169]   MS. reads "Harvey" and "Grieves." Greives had been a student of John Wesley for over three years, but Hervey, also a colleague at Lincoln College, begins appearing regularly in Wesley's diary only at the beginning of Lent, 1734

tion, of the fear of man, of pride, intemperance, and our particular sins, and the several ways whereby the devil deceives us; ri; agreed to meet again at Ford's room next Monday night. 9 Came home with Ford and agreed to have no disputes, but to sconce one another one pence if we did not forbear upon the first sign.[170] 9.15 Wrote diary.

Blessings: the Sacrament with a sick woman; zealous in conversation and avoided disputes; serious in reading Country Parson; attentive in Publice and private prayer; recollected 9 times; temperate, no flesh at supper; Hervey and Greives.

Sins: laid slumbering in bed from 4 to 5; unchaste thoughts.

Ἐκνήψατε δικαίως, καὶ μὴ ἁμαρτάνετε, . . . πρὸς ἐντροπὴν [ὑμῖν] λέγω. I Cor. 15:34.[171]

TUESDAY, APRIL 9. 4 Rose; dressed. 4.15 Business and virtue; ri. 4.30 Private prayer. 4.45 Chapter. 5 E; read Country Parson on resignation.[172] 6 E; read Country Parson, motives to resignation; ri. 7 E and private prayer. 7.15 Public Prayers. 8 E; went to visit the sick woman, religious talk of frequenting the Holy Sacrament, and the church; of daily examination and private prayer, and of family prayer; questioned her how she designed to amend her life; exhortation to her and several other women that were there; read prayers for the sick; ri; called at the Workhouse, and at Smith's. 9 E; wrote diary; private prayer; read Country Parson of the means.[173] 10 Read Country Parson; ri. 11 E; walked, read Country

---

(though he had been "convinced of the Friday fasts" the previous September, about the same time as Ingham; OD III, 106). On 30 March 1734, Hervey had talked with Wesley about the "sermon on the Sacrament" (see note 168), and on 13 April he asked the rector's leave to receive the Sacrament at Christ Church (OD IV, 113, 127). Neither Hervey nor Greives appears to have been part of John Wesley's core group, but here both become involved with Ingham's groups; see also 10 May, where Hervey agrees to meet three times weekly with Ford, Atkinson, and Smith.

170 See 18 May for some indication of specific "signs" they used.

171 "Awake to righteousness, and sin not; . . . I speak this to [your] shame." Ingham's omission of the pronoun may indicate his personalization of the phrase, changing "your shame" to "my shame" (cf. 12 June). This is a footnote to his summary of sins.

172 Part II, "General Directions how to live a holy and Christian life," ch. 3, "Containing a third advice, to give up our selves, souls and bodies entirely to God, with several arguments to persuade us to it"; see Appendix 3.

173 Part II, ch. 4, sec. 2, "Of the means of procuring this knowledge [of God]."

Parson of walking in God's sight,[174] and meditated thereon; ri. 11.45 Private prayer. 12 E; dinner; ri. 1 E; with me, Smyth, Washington, Watson, Atkinson, read John Wesley's treatise.[175] 2 E with them; read Country Parson of resolutions;[176] ri. 3 E and Collect; at Lecture in Greek Testament. 3.45 Walked with Atkinson to search the Court for the will of one Weston of Banbury; ri. 4 E; read Country Parson of resolutions; ri. 5 E; daily examination; private prayer. 5.30 Public Prayers; ri. 6 Supper; ri; no flesh. 7 Divided the Servitors' wages;[177] ri. 8 Went to Smith's, he was engaged; came home. 8.30 Wrote diary; read Norris' first Beatitude;[178] ri. 9 E; wrote diary. 9.15 Private prayer. 9.30.

Blessings: rose; recollected 6 times; fervent in private prayer; zealous in conversing with sick woman; serious resolutions in reading the Country Parson.

Sins: dead in Public Prayers; vain and unchaste thoughts; dissipated.

WEDNESDAY, APRIL 10.   4 Rose; dressed. 4.15 Business and virtue; ri. 4.45 Private prayer. 5 E; meditated of my sins; ri. 6 E; went to John Wesley's to consult him whether I should make the Country Parson's resolutions; he would not have me defer it, but begin this very day, and keep reviewing it and adding to it daily; he advised me to guard chiefly against my strongest temptations, not to multiply resolutions but to secure the main ones; I desired his prayers, which he readily granted;[179] ri. 6.45 Wrote diary; serious. 7 E and private prayer. 7.15 Public Prayers.

---

174   Part II, ch. 5, "Containing a fifth advice, To live alwaies as in God's sight: with the great usefulness of this, to promote a holy life . . . [with] some directions for the practice of this duty."

175   On the Sacrament (see 8 April, note 168).

176   Part II, ch. 1, "Containing the first advice, Seriously to resolve upon a holy life; the necessity of such a resolution, and the great virtue and efficacy of it."

177   Servitors were undergraduates who acted as servants to the fellows and gentleman commoners in return for their board and lodging or a comparable stipend or wages. Ingham was a "Batteler," which ranked between commoner and servitor. See Charles Edward Mallet, *A History of the University of Oxford* (New York: Longmans, Green and Co., 1924–27), vol. 1, 252. Salmon states that "Battlers" were "entitled to no commons, but purchase their meat and drink of the cook and butler" (*Present State,* p. 423). Ingham, however, does mention his "commons"; see 6 March. Cf. *O.E.D.,* s.v. "Battel."

178   See "Christian Blessedness," discourse I on Matt. 5:3 in *Practical Discourses Upon the Beatitudes of Our Lord* (1728), vol. I; see Appendix 3.

179   Wesley's diary entry simply reads: "6.30 Ingham, religious talk. 6.45 . . ." (OD IV, 124). See above, p. 17, note 25, and 12 April below.

8 E; went to the Workhouse, taught the children, read family prayers, and religious talk with the old people of the Sacrament. 9 With the sick woman, religious talk and read prayers for the sick out of Common Prayer and Taylor's *Holy Dying;*[180] gave her sixpence; came home. 9.45 Private prayer for resolutions and courage; ri. 10 E; Watson came, good talk of his affairs. 10.45 Read Country Parson. 11 E; read Country Parson and wrote resolutions. 11.45 Dressed; ri. 12 E and private prayer. 12.15 Hall. 12.30 Meditated of Christ's sufferings; ri. 1 E; with me, Smyth, Atkinson, Washington, and Watson, finished John Wesley's treatise on the Sacrament. 2 E with them, good talk with them and Watson. 2.30 Wrote resolutions. 3 E and private prayer; wrote resolutions; ri. 4 E; went to the Registrar, and the Workhouse; ri. 5 Came home. 5.15 Private prayer. 5.30 Public Prayers. 6 E; Hall. 6.30 Breakfast. 6.45 Read News; ri. 7 E; walked with Watson, good talk. 7.30 At Smith's with Ford, good talk. 8 Good talk (various); ri. 9 Came home. 9.15 Wrote diary and private prayer.

Blessings: rose; recollected 6 times; with John Wesley; zealous and active in doing good at the sick woman's; good resolutions; one meal at 6.30.

Sins: dissipated at Public Prayers; sat too much; inactive with Smith and Ford.

THURSDAY, APRIL 11. 4 Rose; dressed; business and virtue; ri. 4.30 Private prayer. 4.45 Read Country Parson. 5 E; wrote resolutions; ri. 6 E; went to John Wesley's to consult him, whether I should receive the Sacrament at Christ Church today, because it seemed particularly designed for their Servitors; as it was to be administered in the Cathedral, and not a sin to go, he thought the benefits should induce us to go;[181] ri. 6.30 Came home and went to Ford's to ask him if he would go; he began disputing furiously, he would not allow it to be our duty to receive as often as we have opportunity, because we should be obliged to receive four or five times a day,[182] etc; Atkinson was with him but would not dispute, he thought it was not designed for us; came home, displeased at Ford disputing; ri. 7 Wrote diary. 7.15 Public Prayers. 8.15 Dressed. 8.30

---

180 Jeremy Taylor, *The Rule and Exercises of Holy Dying* (1651), ch. V, sec. 7, "Offices to be said by the Minister in his visitation of the sick." See Appendix 3.

181 Wesley's diary takes no notice of this visit.

182 This would seem to be hyperbole on Ford's part, even though Holy Week might have presented more frequent opportunities than was normally the case; cf. 6 April.

Prayer for the Sacrament. 8.45 Went to Smith's, E with him, good talk and read *Meditations*. 9.30 At Christ Church, Public Prayers, Sacrament (this Sacrament was for their Servitors; John Wesley, Hall, and Salmon were there, Mr Battely[183] and their Servitors). 10.45 Came home; ri. 11 E; thanksgiving for the Sacrament; ri. 11.15 Meditated. 11.45 Private prayer. 12 E; dinner. 12.45 With me, Ford, Washington, Watson, Atkinson, Smyth, began Norris' sermon of Religious Conversation;[184] ri. 1.30 Walked with Ford to Smith's for Epigrams;[185] ri. 2 E; at Charles Wesley's with Smith and Carter, began Hales' Contemplation on Christ Crucified;[186] ri. 2.45 Religious talk with Charles Wesley of my resolutions; he advised me to give up all those things by which I had found the greatest advantage this Lent, and whatever hindered my progress; ri. 3 E; walked. 3.30 Carter came, walked with him, good talk. 4 Necessary business; E. 4.15 Wrote resolutions; ri. 5 E and wrote diary. 5.15 Daily examination and private prayer. 5.30 Public Prayers. 6 Supper; ri; no flesh. 7 E; with Smith, religious talk of our Lent Resolutions, which benefited us the most, and which we thought proper to retain; ri. 8 E; compared diaries and good talk; ri. 9 E; came home and private prayer. 9.45.

Blessings: John Wesley; Sacrament; Charles Wesley; reconciled with Ford.

GOOD FRIDAY, APRIL 12.   Set my larum at 3 but was disturbed by drunken persons [so] that I could not sleep, could not rise till 5; disturbed also with dreams. 5 Rose; dressed; business and virtue; ri; wrote diary. 5.45 Private prayer. 6 E; meditated of Christ's sufferings, and my own sins; ri. 7 E; Public Prayers. 8.30 E; private prayer. 8.45 Went to Charles Wesley's. 9 E; prayers for Good Friday[187] with him, Smith, and Carter; ri. 9.15 Read Hale on the circumstances of Christ's sufferings;[188] ri; Charles Wesley showed me his resolutions and resignation, made

---

183   MS. reads "Batley." Oliver Battely was a student of Christ Church, B.A. 1720, M.A. 1723/24, B.D. 1734. See note 189 below, and 15 April, note 4.
184   See 3 November, note 80.
185   See also 15 February.
186   "Of the Knowledge of Christ Crucified" in Matthew Hale's *Contemplations Moral and Divine* (1676); see Appendix 3.
187   See Nelson, *Fasts,* ch. IV.
188   A major portion of Hale's treatise deals with these "circumstances": who it was that suffered, from whom, how, for whom, why, upon what motive, and for what end.

mostly in the Country Parson's words. 10 E; Sermon.[189] 11.30 Began General Examination; ri. 12 Confession; ri. 12.45 Prayer for resignation; ri. 1 E; read my resolutions and protestation, and resigned myself; ri; confirmed my resignation with my own blood;[190] private prayer for courage and perseverance forever; otherwise I washed myself, to represent my repentance and hatred of my past life, and my resolution of becoming a new creature.[191] 1.45 Went to Charles Wesley's with Smith; ri. 2 E; at Charles Wesley's, etc, read Hale on Christ's crucifixion; ri. 2.30 Prayers for the day; ri; religious talk of spending the day. 3 E; walked with Smith, religious talk; came home. 3.30 Public Prayers.[192] 4 E; read Country Parson. 4.15 Hall.[193] 4.30 Daily examination; Atkinson came, read him my resolutions, religious talk about it, exhorted him to make the same; he consented to do it tomorrow, being his birthday, and the twenty-first year of his age. 5 E. 5.15 Private prayer, and for obedience, courage, and resignation; ri. 5.45 General Examination for the past week (dead in Public Prayers and dissipated); ri. 6 E. 6.15 Natt came, asked me to walk with him; told me I did not use him as a friend. 6.30 At Ford's with Atkinson and Washington, religious talk of the Passion Week. 7 E; Smyth came, religious talk of fasting, because he had eaten flesh; I answered his objections; ri. 7.15 Watson came, read Law; ri. 8 E; read Law and religious talk of Christ's Passion; ri. 9 E; private prayer; laid without bed-sheets.

Blessings: recollected 6 times; zealous 6 times in private prayer and meditation; contrite twice;[194] resolutions and resignation; conversation

---

189   Preached by Oliver Battely at Christ Church cathedral. Hearne, *Collections,* vol. 11, 329 (cf. *Statutes,* XVI.1.5).

190   Signing a solemn vow of resignation follows the general pattern suggested in the *Country Parson's Advice* (part II, ch. 1, sec. 3, 4) and is in keeping with the covenant theology of the Puritans. The use of his own blood to confirm this resignation and the subsequent act of washing himself to represent his repentance go beyond the specific injunctions of the Country Parson. Such a covenant, "sealed in blood," is not entirely out of keeping with biblical imagery, pietist theology, or historic customs, but is difficult to verify as a common religious practice during this period. Cf. H. C. Trumbull, *The Blood Covenant* (Philadelphia: J. D. Wattles & Co., 1893). See also p. 168f.

191   Cf. resolutions, pp. 165–69.

192   Apparently a special Good Friday service.

193   An unusual time for Ingham to be in the Hall.

194   Symbols in the Blessings column indicate this was between six and seven and nine and ten in the morning.

with Atkinson blest with success; eat nothing the whole day, and lay upon the bed stocks.[195]

Sins: wandering thoughts in Public Prayers.

SATURDAY, APRIL 13, EASTER EVE.   4.30 Dressed. 4.45 Wrote diary. 5.15 Business and virtue; ri; private prayer; reviewed my resolutions; ri. 6 E; wrote resolutions. 6.45 Atkinson came, showed me his resolutions and read it, religious talk thereupon; ri. 7 Thanksgiving for Atkinson's resolutions, and E; ri. 7.15 Public Prayers. 8 E; religious talk with Mss Harris[196] of the Sacrament; read Country Parson. 8.45 Smith came, good talk (various); ri. 9 E and Collect; read Country Parson on resignation; ri. 10 E with Natt, read Nelson for the day,[197] religious talk. 11 E; went to visit the sick woman, religious talk; ri. 11.45 Private prayer. 12 E. 12.15 Hall. 12.30 Went to Smith's, compared diaries, and good talk; ri. 1 E at Charles Wesley's with Smith and Carter, finished Hale's Contemplation on Christ Crucified; ri. 2 E; walked with Smith, good talk. 2.30 At Charles Wesley's, he persuaded us to leave off flesh supper; we did not entirely consent to it, though we allowed his arguments; ri. 3 E and Collect; Boyce[198] came; breakfast with them three, religious talk. 3.45 With Smith, good talk. 4 Walked; met with Natt, good talk (various). 4.30 Came home; wrote diary; daily examination. 4.45 Ford came. 5 E; private prayer. 5.15 Read Patrick's *Christian Sacrifice;* ri. 5.30 Public Prayers. 6 Eat ¼ dry bread and drank a little water. 6.15 Hall. 6.30 Atkinson read me his resolutions and resignation. 6.45 Dressed. 7 E; at Ford's with Smith, read Goodman; ri. 8 E; read Goodman; ri. 9 E; came home; Atkinson, Ford, and Washington came to watch[199] with me, we read Horneck's meditation before the Sacrament,[200] and private prayer;

195   Bed-stocks refers to the frame of the bed, but the entry at 9 p.m. seems to imply that he lay on an uncovered bedstraw (which served as a mattress).
196   Ingham here uses the abbreviation Mss for Mistress (now commonly abbreviated Mrs.); he otherwise refers to her as Mother Harris (see 24 December, 21 March, and 6 May). Cf. 26 March, and 23 April, note 44.
197   See Nelson, *Fasts,* ch. V ("Easter-Eve").
198   John Boyce [Boyse], son of a former Oxford mayor, a pupil at Christ Church (B.A. 1731, M.A. 1735), and friend of the Wesleys, was in the midst of a controversy concerning his marriage to a woman who was promised to another man. Hearne, *Collections,* vol. 11, 323, 337, 351f.; *Letters,* I, 353.
199   See 6 April, "Resolutions for observing the Passion Week," no. 4.
200   Horneck's *Fire of the Altar,* ch. I, "A preparatory meditation to bring the mind into a serious frame."

ri. 10 E. 10.15 Used his prayer before the Sacrament;[201] ri. 11 They went home, to bed; wrote diary. 11.15 I sit up by myself, and spent the time in private prayer. 11.45 Wrote diary. 12 E; to bed; meditated of the resurrection; ri.

Blessings: recollected 6 times; zealous 4; fervent in Public Prayers thrice; zealous and active in doing good; Atkinson's resolutions and resignation; Charles Wesley; fasted and 3;[202] watched with me, Atkinson, Ford, Washington.

Sins: neglected ejaculatory prayers 4 times; too ludicrous at Charles Wesley's, and with Smith at Ford's.

EASTER SUNDAY, APRIL 14. 6 Rose; dressed. 6.15 Thanksgiving; wrote diary. 6.30 Private prayer and thanksgiving. 7 E; at Ford's with Atkinson and Washington, read Patrick's meditation for Easter day,[203] religious talk of the day, and breakfast; ri. 8 E and Nelson's prayers for the day;[204] ri. 8.15 Read the Country Parson and reviewed my resolutions; ri. 9 E and Collect; Public Prayers. 10 Sermon. 10.30 Sacrament, confirmed my resolutions and resignation in the Country Parson's words;[205] ri. 11.15 Atkinson and Washington came to me to return thanks; we used Patrick's thanksgiving and Nelson's;[206] read Patrick's meditation;[207] ri. 11.45 Read the particulars in the Country Parson[208] and consented to them: B. Ingham. 12 E and private prayer. 12.15 Dinner; ri. 1 Dinner; ri. 1.30 Walked with Smith, good talk (various); ri. 2.15 At Charles Wesley's with Smith and Carter, read sermon. 2.45 He asked me about my resolutions, whether I would give up one flesh meal; I told him I was not fully determined; ri. 3 At Sermon.[209] 3.45 Walked, meditated of God's mer-

---

201 Ibid., [part II], "Prayers and devotions to be used before and after receiving of the holy Sacrament of the Lord's Supper."

202 Refers to his not breaking the Easter Eve fast until three o'clock (with three friends).

203 Patrick's *Christian Sacrifice,* part III, "Meditations and prayers before and after the Communion . . . Easter Day."

204 See Nelson, *Festivals,* ch. XV.

205 This took place in Queen's College chapel (see p. 168; cf. *Statutes,* XVI.2).

206 See *Christian Sacrifice,* part III, "Easter Day . . . The Thanksgiving and prayer afterward"; and Nelson, *Festivals,* ch. XV, Prayer III.

207 See *Christian Sacrifice,* part III, "Easter Day . . . The meditation afterward at home."

208 *Country Parson,* part II, ch. 1, sec. 2.

209 The preacher at this service at St. Peter's in the East was Dr. Euseby Isham, Rector of Lincoln College (Hearne, *Collections,* vol. 11, 329).

cies. 4 E; walked. 4.15 Wrote diary. 4.30 Read chapter and meditated; ri. 5 E; daily examination and private prayer. 5.30 Public Prayers. 6 Supper; ri; no flesh. 7 E; went to Smith's, and Ford, various and useful talk; ri. 8 E; finished Goodman's *Winter Evening Conference* with Smith and Ford; ri; came home. 9 E; thoughts of flesh supper, and private prayers. 9.30.

Blessings: zealous and fervent in Public and private prayer and thanksgiving; confirmed my resolutions at the Sacrament; temperate thrice; no flesh at supper.

Sins: neglected ejaculatory prayers thrice; irrecollected 4 times; wanton at Smith's and inactive; dissipated at Public Prayers; disputed with Charles Wesley.

Resolutions 1734

In the name of God, Amen.[1]

Being, I trust, assisted by God's Holy Spirit to consider the shortness and uncertainty of life, the emptiness and vanity of the world, and all the things of the world; the worth of my soul, and the important concern that lies upon me to provide for its eternal welfare: I see it's absolutely necessary to live a holy and religious life. I cannot be happy forever if I do not do so, and therefore I'm resolved I will [do] so, and nothing shall divert or hinder me forever; the Lord hear me, help me, and be merciful unto me.[2]

This resolution is neither unreasonable or unnecessary; the business indeed which I undertake is difficult, but God is sufficient to enable me to march through all difficulties and to overcome all temptations; and surely the reward annexed to the performance thereof is enough to encourage any man to run through fire and water and to master impossibilities; eternal life, everlasting glory cast down all obstacles; therefore I say again, I do resolve upon a holy and religious life.[3]

Witness Almighty God, the Father, Son, and Holy Ghost, <u>heaven and earth</u>, angels and archangels, the Church militant and triumphant, Amen. Ætatis Anno 22, A.D. 1734, April 12.[4]   B. I.   +

1   The following resolutions, covenant renewal, and resignation, dated 12 April, were transcribed into the diary on 18 April on pages that would immediately precede the entry for 1 May.
2   This paragraph follows the suggestions (and at times the very words) of *The Country Parson's Advice to His Parishioners* (1680), part II, ch. 1, sec. 1; see Appendix 3.
3   Ibid., part II, ch. 1, sec. 2.
4   Ibid., part II, ch. 1, sec. 3, 4.

At my baptism I entered into a solemn covenant with Almighty God. This covenant I do solemnly now renew and take upon myself;[5] and if I do not use my uttermost endeavors to perform it, may I never reap the least advantage from it. I know I shall fall into many sins and diverse temptations, and without God's assistance I shall not be able to do any thing that is good, yet 'tis, if I fall seven times a day, with God's assistance I'll rise again, repent, and amend.

I renounce the devil and all his works, pride, love of greatness and fame, all thoughts of glory, honour, preferment, character, reputation, esteem, even amongst my acquaintances, friends, and relations, when inconsistent with my duty; also anger, malice, revenge, and all other sinful affections of the perverse and corrupt nature, the instruments of the devil to draw us to everlasting damnation.

I renounce the pomps and vanities of the world, with all covetous desires of the same; I'll endeavour to seem little in my own eyes, and be content to be thought so by the whole world; I'll not seek the praise of men, neither will I be pleased with it; whatever condition God places me in, shall content me.[6]

I utterly renounce all proud and vain thoughts of my own worth; I'll not imagine myself to be any other man, or think how I could act in such a state of life, but I'll labour to perform my own part well.

I renounce all the sinful ways of the flesh; lust, adultery, fornication, unchasteness of all kinds; gluttony, drunkenness; sloth; I'll labour against all unchaste thoughts; I'll be temperate in all things, not using the c[reation] for pleasure, but preservation. A little drink makes me merry, therefore I'll watch against all temptation that way. My bed shall be left winter so soon as my body is refreshed with sufficient sleep.[7] I'm subject to intemperance in eating, therefore I must and will guard well against it. I'll be diligent in business, always doing, watchful against temptations, avoiding idleness.

I steadfastly believe all the Articles of the Christian faith and whatever is revealed in Holy Scripture. God's Holy Word and will shall be my study and delight; whatever he forbids, I'll absolutely avoid; whatever he com-

---

[5]   Ibid., part II, ch. 3, sec. 1.5.

[6]   See Phil. 4:11 and John Wesley's *Directions for Renewing our Covenant with God* (1780), sec. IV.2; cf. his *Christian Library* (1753), XXX, 319, in an extract of Richard Alleine's *Vindiciæ Pietatis* (London, 1663), the basis of the Wesleyan "Covenant Service."

[7]   See 10 March.

mands, I'll labour to perform and fulfill. I'll strive to shun even the appearance of all evil, and to do all the good that lies in my power. All my thoughts, words, and will shall be directed to God's glory.

Supposing now I should be sure of gaining the greatest preferment by complying with the customs of the world, and yielding to the humours of great men, I absolutely refuse them. Whatever condition God is pleased to place me in, shall fully content me.[8]

Supposing my friend should desire me, and my mother should importune me, to omit my duty in some respect for the sake of pleasing some great person, or gaining some considerable advantage, I would altogether refuse; and though they should all be set against me, hate me, and persecute me, I'll forsake all to follow my Master and do his Service.[9]

Should I be invited on a Stationary day to breakfast with some great man, my answer should be, I'm engaged. Because I'm delighted with the applause of friends,[10] I'll take care to conceal my charity and other good actions not necessary to be known by them, least I should lose the virtue of such good actions by being pleased with the praise of them.

I utterly renounce all pleasures and diversions which are obstructive of the love of God, especially shooting, etc.[11]

I'll give up whatever hereafter I shall find to be obstructive of my duty, whether it be diversion or any kind of meat. I give up baked pudding with fruit, etc.

I'll not suffer myself to eat one bite at table before I've first fixed the quantity; nor to pick, or eat between meals, unless in case of necessity; every breach of this resolution shall be sconced one pence or the next meal. I'll not allow myself butter or cheese after sufficient meat. I'll not eat flesh on fasting days, but in cases of necessity. I'll always give at the Sacrament if I have anything, but never make the want of money an excuse for not receiving.

(Set apart some time every day for doing good. Set apart a full hour morning and evening and a quarter-hour at noon for devotion;[12] cases of necessity must be excepted.)

8   See note 6 above; and cf. 23 July, summary of sins.
9   See *Country Parson's Advice*, part II, ch. 1, sec. 2.
10   See 1 November (shorthand entry), and 25 March (summary of sins).
11   On the blank page opposite this entry, Ingham later inscribed, "August 13, 1734. Resolved not to go one whole day a-shooting the following winter."
12   See 23 April, at 8 p.m.

After some considerable time spent in making and weighing the resolutions and renewal of my baptismal covenant with fasting and prayer, I did on Good Friday, April 12, A.D. 1734, Ætatis meæ 22, betwixt 1 and 2 in the afternoon in my study at Queen's College, Oxon, on my knees on the floor, take upon myself the said resolutions and renewal of my baptismal covenant; and then and there I did, with all the devotion of my heart and soul, make an entire surrender and resignation of myself and all things belonging to me to Almighty God, protesting and vowing in the following words, that he should have the full guiding and governing and disposing of me and mine forever.[13]

See, O my heart, what thou hast done, observe the bond which thou hast laid upon thyself; it is thy own act and deed, there is no disowning it, or excepting against it; as sure as I now see it with my eyes, it is recorded before God in heaven, and it shall one day be brought forth against me to my everlasting condemnation if I do not discharge and satisfy it.[14]

Go on, O my heart, go on, as thou hast begun, to keep thy resolutions firm, and to pay thy vows unto the most high and be confident that the Lord will prosper thy good desires and endeavours, and reward thee according to his gracious covenant and promise, with everlasting glory and felicity.

April 12, A.D. 1734.

To God the Father, Son, and Holy Ghost, my Creator, Redeemer, and Sanctifier, I do give myself soul and body, and all that belongs unto me, to be guided, governed, and disposed of according to his holy will, and to his honour and glory, and may he be a witness to this my act, which I promise never to revoke, and may I never obtain the least favour from him if I do it not with an upright heart and an unfeigned purpose to make it good to my life's end. Thou art my witness, O my God, be thou also my helper with thy continued grace, and so shall I be faithful to thee according to my heart's desire.[15]

B. Ingham. Amen. Amen. Amen.

All the foregoing things, the resolutions, renewal of my baptism, and the resignation were ratified and confirmed at the Holy Sacrament at the altar in Queen's College Chapel on Easter Sunday, before, betwixt, and after

[13]   See *Country Parson's Advice,* part II, ch. 3, sec. 2.5.
[14]   This paragraph and the following are quoted directly from *Country Parson's Advice,* part II, ch. 1, sec. 3.4.
[15]   Quoted directly from *Country Parson's Advice,* part II, ch. 3, sec. 2.3.

receiving the bread and wine; and that both in the very words of the resignation, and also in the following taken out [of] the Country Parson, whose directions I chiefly followed in this weighty affair, using his prayer frequently for God's assistance.

April 14, 1734.

There is all the reason in the world, O Heavenly Father, that I should give myself entirely to thee, since thou hast not withholden thy Son, thy only Son, from me. There is all the reason in the world, O my blessed Saviour, that I should surrender myself and all I have into thy hands, since thou didst offer thyself a sacrifice upon the cross for me, and dost now offer these holy pledges of the all-sufficient virtue of that sacrifice to me. There is all the reason in the world that I should resign myself to thee, O holy and blessed Spirit, since thou dost offer thyself to be a principle of holiness and life in me. And therefore, as I do now accept with all thankfulness, those great and inestimable favours, and do declare my acceptance of them in the sight of these thy servants and all thy holy angels here present by receiving these tokens and pledges of them according to thy command and institution, so do I give up myself and all I have to thee, and declare it before the face of all these witnesses. And I earnestly desire that even my unworthy self may be accepted through this my poor gift, the perfect sacrifice and oblation of my dearest Saviour, and be sanctified by the Holy Ghost, and be owned by my God, to the everlasting praise of the Holy, Blessed, and Undivided Trinity, whose I am, and whose I will be forever and ever.[16] Amen. Amen. Amen.

Vide [the] third chapter of the second part of the Country Parson's Advice to his Parishioners.

---

[16] This whole paragraph quoted directly from *Country Parson's Advice,* part II, ch. 2, sec. 2.4.

The diary for these two months preceding Ingham's standing for his degree reveals his fervent attempt to implement fully the Wesleyan scheme in both his own and his friends' lives. This leads to increasing numbers of resolutions, Ingham being quite ready and willing to advise others in these matters as well as to struggle to meet his own expectations for himself. Conflict and turmoil are more evident than ever before: early rising, keeping diaries, attending the Sacrament, and other facets of the Wesleyan "method" become a problem for several of the Queen's College associates. Robson, whom John Wesley had been importuning, is still stubbornly uncommitted on many questions, and Ingham's feisty young friend, Ford, "revolts" outright. In the midst of this ferment new friends are added to Ingham's groups; George Dixon, Westley Hall, and James Walker begin to appear regularly in the diary. The full schedule of meetings and group study sessions continues seven days a week. To his former activities, Ingham adds involvement with the poor at Gloucester Green Workhouse and in the Hamel, begins "watching" regularly on Saturday evenings, visits several sick persons in town, and begins attending private sacraments for the sick with the Wesleys and other Methodists. Now fully "convinced" (as Wesley would say), Ingham composes a "Scheme of the Reasonableness of our Practices" (no longer extant), no doubt a rousing *apologia* for Oxford Methodism in its fullest expression.

Ingham is also completing the requirements for his B.A. degree during this period, and the diary entries outline those activities: the speech and lectures he writes, the disputation, the standing for graces and his degree, and the celebrations that follow. He takes time during these last few days at Queen's to show friends through the new college buildings. One last conference with the Wesleys sends him off to the North Country and home. Ingham's daily record during this period helps fill a six-month gap in the extant Wesley diaries beginning in late April.

EASTER MONDAY, APRIL 15. 4.30 Rose; dressed. 4.45 Business and virtue; ri. 5 E and private prayer; wrote diary. 5.30 Read chapter and meditated; ri. 6 E; composed a prayer for Ford standing candidate at the election of Corpus Christi College;[1] ri. 7 E; read Nelson for the day[2] with Natt; ri; religious talk. 8 Public Prayers. 8.45 Walked with Atkinson, religious talk of Natt and Bolton. 9 E and Collect with me, Atkinson, Washington, and Watson, read sermon of Norris of 'The Importance of a Religious Life Considered from the Conclusion'.[3] 10 E with them; Sermon.[4] 10.45 Walked with Atkinson and Washington to enquire after the poor men at Bartlemas House, they were none of them at home;[5] we promised to go at 9 next morning; religious talk.[6] 11.30 Wrote diary. 11.45 Chapter and private prayer. 12 E; dinner, limit the quantity. 1 E with me, Smyth, Atkinson, Washington, and Watson, read Norris on Religious Conversation, and religious talk of temperance; disputed about eating flesh on the Stationary days, and the Church's authority; ri. 3.30 Walked with Atkinson, Washington, and Watson, religious talk of zeal;

1 See 5 April and 20 April.
2 Robert Nelson, *A Companion for the Festivals and Fasts of the Church of England* (1704), ch. XVI (hereafter referred to as *Fasts* or *Festivals*); see Appendix 3.
3 A sermon on Psalm 37:38 in John Norris's *Practical Discourses Upon the Beatitudes of Our Lord* (1728), vol. II; see Appendix 3.
4 The preacher at this service at St. Mary's was Oliver Battely. Thomas Hearne, *Remarks and Collections of Thomas Hearne,* ed. H. E. Salter (Oxford: Clarendon Press, 1914–21), vol. 11, 329.
5 St. Bartholomew's Hospital was built by Henry I in 1126 or 1128 with the "overplus" from his Beaumont Palace (later Whitefriars and Gloucester Green Workhouse). Located about two kilometers east of Queen's College on Cowley Road near St. Clement's, it had been in effect a city almshouse for some hundred years. As this and subsequent entries seem to verify, the eight brethren by this time had begun frequently to live in the city, finding their stipend of nine pence weekly (plus fuel allowance), established in 1367, inadequate to support them in residence. *V.C.H.,* vol. 4, 473–74. Cf. 16, 20, 21 April.
6 Marginal note ("11 E") indicates that ejaculatory prayers were not forgotten at this hour.

ri. 4 E; read chapter. 4.30 Daily examination. 4.45 Private prayer. 5 E; meditated of reading the Holy Scriptures; ri. 5.30 Public Prayers. 6 Supper; ri; agreed with Stonall for milk. 7 At Ford's with Smith, various and useful talk; ri. 8 Greives and Hervey came; religious talk; ri. 9 Good talk with Ford and Atkinson. 9.15 Came home; private prayer; to bed.

Blessings: composed a prayer for Ford; with Natt; went to Bartlemas House; temperate at dinner; zealous in conversation.

Sins: neglected ejaculatory prayers 5 times; irrecollected 5 times; dissipated at Public Prayers; inattentive at Sermon; not limit quantity at supper; indolent with Smith and Ford.

EASTER TUESDAY, APRIL 16.   4 Rose; dressed. 4.15 Business and virtue; ri; wrote diary. 4.30 Private prayer and chapter. 5 E; began *Plain Directions for Reading the Holy Scriptures.* 6 E; read the directions; ri. 7 E; with Natt, read Nelson for the day,[7] and religious talk of the Sacrament and other means of grace; ri. 8 E; Public Prayers. 9 E and Collect; walked with Atkinson and Washington to Bartlemas House, did not meet with the poor people; religious talk and read Thomas à Kempis; ri. 10 Sermon;[8] Watson, Washington, and Smyth came. 11 E; finished Norris on Religious Conversation. 11.45 I finished *Plain Directions for Reading the Holy Scriptures;* ri. 12 E and private prayers; dinner. 1 E; began writing a letter to Charles Burton; finished it; ri. 3 E and Collect; walked with Smith, good talk (various). 3.45 Went [to] Post-Office.[9] 4 E; read chapter; daily examination; private prayer; meditated. 5 E; necessary business; visited Bolton, Sr. 5.30 Public Prayers. 6 E; supper; ri. 7 E; walked with Smith, religious and useful talk. 8 E; drank and compared

---

[7] See Nelson, *Festivals,* ch. XVII.

[8] The preacher at this service at St. Mary's was Mr. George Fothergill, Fellow of Queen's College (Hearne, *Collections,* vol. 11, 329).

[9] During this period, the post office usually operated out of the home (or inn) of the postmaster, changing with each new appointment (*V.C.H.,* vol. 4, 358). William Underwood, butler of Hart Hall, had been appointed to the post in September 1733 succeeding Caleb Colton who had died. Underwood's address in the Government Post Office records is "Bristol Road." (Post Office General Accounts, Post 58.) Underwood later (1758) operated the King's Head Tavern and Inn on the north side of High Street near Carfax (Herbert Edward Salter, *Oxford City Properties* [Oxford: Oxford Historical Society, 1926], pp. 378f.). There was strong local feeling that the letter office, as it was often called, should be near the city center, Carfax, where Colton had also lived. Hearne, *Collections,* vol. 11, 255, 260.

diaries; ri; came home. 9 E and private prayer; thoughts of the Stations, staggered concerning their obligatoriness; troubled.

Blessings: rose; zealous and active in doing good with Natt; at Bartlemas House and to Bolton, Sr.

Sins: vain and unchaste thoughts; intemperate twice; cold in Public Prayers; irrecollected and inconsiderate.

WEDNESDAY, APRIL 17. 4.15 Rose; dressed. 4.30 Business and virtue. 4.45 Troubled about the Stations, raised scruples and objections against them, perplexed; ri. 5.30 Wrote diary. 5.45 Private prayer. 6 E; went to John Wesley's, good talk of study; he advised me to divide my time between composing, reading the Holy Scriptures and the Fathers;[10] Smith came, religious talk of the Stations; he fully convinced us that they are not obligatory betwixt Easter and Whitsuntide;[11] religious talk of temperance; ri. 7 Public Prayers; Washington, Watson, Smyth, and Atkinson came to me; I satisfied them concerning the Stations; Watson made several objections; ri. 8.15 Went to the Workhouse, and visited the sick woman, read prayers, and promised to return on Sunday and give them some instructions of the Sacrament; ri. 9.30 Came home; Watson came, I satisfied him about the Stations; ri. 10.15 Dressed. 10.30 Wrote diary. 11 E; walked, and with Ford, religious and useful talk, and private prayer with him; ri. 12 E; dinner. 1 Washington, Watson, Smyth, and Atkinson came, read the lives of St. Ignatius, Polycarp, Dionysius[12] Areopagite, Clemens, and Origen. 3 E with them; Ford came, various and useful talk, satisfied Atkinson about the Sacrament at St Mary's. 4 E; daily examination; private prayer; meditated. 5 Bolton, Sr, and Dixon came, religious talk of daily examination and confession, read Law thereupon;[13] ri. 5.30 Public Prayers. 6 E; supper; ri. 6.30 Went to Workhouse; ri. 7.30 Came home; went to Ford's, Smith and Atkinson were there, we began

10 Ingham put this advice into practice almost immediately (see 1 p.m. this afternoon; also 19 April, 5 a.m. and 3.15 p.m.).

11 For the next month, Ingham fasts occasionally on Stationary days (more often than not on Fridays), but does not resume the 3 p.m. breakfast regularly until 5 June.

12 MS. reads "Dionisius." "Clemens" is Clemens Romanus (see monthly summary for April 1734). These lives are contained in William Cave's *Apostolici*, vol. I (1677); see Appendix 3.

13 William Law, *A Serious Call to a Devout and Holy Life* (1729), ch. XXIII, "Of the nature and necessity of examination. How we are to be particular in the confession of all our sins" (see Appendix 3).

Castañiza[14] with ejaculatory and private prayers; ri. 8 Read Castañiza; ri. 8.45 Drank; came home. 9 E and private prayer. 9.15 Meditated; ri.

Blessings: satisfied concerning the Stations by John Wesley, and satisfied Washington, Watson, Atkinson, and Smyth; John Wesley; Workhouse; visited sick woman; Bolton and Dixon came; zealous and active at night; admitted Atkinson to meet with Smith and Ford on Wednesdays, Saturdays, and Sundays.

Sins: unnecessarily troubled about the Stations; irrecollected; cold in Public and private prayer; neglected ejaculatory prayers 5 times; broke resolution 15.

THURSDAY, APRIL 18.   4 Rose; dressed. 4.15 Business and virtue, and wrote diary. 4.30 Private prayer. 4.45 Chapter. 5 E; began transcribing my resolutions; ri. 6 E; transcribed resolutions (ri) into diary. 7 E; Public Prayers. 8 E; bottled ale for Smith. 8.30 Breakfast at Smith's, religious and useful talk; ri. 9 E with Smith; came home; transcribed resolutions into diary; ri. 10 E; at Public Prayers and charity sermon at St Mary's;[15] ri. 11.15 Wrote diary. 11.30 Transcribed resignation; ri. 12 E; dinner; ri. 12.45 With me, Washington, Watson, and Atkinson. 1 E; began Dr Knight's sermon on the Reformation of Manners. 2 E; walked with them, finished the sermon; ri. 3 E with them; came home with Washington, called at his room to borrow Francke's[16] *Manuductio ad S. Scripturam;* looked at his diary; ri. 3.30 Wrote diary. 4 E; transcribed resolutions. 4.30 Private prayer. 4.45 Daily examination. 5 E; Bolton and Dixon came, religious talk of daily examination, and the manner of doing it; against vain thoughts and jesting; a dispute about indifferent actions, none such in fact;[17] Dixon was not satisfied; ri. 5.30 Public Prayers.

---

[14] *Spiritual Combat,* purportedly by Juan de Castañiza, has more recently been ascribed to Lorenzo Scupoli; see Appendix 3. Ingham omits the tilde when spelling Castañiza.

[15] The term "charity sermon" at times simply indicated the topic of the sermon, but more often than not referred to an appeal for support of a charitable cause, such as the charity schools or the S.P.C.K. There is no indication of the specific nature of this occasion, though it might be noted that the vice-chancellor, proctors, and several heads of houses had established in Oxford a charity school (Grey-Coat) for boys in 1708 (*V.C.H.,* vol. 4, 444).

[16] MS. reads "Francks."

[17] This agrees with John Wesley's view at this point (see letter to Samuel Wesley, Jr., 17 November 1731, in *Letters,* I, 322).

6 E; religious talk with Natt of business and virtue. 6.15 Supper, no flesh. 7 E with Smith, compared diaries and religious talk of friends. 8 E; read Gother of intemperance;[18] ri; came home; ri. 9 E; wrote diary. 9.15 Meditated and private prayer; ri.

Blessings: rose; recollected twice; zealous in conversation; convinced Bolton and Dixon of the necessity of daily examination; eat no flesh at supper; active with Smith.

Sins: dissipated thrice; wandering thoughts in Public Prayers; spoke rashly of Corpus Christi College Fellows; did not limit quantity at supper.

FRIDAY, APRIL 19. 4 Rose; dressed. 4.30 Business and virtue; ri. 4.30 Private prayer. 4.45 Chapter. 5 E and private prayer for God's blessing upon my present designs and undertakings of reading the Holy Scriptures and the Fathers, and composing a short theme of the reasonableness of our practises, of rising, fasting, etc. 5.15 Began the scheme; ri. 6 E; Public Prayers; read Watson the questions of daily examination;[19] ri. 7 E; wrote scheme; ri. 8 E; read Country Parson; ri. 8.45 Private prayer. 9 E and Collect; private prayer before beginning my study of the Holy Scriptures, composed a prayer for that purpose. 9.45 Began *Manuductionem ad Lectionem S. Scripturæ*, Augusti Hermanni Franckii, S.Th. Prof. Hallensis; ri. 10 E; read Francke; ri. 11 E; read Country Parson; ri. 11.45 Private prayer. 12 E and private prayer. 12.15 Hall. 12.30 Private prayer. 12.45 Meditated. 1 E; with me, Washington, Watson, and Atkinson, began Horneck's sermon on Suffering for Righteousness;[20] ri. 2 E; finished the sermon. 2.15 Taught them the method of daily examination; ri. 2.45 Religious talk with Watson of writing diary and blessings; ri; disputed. 3 E and private prayer. 3.15 Began Ittigius' *Dissertation de Patribus Apostolicis;*[21] ri. 4 E; meditated of Christ's life. 4.15 Daily examination. 4.30 Private prayer. 4.45 Chapter. 5 E; Bolton and Dixon came, read

18 John Gother, *Instructions for Particular States* (1689), ch. VIII, "Instructions for Christians subject to Intemperance"; see Appendix 3.
19 See 28 January, note 180.
20 See Anthony Horneck, *Several Sermons Upon the Fifth of St. Matthew* (1706), vol. I, Sermon X on verse 10, "Blessed are they which are persecuted for righteousness' sake, for theirs is the Kingdom of Heaven." See Appendix 3.
21 A prefatory article by Thomas Ittig, in *Bibliotheca patrum apostolicorum græco-latina, qua continentur* (1690); see Appendix 3. Ingham subsequently read Clement of Rome's "Epistles to the Corinthians" in this source (see 24 April–8 June).

John Wesley's letter of company,[22] and religious talk thereupon; they consented to read religious book thrice a week, to begin with Goodman's Winter Evening Conferences; ri. 5.30 Public Prayers. 6 Breakfast. 6.15 Wrote diary; General Examination (deadness in Public Prayers; anger and intemperence); ri; confessed; ri. 7 E; with me, Washington, Watson, Smyth, and Atkinson; read Law; ri. 8 E; read Law; ri. 8.45 Smith came to tell me that he was going to London in the morning; they went home. 9 Various talk with Watson. 9.15.

Blessings: recollected 12 times; private prayer before beginning my studies; success with Bolton and Dixon.

SATURDAY, APRIL 20.   5 Rose; dressed; business and virtue. 5.15 Blessings; private prayer and thanksgiving. 5.45 Chapter. 6 E; Public Prayers. 6.45 With John Wesley, religious talk. 7 E; breakfast with John Wesley, religious talk.[23] 7.45 Walked with Atkinson, religious talk. 8 E; wrote diary. 8.15 Meditated. 9 E and Collect; read Francke; ri. 10 E; read Francke; ri. 11 E; walked, thought of making my Speech; ri. 12 E and private prayer; dinner. 12.45 Walked with Atkinson and Washington to Bartlemas House, religious talk.[24] 2 Read Ittigius; ri. 3 E and Collect; at Lecture in Sanderson; ri. 4 E; dressed; chapter; daily examination. 5 E; private prayer; thought. 5.30 Public Prayers. 6 E; walked with Washington, religious talk. 6.15 Supper. 7 E; walked with Washington, read Country Parson; ri. 8 E with Washington, read Horneck's *Fire of the Altar;* ri. 8.45 Atkinson came, told us that Smyth would not go to the Sacrament,[25] religious talk thereupon; zealously exhorted them to persevere and pray for him and Ford, now elected Scholar of Corpus Christi

---

[22]   This may be the "Method for Acquaintance," which Wesley wrote in November 1732 (OD III, 30; cf. *Letters,* I, 340). Wesley's general rule was to seek out serious acquaintances and avoid trifling or lukewarm company. In any case, he thought it best not to spend much time *at once* in any company, and to guard especially against the danger of loving company more than God (OD I, 35; see *The Journal of the Rev. John Wesley,* ed. Nehemiah Curnock [London: Epworth Press, 1916], vol. 2, 116; and letter from Wesley to Ann Bolton, 25 August 1771).

[23]   Wesley's diary entry reads: "7 Ingham, tea, talk of Public Prayers. 7.45. . . ." OD IV, 134.

[24]   Marginal note ("1 E") indicates ejaculatory prayers on the hour.

[25]   Ingham did prevail upon Smyth to attend the following day (see 21 April, summary of blessings), as well as the following Tuesday, the beginning of term (see 23 April).

College; ri. 9 E; came home; prayed for all my friends, especially Smyth and Ford; private prayer; went to bed recollected.

Blessings: recollected 9 times; attentive in private prayer; zealous and active to do good; exhorted Atkinson and Washington; prayed for Ford and Smyth.

Sins: rose not; inattentive at Public Prayers; proud and vain thoughts; broke resolution 8 four times.

SUNDAY, APRIL 21.   4 Rose; E; dressed; business and virtue.[26] 4.45 Private prayer. 5 E; wrote diary. 5.15 Meditated and private prayer for the Sacrament. 6 E; dressed; went to Smyth's, religious talk of the Sacrament; ri. 6.45 Meditated. 7 E; Dixon and Bolton came, read Norris' sermon on 'The Importance of a Religious Life', religious talk; ri. 8 E; Public Prayers. 9 Smyth came, read meditations, and prayer for the Sacrament; ri. 9.30 Walked with Smyth and Watson to the Castle; Atkinson and Washington went before; Public Prayers. 10 Public Prayers and Sermon.[27]   11 Sermon and Sacrament; thanksgiving for Smyth. 12 E and Collect; dinner; ri. 1 E; walked with Atkinson, left him at the Workhouse and went to the poor people in St Thomas', began *The Christian Monitor*;[28] ri. 1.45 Came [back] with Atkinson. 2 E; Sermon. 2.45 Walked with Washington and Atkinson to Bartlemas House,[29] could not find the poor people, resolved to go no more;[30] religious and useful talk; came home. 4 E; read chapter; meditated; daily examination. 5 E; private prayer and meditated. 5.30 Public Prayers. 6 E; supper, no flesh. 7 E; walked with Smyth, religious talk. 7.30 Walked with Atkinson, religious talk of Ford, he would scarcely speak to Atkinson, did not receive the Sacrament, neither was determined to receive it on Tuesday. 7.45 Private prayer for Ford, and meditated. 8 E; with me, Watson, read sermon of Norris; ri. 9 Private prayer; ri.

[26]   The H column of recollection resumes at this point and continues through 9 May (see 19 March, note 77). The entries in R column change from the former style; see Appendix 1 (C) and plate 14.
[27]   In going to the Castle, Ingham missed the annual repetition of the Easter sermons at St. Mary's, all of which he had heard the previous week (see Hearne, *Collections,* vol. 11, 329).
[28]   The Hamel in St. Thomas's seems to be the location of these poor people whom Ingham visited every week for the next two months. See 24 April, note 48.
[29]   Marginal note ("3 E and Collect") indicates that prayers were not neglected on the hour.
[30]   See 15 April, note 5.

Blessings: rose; fervent in private prayer twice; success with Smyth and Watson, they both went to the Castle; Sacrament; temperate; no flesh; concerned for Ford.

Sins: broke resolution 8 eight times; cold in Public Prayers; broke resolution 4 twice, resolution 13 twice.

MONDAY, APRIL 22.   5 Rose;[31] dressed; wrote diary; chapter; private prayer. 6 E; read Country Parson; ri; Public Prayers. 7 E; wrote scheme. 7.30 Read Country Parson; ri. 8 Atkinson came, could not meet with Ford, good talk about a method of study; ri. 8.30 Private prayer for myself and friends, Ford; ri. 9 E and Collect; read Francke; ri. 10 E; read Francke; ri. 11 E; went to Workhouse, taught children and read family prayer; ri; came home. 12 E and private prayer. 12.15 Dinner, no flesh; with me, Washington, Watson, and Atkinson. 1 E; read Horneck's eleventh sermon;[32] ri. 1.45 Walked with Watson and Washington, religious talk. 2 E. 2.15 Finished Ittigius' *Dissertation de Patribus Apostolicis.*[33] 3.30 Read Law of the Spirit of the World;[34] ri. 4 E; read Law. 4.15 Private prayer. 4.30 Chapter. 4.45 Daily examination. 5 E; private prayer; meditated. 5.30 Public Prayers. 6 E; walked with Washington, religious talk. 6.15 Supper, no flesh; went to Hervey's. 7 E; at Hervey's, religious talk; Robson and Greives came. 8 Religious talk; ri. 9 Came home. 9.15 Private prayer.

Blessings: fasted and prayed for Ford, myself, and Smyth; went to the Workhouse; eat no flesh; zealous in conversation.

Sins: sloth; broke resolution 8 five times.

TUESDAY, APRIL 23.   5 Rose; dressed; wrote diary; business and virtue; private prayer. 6 E; prayer for the Sacrament; wrote diary. 6.30 Public Prayers. 7 E with Atkinson, he told me that Ford had forbid him his room, etc. 7.15 Went to Broughton, not at home; with John Wesley, religious talk of Ford's fall, he said it was for his good and ours, bid me

---

[31]   Marginal note: "rose not" [at 4].
[32]   See Horneck, *Several Sermons,* vol. I, Sermon XI on Matt. 5:11, "Blessed are you when men shall revile you and persecute you and say all manner of evil against you falsely for my sake."
[33]   Marginal note ("3 E") indicates ejaculatory prayers at 3.
[34]   See *Serious Call,* ch. XVII, "Shewing how difficult the practice of humility is made, by the general spirit and temper of the world. How Christianity requireth us to live contrary to the world."

be of good cheer;[35] ri; came home. 8 Atkinson came, religious talk of Smyth and Brownsword, they both consented to go to the Sacrament. 8.30 Watson came, religious talk of Ford and the Sacrament; ri. 9 E and Collect and prayer for the Sacrament and for Ford, with Watson; ri. 9.30 Went to borrow a book, got one at Peisley's;[36] ri. 9.45 Public Prayers, Sermon, and Sacrament at St Mary's, Washington, Smyth, Atkinson, and Brownsword, several of other houses; Robson not there;[37] I was very bold and not at all concerned at the crowds of gazers;[38] ri. 11.15 Walked with Broughton, religious talk of Ford's fall, etc, and of ourselves; confessed our faults; he advised me to leap out of bed at the first stroke of the larum, and to fall on my knees, and pray for purity;[39] (returned the book). 12 Dinner. 12.45 Atkinson, Washington, Watson, and Smyth came, religious talk. 1 E; began Norris' sermon on the Love of God;[40] ri. 2 E with them;

[35] There is a four-month gap in Wesley's daily diary following 21 April; the monthly summaries in the back of OD IV are the only diary materials we have for this period from Wesley's pen. Ingham's diary thus becomes the primary source for details of Methodist life at Oxford during the next two months.

[36] MS. reads " "Piesley's." Peisley was a bookseller located just east of Queen's College on High Street at the northeast corner of the East Gate. See Salter, *Oxford City Properties*, p. 42 (1734 listing); cf. map in Herbert Edward Salter, *A Cartulary of the Hospital of St John the Baptist* (Oxford: Oxford Historical Society, 1914), vol. 1, plate I, where the name is spelled "Beisley." The Anthony Peisley, bookseller, given *"privilegiatus"* status by the university in 1724, may have been either this person or his father (deceased by 1727; see Hearne, *Collections*, vol. 9, 266; cf. Joseph Foster, *Alumni Oxonienses* [London: Joseph Foster, 1887]).

[37] Wesley also notes this circumstance in his diary: "He missed Sacrament at St Mary's. *Ex illo fluere!*" (OD IV [Summaries], 20). See also 30 May, note 171. This was the beginning of Easter term (see 9 October, note 50).

[38] George Whitefield recalled in *A Short Account of God's Dealings with the Reverend Mr. Whitefield* (London: W. Strahan, 1740), "I was strongly pressed to follow [the Methodists'] good example when I saw them go through a ridiculing crowd to receive the Holy Eucharist at St Mary's" (p. 26). He goes on to explain that, by his own attendance at these occasions, he was set up as a mark for ridicule, since "by this they knew that I was commenced Methodist; for though there is a Sacrament at the beginning of every term, at which all, especially the seniors, are, by statute, obliged to be present; yet so dreadfully has that once faithful city played the harlot, that very few Masters and no undergraduates (but the Methodists) attend upon it" (p. 33). Cf. 9 October, note 50.

[39] See 24 April, summary of blessings, where Ingham writes "on my knees" in place of the symbol =.

[40] "The Measure of Divine Love, with the Natural and Moral Grounds upon which it Stands," a sermon on Matt. 22:37, in *Practical Discourses*, vol. III.

religious talk with Atkinson; ri. 2.30 Wrote diary. 3 E and Collect; finished the preface to Francke;[41] ri. 3.30 Read Country Parson; ri. 4 E; thought of Ford; ri. 4.45 Daily examination. 5 E; private prayer and thanksgiving for the sacrament. 5.30 Public Prayers. 6 E; supper, no flesh. 7 E; Brownsword came, read Norris' sermon of 'The Importance of a Religious Life', and Law upon daily examination; ri. 8 E; he consented to private prayer and daily examination; I promised to call him at 5,[42] and he to set apart that hour morning and afternoon for devotion;[43] he read me some essays and a poem on the affections of his own; good talk of his mistress;[44] recommended Law, Nelson, and Country Parson. 9.15 Wrote diary. 9.30 Private prayer. 9.45.

Blessings: John Wesley; Broughton; Sacrament; easy about Ford, Smyth, and Brownsword.

WEDNESDAY, APRIL 24.   4 Rose; dressed; business and virtue; private prayer; chapter. 5 E; called Brownsword, and necessary business. 5.15 Wrote scheme. 6 E; Public Prayers. 7 E; read Country Parson (ri) and private prayer for resignation; went to the Workhouse,[45] taught and catechized the children and read family prayers; breakfast. 9 E and Collect; read Francke; ri. 10 E; read Francke; ri. 11 E; Disputations; ri. 11.45 Chapter. 12 E and private prayer. 12.30 Dinner; Washington, Watson, Smyth, and Atkinson came. 1 E; finished Norris' sermon of the Love of God; ri. 2 Walked with Washington, religious talk and read Thomas à Kempis. 3 At Broughton's; ri. 3.30 Wrote diary; began St Clement's first Epistle to the Corinthians;[46] ri. 3.45 Greives came, religious talk of Ford, Hervey; he asked me to go to Gambold's with him, fixed Friday;[47] ri. 5 E; daily examination; private prayer. 5.30 Public Prayers. 6 E; supper on bread and milk. 6.15 Went to Workhouse, taught the children and read family prayers, afterward went and read *The Christian Monitor* in the Hamel;[48] ri. 7.30 Came home; at Washington's

---

[41]   The preface to the *Manuductio ad lectionem Scripturæ Sacræ* (1706) is entitled *De impedimentis studii theologici;* see Appendix 3.

[42]   See 21 November, note 102.

[43]   Cf. resolution on pp. 119, 167.

[44]   The term as used here need not imply anything more than "sweetheart" (see *O.E.D.,* s.v. "Mistress"). Cf. 13 April, note 196.

[45]   Marginal note ("8 E") indicates ejaculatory prayers on the hour. See plate 14.

[46]   See 19 April, note 21.

[47]   These plans were apparently altered (see 25 April at 7 p.m., and 30 April).

[48]   A street west of the Castle, about halfway to St. Thomas's church, leading

with Watson, Smyth, and Atkinson, read Law. 8 E; read Law; ri; and Ken on Hell.[49] 9 E; wrote diary. 9.15 Private prayer.

Blessings: rose; kept resolution 9; at the Workhouse and Hamel; I began to leap out of bed at the first ringing of the larum, and falling on my knees, pray for purity, after Broughton's custom.

Sins: vain and unchaste thoughts; intemperate at dinner; broke resolution 8 five times; cold in Public and private prayer. N.B. The headache caused by eating too much at dinner.

Frena gulam et omnem carnis concupiscentiam facilius frenabis.[50]

THURSDAY, APRIL 25. 4 Rose; dressed. 4.15 Business and virtue. 4.30 Private prayer and thanksgiving; chapter. 5 E; called Brownsword, Washington, and Smyth; wrote diary; read Country Parson and meditated. 6 E; read Country Parson; ri. 7 E; dressed. 7.30 Walked with Watson, read Country Parson; ri. 8 E; Public Prayers. 8.45 Breakfast; with me, Washington, Watson, Atkinson, and Smyth. 9 E and Collect; read Norris' sermon on 'Fear of Death'.[51] 10 E; walked with Smyth and Watson, religious talk of simplicity and writing diaries, Smyth not willing to keep one. 10.30 Sermon.[52] 11 Visited Bucher,[53] religious talk. 11.45 Chapter. 12 E and private prayer; dinner; with me, Washington, Watson, Smyth, and Atkinson. 1 E; read Norris on Vanity.[54] 1.45 Walked

---

to the ruins of Osney Abbey. David Loggan's map of Oxford (1675) shows it as a rather broad, though short, thoroughfare lined with small houses and marked by a cross toward the north end. The derivation of "Hamel" is unclear, though it seems this area in medieval times was a hamlet inhabited by workmen associated with the abbey. See Thomas W. Squires, *In West Oxford* (London: A. R. Mowbray, 1928). Ingham's references to the Hamel do not indicate precisely where he carried on his reading program there.

49 See "Of the Sufferings of Hell" in Thomas Ken's *The Retired Christian Exercised in Divine Thoughts and Heavenly Meditations for the Closet* (1737), in Appendix 3.

50 "Bridle the appetite [i.e. gluttony] and you will more easily bridle all fleshly desire." Cf. Charles Dickens, *Nicholas Nickleby* (1838–39), "Subdue your appetites, my dears, and you've conquered human nature" (ch. 5), and James 3:2.

51 "An Effectual Remedy against the Fear of Death" (on Heb. 2:15), in *Practical Discourses,* vol. IV; also published separately in 1733 with the sermon on vanity (see 1 p.m.).

52 This day was the festival of St. Mark the Evangelist (see Nelson, *Festivals,* ch. XVIII). The statutes designated Magdalen College as the location of this service (*Statutes,* XVI.5).

53 Probably Mark Bewsher of Queen's; cf. 11 March.

54 "The Successive Vanity of Human Life," a sermon on Eccles. 11:8, in

with them, good talk; Smyth told us that it was known in College that Ford was (as they called it) revolted.[55] 2.30 Read Clemens Romanus;[56] ri. 3 E and Collect; read Clemens Romanus; ri. 4 E; went to Broughton's, not at home. 4.30 Read chapter; Hervey came, religious talk of going to another Workhouse by Gloucester Green;[57] of an exacter diary, etc; I appointed to go with him on Saturday at 9; of Robson and ourselves; ri. 5.30 Public Prayers. 6 E; daily examination. 6.15 Supper. 7 E; went to Broughton's, not at home; with Greives, talk of going to Gambold's.[58] 7.15 Called at Smith's, not at home; with Charles Wesley, religious talk of Ford, read Rodriguez, satisfied; ri. 8 E; came home. 8.15 Wrote diary; read Rodriguez, 35th chapter. 9 E; private prayer. 9.30.

Blessings: rose; Hervey; Charles Wesley; religious talk with Washington, Watson, Smyth, and Atkinson.

Sins: proud, vain, and unchaste thoughts; malicious thoughts against Natt;[59] cold in Public Prayers.

FRIDAY, APRIL 26. 4 Rose; dressed; business and virtue. 4.45 Private prayer. 5 E; meditated; ri. 6 E; Public Prayers. 7 E; at Broughton's, religious talk of Ford. 7.30 Ford came, he told us the story of his fall, his father and mother the chief causes; religious talk of his great sin, he seemed insensible of it, objected against many things; we exhorted him to go to the Sacrament at Christ Church,[60] he did not consent; ri. 9 He left us; religious talk of him with Broughton, agreed to fast the remaining part of the day and pray for him; ri. 9.30 With Charles Wesley, told him; he thought he would fall lower. 9.45 Came home; thoughts thereupon; told Watson, desiring him to pray for Ford; ri. 10 E, and private prayer for Ford. 10.15 Atkinson came, told him. 11 E; meditated. 12 E and collect. 12.15 Hall. 12.30 Atkinson came, private prayer for Ford; ri. 1 E; with me, Atkinson, Washington, Watson, read sermon [of] Horneck. 1.45 Religious talk with Atkinson of Smyth and Ford; ri. 2 E; read Clemens Romanus; ri. 3 E and Collect; read Clemens Romanus; ri.

Practical Discourses, vol. IV; also published separately in 1733 with the "Fear of Death."

55 Marginal note ("2 E") indicates ejaculatory prayers on the hour.

56 See 19 April, note 21.

57 See 27 April, note 62.

58 Cf. 24 April and 30 April.

59 Marginal note at 12–1 p.m. reads: "broke resolution 13 against Natt." See resolutions on p. 120.

60 Sunday mornings (see 7 October, note 47).

4 E; read chapter; daily examination; private prayer and for Ford; ri. 5 E; read Country Parson; ri. 5.30 Public Prayers. 6 E; Declamation; supper. 6.30 General Examination (indifferent in Public Prayers, and proud, vain, and unchaste thoughts). 6.45 Ford came, religious talk, he was determined to go to the Sacrament at Christ Church, and to meet with us on Wednesdays, Saturdays, and Sundays; and Fridays.[61] 7 With me, Washington, Watson, Smyth, Ford, and Atkinson, E, read Law. 8 E; read Law. 9 E; wrote diary; private prayer for Ford and myself. 9.30.

Blessings: rose; at Broughton's; Ford returned; private prayer for Ford and fasted; zealous with Washington, Watson, Smyth, Ford, and Atkinson; Ford consented to go to the Sacrament at Christ Church.

Sins: broke resolution 8 four times; indifferent in Public and private prayer.

SATURDAY, APRIL 27. 4 Rose; dressed. 4.15 Business and virtue. 4.30 Thanksgiving and private prayer. 5 E; read chapter. 5.30 Meditated. 5.45 Went to Broughton's to talk of Ford; ri. 6 E; walked. 6.15 Public Prayers. 7 E; wrote diary; composed a Theme; ri. 8 E; breakfast at Natt's with Washington, Watson, and Atkinson, religious and useful talk. 9 E; walked with Hervey to a Workhouse on Gloucester Green, set the Master[62] upon reading family prayers morning and evening; ri. 9.30 Walked; met with Gambold, good talk. 10.15 Dressed. 10.30 Transcribed Theme. 11 E; read Country Parson, and private prayer. 12 E and Collect; dinner; Hall. 1 E; with me, Smyth, Washington, Watson, read sermon of Horneck; ri. 1.45 Went to Smith's. 2 E; walked with Smith, religious and useful talk of our friends. 3 E and Collect; at Lecture; ri. 4.15 Walked with Natt, good talk. 4.45 Read chapter. 5 E; daily examination; private prayer. 5.30 Public Prayers. 6 E; religious talk with Brownsword; supper. 7 E; at Smith's with Atkinson and Ford, read Castañiza. 8 E; read Castañiza and religious talk. 9 E; walked with Ford to Corpus Christi College and drank; ri. 9.15 Came home; private prayer. 9.30.

Blessings: rose; recollected 5 times; fervent once in private prayer; zealous for Ford; went with Hervey to do good; met with Gambold; religious talk with Brownsword; Ford met with us.

---

61 This again gave the Wednesday-Saturday-Sunday group four regular participants and the Friday group six.

62 This was James Piggot, a thread-maker who, between 1726 and 1741, employed by contract the poor of at least seven parishes in this workhouse, located in part of the Whitefriars buildings (formerly the Beaumont Palace built by Henry I) on Gloucester Green (V.C.H., vol. 4, 346); cf. 15 April, note 5.

Sins: broke resolution 8 thrice; dissipated in Public Prayers; vain thoughts.

SUNDAY, APRIL 28.   4 Rose; dressed; wrote diary. 4.30 Thanksgiving and private prayer; read chapter. 5 E; General Examination; vain and unchaste thoughts;[63] ri. 6 E; called Brownsword; read Ellis; Ford came, lent him Patrick's *Devout Christian;* read Ellis and meditated; ri. 7 E; went to Charles Wesley's, good talk. 7.30 Christ Church, Public Prayers. 8 E; Public Prayers and Sacrament. 8.45 With Charles Wesley, religious talk of Ford, Smith, etc; ri; came home. 9.30 Read Meditations; and [had] thoughts of friends; ri. 10 E. 10.15 Sermon. 11.15 Meditated. 12 E; dinner. 1 E; walked with Smith and Atkinson to the Workhouse and went to the Hamel, read *Christian Monitor;* ri. 2 E; Sermon. 3 E and Collect; at Ford's, taught him the exacter diary, and religious talk. 4 E; walked. 4.30 Wrote diary. 4.45 Read chapter. 5 E; daily examination; private prayer. 5.30 Public Prayers; prayer, psalm, lessons, collects.[64] 6 E; walked with Natt, religious and useful talk; supper. 7 E; with me, Ford, Atkinson, and Smith, religious talk. 7.30 Read Castañiza's *Spiritual Combat;* ri; drank. 9 E; wrote diary. 9.15 Private prayer. 9.30.

Blessings: rose, Sacrament at Christ Church, Ford there; with Charles Wesley; in the Hamel; taught Ford the exacter diary.

Sins: very vain and unchaste thoughts; cold in Public and private prayer; irrecollected and inactive.

MONDAY, APRIL 29.   4 Rose; dressed; read chapter. 4.45 Private prayer. 5 E; read Country Parson and meditated; ri. 6 E; Public Prayers, prayer, psalm, lessons, collects. 7 E; read Francke; ri. 8 Read Francke; ri. 9 E and Collect; necessary business at Thompson's, tea; ri. 10 E; began to compose a Speech for my degree;[65] ri. 12 E and private prayer; dinner.

---

[63] Marginal note reads: "casting down imaginations."

[64] Ingham here begins to list the parts of the service, indicating by symbol his degree of attention for each part (attentive at prayer, attentive at psalms, indifferent at lessons, cold at collects). In only exceptional cases will the degrees of attention be noted in this edition. Some minor variance in the list, such as the occasional inclusion of the litany and communion, would seem to be indicative of variety in the services themselves.

[65] Ingham wrote this speech in order "to be freed from Exercises" (summary for May 1734). He gave the speech in the Hall on 3 May. Some degree requirements could be waived (see 13 and 14 June), but this speech (declamation?) and the three lectures he composed and read in June (see 30 May and note 168) seem to have been substituted for the required examination under a regent

12.45 With me, Washington, Watson, read Horneck's sermon on Mourning;[66] ri. 1.30 Walked with Smith, good talk. 2 E; walked with Smith, good talk. 3 With Smith, good talk (various). 4 E; walked. 4.45 Read chapter. 5 E; daily examination and private prayer. 5.30 Public Prayers; prayer, psalm, collects. 6 E; walked with Washington, religious talk. 6.15 Supper. 7 E; with Greives, Hervey, Smith, Robson, and Ford, religious talk of the Workhouse. 8 I talked against poets and endeavoured to persuade Robson to go to the Sacrament; ri. 9 Came home. 9.15 Private prayer. 9.30.

Blessings: rose; prevailed with Robson to meet with us at night; recollected thrice; prevailed with Smith to discover to me his love.

Sins: indifferent in Public and private prayer; irrecollected at dinner; vain thoughts.

TUESDAY, APRIL 30. 4 Rose; dressed. 4.15 Wrote diary. 4.30 Business and virtue; private prayer. 5 E; read Country Parson; ri. 6 E; Public Prayers. 6.45 With Charles Wesley, good talk; satisfied. 7.15 Called at Smith's to borrow his watch. 7.30 Went to Greives', breakfast. 7.45 Set forward with Greives to Gambold's, religious talk of the advantage of religious conversation; recommended a diary, he refused; religious talk of Robson and other friends; ri. 10 At Gambold's, religious talk. 10.30 In the church at a wedding;[67] ri. 10.45 Tea with him and Greives, religious talk of temperance, useful to consider before eating, what we are to do next, and also how it tends to God's glory; ri. 11.30 Walked with Greives and Gambold, religious talk of friends, and how to manage them, first to find their temper, and get into their good opinion, and apply to God in prayer, secondly to take occasion from providential accidents. 1 Dinner, religious talk. 1.30 Gambold read family prayers with us and the old woman; ri. 1.45 Came home to Oxford with Gambold and Greives, religious talk of reading the Holy Scriptures; Gambold delineated a sermon which he designed to preach before Lady Harcourt;[68] religious talk of morality and Christianity. 4 At Greives' for my gown and cap; afterward

---

master (*Statutes*, IX.2), which Ingham seems not to have done. Cf. *Statutes*, VI.2.2, which lists two declamations and six lectures as requirements for the master of arts degree.

66 See *Several Sermons*, vol. I, Sermon IV on Matt. 5:4, "Blessed are they that mourn, for they shall be comforted."

67 See 1 April, note 138.

68 MS. reads "Hartcourt."

walked with Gambold to Broughton's and Kebblewell's, religious talk. 4.30 Came home; wrote diary. 5 E; daily examination; private prayer. 5.30 Public Prayers, prayer, psalm, collects. 6 E; supper. 7 E; with Smith and Price,[69] read Norris' 'Importance of a Religious Life'; ri. 8 Good talk (various) with me. 8.45 Drank. 9.15 Came home; private prayer. 9.30.

Blessings: rose; religious talk with Greives and Gambold; Price at Smith's.

Sins: cold in Public and private prayer; unchaste thoughts.

WEDNESDAY, MAY 1.   4 Rose; dressed. 4.15 Wrote diary; business and virtue. 4.45 Private prayer. 5 E and wrote diary. 5.15 Read Country Parson; ri. 6 E; finished the Country Parson; ri. 6.15 Dressed. 6.30 With Charles Wesley, good talk; came home. 7 E; Hervey came, began teaching him the exacter diary; ri. 8 E; Public Prayers, prayer, psalm, lessons, litany, collects. 9 E and Collect; at the Workhouse; ri. 9.45 Dressed. 10 E; Sermon.[70] 10.45 Watson with me. 11 Read Letter on Love,[71] and good talk; ri. 12 E and Collect; dinner. 12.45 With me, Washington, Watson, Smyth, and Atkinson,[72] read Horneck on Mourning;[73] ri. 2 E; got my Speech; ri. 2.45 Went to Smith's,[74] good talk; at Charles Wesley's with him and Carter, began Sales' *Introduction to a Devout Life.* 3.30 Walked with Smith, good talk. 3.45 Went to Workhouse. 4 Taught the children and read family prayers; ri; came home; wrote diary. 5 E; daily examination; meditated. 5.30 Public Prayers, prayer, psalm, lessons, collects. 6 E; supper. 6.45 Visited Bucher;[75] ri. 7 E and private prayer; at Atkinson's with Smith, read Castañiza. 8 E; read Nelson for the day,[76] and Castañiza; ri. 9 E; came home; wrote diary. 9.15 Private prayer. 9.30.

[69] James Price had just matriculated at Christ Church on 2 April; he received the B.A. degree in 1737.

[70] This day was the festival of St. Philip and St. James the Less (see Nelson, *Festivals,* ch. XIX). The university statutes designated Merton College as the location of this service (*Statutes,* XVI.5).

[71] Possibly John Norris, *Letters Concerning the Love of God* (1695); see Appendix 3.

[72] Marginal note ("1 E") indicates ejaculatory prayers on the hour.

[73] See *Several Sermons,* vol. I, Sermon IV.

[74] Marginal note ("3 E") indicates ejaculatory prayers on the hour.

[75] Probably Mark Bewsher; cf. 11 March.

[76] See Nelson, *Festivals,* ch. XIX.

Blessings: rose; taught Hervey an exacter diary; recollected twice; serious six times;[77] zealous with Washington, Watson, Smyth, and Atkinson; at Workhouse twice.

Sins: cold in Public and private prayer; unchaste thoughts; intemperate.

THURSDAY, MAY 2. 4 Rose; dressed. 4.15 Read chapter. 4.45 Private prayer. 5 E; got my Speech; ri. 6 Thoughts of making my Lectures.[78] 6.30 Wrote the Ejaculatory prayers for every hour into Hervey's diary,[79] and Collects, and Resolutions;[80] ri. 7 E; Public Prayers, psalm, lessons, collects. 7.45 Wrote Resolutions for Hervey. 8.15 Breakfast with Hervey, good talk. 8.45 Wrote his diary the new way; ri. 10.15 Came home; translated Kennet. 10.45 Wrote diary. 11 E; Hall. 11.30 Walked with Washington and Watson, religious talk. 11.45 Read Sales. 12 E and private prayer; dinner. 12.45 Washington and Watson came, good talk. 1 Ford came, composed a Theme for him; ri. 2 E; transcribed my Speech; ri. 3 E and Collect; got Speech. 4 E; walked. 4.45 Read chapter. 5 Thought. 5.30 Public Prayers. 6 E; daily examination. 6.15 Supper. 6.45 Private prayers. 7 E; walked with Smith, various and useful talk. 8 E; drank with Smith, and compared diaries; ri. 9 E; came home; private prayer. 9.30.

Blessings: rose; taught Hervey the exacter diary; no flesh at supper.

Sins: cold and dissipated in Public Prayers; unchaste thoughts; dull by eating two apples in the afternoon.

FRIDAY, MAY 3. 4 Rose; to bed. 4.15 Necessary business. 4.45 Private prayer. 5 E; wrote diary. 5.15 Composed a Theme for Ford; ri. 6 E; Public Prayers. 7 E; went to Ford's, breakfast and good talk; came home. 8 With Washington, read Horneck's *Letter of the Primitive Christians;*[81] ri. 9 E and private prayer with Washington; came home. 9.15 Necessary business. 9.45 Read Francke; ri. 10 E; read Francke; ri; Atkinson came, good talk. 11 E with Atkinson; necessary business. 11.30 Got Speech. 11.45 Chapter. 12 E and private prayer. 12.15 Hall. 12.45 I spoke my

[77] Actually seven times according to his hourly entries in the H column.
[78] Three lectures for his degree; see 30 May, note 168.
[79] See p. 119, note 224.
[80] For collects, see pp. 55–59; for resolutions, pp. 119–20.
[81] *The Happy Ascetick . . . to which is Added a Letter . . . concerning the Holy Lives of the Primitive Christians;* see Horneck in Appendix 3.

Speech.[82] 1 E, with me, Washington, Watson, read Norris on 'Worldly and Divine Wisdom';[83] ri. 2 Meditated on Heaven. 2.45 At Ford's, see their Library;[84] ri. 3 E and Collect; read Sales. 3.30 General Examination.[85] 5 E; daily examination; private prayer. 5.30 Public Prayers, prayer, psalm, lessons, collects. 6 E; Hall and supper (General Examination: vain and unchaste thoughts, cold in Public and private prayer); wrote resolutions for the following week. 7 E; with me, Washington, Watson, Smyth, read Law. 8 E; Ford came, read Law. 8.45 Atkinson came, read Law; ri. 9 Religious talk with Ford by myself; ri. 9.15 Wrote diary and private prayer.

Blessings: composed a Theme for Ford; recollected twice; fervent in private prayer; attentive in Public Prayers once; temperate at supper; zealous by reading Horneck; with me, Washington, Watson, Smyth, Atkinson, and Ford; wrote resolutions for temperance.[86]

Sins: rose and went to bed again; broke resolution 8 nine times; cold in Public Prayers.

If I rise in Health and go to bed again, for the next week, I'll sconce myself 1 pence.

SATURDAY, MAY 4.   4 Rose; E; dressed; thanksgiving and private prayer; meditated on the blessings of the past week, and thanksgiving. 5 E; began to draw up a scheme of the blessings of my whole life; ri. 6 E; Public Prayers, prayer, psalm, lessons, collects. 7 E; breakfast at Hervey's, wrote his diary; ri. 8 E; went to Ford's, tea with him, Atkinson and Washington, religious and useful talk. 9 E and Collect; came home; necessary business. 9.30 Read Brownsword's Argument. 10 E; read over Brownsword's Arguments for Generals.[87] 11 E; with Hervey, walked with [him]

---

[82] See 29 April, note 65. Ingham delivered his speech in the Hall, where he had just forgone the noon meal in order to observe the Friday fast. Cf. 29 May at 12:15 p.m. See plate 9.

[83] A sermon on Luke 16:8, in *Practical Discourses,* vol. II.

[84] Ford was a scholar at Corpus Christi College; the library is of interest both for its attractiveness and its collections.

[85] Marginal note ("4 E") indicates ejaculatory prayer on the hour.

[86] In the margin is the symbol for "good resolutions."

[87] "Generals" were exercises required for the B.A. degree, consisting of two-hour disputations on three questions or problems in grammar or logic (sophisms), once as respondent and once likewise as opponent to a respondent his senior, under the moderatorship of a general sophist or bachelor of arts. Two years' standing in the university was prerequisite and the Generals must have been completed three terms before supplicating for the degree. The respondent posted

to Gloucester Green Workhouse, religious talk with the Master,[88] questioned the children, and religious talk with two old people; ri. 12 E; dinner. 12.45 With me, Washington, Watson, read sermon of Horneck;[89] ri. 1.45 Went to Charles Wesley's. 2 E; walked with Charles Wesley to the Castle, heard part of a sermon and family prayers read; came home with him; ri. 3 E and Collect; walked. 3.30 Met with Smith, various and useful talk. 4 Brownsword came, necessary talk. 4.15 Read chapter. 4.45 Daily examination. 5 Private prayer; thought; Public Prayers, prayer, psalm, lessons, collects. 6 Walked with Washington, religious talk. 6.15 Hall. 6.30 Supper at Broughton's, heard Charles Wesley read his diary, and Salmon, and Broughton; religious talk with Broughton of Ford; ri. 7.15 At Atkinson's with Smith, read Castañiza. 8 E; read Castañiza and religious talk. 9 E; came home and went to Washington's with Atkinson, private prayer, began Horneck's *Best Exercise* (we three agreed to watch every Saturday night for May, to begin every hour with ejaculatory prayer and private prayer, and then read Horneck). 10 E and private prayer. 10.15 Read Horneck's *Best Exercise*. 11.15 Private prayer for several virtues; ri. 11.45 Came home; wrote diary [summary].[90]

Blessings: rose, zealous and fervent in private prayer; began a scheme of blessings for my whole life; at Gloucester Green Workhouse with Hervey; went to the Castle with Charles Wesley; saw[91] Broughton, Charles Wesley, and Salmon compare diaries; began watching every Saturday night with Washington and Atkinson.

SUNDAY, MAY 5. 5 Rose; dressed. 5.30 Thanksgiving; private prayer and [prayer] for the Sacrament. 6 E; meditated on God's mercies and perfections; ri. 7 E; walked with Washington, Watson, Atkinson, and Smyth to Christ Church. 7.30 Public Prayers. 8.30 Sacrament; came home; all glad. 9 E and Collect; thanksgiving and psalm. 9.30 Walked with Watson and Atkinson, religious talk; Sermon; ri. 11 Walked with

---

his question a week ahead and at the conclusion was created a general (or senior) sophist. These exercises were formerly called "Variations," or "Disputations in the Parvise," and along with "Answering under Bachelor twice" were the primary exercises for the degree. *Statutes,* VI.1.3–5; cf. John Ayliffe, *The Antient and Present State of the University of Oxford* (London: E. Curll, 1714), II, 117f.

88 James Piggot.

89 Marginal note ("1 E") indicates ejaculatory prayers on the hour.

90 See summary for March 1734, which he had started to "cast up" on 2 April. Cf. 6 May where he starts April summary.

91 MS. reads "see."

Hervey and Walker of Brasenose College,[92] religious talk of company and rising; ri. 12 E and Collect; dinner; walked with Atkinson and Ford[93] to the Workhouse; I went to [the] Hamel, read *The Christian Monitor;* ri. 2 E; Sermon; went to Charles Wesley's with Smith and Carter. 3 Read Sales; ri; walked with Atkinson and Ford, religious talk of the danger of going home and neglecting the means of grace; Ford went home; religious talk with Atkinson of Ford; Atkinson went home; I walked and met with Brownsword, religious talk of reading Nelson, daily examination, rising, and going to the Sacrament at Christ Church. 4.45 Came home; wrote diary. 5 E; daily examination; Public Prayers. 5.45 Private prayer. 6 E; supper, eat flesh; ri. 6.45 Walked with Atkinson, good talk. 7 With me, Atkinson, Smith, and Ford, read Castañiza. 8 E; read Castañiza; taught Ford about inconstancy and indolence and pride and several of his faults; ri. 9 E; wrote diary. 9.15 Private prayer; to bed.

Blessings: rose at 5; recollected 4 times; fervent in private prayer and at the Sacrament at Christ Church; Washington, Watson, and Smyth received comfort at the Sacrament; Watson contrite; in the Hamel; zealous and active to do good for Ford, Walker, etc.

Sins: indulged proud and vain thoughts at Sermon; irrecollected 5 times; intemperate and irrecollected at supper, eat flesh and milk.

MONDAY, MAY 6. 4.45 Rose; dressed; meditated (larum stopped[94] in the night). 5 E and private prayer. 5.15 Began casting up my diary for April.[95] 6 E; Public Prayers. 6.45 Walked with Watson, good talk; came home. 7 E; finished casting up diary; ri; private prayer. 8 E; read Taylor on prayer, private prayer, and intercession;[96] Burchal came, set her upon mending my shirt, and Watson and I gave her a shilling.[97] 9 E and Collect; Watson came, good talk; talk with Mother Harris about the Sacrament, and her daughter; ri. 10 Necessary business. 10.45 Atkinson came, religious talk of friends. 11 E; necessary business. 12 E and Collect; dinner. 12.45 Walked with Brownsword, at the Schools, various talk. 1 E;

---

92   MS. reads "Brazen Nose."
93   Marginal note ("1 E") indicates ejaculatory prayers on the hour.
94   MS. reads "stopt."
95   See monthly summary for April 1734.
96   See Jeremy Taylor, *The Rule and Exercises of Holy Living* (1650), ch. IV, sec. 7, in Appendix 3.
97   In the margin is the symbol for "charitable in relieving the poor."

sat over Redhead[98] and Brownsword doing Generals in the Schools;[99] read Sanderson's Logic. 3 E and Collect; drank with Brownsword and Redhead, read the News; ri. 3.45 Came home; read Clemens; ri. 4 E; wrote a letter to my mother; ri. 5 E; daily examination; Public Prayers, prayer, psalm, lessons, collects. 5.45 Private prayer. 6 E; supper, no flesh. 6.30 Considered what to read. 7 E; at Hervey's with Greives, Smith, and Walker, learned and useful talk. 8 Ford came, religious talk of the first Christians, of Law, etc, of dying persons; Walker said he would ask leave to go to the Sacrament at Christ Church. 9 Came home. 9.15 Private prayer. 9.30.

Blessings: intercession for friends; good advice to Mother Harris; set Burchal upon mending my shirt; sat over Brownsword and Redhead; fervent in private prayer; temperate at dinner and supper; considered before I went what to read at Hervey's; zealous and active in conversation; serious talk.

Sins: not rise;[100] trifling business; irrecollected.

TUESDAY, MAY 7. 4 Rose; dressed. 4.15 Wrote diary. 4.30 Business and virtue. 4.45 Private prayer. 5 E; began to compose my first sermon on Matthew 19.17 by way of a *genesis problematica solitaria;* ri. 6 E; Public Prayers. 6.45 Meditated. 7 E; went to Broughton's, not at home; went to Gloucester Green Workhouse, began reading the family prayers, the Master[101] promised to continue it; ri. 7.30 With Hervey, religious talk of Walker and how to manage him, ri; came home. 8 Breakfast. 8.15 Necessary business. 8.30 Read Francke; ri. 9 E and private prayer; read Francke; ri. 10 E; read Francke; ri. 11 E; Disputations, answered;[102] ri. 11.45 Read chapter. 12 E and private prayer; dinner. 12.45 With me, Watson and Washington. 1 E; began Jenkin's *Christian Religion.* 2 With Smith, various and useful talk. 3 E and Collect; came home. 3.15 Read Clemens Romanus. 4 E; meditated. 4.30 Daily examination; Hervey came to invite me to breakfast with Walker. 4.45 Private prayer. 5 E; read chapter. 5.15 Public Prayers, prayer, psalm, lessons, collects. 5.45 Declamation. 6 E; supper. 6.45 Went to Smith's. 7 E; with Smith, com-

[98] John Redhead, Queen's College, B.A. 1735.
[99] See 4 May, note 87.
[100] MS. reads "rose."
[101] James Piggot.
[102] Ingham was the respondent; probably a collegiate disputation and certainly not the "Determinations" (cf. 1 March, note 4).

pared diaries; ri. 8 E; read sermon of Glanvill's; ri. 9 Came home; private prayer; to bed.

Blessings: rose; began composing a sermon; at Gloucester Green Workhouse, began family prayers; refused to breakfast with Thomas;[103] set Burchal upon mending shirts.[104]

Sins: irrecollected the whole day and intemperate at dinner and supper; indolent; talk without consideration; unchaste thoughts.

WEDNESDAY, MAY 8.   4 Rose; dressed; wrote diary; business and virtue; private prayer. 5 Drowsy, could not study. 6 E; Public Prayers, psalm, lessons, litany, collects. 7 E; went to Workhouse, read family prayers and taught children. 7.30 To Gloucester Green Workhouse, read family prayers; went to Hervey's. 8 E; walked with Hervey to breakfast with Walker, learned and useful talk. 9 Came home. 9.30 Composed an Opposition; ri. 10 E; Opposition and Arguments; ri. 11 Disputations; ri. 11.45 Read chapter. 12 E and private prayer; Hall. 12.30 Private prayer. 12.45 Washington, Watson, and Smyth came. 1 E; read Jenkin; ri. 2 E; Smith came, wrote Arguments for him; ri. 3 E and Collect and private prayer; read Clemens [Romanus]; ri. 4 E; read Clemens; ri. 4.45 Daily examination. 5 E; private prayer; began Rodriguez on Humility; ri. 5.30 Public Prayers, prayer, psalm, lessons, collects. 6 Supper. 6.45 Walked with Washington to Workhouse; ri; came home. 7.30 At Washington's with Watson and Atkinson. 8 E; read Horneck's *Letter of the Primitive Christians;* ri. 9 Walked with Atkinson, religious talk. 9.15 With Watson, Thompson, and Hodgson, various talk of authors; ri. 9.45 Private prayer.

Blessings: rose; Workhouse, and Gloucester Green Workhouse; Washington went to the Workhouse; zealous with Washington, Watson, and Atkinson.

Sins: slept from 5 to 6; trifling at Walker's; various talk with Thompson; broke resolutions 16 and 3.

Be zealous unto death and the Lord shall give thee a crown of life.[105]

THURSDAY, MAY 9.   4 Rose; dressed; business and virtue; private prayer; meditated. 5.15 Hervey came to consult me, whether after reproving a man for swearing, if he did not desist, he ought to leave the company?; religious talk of Walker and Greives; we agreed to tell one another our

---

103   In the margin is the symbol for "conquest over lawful things."
104   In the margin is the symbol for "charitable in relieving the poor."
105   Cf. Rev. 2:10; James 1:12.

faults and to pray for one another; ri. 5.45 Wrote sermon; ri. 6 E and wrote diary. 6.15 Composed sermon; ri. 7 E; Public Prayers. 7.45 Went to Walker's, he was engaged. 8 E; went to Hervey's, breakfast and religious talk. 9 E with Hervey; came home. 9.15 Atkinson came, told me that he was chosen Larder-man.[106] 9.45 Read Francke. 10 E; read Francke; ri. 11 E. 11.15 Read Rodriguez; ri. 11.45 Chapter. 12 E and private prayer; dinner; Washington, Watson, and Smith came. 1 E; read Jenkin. 1.15 Ford came, religious talk with him about asking leave of the President[107] to go to Christ Church; Washington and Watson pressed him, Washington would make his Theme, Watson would translate him a Narrare;[108] we could not all prevail. 2 They went away; I used a great many arguments, but could not prevail; I represented to him the danger he was in, and showed him the consequences of falling off; at last prayer and love and <u>concern</u> prevailed with him to go. 3.30 Private prayer with Ford for humility and good success. 3.45 Ford went to ask leave; I continued <u>on my knees</u> in prayer for him. 4 E; Ford came, the President told him he would give him an answer before Sunday; we returned thanks together for this great blessing, that Ford was enabled to go; ri; Washington came and brought the Theme, Ford transcribed it with me; I read Rodriguez; Ford went home. 5 E; daily examination; private prayer; Public Prayers. 6 Supper.[109] 7 E; at Greives' with Walker, Hervey, Ford, and Robson, read John Wesley's letter of Company,[110] and religious talk; ri. 9 Came home; wrote diary; private prayer. 9.30 To bed.

Blessings: rose; Hervey and I agreed to tell one another our faults; Atkinson chosen Larder-man; Ford overruled to ask leave of the President to go to the Sacrament at Christ Church; religious talk at Greives' with Ford, etc.

FRIDAY, MAY 10. 4 Rose; dressed; private prayer; meditated of God's goodness; ri. 5 Meditated of judgment; ri. 6 E; Public Prayers, prayer, psalm, lessons, litany, collects. 7 E; with Ford, wrote a letter for his father to excuse him from going home; and breakfast with him. 9 E and

106 This may refer to the person in charge of the larder or provision store, although this position seems to have been intended for a college servant (*larder-narii* in *Statutes of Queen's College,* p. 32). The charges listed in the Buttery Books are divided *e Lardario* and *e Promptuario.*
107 John Mather (M.A. 1699) was president of Corpus Christi College, 1715–48.
108 See 31 January, note 187.
109 In the margin is the symbol for "conquest over lawful things."
110 See 19 April, note 22.

collect with Ford; came home; read Francke; ri. 10 E; read Francke; ri. 11 E; Disputations; ri. 12 E and private prayer; dinner; ri; went to the Schools. 1 Sat over Brownsword and Redhead doing Generals;[111] ri. 3 Drank Coffee with them, read News. 4 E; read Clemens [Romanus]. 4.30 Chapter. 4.45 Daily examination. 5 E; private prayer; read Rodriguez. 5.30 Public Prayers. 6 E; Hall. 6.15 With Hervey, religious talk, promised that he should meet with me, Ford, Smith, and Atkinson on Wednesday, Saturday, and Sunday nights; necessary talk about Walker; ri. 7 E; with me, Ford, Washington, Watson, Smyth, and Atkinson read Law; ri. 8 E; read Law and good talk of singing psalms.[112] 9 General Examination (intemperate, irrecollected, idleness, and laying on the bed); private prayer.

Blessings: rose; wrote letter for Ford; agreed with Hervey to meet on Wednesdays, Saturdays, and Sundays; with me, Ford, Atkinson, Washington, Watson, and Smyth.

Sins: irrecollected; various talk; cold in Public Prayers; intemperate.

SATURDAY, MAY 11.   4 Rose; dressed; planned; blessings, thanksgiving, and private prayer. 5 E; composed sermon; ri. 6 E; Public Prayers, prayer, psalm, lessons, collects. 7 E; composed sermon; ri. 8 E; necessary business about breakfast. 8.45 Hervey and Walker came. 9 Breakfast and religious talk of the Sacrament; ri. 9.30 Necessary business. 9.45 Wrote diary. 10 E; read Francke; ri. 11 E; walked. 11.45 Read chapter. 12 E and private prayer; dinner; Declamation. 1 E; with me Washington, Watson, and Smith, read Jenkin. 2 Walked with Washington, Watson, and Smith to visit Blair, sick at Littlemore,[113] read Patrick's meditation by the way; various and useful talk with him; religious and useful talk as we came back; ri. 4 Necessary business. 4.15 Wrote diary. 4.30 Meditated and necessary business; ri. 5 E; daily examination; private prayer. 5.30 Public Prayers. 6 E; supper. 7 E; read Milton. 7.30 Smith, Ford, Atkinson, and Hervey came. 8 E; read Castañiza and religious talk; ri. 9 E. 9.15 Washington and Atkinson came, private prayer. 9.30 Read Horneck's *Best Exercise*;[114] ri. 10.45 Private prayer. 11 Thanksgiving. 11.15 To bed.

[111]   See 4 May, note 87.
[112]   See 17 May, at 4 a.m.
[113]   MS. reads "Little-More." This is about four kilometers southeast of Magdalen Bridge on the outskirts of Oxford.
[114]   Marginal note ("10 E and private prayer") indicates that this hourly exercise was not neglected.

Blessings: rose; good success with Walker; visited sick Blair; gave two commons to poor persons;[115] watched and fervent in private prayer with Washington and Atkinson; recollected twice.

Sins: irrecollected; dissipated in Public Prayers; unchaste thoughts.

SUNDAY, MAY 12. 6 Dressed. 6.30 Wrote diary; private prayer and [prayer] for the Sacrament. 7 E; walked with Washington, Watson, and Smith to Christ Church. 7.30 Public Prayers. 8 Public Prayers and Sacrament. 8.45 Thanksgiving with Smith. 9 E and collect; breakfast with Smith, read Patrick; ri. 10 E; Sermon.[116] 10.45 Walked with Ford, religious talk. 11.45 Meditated. 12 E and Collect; dinner; went to the Hamel. 1 E; finished *The Christian Monitor;* ri. 2 E; Sermon. 3 E and collect; at Charles Wesley's with Smith and Carter, read Sales. 4 E; meditated, heavy. 5 Daily examination; private prayer. 5.30 Public Prayers. 6 E; religious talk with Washington; ri. 6.15 Supper. 7 E; at Smith's with Ford, Atkinson, Hervey, and Evans. 8 E; read Castañiza; ri. 8.45 Walked with Hervey, religious talk of Robson and Walker; ri. 9 Came home; thought; private prayer; to bed.

Blessings: the Sacrament; at the Hamel; religious talk at Smith's with Atkinson, Ford, Hervey, and *Evans.*[117]

Sins: wandering thoughts and irrecollected; intemperate twice.

MONDAY, MAY 13. 4 Rose; dressed; private prayer; business and virtue; wrote diary; read chapter. 5 E; composed sermon; ri. 6 E; Public Prayers, prayer, psalm, lessons, collects. 7 E; at a sale of books; ri. 8 E; read Rodriguez; ri; private prayer. 9 E and Collect; read Sanderson's *De themate simplici*[118] with Washington, Watson, and Atkinson, religious talk. 10 E; read Francke; ri. 11 E; Disputations; ri. 12 Dinner; with me, Watson, Washington, and Smyth,[119] read Jenkin; ri; Ford came, various talk. 2 E; went to Smith's, necessary talk; ri. 3 E and Collect; walked with Smith

---

115 See Glossary, s.v. "Commons." The recipients, occasion, or means of effecting this act of charity are not evident in his hourly entries; see also 23 May.

116 The preacher at St. Mary's on this occasion was Dr. Thomas Tanner, Bishop of St. Asaph, who was ill at the time. Hearne, *Collections,* vol. 11, 342.

117 Ingham underlined Evans's name, no doubt emphasizing his return to the group. See 4 April, note 149.

118 *De factione simplicis thematis* is the first section of the Appendix (*De usu logicæ*) to Robert Sanderson's *Logicæ artis compendium* (cf. Wesley's translation in his *Compendium of Logic,* Appendix, sec. 1, "Of Treating on a Simple Theme").

119 Marginal note ("1 E") indicates ejaculatory prayers on the hour.

and Evans, mostly religious talk; came home. 4 E; read Rodriguez; ri. 5 E; daily examination; private prayer. 5.30 Public Prayers, prayer, psalm, lessons, collects. 6 Supper. 7 E; with me, Smith, Hervey, and Greives, religious and useful talk. 8 E; Ford came, read Norris' sermon on 'Despisers of Those that are Good';[120] ri. 9 E; religious talk with Ford about receiving the Sacrament in the morning with a sick person.

Blessings: rose; recollected thrice; temperate at supper; religious talk with Smith, Ford, Hervey, and Greives.

Sins: neglected private prayer at noon; trifling at Smith's.

TUESDAY, MAY 14.   4 Rose; dressed; thanksgiving and private prayer; business and virtue; chapter.[121] 5 E; composed sermon; ri. 6 E; Public Prayers, prayer, psalm, lessons, collects. 7 E; necessary business; read Meditation on the Sacrament[122] with Ford; ri. 8 E and Collect; breakfast with me, Ford and Washington, good talk. 8.45 Walked with Ford to the Workhouse to receive the Sacrament; Mr Hughs did not come; read Meditations and religious talk. 9.30 We went home; I walked with Hervey to Gloucester Green Workhouse; religious talk; then we went to the School, taught the children; afterwards we went to another School, taught the children; ri. 10.45 Went to the Workhouse, religious talk with Hervey and Atkinson, read Meditations. 11.15 Hughs came, I, Hervey, and Atkinson with three women and the clerk[123] received the Holy Sacrament with the sick person; ri (Ford could not come). 11.45 Came home with Atkinson, religious talk; wrote diary. 12 E and Collect and private prayer; dinner. 1 E; with me, Watson, and Smyth, read Jenkin. 2 E; looked over my books; ri. 3 E and Collect and private prayer; read Rodriguez; ri. 4 Walked. 4.45 Chapter. 5 E; daily examination; private prayer. 5.30 Public Prayers, prayer, psalm, lessons, collects. 6 E; supper. 7 E; with Smith, good talk (various) of ourselves and friends. 8 E; compared diaries and good talk (various). 9 E; came home; private prayer; to bed.

Blessings: rose; fervent in private prayer; visited the Workhouse and

---

[120] "The Honour Due to Good Men, and the Great Crime of Treating them with Scorn and Contempt," a sermon on 2 Tim. 3:3, in *Practical Discourses*, vol. III.

[121] At this point the D column, rating his hourly temper of devotion, is given the heading S, measuring essentially the same sense of spiritual attentiveness under the term "Simplicity"; see Appendix 1 (D) and plate 15.

[122] See 10 March, note 38.

[123] MS. reads "clark."

two schools; the Sacrament with a sick person; attentive in Public and private prayer; recollected thrice.

Sins: broke resolution 9 twice, 8 four times, 1 twice, 3 once, 5 once, 15 twice, 14 once.

WEDNESDAY, MAY 15.   4 Rose; dressed; E; wrote diary; private prayer; chapter. 5 E; <u>called;</u>[124] composed sermon; ri. 6 E; Public Prayers, prayer, psalm, lessons, litany, collects. 7 E; at the Workhouse, read family prayers. 8 Breakfast with Charles Wesley, religious and useful talk; ri; transcribed a prayer. 9 E and collect; came home; meditated. 10 E; read Francke; ri. 11 E; walked. 11.45 Read chapter. 12 E and private prayer; dinner; with me, Watson and Smyth. 1 E; read Jenkin. 1.45 Meditated. 2 E; read Horneck on Watching.[125] 3 E and Collect; read Horneck; ri. 4 E; went to Workhouse, taught children, read family prayers, and religious talk with two sick persons; ri. 5 Came home. 5.15 Dressed. 5.30 Public Prayers, prayer, psalm, lessons, collects. 6 E; daily examination; private prayer; supper. 7 E; with Atkinson, religious talk. 7.30 Smith, Evans, and Hervey came, read Castañiza, and religious talk. 8 Ford came; E; read Castañiza, and religious talk. 9 E; came home; private prayer; meditated of death; ri. 10 R R;[126] disturbed in the night by drunkards.

Blessings: rose; at Workhouse twice; at Gloucester Green Workhouse; breakfast with Charles Wesley; recollected thrice; zealous in conversation; R R.

Sins: vain and unchaste thoughts; seemed angry at Watson, broke resolution 11; dissipated at Public and private prayer; irrecollected at supper.

THURSDAY, MAY 16.   6 Rose; dressed; wrote diary; private prayer, and chapter. 7 E; read Rodriguez. 7.15 Public Prayers, prayer, psalm, lessons, collects. 8 Lecture.[127] 8.30 With Smith, private prayer and Meditation before the Sacrament; walked with Smith to a sick person, received the Holy Sacrament with him, Charles Wesley, and the person; ri. 9.45

124   See 21 November, note 102. Through May, Ingham does not indicate whom he called. Cf. 20 June.
125   See The Happy Ascetick, part 2, "The Extraordinary Exercises of Godliness," ch. III, "To use Watching, or abstinence from sleep."
126   The entry "R R" might mean "[confirmed] Resolutions and Resignation" (cf. 12 April, summary of blessings, and 14 April at 10 a.m.). The four times it is used (cf. 16 and 20 May, and 7 June) give no clue as to its precise meaning other than that it comes at the end of the day and can be summarized under Blessings.
127   Perhaps a university lecture (see 14 February, note 204).

Meditated with Smith and the sick person; came home. 10 E and private prayer and thanksgiving; read Rodriguez. 11 E; walked; met with Natt and Bolton, Sr, religious talk. 11.45 Read chapter. 12 E and private prayer; Hall. 12.30 Meditated. 12.45 Intercession. 1 E; with me, Smyth and Watson, read Jenkin; ri. 1.30 With Smith, religious talk. 1.45 Began the Penitential Office for the 16th Day of the Month the first time together, designing to continue it;[128] ri. 2.45 Walked to the Workhouse, taught the children, read to the old people on the Sacrament; religious talk with the sick person. 4 E; wrote diary. 4.15 Meditated. 4.30 Ford came, necessary talk. 4.45 Chapter. 5 E; daily examination; private prayer; Public Prayers, prayer, psalm, lessons, collects. 6 E; religious talk with Washington. 6.15 Supper. 7 E; with Smith, good talk. 7.30 Hervey, Walker, Ford, and Greives came, read Meditation on the Sacrament,[129] began Norris on Humility; ri. 8.45 Came home with Ford; ri. 9.15 Wrote diary. 9.30 R R.

Blessings: the Sacrament with a sick person; fasted[130] and used the Penitential Office for the 16th Day of the Month; fervent in private and Public Prayers; at the Workhouse; recollected thrice; R R.

Sins: did not rise at 5.

FRIDAY, MAY 17.   4 Rose; dressed; psalm;[131] private prayer; thanksgiving; meditated. 5 E; wrote diary. 5.15 Composed sermon; ri. 6 E; Pub-

---

[128] Widespread interest in a revival of the penitential discipline of the Early Church can be seen in many publications of the period, such as Nathaniel Marshall, *The Penitential Discipline of the Primitive Church* (1714), William Wogan, *The Right Use of Lent* (1732), Thomas Deacon, *A Compleat Collection of Devotions* (1734), and John Kettlewell, *A Companion for the Penitent* (1728). None of these, however, mentions an office for the sixteenth day of the month; the source of that practice as well as the publication mentioned here by Ingham both remain unidentified. Cf. 1 April at 7:45 a.m., and 16 July and 16 August. In a list of resolutions "as to times" from 1732–33, Wesley noted "On the 16th Day, Wog[an] at 11, etc." OD III, iii.

[129] Marginal note ("8 E") indicates ejaculatory prayers at the hour.

[130] Marginal notes: at 8–9 a.m., "no breakfast"; at 12–1 p.m., "no dinner."

[131] This may correspond to the "morning hymn" he used rather regularly through the winter (see 25 November, note 107, and 10 May at 8 p.m.). Richard Morgan, Jr., claimed that the Methodists at Oxford "[sang] Psalms and read some piece of divinity" from five to eight every morning, one of many claims that John Wesley stated were "not only false, but I fear were known so to be when he related them as true" (*Letters*, I, 365, 368). Wesley's diary does, however, indicate either "psalm" or "hymn" quite regularly as part of his early morning routine during this period (OD IV, passim).

lic Prayers, psalm, lessons, litany, collects. 7 E; composed sermon; ri. 8 E; composed sermon; ri. 8.30 Necessary business and gave threepence to a poor woman. 9 E, Collect, and private prayer; read Francke; ri. 10 E; read Francke; ri. 11 E and private prayer. 11.15 Disputations; ri. 12 E and Collect; Hall. 12.30 Read Horneck of Fasting. 1 E; with me, Washington, Watson, and Smyth, read Jenkin; ri. 2 E; finished Horneck on Fasting.[132] 2.45 Necessary business. 3 E and private prayer; with me, Smyth and Atkinson, breakfast[133] and religious talk. 3.45 Walked. 4.45 Came home; chapter. 5 E; daily examination; private prayer. 5.30 Public Prayers. 6 E; supper. 6.15 General Examination (intemperate; ir-recollected; unchaste thoughts); wrote diary; made resolutions for the week. 7 E; with me, Washington, Watson, Smyth, and Atkinson, read Law; ri. 8 Ford came, E, read Law and religious talk. 9 E; wrote diary. 9.15 Private prayer.

Blessings: rose; simple 15 times; recollected 4 times;[134] gave three-pence to a poor woman; with me Ford, Washington, Watson, Smyth, and Atkinson; fasted till 3.

Sins: dissipated at Public and private prayers once.

SATURDAY, MAY 18. 4 Rose; dressed; business and virtue; thanksgiving and private prayer. 5 E; composed sermon; ri. 6 E; Public Prayers, prayer, psalm, lessons, collects. 7 E; finished my first sermon, on Matthew 19, verse 17, and began transcribing it fair over. 8 E; breakfast at Natt's with Ford, Washington, Watson, and Atkinson, good talk. 9.15 Came home; E and Collect; read Francke. 10 E; read Francke; ri. 11 E; with Brough-ton, religious talk of friends. 11.30 With Hervey, religious talk of our-selves and friends; ri. 12 E; dinner; Declamation. 1 E; with me, Wash-ington, Watson, and Smyth, read Jenkin. 2 E; walked with Washington

132 See *The Happy Ascetick,* part 2, "The Extraordinary Exercises of Godli-ness," ch. II, "To subdue the body by fasting."

133 This is Ingham's first regular observance of a Stationary fast day since 19 April (see 17 April, note 11).

134 Ingham here begins to summarize the positive entries in the S and R col-umns—see Appendix 1(D). The total number of hourly ratings of 6 or better in the Simplicity column is noted here under Blessings, as is the total number of Recollection entries with the top three degrees of attention (attentive, fervent, or zealous). He occasionally records an incorrect total, such as on 18 May: there are actually seventeen entries of 6 or better, but he apparently overlooked the last three which are somewhat obscured by the encroachment of entries from another column. He also adjusted the criteria occasionally (see 19 May, note 139).

and Watson, religious talk. 2.45 Meditated. 3 E and Collect; meditated on faith; ri. 4 E; meditated. 4.30 Daily examination; private prayer. 5 E; read Rodriguez. 5.30 Public Prayers, prayer, psalm, lessons, collects. 6 E; dressed; supper, no flesh; ri. 7 E; at Hervey's with Ford, Atkinson, Smith, and Evans, finished Castañiza's *Spiritual Combat,* and religious talk. 8 E; began Young's *Poem on the Last Day.* 9 E; good talk with Smith; walked with Ford to Corpus Christi College and drank, good talk. 9.30 Went to Atkinson's, and Washington, religious talk and private prayer. 9.45 Read Horneck's *Best Exercise.* 10 E and private prayer. 10.15 Read Horneck; ri. 11 E and private prayer. 11.15 Read Horneck. 11.30 Private prayer and thanskgiving. 11.45 Came home; private prayer and to bed.

Blessings: rose; sweet meditations; simple 14 times; recollected 5 times; zealous in conversation with Hervey, etc; Atkinson, Washington, and I agreed to remember one another of God by signs, laying our hand upon our face, looking up or at one another, and also if we heard one another revile or say anything of another which doth not tend to God's glory, to give a clap with our hands;[135] zealous in conversation and private prayer with Atkinson and Washington.

Sins: careless at Natt's; intemperate at dinner.

SUNDAY, MAY 19. 5 Rose; dressed. 5.15 Wrote diary. 5.45 Psalm and private prayer. 6 E; meditated on God's perfections; confession and prayer for the Sacrament. 7 E; dressed; private prayer for Watson; walked with Washington, Watson, and Smyth to Christ Church. 7.30 Public Prayers, prayer, psalm, lessons, litany, collects. 8.15 Sacrament. 8.45 Thanksgiving with Smith, and breakfast. 9 E and Collect; at Gloucester Green Workhouse, read family prayers, and religious talk with Piggot, and read the Country Parson on hell's torments.[136] 10 E; at Sermon; walked with Watson and Atkinson,[137] religious talk of rising and making resolutions against those sins which most beset us, and sconcing ourselves for breaking them. 11.45 Wrote diary; private prayer. 12 E and Collect; dinner; walked with Atkinson to Workhouse, religious talk. 1 E; began Ellis'

---

135 The symbol for "good resolutions" is placed in the margin at this point. See 8 April for another expression of concern over disagreements between friends.
136 Part I, ch. 4, "Containing a fourth argument to a holy life: The consideration of the future punishments of wicked men, viz. that their torments are extream and intolerable, without ceasing and without end." See *The Country Parson's Advice to His Parishioners* (1680), in Appendix 3.
137 Marginal note ("11 E") indicates ejaculatory prayers on the hour.

Communicant[138] in the Hamel. 2 E; came with Atkinson to the Sermon. 3 E and Collect; at Charles Wesley's with Smith, read Sales. 4 E; walked. 4.30 Came home; wrote diary. 4.45 Read chapter. 5 Meditated; daily examination; private prayer. 5.30 Public Prayers, prayer, psalm, lessons, collects. 6 E; religious talk with Washington. 6.15 Supper. 7 E; walked with Atkinson, religious talk; at Ford's with Atkinson, Smith, Evans, read Nelson. 8 Hervey came, E, finished Young's *Poem on the Last Day,* and religious talk; ri. 9 E; drank; came home; private prayer; to bed.

Blessings: rose; simple 7 times;[139] recollected 8 times; fervent in private and Public Prayers; the Holy Sacrament at Christ Church; at Gloucester Green Workhouse; Watson overruled to go to the Sacrament; at Charles Wesley's.

Sins: eat too much at supper; broke resolution 8 three times, 9 once, 1 once.

MONDAY, MAY 20. 4 Rose; dressed; wrote diary; private prayer; read chapter. 5 E; transcribed sermon. 6 E; walked; Public Prayers, prayer, psalm, lessons, collects. 7 E; transcribed sermon. 8 E; breakfast with me, Greives, religious talk. 9 With me, Washington, Watson, and Atkinson, read Sanderson. 10 E; read Francke; ri. 11 E; walked. 11.45 Came home; read chapter. 12 E; dinner. 1.30 Ford and Washington with me, various and useful talk. 2.45 Took a walk with Ford and Washington, religious talk. 3 Psalm, and read Thomas à Kempis; ri; came home. 4 E; meditated. 5 E; daily examination; private prayer. 5.30 Public Prayers, prayer, psalm, lessons, collects. 6 E; supper; religious talk with Bolton; ri. 7 E; at Walker's with Smith, Hervey, and Ford. 8 Read Nelson on the Rogation Days,[140] private prayer, and religious talk. 9 Came home; walked with Smith and Ford, good talk. 9.15 Composed Arguments for Ford. 9.45 Private prayer; to bed.

Blessings: rose; simple 7 times;[141] recollected 3 times; (R R).

TUESDAY, MAY 21. 4 Rose; dressed; psalm; private prayer; business and virtue. 5 E; transcribed sermon. 5.45 Ford came for his Arguments; ri. 6

---

138 Clement Ellis, *The Communicant's Guide* (1685); see Appendix 3.

139 For two days, Ingham adjusts his criterion for "Simplicity" to include only ratings of 7 or better (cf. 17 May, note 134).

140 See Nelson, *Fasts,* ch. VI. Rogation Days are the Monday, Tuesday, and Wednesday before Holy Thursday (Ascension Day); Ingham did not fast at all on Monday, and only until noon on Tuesday.

141 See note 139 above.

E; Public Prayers, prayer, psalm, lessons, collects. 7 E; went to Smith's good talk. 7.45 With Charles Wesley, religious talk. 8 Came home. 8.15 Read Rodriguez. 8.45 Private prayer. 9 E and Collect; with me, Washington, Watson, and Atkinson, read Sanderson, and religious talk. 10 Religious talk with Atkinson. 11 E; walked. 11.45 Private prayer. 12 E; dinner. 1 E; with me, Washington, Watson, and Smyth, read Jenkin; ri. 2 E; slept. 3 E and collect; meditated. 3.30 Read Clemens [Romanus]. 4 E. 4.30 Bolton came, religious talk. 5 E; daily examination; private prayer. 5.30 Public Prayers, prayer, psalm, lessons, collects. 6 E; supper. 7 E; with Smith, mostly religious talk. 8 Compared diaries, and walked. 9 Came home. 9.15 Wrote diary.

Blessings: rose; Bolton promised to go to the Sacrament at St Mary's.
Sins: vext with Ford for carping at the Arguments I made him.

WEDNESDAY, MAY 22.   4 Rose but very sleepy, laid down again. 5 Dressed; psalm; wrote diary; private prayer. 5.30 Read Rodriguez. 6 E; Public Prayers, prayer, psalm, lessons, litany, collects. 7 E; read Rodriguez; ri. 8 E; at the Workhouse, read family prayers, etc; ri; at Gloucester Green Workhouse. 9 E and Collect; read Sanderson with Washington, Watson, and Atkinson, and religious talk. 10 E; read Francke, and thoughts of doing good. 11 E; walked with Natt, religious talk of the Sacrament; ri. 12 E and private prayer. 12.15 Hall. 12.30 Read Rodriguez. 1 E; with me, Washington, Watson, and Smyth, read Jenkin. 2 E; read Jenkin. 2.45 Private prayer for the Rogation and Stationary days; with me, Washington, Watson, Smyth, and Atkinson. 3 Breakfast. 3.30 Atkinson, religious talk, and private prayer for Bolton; ri. 4 E; read Rodriguez, and meditated; ri. 5 E; daily examination; private prayer. 5.30 Public Prayers, prayer, lessons, psalm, collects.[142] 6 E; supper, refused dainties. 6.45 Walked. 7 E; with me, Hervey, Smith, Evans, Ford, Atkinson; J Whitaker sent for me. 8 I went to sit with him, religious talk. 8.30 Came home; religious talk with Hervey, etc. 9 E; with me, Washington and Atkinson, private prayer, read Horneck. 10 E and private prayer; read Horneck. 10.45 Private prayer and thanksgiving. 11 Private prayer and wrote diary. 11.30.

Blessings: simple 16 times; recollected 8 times; refused dainties at supper; zealous and active in conversation with Natt, and with J Whitaker; at the Workhouse and Gloucester Green Workhouse; attentive and fer-

---

[142] The alteration in the order these are listed would not necessarily imply any change in the service itself.

vent in private prayer; fasted till 3 and temperate afterwards; watched till 11 with me, Washington and Atkinson, zealous talk [Go on and prosper].[143]

Sins:[144]

HOLY THURSDAY, MAY 23. 5 Rose; psalm and meditated; dressed, thanksgiving. 6 E; private prayer. 6.15 Read Nelson,[145] and private prayer. 6.30 Necessary business. 6.45 Atkinson and J Whitaker came to breakfast with me, religious talk, showed him the Chapel and Library.[146] 8 E and Public Prayers. 8.45 Bolton came to breakfast with me, religious talk. 9.30 Necessary business. 10 E; Sermon.[147] 10.45 Walked with Washington, religious talk. 11 E; Ford met us, religious talk. 11.45 Wrote diary; private prayer. 12 E and thanksgiving. 12.15 Dinner. 12.45 With me, Washington,[148] Watson, and Smyth, read Jenkin. 2 E; with John Wesley, necessary talk. 2.15 With Smith, good talk; walked with Smith and Evans, religious talk of friends. 2.45 With Hervey, various talk. 3.30 Came home; read Rodriguez. 4 E; read Rodriguez. 5 E; daily examination; private prayer. 5.30 Public Prayers, prayer, psalm, lessons, collects. 6 E; supper; went to Ford's, with Smith, Hervey, and Walker, read part of Beveridge on the Stations;[149] ri. 8.45 Walked with Smith, Hervey, and Walker, good talk; religious talk with Hervey of resolutions, advised him not to insert anything about eating; ri. 9.30 Came home; wrote diary. 9.45.

Blessings: zealous and active in conversation; good success with Bolton; gave two commons to two poor people.[150]

[143] 1 Kings 22:15; 2 Chron. 18:14. These words of the prophet Micaiah, footnoted to the last entry under Blessings, are strangely taken out of context, having been spoken in scorn to mimic the prophets surrounding King Ahab.

[144] Nothing is listed under this heading for this day.

[145] This day was the festival of the Ascension of Our Lord Jesus Christ (see Nelson, *Festivals,* ch. XX).

[146] See 7 April, note 165. The new library building, one of the most splendid in the university, was finished in the last decade of the seventeenth century.

[147] Festival of the Ascension of Our Lord Jesus Christ. The statutes stipulate that the sermon before the university on this day should be preached at Christ Church cathedral.

[148] Marginal note ("1 E") indicates ejaculatory prayers on the hour.

[149] The monthly summary for May indicates that this was "De jejunio quartæ ac sextæ feriæ," book III, ch. X, of William Beveridge's *Codex canonum ecclesiæ primitivæ vindicatus ac illustratus* (1678); see Appendix 3.

[150] Ingham did not forgo his own meals in order to carry out this charitable act; see also 11 May and cf. 6 March.

Sins: irrecollected and inconsiderate; unchaste, proud, and vain thoughts.

FRIDAY, MAY 24.   4 Rose; dressed; psalm, private prayer; business and virtue. 4.45 Called. 5 E; Atkinson came, religious talk of Smyth and Watson. 5.30 Transcribed sermon. 6 E; Public Prayers, prayer, psalm, lessons, litany, prayers;[151] religious talk with Watson. 7 Hervey came, religious talk of friends. 8 E; meditated and prayer for the Sacrament. 8.30 At Smith's, religious talk. 9 E and Collect; received the Holy Sacrament at a sick person's with his wife, John Wesley, Charles Wesley, Broughton, Salmon, Smith, and Evans; ri. 9.30 Thanksgiving at Charles Wesley's with John Wesley, Broughton, and Salmon; ri; came home. 10 E; transcribed sermon; ri. 11 Transcribed sermon. 11.45 Private prayer. 12 E and Collect; dinner. 1 E; with me, Washington, Watson, and Smyth, read Jenkin. 2 Good talk with me, Watson. 2.30 Read Clemens [Romanus]. 3 E and Collect; read Clemens. 4 E; with Dixon and Bolton, read the third chapter of Law's *Serious Call;* ri. 4.30 Came home; read Clemens. 5 E; daily examination; private prayer. 5.30 Public Prayers, prayer, psalm, lessons, collects. 6 Hall; supper on ¼ bread and butter. 6.15 General Examination and private prayer. 7 E; at Washington's with Watson, Smyth, and Atkinson, read Law. 8 E and private prayer; read Law and religious talk. 9 E; came home; meditated and private prayer; to bed.

Blessings: rose; simple 14 times; recollected 8 times; zealous in conversations; the Holy Sacrament.

Sins: broke resolution 8 thrice.

SATURDAY, MAY 25.   4 Rose; dressed; psalm; wrote diary; business and virtue; thanksgiving and private prayer. 5 E; transcribed sermon; ri. 6 E; Public Prayers, prayer, psalm, lessons, collects; went to John Wesley's. 7 Breakfast with him, religious talk of the obligations of the Apostolic Church; every particular Church may conform to it entirely;[152] every member of any particular Church may conform so far as he is at liberty;

---

[151] The usual entry would read "collects."

[152] Cf. Wesley's "Of the Weekly Fasts of the Church": "The rites of the Church universal ought to be observed by all particular churches. For it is not in the power of any particular church to reject what is established by the Church universal. By so doing, it would become schismatical, disjoining itself from the Body of Christ" (p. 2 in back of John Wesley MS., Colman Collection XII, MA). See also Wesley's Sermon 39 on "Catholic Spirit" in which he distinguishes between "essentials" and matters of "opinion," the gist of this conversation with Ingham.

in particular instances we must consider their nature and necessity; fasting is always necessary, standing on Sundays[153] only decency; religious talk of watching—acceptable, but not necessary for all; religious talk of our friends; ri; came home. 8 E; wrote diary. 8.15 Read Rodriguez and thought. 9 E and Collect; Washington came, religious talk. 9.15 Thought. 9.30 Transcribed sermon. 10 E; transcribed sermon; ri. 11 E; transcribed sermon. 11.45 Private prayer. 12 E and Collect; dinner. 1 E; with me, Washington, Watson, and Smyth, read Jenkin; ri. 2 E; transcribed sermon; ri. 3 E and Collect; finished transcribing sermon; ri. 4 E; with Dixon, Bolton, and Hall, read Law. 5 E; daily examination; private prayer; Public Prayers, prayer, psalm, lessons, collects. 6 Supper; walked with Atkinson to Evans', good talk. 7 Smith came, read Ken's Meditation on the Sacrament.[154] 8 E; read the Life of an Apostate;[155] ri. 9 E; came home. 9.15 At Washington's with Atkinson, private prayer. 9.30 Read Horneck. 10 E and private prayer. 10.15 Read Horneck's *Best Exercise.* 11.15 Private prayer. 11.30 Came home; to bed. 11.45.

Blessings: rose; with John Wesley; finished my first sermon, on Matthew 19:17; watched till 11.30 with Washington and Atkinson; zealous in conversation and fervent in private prayer; recollected 7 times; simple 18 times; gave two pence to poor woman.

Sins: wandering thoughts at Public Prayers; lazy and irrecollected; vain thoughts; broke resolution 8 thrice.

Continue instant in prayer.[156]

SUNDAY, MAY 26. 5 Rose; dressed; psalm; wrote diary; private prayer. 6 E; thanksgiving. 6.15 Meditated on God's perfections and mercies. 7 E; meditated on death, judgement; dressed. 8 E; Public Prayers, prayer, psalm, lessons, litany, collects, com[munion][157] 9 E and Collect; walked with Watson to Gloucester Green Workhouse, read Ellis on the Sacrament, and religious talk. 9.45 At the Castle with Watson, Washington, Smyth, Ford, and Atkinson; Public Prayers. 10 Public Prayers and Sermon. 11 Sermon and Sacrament. 12 Came home; dinner; walked with

---

153   Standing at the reading of the Gospel, and so on.

154   See "Of the Holy Eucharist" in Ken's *The Retired Christian.*

155   See Richard Sault, *The Second Spira* (1693), in Appendix 3; Ingham subsequently refers to this work as "Death of an Apostate" (e.g., on 30 May) but uses the usual title in the monthly summaries for May and June.

156   Rom. 12:12.

157   The time of this service would seem to indicate Queen's College as the location rather than Christ Church. See also 2 and 4 June.

Watson and Atkinson. 1 E; to Workhouse, read Ellis in the Hamel. 2 E; Sermon. 3 E and Collect; at Charles Wesley's with Smith and Carter, read Sales; ri; came home. 4 E; necessary business; with Bolton, Dixon, and Hall, read the last chapter of Law's *Serious Call*,[158] and religious talk. 5 E; private prayer and thanksgiving; wrote diary. 5.30 Public Prayers, prayer, psalm.[159] 6 Religious talk with Washington and Natt. 6.15 Supper. 7 E; at Smith's with Atkinson, Evans, and Hervey, began *The Life of Monsieur de Renty;* ri. 9 E; came home; private prayer; to bed.

Blessings: rose; recollected 12 times; simple 15 times; fervent and zealous in private prayer and the Sacrament; Watson went to Gloucester Green Workhouse and the Hamel; religious talk with Bolton, Dixon, and Hall; temperate at supper; to bed [early]; Charles Wesley's.

Sins: intemperate at dinner; inattentive at and in Public Prayers; cold at night in conversation.

MONDAY, MAY 27.   4 Rose; dressed; wrote diary; business and virtue; private prayer; called. 5 E; Washington came, religious talk of resolutions, read him mine, read Rodriguez. 5.45 With John Wesley, religious talk of Washington's and Hervey's resolutions; ri. 6 E; Public Prayers, prayer, psalm, lessons, collects. 7 E; read Rodriguez. 7.45 Walked with Watson to Workhouse, taught children and read family prayers. 8.45 Went to Gloucester Green Workhouse with Watson, read family prayers; came home. 9.30 With me, Hervey, Washington, and Atkinson, religious talk of resolutions, and private prayer for serious consideration; read my resolutions; ri. 10 E and private prayer for resolutions, etc; ri. 10.45 With Atkinson. 11 E; read Rodriguez. 11.30 Walked with Watson, read the letter he wrote[160] to his mistress;[161] ri. 12 E; Hall. 12.30 Read· Rodriguez; with me, Washington, Watson, and Smyth, read Jenkin. 1.45 Went[162] to Smith's, walked with him, good talk. 2.45 Came home and walked with Atkinson and Washington to Hervey's. 3 E and private prayer for resolutions, etc; ri. 3.30 Breakfast, religious talk. 4 E; came home. 4.30 With Bolton and Dixon, began Law's *Christian Perfection,*

---

[158] Ch. XXIV, "The conclusion. Of the excellency and greatness of a devout spirit."
[159] This deviation from the normal entry does not necessarily indicate an alteration in the service itself.
[160] MS. reads "writ."
[161] See 23 April, note 44.
[162] Marginal note ("2 E") indicates ejaculatory prayer on the hour.

and disputed; ri. 5 Came home. 5.15 Wrote diary; daily examination. 5.30 Public Prayers, prayer, psalm, lessons, collects. 6 E; with Bolton and Dixon, religious talk of reading and of company; they would not consent to meet with Atkinson and Watson, but with me as oft as I would; they promised to read *The Gentleman Instructed* at nights by themselves. 6.30 Supper. 6.45 Private prayer. 7 E; at Hervey's with Greives and Walker, good talk of Walker's brother and his contempt of the world, and way of living; good talk with Greives of the nature of penal laws. 9 Came home. 9.15 Private prayer. 9.30 Lay meditating to 10 and afterward.

Blessings; rose; recollected 5 times; at Workhouse and Gloucester Green Workhouse with Watson; with John Wesley; Atkinson and I fasted and prayed with Washington and Hervey who were beginning to make resolutions.

TUESDAY, MAY 28. 4 Trust not to thine own strength, but be humble.[163] 5.15 Rose; dressed. 5.30 Wrote diary. 5.45 Private prayer. 6 E; thought; Public Prayers, prayer, psalm, lessons, collects. 7 E; necessary business; wrote a Supposition; ri. 8 E and private prayer; breakfast with me, Bolton and Dixon. 9 Religious talk; Bolton consented to go to the Sacrament at St Mary's,[164] and Dixon if he was well. 9.30 Thought, and read Francke. 10 E; read Francke. 11 E; Disputations; ri. 12 E and Collect; dinner. 1 E; with me, Washington, Watson, Smyth, finished the first volume of Jenkin's *Christian Religion.* 1.45 Walked with Washington and Watson. 2 E; met with Gambold, religious talk of particular providence and some instances; ri. 2.45 Private prayer and meditated. 3 E and Collect; read Francke; ri. 4 E; drowsy and slumbered. 5 E and private prayer; daily examination. 5.30 Public Prayers, prayer, psalm, lessons, collects. 6 Supper. 7 Walked with Smith, religious talk of friends. 8 E; compared diaries, and religious and useful talk; ri. 9 Came home. 9.15 Thought. 9.30.

Blessings: convinced of my inability to do anything of myself by not hearing the larum, nor rising at 4, for last night I boasted before Walker (complaining that he could not rise, nor hear his larum) that I never

163 This might be a quotation or perhaps Ingham's own words summarizing Rodriguez's treatise on humility which he was reading. Cf. shorthand entry dated 1 February 1733/34.
164 The Sacrament to be administered on 29 May (see also 30 May, note 171).

missed hearing my larum; good success with Bolton and Dixon; with Gambold; recollected 6 times; simple 12 times; met with a sentence in Francke pertinent to the discourse I had with Gambold; Dixon read the eleventh chapter of I Corinthians about the Sacrament.

WEDNESDAY, MAY 29.   4 Rose; dressed; psalm; meditated; private prayer. 5 E; called. 5.15 Meditated. 6 E; read Rodriguez; ri. 7 E; finished Rodriguez on Humility; dressed. 8 Public Prayers. 9 Religious talk with Atkinson; with Bolton and Dixon about going to the Sacrament at St Mary's, could not prevail with them; came home and prayed for them; Dixon came, religious talk with him, used a great many arguments; sent him for Bolton, he could not get him to come; he came again, religious talk of the Methodists. 10 Went with Dixon to Chapel, Public Prayers and Sermon.[165] 12 Came home; dressed. 12.15 Dinner and heard a Speech in the Hall.[166] 1.15 With me, Washington, Watson, and Atkinson. 1.30 Walked and religious talk. 2 Went to Gloucester Green Workhouse, left Washington and Watson there; Atkinson and I went to Workhouse, taught children and read family prayers; they convinced me that a spirit came. 3 Walked with Atkinson, mostly religious talk. 4.15 With Bolton, various talk; Dixon not at home. 4.30 Came home; wrote diary. 4.45 Read chapter. 5 E; daily examination; private prayer. 5.30 Public Prayers, prayer, psalm, lessons, collects. 6 Walked with Watson; supper. 7 E; at Hervey's with Atkinson, Smith, and Evans, read *The Life of Monsieur de Renty;* ri.[167] 9 E; came home. 9.15 Private prayer; could not sleep.

Blessings: rose; zealous and active in conversation with Dixon and Bolton; at Gloucester Green Workhouse and Workhouse.

Sins: irrecollected and intemperate; pulled my clothes in pieces; indolent.

THURSDAY, MAY 30.   4 Rose; sleepy, went to bed till 6; dressed; psalm; business and virtue. 6.30 Wrote diary. 6.45 Private prayer. 7 E; Public Prayers; necessary business. 8 E; breakfast with me, Smith and Evans,

---

[165] This day was the commemoration of the birth (1630) and restoration (1660) of Charles II. Thus no fast was kept, even though it was a Stationary day. Rather than attend the Sacrament at St. Mary's, Ingham attended Queen's College chapel with Dixon and noted that he was "indifferent" during the prayers and sermon.

[166] See 29 April, note 65.

[167] Marginal note ("8 E") indicates ejaculatory prayers on the hour.

mostly religious talk. 9 E and Collect; began to transcribe my three Lectures for my degree;[168] ri. 11 E; transcribed Lectures; ri. 12 E and private prayer; dinner. 12.45 With me, Atkinson, Washington, Watson, and Smyth, E, began the second volume of Jenkin's Reasonableness of Christianity.[169] 2.15 Tea with Natt, good talk. 3 E and Collect; read a sermon of Tillotson's. 4 E and religious talk. 4.30 Came home; read Bible. 5 E; daily examination; private prayer; Public Prayers, prayer, psalm, lessons, collects. 6 E; supper. 6.45 With Hervey, Walker, Smith, and Robson at Greives', learned talk and read the Death of an Apostate,[170] and various and useful talk; ri. 9.15 Came home; transcribed a prayer for humility, and wrote diary.

[Blessings: Robson prevailed with by Hervey.][171]

FRIDAY, MAY 31.   4 Rose; psalm; business and virtue; meditated. 5 Drowsy and slept.[172] 6 Private prayer; transcribed Lectures; Hervey

---

[168] Ingham's three lectures, given on 6, 7, and 8 June, along with the "Speech" he delivered on 3 May, seem to have excused him from the required examination for the B.A. degree (see 29 April, note 65). The lectures were on the tenth satire of Juvenal, the design of which Dryden summarized in a preface to his translation: "to represent the various wishes and desires of mankind [riches, honours, eloquence, fame, long life, beauty]; and to set out the folly of 'em, [showing] how frequently they have prov'd the ruin of those that own'd them," and concluding that all one needs for happiness is "health of body and mind." *The Satires of Decimus Junius Juvenalis* (London: Jacob Tonson, 1697), p. 244.

[169] Previously referred to as *Christian Religion;* cf. Robert Jenkin in Appendix 3.

[170] Cf. 25 May (and see note 155).

[171] This entry is a footnote to the 7–9 p.m. meeting. John Wesley also had a continuing concern for Robson, as seen in his diary summary of important events for May:

25. Robson not rise.
26. In tears. Resolved again.
29. He missed Sacrament at St. Mary's.
30. Robson not rise. No more?

On 5 June "Robson rose" and on the sixth was "convinced and affected," but the subsequent entries through June and July show a great deal of fluctuation in Robson's zeal (OD IV [Summaries], 21–23). See also Wesley's letter to William Law on 26 June 1734 asking for advice on how to proceed with the recalcitrant student who admits, "with all composure, that he is not in a salvable state, and shows no concern" (*Letters*, I, 386–88; see also pp. 391–93 for John Clayton's advice to Wesley).

[172] In the Simplicity column for this hour, Ingham has rated his temper of devotion as 0; cf. Appendix 1.

came to read my resolutions. 7 Public Prayers, prayer, psalm, lessons, litany, collects. 8 E; breakfast with me, Hervey, Washington, and Atkinson, religious talk of resolutions. 9 E and read the last chapter of Rodriguez; ri; they fixed the time on Saturday night, 10 to 11, for resolutions and resignation. 10 E and private prayer; necessary business. 10.15 Composed Lecture; ri. 11 E; composed Lectures; ri. 12 E and private prayer. 12.15 Dinner. 12.45 With me, Washington, Watson, Atkinson, and Smyth. 1 E; read Jenkin; ri. 2.30 Composed Lectures. 3 E and Collect; with Dixon, Bolton, and Hall, read Law. 4 E. 4.15 Walked. 4.45 Read Bible; ri. 5 E; daily examination; private prayer; Public Prayers, prayer, psalm, lessons, collects. 6 E; supper and General Examination and wrote diary. 7 E; with me, Atkinson, Washington, Watson, Smyth, and Ford, good talk and read Law. 8 E; read Law's *Serious Call;* ri. 9 E; composed Lecture; ri. 10.30 Private prayer.

Blessings: recollected 7 times; Ford came, would not go home to his father's.

SATURDAY, JUNE 1.   4 Rose; dressed; business and virtue; thanksgiving and private prayer. 5 E; composed Lectures; ri. 6 E; with John Wesley, read my sermon on Matthew 19:17. 7 Came home; Public Prayers, prayer, psalm, lessons, collects; walked with Watson to Workhouse and Gloucester Green Workhouse; ri. 9 Received £10. 10*s.* and necessary business; ri.[173] 10 E; composed Lecture; ri. 11 E; finished three Lectures for my degree. 11.30 Walked. 12 E and private prayer; dinner. 12.45 With me, Atkinson, Washington, Watson, and Smyth. 1 E; read Jenkin; ri. 2 E with me, Washington and Hervey, read their resolutions and considered them, and religious talk of making[174] the resignation; ri. 4 E; transcribed abridgement of a sermon. 4.30 Meditated. 5 E; daily examination; private prayer. 5.30 Public Prayers, prayer, psalm, lessons, collects. 6 E; supper; walked with Atkinson, religious talk. 7 With me, Atkinson, Ford, Smith, Evans, and Hervey, read *The Life of Monsieur de Renty;* ri. 9 E; with me, Atkinson, private prayer; read Nelson; ri. 10 E and prayer for Hervey and Washington. 10.30 Meditated. 10.45 Private prayer. 11 Thanksgiving. 11.15 To bed.

Blessings: rose; with John Wesley; at Workhouse and Gloucester Green Workhouse; received some money; recollected 8 times; resolved

---

[173] The notice of this gift of ten guineas is accompanied by the symbol for "success in temporal affairs" in the margin.

[174] Marginal note ("3 E") indicates ejaculatory prayers on the hour.

to examine my resolutions once a month on Friday;[175] watched with Atkinson and prayed for Washington and Hervey who were making a resignation of themselves to Almighty God. N.B. Atkinson stood sentry[176] all night by my bedside in two chairs.

Sins: irrecollected and dissipated in Public Prayers.

WHIT SUNDAY, JUNE 2. 5 Rose; dressed. 5.30 Thanksgiving and wrote diary. 6 E; private prayer. 6.30 Breakfast with Charles Wesley, religious talk of ourselves and friends; ri; came home. 7.15 Meditated. 8 E; Public Prayers, prayer, psalm, lessons, litany, collects, com[munion].[177] 9 Sermon in the Chapel, and Sacrament.[178] 10 With me, Washington, private prayer for resignation, for courage, contempt of worldly things, and read meditation for the day;[179] ri; Washington went home. 11 E; Atkinson came, religious talk of friends. 11.30 Thanksgiving with Atkinson; ri. 11.45 Meditated. 12 E and Collect; dinner. 1 E; walked with Watson to Hamel, read a sermon. 2 E; at Sermon. 3 E and Collect; with Bolton and Dixon, read Law, and religious talk of private prayer and daily examination. 4.45 Meditated. 5 E; daily examination; private prayer. 5.30 Public Prayers, prayer, psalm, lessons, collects. 6 Walked with Dominus Black, learned talk; supper. 7 E; at Smith's with Ford, Atkinson, Hervey, and Evans, finished *The Life of Monsieur de Renty*. 8 E; read Norris on the Love of God;[180] ri. 9 E; came home; religious talk with Atkinson, private prayer. 9.45.

Blessings: rose; with Charles Wesley; recollected 11 times; the Sacrament; fervent in Public and private prayer; attentive at Sermon; in the Hamel; comforted Washington fearing God had forsaken him because he was dull in making the resolutions; prevented from laughing immoderately at Smith's.[181]

Sins: irrecollected and intemperate at dinner; burst into laughter at Smith's.

---

175 In the margin is the symbol for "good resolutions."
176 MS. reads "century," an obsolete form (see *O.E.D.*, s.v. "Century").
177 See 26 May, note 157.
178 This service at Queen's College chapel is the second time that day Ingham had received the Sacrament there.
179 See Johann Gerhard, *Gerhard's Meditations and Prayers* (1695), ch. 22, "Of the descent of the Holy Ghost" (Acts 2:4); see Appendix 3.
180 See 23 April, note 40.
181 In the margin is the symbol for "prevented from sin."

WHITSUN MONDAY, JUNE 3.   6.15 Dressed. 6.30 Confession and private prayer; ri. 7 E; prayer for the Sacrament. 7.15 Went to Christ Church; ri. 7.30 Public Prayers. 8 Public Prayers and Sacrament, <u>contrite</u>; came home with Broughton, religious talk. 9 E and Collect, thanksgiving after the Sacrament, and meditated; ri. 10 E; at Sermon. 10.45 Walked with Washington and Atkinson, religious talk. 11.30 Wrote a prayer for Smith. 12 E and private prayer; dinner. 1 E; with me, Washington, Watson, and Atkinson, read Jenkin; ri. 2 E; read Jenkin; ri. 3 E and Collect; read Jenkin; ri. 3.45 Walked with Washington, religious talk. 4 E; with Dixon, religious talk; Bolton not at home. 4.15 Wrote prayers. 5 E; daily examination; private prayer. 5.30 Public Prayers, prayer, psalm, lessons, collects. 6 E; gave Watson a prayer to transcribe. 6.15 Supper. 7 E; at Robson's with Smith, Greives, Hervey, and Ford, read Nelson for the day and used the prayers;[182] ri; drank. 9 Walked with Ford, religious talk. 9.30 Private prayer, to bed. 10.30.

Blessings: convinced of my utter inability to rise by hearing the larum at 4 and not being able to stir; I forgot to pray for help last night; I also waked at 5 but could not rise, so that I laid till Atkinson came and knocked at my door, and then I was heartily sorry at myself and penitent; + received the Holy Sacrament at Christ Church very devoutly; fervent in Public and private prayer; devout in meditating; thankful; zealous to do good; not intemperate; burnt my fingers and bore it patiently;[183] prevailed with Robson to promise to meet with us on Thursday night;[184] Hervey told me of a private Sacrament tomorrow, and John Wesley promised to stay till his brother and I come to them.

WHITSUN TUESDAY, JUNE 4.   4.15 Rose; dressed; wrote diary; business and virtue. 5 E; private prayer and thanksgiving. 6 E; walked; read Meditations; ri. 7 E; looked over a Boy's exercise.[185] 7.45 Meditated. 8 E; Public Prayers, prayer, psalm, lessons, collects, com[munion].[186] 8.45 With Charles Wesley. 9 Breakfast and religious talk and prayer for the Sacrament; ri. 9.15 Walked with him to a sick person; he read to her

---

182   See Nelson, *Festivals,* ch. XXII.
183   Marginal symbol indicates "prevented from sin."
184   Robson appears not to have fulfilled his promise in the three weeks before Ingham left Oxford; this is the last mention of him in the diary.
185   No doubt referring to one of the Poor Boys at Queen's, the name given to scholars who had entered on (were supported by) the foundation and who hoped as B.A.'s to become Taberdars and as M.A.'s, fellows.
186   See 26 May, note 157.

till John Wesley, Hall, Broughton, Salmon, Ford, Hervey, and Greives came, then we received the Blessed Sacrament; ri. 10 Sermon; ri. 11 Walked with Washington and Watson, religious talk; ri. 12 E and private prayer. 12.15 Dinner. 1 E; with me, Washington, Watson, and Atkinson, read Jenkin. 2 E; read Jenkin and religious talk. 3 E and Collect and private prayer. 3.15 Read Jenkin; walked with Washington. 4 E; with Dixon and Bolton, read Law, and religious talk; ri. 5 E; daily examination; private prayer; Public Prayers, prayer, psalm, lessons, collects. 6 E; religious talk with Washington; ri; supper. 7 E; at Smith's, good talk. 8 E; compared diaries; ri. 9 E; walked. 9.30 Private prayer and good talk with Watson; ri.

Blessings: rose; recollected 8 times; fervent in private prayer; the Sacrament with a sick woman; zealous to do good.

Sins: vain thoughts, and intemperate.

WEDNESDAY, JUNE 5. 4 Rose; dressed. 4.30 Wrote diary; read chapter; business and virtue. 5 E; private prayer; read *Plain Directions for Reading the Holy Scriptures;* ri. 6 E; with John Wesley, good talk about learning Hebrew. 7 E; walked with Rooke,[187] learned talk. 7.15 Public Prayers, prayer, psalm, lessons, collects. 8 E; at the Workhouse, taught children and read family prayers; came home. 9 E and Collect; read Sanderson with Atkinson and Washington, and religious talk. 10 E; went to Hervey's to begin to learn Hebrew with him and Greives, talked about it; looked into some liturgies of the Primitive Church; used some private prayer before we began; read over the letters, but could not go on; ri. 12 E and Collect; Hall. 12.30 Private prayer and read. 1 E; with me, Washington, Watson, and Atkinson, read Jenkin. 2 E; read Jenkin. 2.45 Smyth came, private prayer. 3 Breakfast and read Nelson for the Ember Days.[188] 4 E; with Dixon and Bolton, read Law, and religious talk. 5 E and daily examination; private prayer; Public Prayers. 6 Necessary business; supper on milk and bread; at the Workhouse, taught children and read family prayers. 7.30 At Ford's with Atkinson, Hervey, Smith, and Evans, began a collection of testimonies for the Primitive Church,[189] and religious talk of the Stations. 8.45 Walked with Smith and Evans. 9.15 Came home; thought; private prayer. 9.45.

187 MS. reads "Rook." Robert Rooke, Queen's College, B.A. 1733 (*Scholaribus Grindallianus,* 1732–33).
188 See Nelson, *Fasts,* ch. VII.
189 See the appendix to Thomas Deacon, *A Compleat Collection of Devotions Both Public and Private* (1734), in Appendix 3.

Blessings: rose; with John Wesley, he persuaded me to begin and learn the Hebrew tongue; began with Hervey and Greives with private prayer.

THURSDAY, JUNE 6.   6 Hervey came, religious talk. 6.15 Dressed. 6.30 Wrote diary; private prayer. 7 E; necessary business; Public Prayers, prayer, psalm, lessons, collects. 7.45 With Watson. 8 E; read Meditations, and prayer for the Sacrament. 8.30 Went to receive the Holy Sacrament with a poor woman (John Wesley, Charles Wesley, Broughton, Hall, Salmon, Washington, Watson, Atkinson, Greives, and two women). 9 Sacrament. 9.30 Thanksgiving at Hervey's, and religious talk; consulted with John Wesley about learning Hebrew, he agreed that I should defer it till Lent; Hervey and I agreed to write to each other; afterward I went to the Workhouse. 12 E and Collect; dinner; read first Lecture.[190] 1 E; with me, Atkinson, Washington, Watson, and Smyth, read Jenkin. 2 Good talk with Watson. 2.15 Washington, Smyth, and Watson came to be convinced of the obligation of the Stations; we first read Dr Hammond's judgment of the Church, then we read Bishop Beveridge, afterward we read John Wesley's treatise on the Stations;[191] Smyth disputed very much and left us before we finished it; ri. 5 E; daily examination; private prayer. 5.30 Public Prayers, prayer, psalm, lessons, collects. 6 E; supper. 7 E; with me, Hervey, Smith, Ford, and Walker, religious talk and read Norris on 'Religious Singularity'. 9 Religious talk with Ford of the Stations, of a diary, daily examination, etc; reconciled him. 10 E; read Law on rising;[192] ri; private prayer.

Blessings: Hervey came and raised me at 6; the Sacrament; John Wesley; Hervey; at Workhouse; Washington and Watson convinced of the Stations; Ford reconciled once more; zealous with Smyth.

Sins: rose at 4 and went to bed again; irrecollected.

FRIDAY, JUNE 7.   5 Rose; dressed; wrote diary; read chapter; private prayer. 6 E; necessary business; Public Prayers, prayer, psalm, lessons, litany, collects. 7 E; necessary business about my books. 8 E; walked

190   See 30 May, note 168.
191   Extracts from all three of these are contained in Deacon's appendix (see 5 June at 7:30 p.m.). The Hammond extract is from his *Practical Catechism* (1644), book 2, sec. 1 (see Appendix 3); the section from Beveridge is from book III, ch. X, of *Codex canonum;* and the Wesley item is sec. 3 of his "Essay upon the Stationary Fasts" (cf. John Wesley MS., Colman Collection XII, MA).
192   *Serious Call,* ch. XIV, "Concerning that part of devotion which relates to times and hours of prayer. Of daily early prayer in the morning."

with Washington to Gloucester Green Workhouse, taught the children, read family prayers, and religious talk; ri. 9 E; read Lectures; Hervey came, religious talk of Ford and ourselves; ri. 10.15 Necessary business. 11 E; meditated on my sins and Christ's sufferings; ri. 12 Private prayer. 12.15 Hall; read second Lecture.[193] 1 E; with me, Washington, Watson, Atkinson, and Smyth, read Jenkin. 2 E; read Jenkin; necessary business. 3 E and private prayer; breakfast and read Jenkin. 4 E; with Dixon and Bolton, read Law; ri. 5 E; daily examination; private prayer. 5.30 Public Prayers, prayer, psalm, lessons, collects. 6 Declamation. 6.15 Supper; Ford came to consult with me about going home, religious talk and encouraged him. 7 E; with me, Atkinson, Washington, Watson, Smyth, and Ford, read Law, and religious talk. 8 E; read Law, and religious talk. 9 Good talk with Watson; private prayer; R R.[194]

Blessings: rose; fervent in private prayer; at Gloucester Green Workhouse with Washington; zealous and active in conversation; recollected 8 times; encouraged Ford; R R.

Sins: unchaste thoughts frequently occurred.

SATURDAY, JUNE 8. 4 Rose; wrote diary; business and virtue; thanksgiving and private prayer. 5 E; began the second of St Clement's Epistles;[195] Smith came to tell me of a Sacrament; ri. 6 E; necessary business; Public Prayers, prayer, psalm, lessons, collects. 7 E; finished St Clement's Second Epistle. 8 E; various business. 8.30 Went to Hervey's, used a prayer for the Sacrament and then went to the sick person. 9 Sacrament; religious talk with Broughton of Ford. 9.30 Meditated. 10 E; vain thoughts, and meditated; ri. 11 E; walked. 11.45 Meditated. 12 E and private prayer; dinner; read third Lecture.[196] 1 E; with me, Atkinson, Washington, Watson, and Smyth, read Jenkin. 2 E; meditated; read Beveridge's Canons of the Primitive Church, and on the Stations.[197] 4.30 General Examination. 5 Daily Examination; private prayer. 5.30 Public Prayers. 6 Supper. 7 At Smith's with Atkinson, Hervey, and Evans, good talk and read Nelson. 8 E; read Nelson, and religious talk; ri. 9 E; came home. 9.15 With me, Atkinson and Washington, private prayer. 9.30 Read Horneck. 10 E and private prayer. 10.15 Read Horneck's

---

193 See 30 May, note 168.
194 See 15 May, note 126.
195 See Thomas Ittig, *Bibliotheca patrum apostolicorum.*
196 See 30 May, note 168.
197 See 23 May, note 149.

Best Exercise. 11 E and private prayer and thanksgiving. 11.30 To bed. 11.45.

Blessings: rose; recollected 8 times; the Holy Sacrament; fervent in private prayer; watched with me, Atkinson and Washington; denied myself of eating cherries and bought two books to give away; [the Provost gave Washington, etc, leave to go to the Sacrament at Christ Church].[198]

Sins: irrecollected; vain and unchaste thoughts frequently; spoke of my neighbour's faults without tenderness.

TRINITY SUNDAY, JUNE 9.   5 Rose; psalm; dressed; meditated. 6 E; wrote diary. 6.15 Private prayer. 6.30 Thanksgiving; read Nelson[199] and prayer for the Sacrament. 7 Breakfast at Charles Wesley's, good talk uninterrupted; ri. 8 At Christ Church, Public Prayers, heard the Ordination Sermon, attended at the Ordination;[200] afterward received the Holy Sacrament; ri. 11.30 Walked with Washington, Watson, and Atkinson, religious talk; wrote diary. 12 E; thanksgiving. 12.15 Dinner. 1 E; went to the Hamel, read a sermon; ri. 2 At Sermon.[201] 2.45 With Dixon and Bolton. 3 E; read Law and religious talk of the Church and of the Sacrament at St Mary's, etc; ri. 5 E; daily examination; private prayer; Public Prayers. 6 E; religious talk with Bolton and Brownsword; ri. 7 E; at Evans' with Smith, Atkinson, Ford, and Hervey. 8 E; read Extracts for the Primitive Church.[202] 9 E; religious talk with Smith. 9.15 Looked over the *Collection of Devotions.* 10.30.

Blessings: rose; in the Hamel; fervent in private prayer; the Sacrament; recollected 8 times; zealous for Bolton and Dixon and Brownsword.

MONDAY, JUNE 10.   5 Rose; dressed. 5.15 Private prayer. 5.45 Read *Collection of Devotions.* 6.30 Public Prayers; went to Smith's and Charles Wesley's, religious talk of friends. 7.30 Read *Collection.* 8 E; necessary business. 8.45 Breakfast with me, Bolton and Dixon, religious talk. 9.30 Went to St Mary's, Public Prayers. 10 Latin Sermon, and

---

198   This note is in the Blessings column at 1 p.m. Joseph Smith was provost of Queen's College, 1730–56.

199   See Nelson, *Festivals,* ch. XXIV.

200   Ordinations occurred on the Sundays following the four seasonal observances of Ember Days: in Lent, after Whitsunday, in September, and in December. Nelson, *Fasts,* ch. III.

201   The statutes designated New College as the location of the sermon before the university on Trinity Sunday (*Statutes,* XVI.5).

202   See the appendix to Thomas Deacon, *Compleat Collection,* in Appendix 3.

Sacrament.[203] 11.15 Private prayer and Thanksgiving with Watson. 11.45 Necessary business. 12 Dinner. 12.45 With me, Atkinson, Washington, Watson, and Smyth. 1 E; read Jenkin, and religious talk of spirits and temperance; ri. 3 E and Collect; necessary business; began Mr Reeves' *Apologies*. 4 E; read Reeves' Preface. 5 E; daily examination; private prayer. 5.30 Public Prayers. 6 Supper. 7 At Walker's with Smith, Hervey, and Ford, various and useful talk. 8 E; read a sermon of Norris; ri; walked with Smith, mostly religious talk. 9.15 Walked with Ford, religious talk how he should behave himself at home. 10 Private prayer.

Blessings: rose; zealous for Dixon and Bolton, etc; the Holy Sacrament at St Mary's; Hervey gave good advice at Walker's when we were trifling.

Sins: irrecollected; neglected ejaculatory prayers; cold in Public and private prayer; trifling at Walker's.

ST BARNABAS TUESDAY, JUNE 11. Very much disturbed in the night by frightful dreams and irregular persons, so that I could not sleep for several hours. 5.45 Rose; dressed; psalm; wrote diary. 6 Private prayer, and for my birthday, private prayer and thanksgiving. 6.30 Wrote resolutions for Ford going into the country; ri; dressed; prayer for the Sacrament. 8 E; Public Prayers. 8.45 Religious talk with Dixon and Bolton of the Sacrament at St Mary's; ri. 9 Breakfast with me, Washington, and Smith, good talk. 10 Private prayer with me, Atkinson, for the Sacrament; afterward we went to St Mary's, Public Prayers and Sermon, John Wesley preached.[204] 11 The Blessed Sacrament. 11.45 Thanksgiving. 12 E; dinner; meditated. 1 E; with me, Atkinson, Washington, Watson, and Smyth, read Jenkin. 2 E; walked with Washington, religious talk.

---

203 This was the service at the beginning of Trinity term (see 9 October, note 50).

204 This day was the feast of St. Barnabas the Apostle (see Nelson, *Festivals*, ch. XXV), and also the anniversary of the accession of George II to the throne in 1727. Charles Wesley reported to his brother Samuel that John had been "much mauled, and threatened more for his Jacobite Sermon on the 11th June." *Original Letters by the Rev. John Wesley and his Friends*, ed. Joseph Priestley (Birmingham: T. Pearson, 1791), p. 15. Although the occasion might have lent itself to the expression of Jacobite sympathies, the text of Wesley's sermon ("The One Thing Needful," on Luke 10:42) as we have it in Charles's transcription gives no hint as to what might have caused such an uproar. See Sermon 146.

3 E; necessary business. 3.30 Read Reeves' Preface. 4 E; read Reeves; ri. 5 E; daily examination; private prayer. 5.30 Public Prayers, prayer, psalm, lessons, collects. 6 Supper, necessary talk about my degree. 7 E; walked with Smith. 8 Good talk, compared diaries and good talk; ri. 9 Wrote diary; meditated, and private prayer. 9.45.

Blessings: zealous for Dixon and Bolton; the Sacrament at St Mary's; Washington regarded not his tutor's threats; recollected 10 times.

Sins: dissipated in Public Prayers.

WEDNESDAY, JUNE 12. 5 Rose; dressed; necessary business; private prayer. 6 Necessary business; Public Prayers. 7 Wrote questions for Disputation. 7.45 Walked with Washington and Atkinson to a Sacrament with John Wesley, Charles Wesley, Hall, and Hervey; ri. 8.30 To Workhouse; called at Smith's; ri; came home. 10 E; composed an Opposition. 11 E; Disputations. 12 Watson with me, read Law and used the Stationary prayer.[205] 12.30 Hall. 12.45 Read Reeves. 1 E; with me, Washington, Watson, Smyth, and Atkinson, read Jenkin. 2 E; read Jenkin. 2.45 Private prayer. 3 E and Collect; breakfast and religious talk. 3.45 Necessary business. 4 E; wrote a Supposition. 5 E; daily examination; private prayer; Public Prayers. 6 Supper. 7 With me, Atkinson, Smith, Evans, Hervey, and Ford. 8 E; read Extracts upon the Primitive Church, and disputed. 9 E; wrote a Supposition. 10.30.

Blessings: received the Blessed Sacrament with a sick woman.

Sins: indolent and irrecollected; indulged unchaste thoughts.

Πρὸς ἐντροπὴν γράφω.[206]

THURSDAY, JUNE 13. 5 Rose; dressed; private prayer. 5.45 Began Justin Martyr's 'Apology for the Christians'; ri.[207] 7.15 Public Prayers; finished Justin Martyr's 'Apology', translated by Mr Reeves.[208] 8.15 At Dixon's with Bolton, various talk; breakfast with Dixon and Dominus Collinson,[209] various talk. 9.30 Wrote Supposition. 10 E; began Tertullian's 'Apologetic', translated by Mr Reeves; ri. 11 E; walked. 11.45 Meditated and private prayer. 12 E; dinner; with me, Atkinson, Washington, Watson, and Smyth. 1 E; read Jenkin, and religious talk. 2 E;

---

205 See 31 October, note 73.
206 "I write this to [my] shame"; cf. 1 Cor. 4:14, 6:5 (see also 8 April, note 171).
207 Marginal note ("6 E") indicates ejaculatory prayers on the hour.
208 See William Reeves in Appendix 3.
209 William Collinson, Queen's College, B.A. 1732.

Disputation for my degree;[210] ri. 3 E; wrote Epistle and stood for my Grace;[211] Thomas and I had it granted.[212] 4 E; with Hervey, religious talk and private prayer; came home. 4.45 Read Nelson. 5 E; daily examination; private prayer. 5.30 Public Prayer, prayer, psalm, lessons, collects. 6 Supper; necessary business. 7 Walked with Watson, good talk about his love affair; he had received a letter from his mistress,[213] she left it to his choice; I exhorted him never to think of it more, but to dedicate himself to God. 8 E; at Thomas' with Mayo,[214] we treated the six senior Scholars,[215] various talk; we sit from 8 to 12; I was pretty well recollected.

Blessings: rose; Atkinson was called up by Mr Benn,[216] and was not discouraged; Watson at last received a letter from his mistress which put an end to his troubles; I got my Grace in the House; preserved from drunkenness and wantonness.

FRIDAY, JUNE 14. 6 Dressed; Public Prayers, prayer, psalm, lessons, litany, collects. 7 E; private prayer; read Tertullian. 8 E; read Tertul-

---

210 Undergraduates were required, upon being created general sophist, and until they were promoted to the bachelor's degree, to dispute at least once each term in the Parvises (*Statutes*, VI.1.4). These were called "Juraments." This summer term was the sixteenth term since Ingham had matriculated in November 1730 (see *Statutes*, VI.1.1; see also note 211).

211 The Latin epistle was no doubt a supplication for his grace (see 1 January, note 151). The House of Congregation (of regent masters) could grant a dispensation (grace) from any one of a number of statutory requirements for degrees. The records indicate that Ingham on this occasion was excused from two terms of the residence requirement, a rather common allowance at that time. *Supplicat &c. . . . ut gratiore secum dispensetur pro absentia duorum Terminorum. Causa est quod seriis negotiis impeditur eisdem vacare non licuit.* "Register of the Acts of Congregation," BH (E.W. 1a), fol. 69 recto (University of Oxford Archives); see also *Statutes*, IX.4.2(no. 1). Ingham had apparently been absent during Michaelmas term, 1732, as there are no entries for him in the college battel books for that period. Since the college records are not complete during this decade, we cannot tell which other term Ingham missed.

212 Symbol in margin indicates "success in temporal affairs."

213 See 23 April, note 44.

214 John Mayo, Queen's College, B.C.L. 1737.

215 Taberdars. These "treats" were soon to be superseded by payments in money, made in lieu of this public mode of celebrating an occasion. John Richard Magrath, *The Flemings in Oxford* (Oxford: Oxford Historical Society, 1904–24), vol. 1, 249; vol. 2, 81.

216 MS. reads "Ben." Robert Benn was a fellow of Queen's, B.A. 1718, M.A. 1721/22, B.D. 1738, D.D. 1739.

lian. 9 Private prayer. 9.15 Read Tertullian. 9.30 Went to the Schools, walked in the Pig Market,[217] and Stood for my Grace till 12; ri. 12 Came home; read Tertullian. 12.45 Private prayer. 1 E; with me, Washington, Watson, Smyth, and Atkinson, read Jenkin. 2 E; read Jenkin. 2.30 Went to Charles Wesley's with Smith and Carter.[218] 2.45 Private prayer. 3 Breakfast, read Sales; walked with Smith, and religious talk. 4 E; with Hervey, religious talk and private prayer. 5 E; daily examination; private prayer. 5.30 Public Prayers. 6 E; Declamation; General Examination; finished Reeves' Tertullian's 'Apologetic'; ri. 7 E; with me, Atkinson, Washington, Smyth, Watson, and Ford, read Law; ri. 8 E; read Law's *Serious Call,* and religious talk. 9 Private prayer and meditated. 9.30.

Blessings: got my Grace in the University; made several acts of self-denial; zealous in conversation; to bed.

Sins: irrecollected; cold in Public and private prayer.

SATURDAY, JUNE 15.   4 Rose; dressed; wrote diary; business and virtue; private prayer and thanksgiving; meditated. 5 Meditated; went to John Wesley's, religious talk of friends. 6 Religious talk with Atkinson. 6.15 Public Prayers, prayer, psalm, lessons, collects. 7 E; religious talk with Watson; with Dixon; walked with Washington and Atkinson to Smith's, religious talk of meeting at nights with those gentlemen in Queen's College on Fridays and Sundays.[219] 9 E and Collect; religious talk with

---

[217]   The lobby of the Divinity School. The supplicant candidate was "to stand in the Proscholium or Pig-market, vulgarly so called, during the whole time of the Congregation, *nudato capite* [head uncovered], until his Grace be either granted or denied" (Ayliffe, *Present State,* II, 143; cf. *Statutes,* IX.3.1). Ingham had requested a dispensation from the stated requirements for attendance at the public lectures, a grace that was granted pro forma at this time because of the less than diligent performance of many of the lecturers. Symbol in margin indicates "success in temporal affairs." The entry in the university records reads, *Supplicat &c. . . . ut gratiore secum dispensetur pro minus diligenti Publicorum Lectorum Auditione. Causa est [quod illi seriis negotii impedito eisdem vacare liciut].* "Register of the Acts of Congregation," BH (E.W. 1ᵃ), fol. 68 verso. See also Thomas Wilson, *The Diaries of Thomas Wilson, D.D. 1731–37 and 1750,* ed. C. L. S. Linnell (London: S.P.C.K., 1964), p. 111; and *Statutes,* IX.4.2 (no. 4, "For a loose attendance on the Public Readers").

[218]   This is Ingham's first afternoon meeting and breaking of the fast with Charles Wesley since Easter Eve, 13 April.

[219]   Smith was resident at Christ Church. The plan was begun the following evening.

Charles Wesley of friends. 9.45 Went to my tutor's to get out my accounts,[220] and necessary business. 11 E; walked. 12 Dinner. 1 E; with me, Washington, Watson, and Smyth, finished Jenkin's second volume of *The Reasonableness of the Christian Religion,* and then used a prayer for faith.[221] 2.30 Necessary business. 3 E; at Dixon's with Hall and Bolton, read Law, and disputed of predestination and morality. 5 E; daily examination; private prayer. 5.30 Public Prayers. 6 Read Nelson, and supper. 7 With me, Smith, Evans, Ford, Atkinson, and Hervey,[222] read Extracts for the Catholic Church.[223] 9 E; religious talk with Ford; private prayer. 9.45.

Blessings: rose; recollected thrice; success with Smith, Atkinson, and Washington; temperate.

Sins: cold and dissipated in Public Prayers; trifling; sit up too late.

SUNDAY, JUNE 16. 4 Rose; could not abide up, but to bed again. N.B. Resolved to allow myself at least 6½ or 7 hours [sleep]. 5 Dressed; meditated. 5.45 Private prayer. 6 E; necessary business. 6.30 Breakfast with me, Charles Wesley and Atkinson. 7 Religious talk of friendship, and read Sales; ri. 8 Public Prayers. 9 E and Collect; went to the Castle with Watson, religious talk; there were 21 Gown Men.[224] 10 Public Prayers, Sermon, and Sacrament. 12 Came home. 12.15 Dinner. 12.45 Wrote diary. 1 E; went to the Hamel, read Country Parson. 2 E; Sermon. 3 E; began Reeves' Minutius Felix.[225] 4 E; with Dixon, read Law; ri. 5 E; daily examination; private prayer. 5.30 Public Prayers. 6 E; supper; finished Minutius. 7 E; at Smith's with Atkinson, Ford, Evans, and Hervey, read Extracts for the Primitive Church. 9 E; came home; necessary business; private prayer. 9.30.

---

220 Tutors usually acted as financial agents for their students, paying their bills for clothes and other necessities from money sent by the parents, reckoning up their accounts every quarter or so. See Thomas Salmon, *The Present State of the Universities* (London: J. Roberts, 1744), p. 436f.; Robert Howard Hodgkin, *Six Centuries of an Oxford College* (Oxford: Basil Blackwell, 1949), p. 124.

221 An ironic, though perhaps not unexpected, reaction to reading Jenkin's book.

222 Marginal note ("8 E") indicates ejaculatory prayers at the hour.

223 See appendix to Thomas Deacon, *Compleat Collection.*

224 University students.

225 MS. reads "Fælix." "The Octavius of Minutius Felix," in vol. II; see William Reeves in Appendix 3.

Blessings: Charles Wesley; the Sacrament; Atkinson, Watson, and Washington agreed to go twice a week to Gloucester Green Workhouse, and contribute sixpence a month to maintain some poor children at school.

Sins: unchaste [thoughts] and idleness; dissipated at Public Prayers.

MONDAY, JUNE 17.   5 Rose; dressed; private prayer; business and virtue. 6 E; Public Prayers; necessary business; with Charles Wesley, asked him whether I should go to London; he thought not; with Smith, good talk; necessary business[226] getting Scios.[227] 8.15 Breakfast with Natt, good talk (various). 9 E and Collect; went to the Schools, stood for my Bachelor's Degree,[228] got it. 11.30 Came home; wrote diary; thanksgiving. 11.45 Necessary business. 12 Necessary business and dinner. 1 E; with me, Washington, Watson, and Smyth, read Law. 2 E; walked with Watson, religious talk. 2.45 Walked with Smith and Evans, religious and useful talk. 3.30 Mostly religious talk with Smith. 4 With Hervey, religious talk and private prayer. 4.45 Wrote diary. 5 E; daily examination; private prayer. 5.30 Public Prayers. 6 Supper. 7 Walked with the Bachelors, various and useful talk. 8 E; in the Taberdars' Common Room,[229] treated the Bachelors, various talk till 11.30.[230]

Blessings: got my B.A. degree; zealous in conversation; preserved from drunkenness and pretty recollected.

Sins: not rise;[231] irrecollected; neglected Ejaculatory prayers.

TUESDAY, JUNE 18.   5.30 Rose; dressed; wrote diary; private prayer. 6 Walked; Public Prayers. 7 E; breakfast with John Wesley, religious

---

[226]   Marginal note ("8 E") indicates ejaculatory prayers on the hour.

[227]   On presentation day, the candidate in the arts was required to have formal testimonies from nine B.A.'s, depositing in the Apodyterium or outer room of the Congregation House on their knees before the proctors, as to the fitness of the candidate for the degree. The inquiry as to whether or not the candidate was *aptus et idoneus moribus et scientia* was to be answered by a whisper in the proctor's ear: *scio* (I know), *credo* (I believe), or *nescio* (I do not know). Five *nescios* would serve to reject the candidate. See Ayliffe, *Present State,* II, 148; Magrath, *Flemings,* vol. 3, 65, note 6; cf. *Statutes,* IX.3.3, and IX.5.7.

[228]   MS. reads "Batchelor's." A symbol in the margin indicates "success in temporal affairs."

[229]   MS. reads "Tabardar's." The Taberdars were members of the foundation chosen from among the Poor Boys after becoming B.A.'s.

[230]   Marginal note: "not drunk."

[231]   MS. reads "rose."

talk. 8 With me, Atkinson, religious talk; necessary business. 9 Necessary business. 10 E; began Vincentius Lirinensis.[232] 11 E; walked and necessary business. 11.45 Private prayer. 12 E and Collect; dinner. 12.45 With Hervey, necessary business. 1 E; with me, Atkinson, Washington, Watson, and Smyth, read Law. 2 E; finished Law's *Serious Call*, disputed about the Stations, religious talk. 3 With Atkinson. 3.30 With Natt, tea, and read the Death of an Apostate.[233] 4 With him and Atkinson, and religious talk. 5 E; daily examination; private prayer. 5.30 Public Prayers, prayer, psalm, lessons, collects. 6 Supper. 7 With Charles Wesley, good talk. 7.15 Walked with Smith, religious and useful talk. 8 Compared diaries with Smith, and religious talk. 9 E; came home; good talk with Atkinson and Watson. 9.30 Private prayer.

Blessings: with John Wesley; zealous to do good.

Sins: irrecollected; intemperate.

WEDNESDAY, JUNE 19. 4.15 Rose; dressed; psalm; wrote diary; business and virtue. 5 E; private prayer. 5.15 Finished Vincentius Lirinensis, translated by Reeves. 6.30 Public Prayers; religious talk with Watson. 7 E; Smyth came, religious talk, satisfied him; ri. 8 Went to the Workhouse, taught and read family prayers. 9 E and Collect; with Smith, religious and useful talk; Charles Wesley came, walked with him, and religious talk of friends, and going home; with John Wesley, religious talk; got some prayers to be used before reading at nights. 10 E; with Dixon and Bolton, read the Death of an Apostate, and religious talk of my friends, and how they should proceed; ri. 11.45 Came home and necessary business. 12 E and Collect; meditated. 1 E; with me, Atkinson, Washington, Watson, and Smyth, read the Death of an Apostate. 2 Religious talk with Washington, Watson, and Smyth. 2.45 Private prayer. 3 E and Collect; breakfast with me, Washington, Watson, Smyth, and Atkinson, religious talk, and dressed. 4 E; with Bolton and Dixon, read Law, and religious talk; they consented to rise at 5.30, read Nelson, and use private prayer. 5 E; daily examination; private prayer. 5.30 Public Prayers. 6 Supper. 6.30 Went to Workhouse. 7.15 At Evans' with Hervey, Smith, and Ford, religious talk. 8 E; read Extracts, and religious talk. 9 E; walked with Ford, religious talk. 9.30 Came home; private prayer.

---

[232] "The Commonitory of Vincentius Lirinensis," in vol. II; see Reeves in Appendix 3.
[233] See 25 May, note 155.

Blessings: rose; twice at the Workhouse; good success with my friends; zealous and active.

Sins: dissipated in Public Prayers, and irrecollected.

THURSDAY, JUNE 20.   4 Rose; dressed; meditated.   4.30 Wrote diary. 4.45 Necessary business. 5 E; private prayer. 5.15 Dressed. 5.30 <u>Called</u> Dixon and Bolton; necessary business, and private prayer. 6 E; breakfast at Ford's with Smith, religious and useful talk. 7 Came home; Public Prayers. 7.45 Called at John Wesley's, necessary business. 8 E; went with Smith to Gambold's,[234] religious and useful talk of resolutions, etc. 10.30[235] At Gambold's, eat, religious and useful talk. 11 Read Ephraem Syrus. 12.30 Dinner with Gambold, Charles Wesley, Broughton, and Smith, religious talk of meditation. 1 E with Charles Wesley, and religious talk. 2 E; read Bishop Hall on Meditation with Charles Wesley, etc, and resolved to meditate a full hour every day. 3 E; tea; religious talk. 4 Came home with Smith, E, and religious talk.[236] 6 E; daily examination; private prayer. 6.45 Supper at Smith's. 7 E; necessary business. 7.15 At Ford's with Hervey, religious talk. 9 E; walked with Ford, religious talk. 9.30 Laid with Washington, private prayer. 9.45 To bed.

Blessings: Bolton and Dixon got up; with Charles Wesley, resolved to meditate an hour, he advised me never to be irrecollected two hours together, but to set apart ½ [hour] to recover myself; religious talk with Gambold; got Smith to fix a week for resolutions before I go into the country; Ford should have provided me a supper, but did not,[237] I supped with Smith; Washington was not gone to bed at 9.30.

FRIDAY, JUNE 21.   4.30 Psalm; dressed. 5 E; business and virtue; read Greek Testament. 5.30 Private prayer. 5.45 Meditated. 6 E; Public Prayers. 7 E; walked with Natt, religious and useful talk. 7.15 Wrote diary. 7.30 Necessary business. 8 E; at Workhouse, taught, and read family prayer. 9.15 At Smith's, composed Arguments. 10 E; composed a Theme. 11 E; necessary business. 12 E and Collect; meditated on Christ's sufferings, and private prayer. 1 E; with me, Atkinson, Washing-

---

[234]   At Stanton Harcourt.

[235]   At this point the diary returns to the original paragraph format for four pages, the many columns of the "exacter" style not returning until 10 July.

[236]   This is the only instance in this diary up to this point of Ingham missing the evening chapel service. Cf. 29 January, note 181.

[237]   See 23 June, at 6:15 p.m.

ton, Watson, and Smyth, read a sermon. 2 E; necessary business with Smith. 2.30 Came home; meditated. 2.45 Private prayer. 3 E; breakfast with me, Washington, Watson, and Smyth, religious and useful talk, and disputed about the Stations.[238] 4.30 With Dixon and Bolton, read Country Parson, and religious talk. 5 E. 5.15 Daily examination. 5.30 Public Prayers. 6 E; Declamation, and supper. 6.30 Necessary business. 6.45 With me, Ford, good talk. 7 At Washington's with Smith, Ford, and Watson, religious talk, and read Country Parson, and religious talk of resolutions; ri. 8.45 Walked with Smith, religious talk. 9 E. 9.15 Came home; private prayer with Washington, and laid with him. 9.45 To bed.

SATURDAY, JUNE 22. 5 Rose; dressed; business and virtue; read Greek Testament; private prayer. 5.45 Composed Arguments. 6.15 Public Prayers. 7 E; breakfast with John Wesley, religious and useful talk. 8 Necessary business. 9 E and Collect; settled affairs. 10 Wrote a letter to Charles Burton. 11.45 To Ford's, meditated. 12.30 Dinner. 1 E; came home; put up my goods. 3.30 With Charles Wesley and Smith, necessary talk. 4 E; necessary business with Hervey, religious talk. 4.30 Wrote out the marks for the Blessings for Hervey.[239] 4.45 Daily examination. 5 E; meditated, and private prayer. 5.30 Public Prayers. 6 Religious talk with Watson. 6.15 Went to Hervey's, supper, wrote him the scheme of daily examination.[240] 7 Ford and Evans came, finished Deacon's Extracts, and religious talk, used a prayer for perseverance; ri. 9 E; called at Broughton's, religious talk. 9.15 Came home; private prayer with Washington. 9.30 To bed.

SUNDAY, JUNE 23. 5 Rose; dressed; meditated; private prayer. 6 Called Dixon and Bolton. 6.15 Wrote diary. 6.30 Meditated. 7 E; went to Charles Wesley's. 7.30 Public Prayers. 8 Public Prayers and Sacrament.[241] 9 Breakfast with Charles Wesley, religious talk; he gave me Rodriguez on Humility. 10 E; at Sermon. 11 E; wrote. 12 E; dinner at Smith's, religious talk with him; he fixed the first week of next month for Country Parson's resolutions. 1 E; with Smith at Atkinson's, good talk. 2 E; Sermon. 2.45 At John Wesley's with Charles Wesley, they gave me

238 Watson was perhaps the most convinced proponent of the Stations, Smyth the least; see 27 March, 17 April, and 5 June.
239 See list of symbols, plate 4.
240 See 28 January, note 180.
241 At Christ Church.

little books to give away; John Wesley gave me Thomas à Kempis in Latin;[242] parted with them. 3.15 With Smith, private prayer and religious talk. 3.30 With Atkinson, Watson, and Bolton, read a sermon of Horneck's, and religious talk; Bolton consented that they should call him up. 5 E; thanksgiving and private prayer. 5.30 Public Prayers. 6 Necessary business. 6.15 Supper at Ford's, religious talk. 7.15 At Smith's with Ford, Washington, Watson, Evans, and Hervey, read Bishop Hall on Meditation, and religious talk; prayed for perseverance. 9 Drank with Ford. 9.15 With Atkinson, Washington, Watson, and Ford, necessary and useful talk. 9.30 Private prayer with Washington; to bed.

[242] From the time of his becoming a corresponding member of the S.P.C.K. in 1732, John Wesley regularly ordered sizable quantities of books from their list of books "For the Use of the Poor" and had in fact just sent in an order on 19 June to replenish his stock of giveaway items. See *Letters*, I, 726–33; cf. *An Account of the Origin and Designs of the Society for Promoting Christian Knowledge* (1734) in which prices are listed for "singles" and "per hundred." See also 10 August, note 84. In November 1733 Wesley had also bought three copies of Thomas à Kempis for five shillings (although he already owned one), apparently intending them to be gifts (John Wesley MS., Colman Collection XVIII, p. 65, MA).

The last three months of this diary display Ingham's attempt to transplant the Oxford Methodist lifestyle to Ossett, his hometown near Wakefield in Yorkshire. He immediately introduces study sessions and family prayers in his mother's house every evening; some of the neighbors begin to attend before a month has passed. He begins teaching the children of the town (including his own sister) how to read and write, and considers setting up a school. He tries to maintain some semblance of the disciplined life of meditative piety so carefully cultivated at Oxford, but soon discovers the added trials and temptations of this new setting where "even those who pass for good Christians are sunk deep in a dead indifferency." The daily record of his diary reflects the continual turmoil as well as the occasional triumphs of his spiritual combat. In mid-July Ingham draws up a schedule of "Rules for Spending my Time" to help adjust to the new surroundings. His daily "recollections" frequently indicate his failures. A month after "methodizing" his time, several continuing problems are reflected in the "resolutions for the following week" that result from his self-examination on 23 August.

Interspersed among all of this intentional discipline is a round of daily activities typical of country life: hunting, hewing trees, harvesting crops, visiting neighbors, sightseeing, and shopping. This section of the diary is bracketed by two trips to visit the Wesleys at the Epworth rectory. On the way north from Oxford, Ingham follows the route usually taken by the Wesley brothers, often eating at the same inns and staying overnight with the same friends. At the end of the diary, he journeys from Ossett to Epworth in company with John and Charles and spends several days in the Wesley household, following a schedule of activities that is not much different from his accustomed round.

MONDAY, JUNE 24.   4.30 Rose; dressed. 5 Private prayer with Washington, Watson. 5.15 Set forward for the North;[1] Washington and Watson came with me about two miles; religious talk and prayed at parting; afterwards I missed[2] my way, and by that means met with a Boy[3] going to Coventry; he let me ride with him; we dined at Banbury. 6.45 At Coventry, wrote a letter to Joseph Alleine.[4] 8 Religious talk with a stranger against swearing. 9 Supper. 9.30 Private prayer; to bed.

TUESDAY, JUNE 25.   4.30 Rose; walked to Leicester, and dinner at Alderman Smith's,[5] religious talk with his wife, the son not at home. 3.30 Walked to Segshill;[6] meditated a little by the way; met with no one. 8 Supper. 9.30 To bed.

WEDNESDAY, JUNE 26.   Walked to Red Lodge[7] to dinner, religious talk with the owners. 4 To Newark; walked with a butcher to Collingham.[8] 9.30 Supper; to bed.

THURSDAY, JUNE 27.   Walked to Gainsborough,[9] dinner with Miss

---

[1]   Ingham's route and method of travel (walking) conformed to the Wesley brothers' usual pattern.

[2]   MS. reads "mist."

[3]   This may refer to a Queen's College Poor Boy; cf. 4 June, note 185.

[4]   Ingham was writing "on Wesley's account" (see monthly summary for June 1734). The name is spelled the same as that of the seventeenth-century Nonconformist friend of Wesley's grandfather, but there is no indication whether this person might be a descendant.

[5]   Henry Smith, baker in Shambles Lane, was the father of William Smith, one of John Wesley's students at Lincoln College. He had been an alderman since 1705 and had served as mayor of Leicester in 1730. *Roll of the Mayors of the Borough and Lord Mayors of the City of Leicester, 1209–1935,* comp. Henry Hartopp (Leicester: E. Backus, 1936), p. 141. Wesley frequently stopped at the Smiths'.

[6]   Now called Six Hills, seventeen kilometers north of Leicester on Foss Way, another regular stop for the Wesleys. John Cary's map of Leicestershire lists this place as "Sax or Segs Hill" (*Antiquities in Leicestershire,* ed. John Nichols, vol. VII of *Bibliotheca Topographica Britannica* [London: J. Nichols, 1790], facing p. 424).

[7]   An inn twelve kilometers south of Newark, visited often by the Wesleys and still operating today under the same name.

[8]   Ingham would have had a choice of several inns at Collingham (South and North), including the White Hart, the King's Head, and the Royal Oak (the latter two are still operating).

[9]   MS. reads "Ganesbro."

Wesley;[10] thence to Epworth; stayed there three days at Mr Wesley's; read Gother, and Dr Waterland on the Nature of the Sacraments; much religious talk with Mrs Wesley and some with Kezzy,[11] some with the old man;[12] very well entertained.

MONDAY, JULY 1. 3.30 Rose; private prayer; breakfast. 4 Rode to Doncaster with their wagon going for coals. 8 With Mr Fox, delivered a letter. 8.30 Walked to Wakefield. 3.30 Dressed. 4 At J Wright's, tea. 6 Came to Ossett.[13] 8 Religious talk with my friends of family prayer; ri. 9 Began and read family prayers. 9.15 Private prayer; to bed.

Blessings: got safe home and began to read family prayers; we stood at reading the chapter.[14]

TUESDAY, JULY 2. 5 Rose; dressed; private prayer. 5.30 Read family prayers. 5.45 Wrote diary. 6 E; read Nelson.[15] 7 E; meditated. 7.45 Breakfast with mother, and religious talk. 11 E; various talk with strangers. 12 E and Collect; dinner at brother William's, religious talk. 1 E; slept. 2.30 Began Cave's *Primitive Christianity*. 4.30 Walked with Joseph.[16] 5.30 Daily examination; private prayer. 6.30 Supper. 7 E; read Cave. 8.30 Religious talk with my mother and Hannah.[17] 9.15 Read family prayers. 9.45 To bed.

WEDNESDAY, JULY 3. 5.30 Dressed; business and virtue; read Nelson;

10 Emilia Wesley (John's sister, age forty-one) had established a boarding school in Gainsborough in 1731. See George Stevenson, *Memorials of the Wesley Family* (London: S. W. Partridge & Co., 1876), pp. 268–70.

11 Susanna, mother of John and Charles, and Kezia Wesley, another of the Wesley sisters, age twenty-four or twenty-five.

12 Samuel Wesley, Sr., mentions this visit by Ingham in a letter to Westley Hall on 11 July, mentioning that when Ingham, Hall, and the Wesley brothers came to Epworth at fair time in August, he hoped to provide the Sacrament weekly for their benefit. Luke Tyerman, *The Life and Times of the Rev. Samuel Wesley* (London: Simpkin, Marshall & Co., 1866), p. 427.

13 MS. reads "Osset"; listed as "Osleset" in the Domesday Book. W. Bawdwen, *A Translation of the Record called Domesday, so far as relates to the County of York.* . . . (Doncaster: W. Sheardon, 1809), pp. 15–16. The Ingham home was at 7–9 Town End, just off the Wakefield–Dewsbury Road. P. H. Taylor, *Wesley Street Chapel, Ossett, Diamond Jubilee 1868–1928* (Ossett, Yorkshire: S. Cockburn & Son, n.d.), p. 5. See plate 18.

14 See conversation with John Wesley on 25 May.

15 During July, Ingham read Nelson's *Practice of True Devotion* (1698); see Appendix 3 and monthly summary for July 1734.

16 William and Joseph were his older brothers.

17 Hannah Ingham, one of his younger sisters.

private prayer. 6.30 Meditated. 7 Read family prayers and meditated. 8 E; read Nelson, and private prayer. 9 E and Collect. 9.15 Wrote letters to Ford, Smyth, and Smith. 12 E and Collect; meditated and private prayer. 1 Read Cave; ri. 3 E and Collect; breakfast;[18] various and useful talk with my mother and Hannah. 5 E; daily examination; meditated; private prayer. 6 E; supper on milk and bread. 6.30 Walked. 7 Read Cave. 8 Religious talk with my mother and Hannah. 9 Read family prayers and religious talk. 10 Private prayer; to bed.

THURSDAY, JULY 4.   5.30 Rose; dressed; business and virtue. 6 E; read Nelson, and private prayer. 6.30 Meditated. 7 E; read family prayers; read Cave. 7.45 Breakfast. 8 E; wrote letters to Washington, Watson, and Atkinson. 10 Read Cave. 11 Walked. 12 E and Collect; dinner. 1 Waited to send the letters to Oxford, but was disappointed;[19] read Cave. 6 E; daily examination; read Nelson, and private prayer. 7 Read Cave, and supper. 8.30 Religious talk with my mother. 9 Read family prayers. 9.15 Various and useful talk. 9.45 Private prayer.

FRIDAY, JULY 5.   5 Rose; dressed; business and virtue; read Nelson. 6 Private prayer; meditated. 7 Read family prayers. 7.30 Read Cave. 8.45 Private prayer. 9 E and Collect; read Cave. 12 E and Collect; finished Cave's *Primitive Christianity*. 12.15 Meditated, and private prayer. 1.15 Began Tully *Of the Nature of the Gods,* English.[20] 2.45 Private prayer. 3 Breakfast. 3.15 Walked. 3.30 Slept. 5.30 Read Nelson. 6 E; daily examination; private prayer. 6.30 Read Tully. 7 Read Bible. 8 Supper, and walked. 9 Religious talk; read family prayers. 9.30 Private prayer; to bed.

SATURDAY, JULY 6.   5 Rose; dressed; read Nelson; private prayer. 6

[18] Ingham observed the fast here on his first Wednesday at home, and continued to observe the Stations faithfully throughout the rest of the time recorded in this diary.

[19] Postal service for Ossett was provided through Wakefield, as markings on the extant Ingham letters indicate (see also p. 289 and 5 August at note 71). Neither Ossett nor Wakefield was on one of the "great" post roads or even a main cross route, so service would probably have been somewhat infrequent and perhaps (as this entry shows) irregular. See Howard Robinson, *The British Post Office* (Princeton, N.J.: Princeton University Press, 1948), pp. 104ff.; see also *The Traveller's Pocket Companion* (London: J. Hodges, 1741) for maps and comments about post roads, carriers, and service.

[20] There appears to have been only one edition (1683) of Cicero's *De natura deorum* translated into English at this time; see Appendix 3.

Read Law on rising,[21] and religious talk with my brothers.[22] 7 Read family prayers. 7.15 Read Tully; breakfast. 8 Necessary business. 9 E, Collect, and private prayer. 9.15 Methodized my time.[23] 10 E; religious talk and read Nelson with Jeremy Ellis. 11 Walked and meditated on thanksgiving. 11.45 Private prayer. 12 E and Collect; dinner. 1 Walked to Isaacs', meditated. 2 Various talk with them; tea, and religious talk. 6 Came home. 7 E; daily examination; read Nelson, and private prayer. 8 Supper; read a sermon to our family, and religious talk. 9 Read family prayers, and religious talk. 9.45 Private prayer; to bed.

SUNDAY, JULY 7. 6 Dressed; meditated and private prayer. 7 Read family prayers, and breakfast. 8 E; read a sermon. 9 Walked to Wakefield Church. 10 Public Prayers, Sermon, Sacrament. 1 Dinner at Wright's. 2 Sat and slept. 3.15 Public Prayers, and Sermon. 5 Drank. 5.30 Came home. 6.30 Wrote diary; daily examination; meditated; private prayer; read Nelson. 7.30 Supper. 8 E; read a sermon to our family, and religious talk. 9 Family prayers. 9.15 Various talk. 9.45 Private prayer. 10 To bed.

Blessings: began to go to the Sacrament at Wakefield; religious talk with William Wilby[24] and our family.

MONDAY, JULY 8. 5.45 Dressed. 6 Read Nelson; private prayer; meditated. 7 Read family prayers. 7.30 Transcribed diary. 8.30 Began to learn shorthand;[25] ri. 9 E and private prayer. 9.15 Read Tully. 10 E; unloaded hay. 11 E; walked; meditated. 12 E and Collect; dinner. 12.45 Shorthand. 2 Read Tully. 3 E and Collect. 3.30 Read Beveridge's sermon on the Common Prayer with our family; ri. 5 E; read Nelson. 5.15

---

21 William Law, *A Serious Call to a Devout and Holy Life* (1729), ch. XIV, "Of daily early prayer in the morning"; see Appendix 3.

22 Besides two older brothers, Ingham had a younger, John.

23 Part of Ingham's continuing effort to follow the first rule of Jeremy Taylor in *The Rule and Exercises of Holy Living* (1650; see Appendix 3), adopted by Wesley and the Methodists: "Care of our time" (ch. 1, sec. 1). See the outline of his schedule as contained in Ingham's letter to John Wesley in Appendix 4. Cf. 26 September, 28 February, 31 December, and 13 July.

24 The rug-maker mentioned in the letter to Wesley on p. 289.

25 This is a puzzling entry in view of his having studied and used Weston's shorthand for nine months at this point. Perhaps he was beginning to learn a new system, but more likely he is simply referring to taking up the study once again, now at home. Cf. 29 August and note 122, where he studied shorthand with Charles Wesley, who used Byrom's system.

Daily examination and private prayer. 6 E; supper; various talk with my mother. 7 At brother William's, necessary business, various talk. 8.45 Came home. 9 Read family prayers. 9.15 Good talk. 9.45 Private prayer. 10 To bed.

TUESDAY, JULY 9. 5 Rose; dressed. 5.15 Read Nelson; private prayer. 5.45 Meditated. 7 Read family prayers; breakfast; read *Plain Directions for [Reading] the Scriptures;* ri. 8.15 Meditated. 8.30 Idle.[26] 9.15 Read Tully; ri. 11.45 Dinner. 12.30 Read a sermon of my own to my mother and Hannah. 1 Meditated. 1.30 Shorthand. 2 E; finished Tully *Of the Nature of the Gods;* ri. 3 Walked with John, various and useful talk. 5.45 Eat. 6 E; daily examination; read Nelson and meditated. 6.45 Private prayer. 7 E; walked. 7.30 Supper. 8 E; began Bishop Wilson's *Catechism*[27] with our family; ri. 9.15 Read family prayers. 9.45 Private prayer; to bed. 10.

Blessings: good success with our family; [rose].[28]

WEDNESDAY, JULY 10.[29] 6.45 Dressed; read Law on rising;[30] ri. 7 Read family prayers. 7.30 Meditated. 8 E; meditated of death, and private prayer. 9 E and Collect; began to study the Greek Testament according to Francke's directions.[31] 10 E; read Francke; ri. 11 E; began to teach William Wilby's children to read, promised to catechize them; ri. 11.30 Shorthand; ri. 12 E and private prayer. 12.15 Meditated; private prayer. 1 E; began the Greek Testament; ri; only reading the verses

---

[26] This entry is accompanied by the symbol for the degree of attention, "dead."

[27] See Thomas Wilson, *The Principles and Duties of Christianity* (1707) in Appendix 3.

[28] Marginal note at 5 a.m.

[29] On this day, Ingham resumed the "exacter"-style diary with columns.

[30] *Serious Call,* ch. XIV. In the Resolutions Broken column, Ingham has entered for this hour, "idleness."

[31] See August Hermann Francke's *Manuductio ad lectionem Scripturae Sacrae* (1706), ch. II, sec. iii, para. 7, which recommends reading the Greek Testament first with respect to the *letter* of scripture (a study with three branches: grammatical, historical, and analytical), and second with respect to the *spirit* of the Word (in its expository, doctrinal, inferential, and practical aspects). In the "grammatical" section, Francke suggests acquiring a knowledge of the Greek Testament quickly (within three months if possible), using either Johannes Leusden's *Compendium Græcum Novi Testamenti* (1677) or studying the verses asterisked in Leusden's edition of the Greek Testament (which together comprise all the words used by sacred writers). See 1 p.m. below.

marked in Leusden.[32] 2 E; read Greek Testament; ri. 2.45 Private prayer. 3 E; breakfast. 3.15 Brother Isaacs and Susy came, stayed till 6.30, various talk. 6.30 Daily examination, and read Nelson. 7 Private prayer. 7.15 Meditated. 7.30 Supper. 8 E; read *Catechism* with our family, and religious talk. 9 Read family prayers. 9.15 Religious talk. 9.30 Private prayer. 9.45 To bed.

THURSDAY, JULY 11. 5 Rose and went to bed again. 6.30 Dressed. 7 E; read family prayers; meditated; private prayer. 8 E; breakfast. 8.15 Shorthand. 8.45 Private prayer. 9 E and Collect; read Greek Testament. 10 E; read Greek Testament. 11 E; at Wilby's; ri. 11.30 Walked. 11.45 Private prayer. 12 E and Collect; dinner; read John the Catechism. 1 E; shorthand; ri. 2 E; read Greek Testament. 3 E and private prayer. 3.10 Read Greek Testament; ri. 4 E; walked and began Milton's *Paradise Lost.* 5 E; read Nelson. 5.30 Daily examination; private prayer. 6 E; supper; various talk and meditated on the vanity of the world. 8 E; read Wilson's *Catechism* with our family. 9 E; read family prayers. 9.15 Good talk. 9.30 Private prayer. 9.45 To bed.

FRIDAY, JULY 12. 5.45 Rose; dressed. 6 E; meditated and private prayer. 6.30 Began a letter. 7 E; read family prayers and religious talk with Joseph. 7.30 Wrote letter. 8 E; finished letter to Smith. 9 Meditated on the vanity of the world, and private prayer. 10 E and private prayer. 10.10 Read Greek Testament; ri. 11 E and private prayer. 11.05 At Wilby's; ri. 11.30 Began to hear my sister Hannah read a chapter; to continue. 11.45 Private prayer. 12 E and Collect; meditated on Christ's sufferings; ri. 1 Private prayer. 1.15 Read Greek Testament; ri. 2 E; read Greek Testament. 2.45 Private prayer. 3 E and Collect; breakfast. 3.15 Shorthand; ri. 4 E; read Law on rising with Joseph and Hannah, and religious talk. 5 E; meditated. 5.30 Daily examination, private prayer, and thanksgiving. 6 E and private prayer; General Examination of my resolutions, confession and private prayer. 7 E; walked. 7.30 Supper. 8 Went with Joseph, good talk. 9 Read family prayers. 9.15 Religious talk with John. 9.30 Private prayer; to bed.

[32] Leusden's edition, in Greek and Latin parallel columns, has asterisks before verses containing the 1,686 Greek words used only once in the New Testament (noted with a dagger), and a grammatically significant location (not always the first occurrence) of the other 3,270 Greek words that are used more than once (noted with a double dagger). See 6 August, note 73.

Blessings: recollected 12 times; fervent in private prayer 6 times; temperate twice; zealous in conversation; comforted in meditation; diligent.

Sins: did not rise at waking.

SATURDAY, JULY 13.   5 Rose; dressed; wrote diary; thanksgiving for the blessings, and private prayer.[33] 6 E; began to compose a sermon on self-denial. 7 E; read family prayers. 7.15 Breakfast, and read Nelson. 7.45 Composed sermon. 8 E; meditated on self-denial. 9 Could not study. 9.30 Read Greek Testament; meditated. 10 Private prayer; read Greek Testament; ri. 11 E; at Wilby's; ri. 11.30 Dinner. 12 E and Collect; dressed. 12.30 Private prayer; shorthand. 1 E; rode[34] to Batley to see Mr Rhodes;[35] called at Dickinson's; rode to Dewsbury with Rhodes to bury a corpse; stayed till 6, then rode to Batley; supper, good talk (various). 8.30 Came home. 9.30 Read family prayer. 9.45 Private prayer. 10 To bed.

SUNDAY, JULY 14.   5.45 Rose; dressed. 6 E; psalm. 6.15 Thanksgiving and private prayer; meditated. 7 E; read Nelson, and family prayers. 7.30 Walked. 8 E; breakfast. 8.15 Meditated on faith; ri. 9 Collect and private prayer. 9.15 Read Wilson's Catechism. 10 E; Public Prayers and Sermon. 12 Dinner. 12.30 Meditated. 2 Read Catechism. 2.45 Public Prayers and Sermon. 4.15 With me, William, Joseph, and Joshua Smithson, various talk (idle). 6 Daily examination, meditation, and private prayer. 7.30 Read Wilson's *Catechism* to our family, and supper. 9 E; read family prayers. 9.30 Private prayer; to bed.

MONDAY, JULY 15.   5.15 Rose; dressed; meditated, and private prayer. 6 E; meditated and composed sermon. 7 E; read family prayers; composed sermon and breakfast. 8 Taught children, and private prayer. 9 E and Collect; read Greek Testament. 10 E; read Greek Testament. 11 E; at Wilby's; ri. 11.45 Private prayer. 12 E and Collect; dinner and walked. 1 Private prayer; began Norris' Beatitudes and Discourses.[36] 2

[33]   Marginal note in Blessings column: "rose."
[34]   MS. reads "rid," here and elsewhere transcribed "rode."
[35]   See 21 September, note 33.
[36]   See John Norris, *Practical Discourses Upon the Beatitudes of Our Lord* (1728), in Appendix 3. This collection of writings was published under several titles, beginning with a one-volume work on the Beatitudes entitled *Christian Blessedness* (1690), to which then were subsequently added three more volumes of *Practical Discourses Upon Several Divine Subjects.* The four-volume set was

Private prayer; read Greek Testament; ri. 3 Slumbered and slept.[37] 5 E; eat; walked and meditated. 6 E; daily examination; private prayer; read Norris. 7 E; supper and walked. 8 Read Norris; ri. 9 Read family prayers; meditated. 9.45 Private prayer. 10 To bed.

Blessings: rose; began to teach James Blackburn to read; fervent in private prayer; recollected 6 times.

Sins: eat too much; slept.

TUESDAY, JULY 16. 5.15 Rose; dressed; wrote diary. 5.45 Private prayer. 6 E; composed sermon; ri. 7 E; read family prayer and composed sermon; ri. 8 Composed sermon. 8.30 Meditated on my infirmities; ri. 9 E and private prayer for 16th day. 9.15 Read Greek Testament. 10 E; Greek Testament. 11 E; at Wilby's; ri. 11.30 Shorthand; ri. 12 E and Collect; meditated; read the book of Judith. 1 E. 1.15 Used the Penitential Office for the 16th Day of the Month in full, and read a chapter in Law; ri. 3 E and Collect; breakfast. 3.30 Read a sermon on Method[38] with my mother, etc; Godley[39] came, tea, little talk. 5.30 Daily examination and private prayer. 6 Set Hannah France and Susy Wilby to writing, and taught. 7 E; supper; religious talk at Wilby's. 8 E; catechized John and Hannah, and religious talk. 9 E; read family prayers. 9.15 Good talk. 9.30 Private prayer; to bed. 10 Thoughts of death; vain and proud thoughts; waked till 12.

Blessings: recollected 8 times; fervent in private prayer twice; performed the Penitential Office; began to teach two to write; religious talk with our family.

Sins: trifled two hours at night; proud thoughts in bed. S P[40]

WEDNESDAY, JULY 17. 6 Rose; dressed; read the last chapter of Rodriguez. 7 Read family prayers; read Law; ri. 8.45 Private prayer. 9 Read Miranda's character;[41] ri. 9.45 Greek Testament. 10 E; read Greek

---

sometimes published with these titles retained and at other times under the combined title, *Practical Discourses upon the Beatitudes of our Lord.*

[37] Ingham entered 1 as his rating in the Simplicity column; cf. 14 August, note 96.

[38] See *The Way of Living in a Method, and by Rule* (1722), in Appendix 3.

[39] John Godley, curate of Ossett, of whom Ingham once remarked to Charles Wesley, "You know, I believe, that he is misnamed." Luke Tyerman, *The Oxford Methodists* (London: Hodder and Stroughton, 1873), p. 87; see also John F. Goodchild, *The History of Ossett Church* (Ossett, Yorkshire: n.p., 1965), p. 9.

[40] See 22 July, note 45.

[41] Law, *Serious Call,* ch. VIII.

Testament; ri. 11 E; taught at Wilby's. 11.45 Private prayer. 12 E; began Bishop Hall on Meditation. 1 Partly meditated. 2 Finished Bishop Hall on Meditation; ri. 2.45 Private prayer. 3 E and Collect; breakfast. 3.30 Eat berries; ri. 4 Walked. 4.45 Began to write rules for spending my time; finished.[42] 6.15 Daily examination, private prayer, and meditated. 7 Supper; various talk with our family. 8 Read Bible, and religious talk. 9 Read family prayers. 9.15 Religious talk with Joseph. 9.30 Private prayer; to bed.

Blessings: recollected 5 times; contrite for unchasteness; fervent in private prayer; urged resolutions; zealous in conversation.

Sins: neglected ejaculatory prayers; idled an hour.

[Rules for spending my time][43]. . . to rise . . . -tion at night . . . to observe . . . time- . . . compose sermon. 7 Family prayers, compose [sermon] . . . teach Wilby's [children] . . . Norris. 1 Shorthand. . . . -t. 6 Meditate. 7 Supper and . . . family. 9 Family prayers; private prayer, and to bed. . . . meditate on Christ's sufferings. . . .

THURSDAY, JULY 18. 5.15 Rose; dressed; wrote diary. 5.45 Private prayer. 6 Meditated on the bed. 7 Read family prayers. 7.30 Wilby shaved me. 8.30 Breakfast. 9 E and private prayer; meditated. 9.30 Dressed and rode with my mother to see Isaacs; various talk; stayed till 6.30, came home. 7.30 Vain thoughts. 8.15 Began Alleine's *Sure Guide to Heaven* with our family; ri. 9.15 Read family prayers. 9.30 Private prayer. 9.45 To bed.

FRIDAY, JULY 19. 6 Rose; dressed; meditated; read Nelson. 6.45 Private prayer. 7 E; read family prayers. 7.30 Vain thoughts. 8 E; meditated on my sins, and private prayer for zeal. 9 E and Collect; read Greek Testament. 10.15 Necessary business. 11 At Wilby's. 12 E and Collect; meditated on Christ's sufferings, and private prayer. 1 Necessary business. 2 E; read Greek Testament, and private prayer. 3 Breakfast. 3.30 Walked. 4 Read Greek Testament. 4.30 Eat fruit. 5 E; daily examination; read Law; meditated; read Country Parson, and meditated. 6.30

---

[42] See below, following this day's entry, for the transcription of what remains in the diary of Ingham's listed schedule and rules, originally entered on the verso of the leaf containing the entries for 1–4 August.

[43] These are the fragmentary remains, on a partially removed page, of the results of Ingham's having "methodized" his time on 6 July and 17 July. See the fuller transcription of this outline in his letter to John Wesley in Appendix 4. See also 28 February, 31 December, and 26 August.

Private prayer. 7 Meditated on vanity; ri. 7.45 Supper. 8 Walked, read Alleine, and meditated. 9 Meditated. 9.30 Read family prayers. 9.45 Private prayer. 10 To bed.

Blessings: recollected 5 times; fervent in private prayer thrice; sorrowful for my sins; affectionate in meditation twice; denied myself at supper; began to teach Mary Wilby to write, and my sister Hannah.

Sins: laid long.

SATURDAY, JULY 20. 7 Read family prayers. 7.30 Meditated. 8.30 Breakfast. 9 Psalm and private prayer; meditated. 10 E; read Greek Testament; ri. 11.15 At Wilby's and taught; ri. 12 E and private prayer. 12.15 Dinner. 12.45 Went to make hay; ri. 2 Dressed; went to brother William's. 3 Began Law's *Serious Call.* 4.30 Tea. 5.30 Came home; meditated and psalm. 6 E; daily examination; private prayer; psalm. 7 Supper; meditated. 7.45 Religious talk with Molly Harrup, got her to call me up.[44] 8.45 Read Alleine with our family; ri. 9.30 Read family prayers. 10 Private prayer. 10.15 Read Law and meditated; ri.

SUNDAY, JULY 21. 7 Dressed. 7.15 Read family prayers. 7.30 Private prayer; meditated. 8 Breakfast. 8.30 Walked with William Wilby, religious talk. 9 Read Alleine; ri. 9.45 Private prayer. 10 E; Public Prayers and Sermon. 11.45 Private prayer. 12 E; dinner. 1 Read a sermon to our family; ri. 2.30 Public Prayers and Sermon. 4 Sat with strangers, various talk. 5.30 Read a sermon with our family; ri. 6 E; daily examination and private prayer; meditated. 7 Read with our family, Alleine. 8 E; read, and religious talk with our family; ri. 9 Family prayers. 9.15 Private prayer.

MONDAY, JULY 22. 4.45 Rose; dressed. 5 Psalm; wrote diary. 5.15 Meditated. 5.45 Private prayer. 6 E; composed sermon. 7 E; read family prayers. 7.15 Breakfast; composed sermon. 8 Taught. 8.10 Shorthand; ri. 8.45 Private prayer. 9 Necessary business. 9.30 Entertained foolish and unchaste thoughts; S P.[45] 11.15 At Wilby's; ri. 11.45 Dinner. 12 Taught. 12.30 Read Norris; ri. 2 Read Greek Testament; ri. 4 E; went to see Jeremy Ellis, religious and useful talk, gave him one shilling. 6.30 E; daily examination; private prayer. 7 E; supper. 7.30

[44] Ingham apparently arranged to have Molly assist his attempts at early rising by waking him in the morning (see the similar arrangements and phraseology on 23 June regarding Bolton).
[45] The "S P" in the summary of sins at the end of the day seems to indicate "sincere penitence." Cf. 16 July.

Walked and meditated. 8 E; read Alleine with our family, and religious talk; ri. 9.15 Read family prayers. 9.30 Religious and useful talk with our family; ri. 10.30 Private prayer; to bed.

Blessings: rose; gave Jeremy Ellis a shilling; zealous with our family.

Sins: spent almost two hours in vain and unchaste thoughts and then S[incere] P[enitence].

TUESDAY, JULY 23.   4 Rose; dressed; wrote diary; meditated on God; ri. 4.45 Private prayer. 5 Meditated on humility, and my sins and infirmities. 6 E; composed sermon. 6.45 Private prayer. 7 E; read family prayers. 7.15 Composed sermon; ri. 8.15 Breakfast. 8.30 Walked. 8.45 Private prayer. 9 Read Greek Testament; ri. 10 E; read Greek Testament; ri. 11 E; at Wilby's; ri. 11.30 Walked. 11.45 Private prayer. 12 Dinner and walked. 1 E; read Norris; ri. 2 Mr Godley came, various talk. 2.45 Went to Wakefield to buy some books at Stringer's;[46] tea and various talk; ri. 7.30 Supper. 8 E; daily examination; private prayer; gave James Blackburn[47] a New Testament; various and useful talk with Mary France, promised to teach their John two lessons a day, if he would come. 9.15 Read family prayers. 9.45 Private prayer; to bed. 10 Meditated. 11 Private prayer; thanksgiving.

Blessings: received a letter from Smith; rose; fervent in private prayer; gave Blackburn a New Testament; zealous in private prayer in the night, and contrite.

[Sins:] entertained thoughts of preferment.[48]

WEDNESDAY, JULY 24.   4.30 Rose; dressed; psalm. 5 Wrote diary and private prayer. 5.30 Meditated. 6 Thoughts of writing to John Wesley; ri. 7 E; read family prayers. 7.30 Pared my nails; ri. 8 E; meditated on my sins; ri; confession and private prayer. 9 Taught. 9.15 Read Greek Testament; ri. 10 Psalm and Collect; necessary business in setting up a shelf. 11.15 at Wilby's. 12 E; meditated on Christ's sufferings, and private prayer; ri. 1 E; read Greek Testament; ri. 2 E; read Greek Testament; ri. 2.45 Private prayer. 3 Breakfast. 3.30 Read Norris; ri. 4 E; wrote a prayer for John. 4.15 Walked; vain thoughts; ri. 5 E; daily examina-

---

[46] Ed Stringer's stationer shop was where Ingham received his mail; see p. 289, postscript to the letter.

[47] Marginal note reads: "In part fulfilled my vow, made in my journey, to go to the poor." Nothing in the diary indicates precisely when or where this vow was made, presumably between 24 June and 1 July. Cf. 10 August, at note 84.

[48] Cf. resolution on p. 166, and also 14 March, summary of blessings.

tion. 5.30 Private prayer. 5.50 Meditated. 6 E; meditated on temperance and death; ri. 7 Supper; religious talk with our family; ri; walked; taught. 8 Walked and read Alleine, religious talk; set them upon private prayer twice a day, and daily examination; ri. 9 Read family prayers. 9.20 Private prayer. 9.45 To bed.

Blessings: rose; contrition; began to teach John France twice a day; zealous in religious talk; fervent in private prayer thrice; prevented from lending my gown to act a play in.[49]

Sins: neglected ejaculatory prayers 5 times; broke resolution 8 five times.

THURSDAY, JULY 25. 4.45 Rose; dressed. 5 Wrote diary; private prayer; read Nelson; ri. 6 Necessary business. 6.15 Composed a letter to John Wesley. 7 E; read family prayers; wrote letter; taught. 8 E; breakfast. 8.15 Taught; wrote letter. 8.45 Private prayer. 9 At Wilby's. 9.45 Dressed. 10.30 Rode to Dewsbury; met with Mr Thomas, promised to go see him; Public Prayers. 12 Went with Mr Rhodes to the Crow Nest,[50] dinner with him, the Captain, and Lady, various talk; Mr Coleby came, various talk; I drank and talked little. 7 Came home. 7.45 Supper. 8 E; daily examination; private prayer. 8.30 Read the catalogue of books to be sold next day at Pontefract.[51] 9 Read family prayers. 9.30 Private prayer; to bed.

FRIDAY, JULY 26. 5.30 Dressed; private prayer. 6 Meditated; read family prayers, and breakfast; rode to Pontefract with Thomas and Burnell,[52]

---

49   This no doubt refers to his Oxford gown; cf. 18 September, note 29.
50   MS. reads "Crow Nests." The Crow Lees estate upon which sits this imposing home was held almost continually by the Bedford family from 1571 to about 1800, at which point it was purchased by Mr. Thomas Hague, whose descendants later sold it to the Dewsbury Corporation for use as a public park. Samuel Joseph Chadwick, *Handbook to Dewsbury and the Neighbourhood* (Dewsbury, Yorkshire: Dawson and Sons, 1893). My appreciation to Mr. Stanley T. Dibnah, Chief Librarian and Curator for the Kirklees Metropolitan Council Libraries and Museums Service, for this information. See also the description given in N. B. L. Pevsner, *The Buildings of England: Yorkshire, the West Riding* (Harmondsworth: Penguin Books, 1959), p. 180.
51   MS. reads "Pomfret," a phonetic spelling of the city name.
52   MS. reads "Burnel." Richard Burnell (1689–1773) was for the last forty-nine years of his life master of a school in Dewsbury, established in 1724 by John Wheelwright. "Thomas" might be either Jonas Thomas, who was elected trustee of the Dewsbury school in 1729, or Rev. Joseph Thomas, who in 1743 accompanied Burnell to York for an interview with the archbishop concerning

learned talk. 10 At the sale, bought not a book; ri. 12 Went with them to see the Castle.[53] 12.30 Dinner with them, Dr Rogers, and Mills; two Leeds booksellers and Rhodes came, learned and useful talk; Rhodes defrayed my charges. 3 Went again to the sale, bought nothing. 5 Drank. 5.30 Came home with Rhodes, Thomas, and Burnell, learned talk (various). 8.30 At home; supper, various talk. 9.15 Read family prayers. 9.30 Private prayer. 9.45 To bed.

SATURDAY, JULY 27.   6 I was waking at 4.30 and would not rise, Oh! Shame! 6.15 Dressed. 6.30 Wrote diary. 6.45 Vain thoughts. 7 E; read family prayers. 7.15 Read Law; ri; private prayer and thanksgiving. 8 E; breakfast; wrote letter to John Wesley; ri. 9 E; wrote letter. 10 Finished letter to John Wesley.[54] 11 E; at Wilby's; ri. 11.45 Private prayer and intercession for Ford. 12 Dinner. 12.30 Taught. 1 E; read Norris. 2 E; made hay. 3 Private prayer. 3.15 Read Greek Testament; ri. 4.30 Slept. 5.45 Daily examination. 6 E; private prayer. 6.20 Meditated on death; ri. 7 E; supper and walked; ri. 8 Walked and at brother William's, religious and useful talk. 9 Came home; read family prayers. 9.30 Private prayer for faith. 9.45 Read Law. 10 E and private prayer. 10.25 General Examination of my resolutions;[55] ri. 11 Private prayer of resignation and for grace; ri. 11.20 Began to cast up my diary for May.[56] 12 Private prayer for death, and thanksgiving; ri. 12.30 To bed.

Blessings: recollected 12 times;[57] fervent in private prayer thrice; watched.

Sins: laid on the bed.

---

school business. W. Pickles, *History of the Wheelwright Grammar Schools* (Leeds: Garforth, 1973), pp. 7f.

53   Pontefract Castle, dating to Norman days, was a strategic stronghold in the North and often the target of rebellious forces. Best known perhaps as the site of the alleged murder of Richard II during the winter of 1399/1400, it was laid to ruin after royalists surrendered it upon the execution of Charles I in 1649.

54   This letter was published by Tyerman in *The Oxford Methodists,* pp. 57–58. Besides the wrong date (27 February), there are several other glaring errors and omissions in his transcription, especially in the paragraph containing Ingham's "methodized" schedule. The correct text, with additional details from this diary in brackets, is in Appendix 4 below.

55   Ingham here is "watching" as he did at Oxford, preparing for Sunday; cf. 23 August.

56   See monthly summary for May 1734 and plate 16.

57   Actually eleven times.

SUNDAY, JULY 28. 6 Rose; dressed. 6.30 Psalm and wrote diary. 6.45 Private prayer and thanksgiving. 7 E; read Alleine with our family [and] Wilby, and private prayer. 8 E; breakfast with me, Wilby, religious talk. 8.15 Walked with him. 9 Religious talk; read the Country Parson on the joys of heaven;[58] ri. 9.45 Private prayer. 10 E; Public Prayers and Sermon. 12 Dinner at Low Laithes,[59] various and useful talk. 2.15 Came home. 2.45 Public Prayers and Sermon. 4.15 Eat. 4.45 Walked with Wilby, religious talk and read the Country Parson on the means;[60] ri. 6 E; daily examination. 6.15 Private prayer and psalm. 6.45 Meditated. 7 Supper. 7.30 Read Alleine; ri. 8 Read Alleine with our family, and religious talk; ri. 9 Read family prayers. 9.15 Private prayer. 9.30 To bed.

MONDAY, JULY 29. 6 Read Nelson. 6.15 Wrote diary. 6.30 Psalm and private prayer. 6.50 Meditated. 7.15 Read family prayers. 7.30 Meditated on judgement; ri. 8.30 Taught. 8.45 Private prayer; resolve to rise at first call, not to lay on the bed two nights; to fix quantity before eating; not to sit on the bed in the daytime.[61] 9 E; read Greek Testament; ri. 10 Trifled. 10.20 Read Greek Testament. 11 E; at Wilby's; ri. 11.30 Religious talk with my mother and Hannah of fasting, the Sacrament, and daily examination; ri. 12 E, Collect, and private prayer; General Examination, and read Taylor on chastity;[62] ri. 2 Private prayer. 2.20 Transcribed my diary for May. 3.30 Private prayer and psalm. 4 E; cast up my diary for June;[63] ri. 5 E; daily examination. 5.30 Private prayer,

---

58   See *Country Parson's Advice,* Part I, ch. 5, "Containing a fifth argument to a holy life, from the consideration of those great rewards God hath prepared for good men, in the other world."
59   Also called "Low Lathes" or "Low-land" on contemporary tombstones in the area (see Smithson tombstones in Dewsbury churchyard). Just two kilometers north-northeast of Ingham's home, this territory was from medieval days a hunting estate known as New Park. See also 12 August, note 88, and plate 18.
60   Part II, ch. 4, sec. 2, where the means of attaining the knowledge of God are discussed: "1. Reading the Holy Scriptures. 2. Reading good books. 3. Hearing of good sermons and good discourses. 4. Frequent conferring with serious Christians. 5. Meditating upon the good things we hear and read. 6. Prayer, which ought never to be omitted. 7. Regulating our lives according to this knowledge."
61   Symbol in margin indicates "good resolutions."
62   Taylor, *Holy Living,* ch. II, sec. 3, "Of Chastity."
63   See monthly summary for June 1734 and plates 16 and 17. At this point, Ingham reinstituted the H column of hourly recollection for one page only (through 31 July). See 19 March, note 77.

and for good resolutions; ri; meditated. 6 E; breakfast.[64] 6.30 Thought how I could <u>manage a school</u>.[65] 7 E; taught. 7.15 Read Norris; ri. 8 E; finished Alleine's *Sure Guide to Heaven* with our family and William Wilby, and religious talk. 9 E; read family prayers. 9.15 Private prayer. 9.30 To bed.

Blessings: wrote good resolutions; fasted till 6; promised to teach James Fozard's son to read.

TUESDAY, JULY 30. 5 Rose; dressed. 5.15 Wrote diary. 5.25 Psalm. 5.30 Private prayer. 5.45 Meditated. 6 E; composed sermon; ri. 7 E; read family prayers; composed sermon. 8 E; breakfast; taught. 8.30 Walked. 8.45 Private prayer. 9 E and Collect; read Greek Testament. 10 E; read Greek Testament; ri. 11 E; at Wilby's. 11.30 Walked. 11.45 Private prayer. 12 Dinner. 12.30 Taught; read Norris. 1.45[66] 2.15 E; read Greek Testament. 3 Private prayer. 3.15 Greek Testament. 4 Walked. 4.15 At Wilby's.[67] 4.45 Various talk with our family. 5 E; daily examination. 5.30 Entertained vain thoughts. 6 Taught. 6.15 Private prayer. 6.30 Supper. 6.45 Went to brother William's, various and useful talk. 8.30 Came home; began Ellis' *Communicant's Guide* with our family; ri. 9.15 Read family prayers. 9.30 Various talk. 9.45 Private prayer.

WEDNESDAY, JULY 31. 5 Dressed. 5.15 Wrote diary; meditated on <u>omnipresence</u>; ri. 5.45 Private prayer. 6 E; composed sermon and read family prayers; ri. 8 E; meditated on my sins, and private prayer and confession. 9.05 Read Greek Testament. 10 E; read Greek Testament. 11 E; at Wilby's; ri. 11.30 France's; ri. 12 Private prayer. 12.10 Medi-

[64] Marginal note in Blessings column: "fasted to 6."

[65] Ingham did manage a school for Wesley in Georgia in 1736 (Tyerman, *Oxford Methodists*, p. 79) and upon his return to England founded a school for the children of Ossett, which eventually became Ossett Grammar School. He appears to have raised subscriptions for the project in 1737 and began operations the following year. See letter from John Thorold to Betty Hastings, 17 January 1737/38, in George Hastings Wheler, *Hastings Wheler Family Letters* (London: Privately printed, 1929); see also D. N. R. Lester, *The History of Batley Grammar School 1612–1962* (Batley, Yorkshire: J. S. Newsome & Son, n.d.), p. 53. Appreciation is extended to Beatrice Scott of Boston Spa for pointing me to this material. See also Goodchild, *Ossett Church*, p. 9.

[66] This time entry is followed only by the sign = which may mean "on my knees"; cf. "Resolutions for Lent," p. 119, note 220.

[67] Marginal note in the Blessings column: "taught."

tated and taught. 1 E and private prayer. 1.05 Read Greek Testament. 2 E; Greek Testament. 2.45 Private prayer. 3 Breakfast. 3.30 Walked. 4.15 Cast up diary. 5 E; daily examination; meditated. 5.45 Slept. 7.30 Supper. 7.45 Private prayer. 8 E; read Ellis with our family and William Wilby, and religious talk. 9 Read family prayers. 9.15 Private prayer; to bed; could not sleep till after 12.

THURSDAY, AUGUST 1.[68] 6 Dressed. 6.15 Wrote diary. 6.45 Private prayer. . . . 8 E; taught; at Wilby's. . . . 9 Walked. 9.15 Various business and . . . rode to Joseph's, various and useful talk . . . eat a scalding. . . . 8 Taught. 8.15 Read Ellis. . . . 9 E. 9.20 Read family prayers. 9.30. . . .

FRIDAY, AUGUST 2. 6.45 Dressed. 7 E; meditated. 7.20. . . . 8 Taught. 8.15 Meditated on my [sins]. . . . 9 Private prayer on my knees. 9.45 Read Law. . . . 11.15 At Wilby's. 11.40. . . . 12 Private prayer. 12.10 Meditated on Christ's [sufferings]. . . . 1 Private prayer. 1.15 Meditated on death. . . . 3 E. 3.10 Breakfast. 3.30 Walked; thought of. . . . 4 E; with me, read Law of. . . . 5 E; daily examination. 5.30 Private prayer. 6 E; meditated. 7 E; supper. 7.30 Began Milton. . . .[69] 8.15 Received a letter from. . . . 8.45 Read Ellis with our family. . . . 9.15 Read family prayers. 9.30 Various and useful talk. . . . 10 Private prayer. 10.15 Read a chapter; ri. . . .

SATURDAY, AUGUST 3. 6.30 Dressed. 6.45 Private prayer. 7.10. . . . 8 Breakfast. 8.05 Taught; meditated on judgement. . . . 9 Private prayer. 9.15 Walked; vain thoughts. . . . 10 E; read Greek Testament; ri. 11 E; at Wilby's; ri. 12 Dinner; various talk with John. 1 M[editated]. . . . 3.15 Private prayer; read Law, felt. . . . 6.15 Daily examination and private prayer. 7 Supper, and meditated on. . . . 8 Finished Ellis' *Communicant's* [*Guide*] with our family and William Wilby. 9 Read family prayers. 9.30 Meditated; private prayer. 10 General Examination and reviewed. . . . [11].45 Wrote diary and thanksgiving.[70]

[SUNDAY, AUGUST 4. Between 8 and 9] . . . read it. . . .
  Sins: inattentive and cold in Public Prayers; . . . vain thoughts.

[68] The page containing the entries for the next four days has been cut out of the diary, except for a narrow strip 26–35 mm wide. Cf. 7 and 8 March and 17 July, note 43.

[69] Book 2 of *Paradise Lost;* see Appendix 3 and monthly summary for August 1734.

[70] Ingham appears again to be "watching" on the Saturday night.

MONDAY, AUGUST 5.   5.30 Dressed and wrote diary. 6 E; psalm; private prayer. 6.30 Meditated; family prayers. 7 E; wrote a letter to Charles Burton. 8 Taught and breakfast. 8.30 Letter. 8.45 Private prayer. 9 Finished letter to Charles Burton. 10 E; wrote a letter to John Ford; ri. 11.15 At Wilby's. 11.45 Wrote diary, and intercession for Ford and Smyth. 12 Dinner. 12.30 Taught. 1.15 E; Shorthand; ri. 2 E; read Greek Testament; ri. 3 Private prayer. 3.15 Read Greek Testament; ri. 4 E; walked and various business. 5 Necessary talk with my mother. 5.15 E; daily examination. 5.30 Private prayer. 5.50 Read chapter. 6 E; meditated on judgment; ri. 7 E; supper. 7.15 Walked with Joseph, learned talk (various). 8 E; read Country Parson with our family and William Wilby, religious talk. 9 E; read family prayers. 9.10 Good talk (various) of spirits. 9.45 Private prayer.

Blessings: N.B. When I had finished my letters and was going with them to Wakefield, that instant my mother called in a woman that was going there, who took them;[71] devout in family prayers; zealous in conversation; fervent in family prayers and private prayer.

TUESDAY, AUGUST 6.   6 Rose; dressed; private prayer.[72] 6.35 Meditated on the Methodists. 7 E; taught. 7.20 Read family prayers; taught and breakfast. 8 E; pared apples; ri. 8.45 Private prayer. 9 Finished verses in Leusden's Greek Testament marked with an asterism;[73] ri. 10.30 Went to glean in the field. 12 E; dinner. 12.30 At Wilby's; ri; wrote diary. 1 E; shorthand; ri. 2 Necessary business. 2.15 Private prayer. 2.20 Began to read a little of the Greek Grammar,[74] the declensions and conjugations. 4 E; walked; vain thoughts. 5 Necessary business. 5.15 Daily examination. 5.30 Slumbered. 6 Private prayer. 6.20 Meditated on God's attributes. 7 E; supper; read Milton; ri. 8 Various and useful talk. 8.40 Read Country Parson; ri. 9.15 Read family prayers. 9.30 Private prayer; to bed.

71   In margin here, as also at 10 a.m. above, the symbol for "success in temporal affairs." See 4 July, note 19.
72   Ingham here entered two identical abbreviations for private prayer.
73   "Asterism" usually refers to a cluster of three asterisks used to direct attention to important passages. In Leusden, a single asterisk is used in each case for this purpose. See also 10 July, note 32.
74   Marginal note ("3 p") indicates private prayer on the hour. The grammar he was reading may have been an edition of *Græcæ grammatices rudimenta in usum Scholæ Westmonasteriensis;* see Appendix 3.

WEDNESDAY, AUGUST 7. 5 Rose; dressed; wrote diary. 5.25 Psalm.
5.30 Private prayer. 5.45 Read chapter. 6 E; composed sermon; ri. 7 E;
read family prayers, and taught. 8 E; meditated on my sins; ri. 8.45 Private prayer. 9 E; read Grammar; ri. 11 E; walked. 11.30 Read Law;
ri. 12 E; read Law. 12.15 Meditated and private prayer. 1 Read Grammar and taught. 2.45 Private prayer. 3 E; breakfast. 3.30 Walked. 4
Shorthand. 5 E; daily examination; private prayer; psalm; read chapter.
6 E; meditated on the creation; ri. 7 Various and useful talk with Molly
Harrup. 7.15 Supper. 7.30 Walked. 8 Walked, and various and useful
talk with our family. 9 E; read family prayers. 9.15 Various talk with
our family. 9.45 Private prayer.

Blessings: rose; recollected thrice; began to teach Hannah Cunningham to read.

Sins: indulged vain thoughts of being a fine poet,[75] etc; irrecollected
9 times; idle at night.

THURSDAY, AUGUST 8. 4.45 Rose; dressed. 5 E; wrote diary. 5.15
Psalm; private prayer; read chapter. 6 E; composed sermon, and thought.
8 E; loaded corn. 9.25 Private prayer and psalm. 9.45 Necessary business. 10 E; read Grammar; ri. 11 Taught. 11.15 Walked. 11.45 Private prayer and psalm. 12 Read Norris and dinner. 1 E; unloaded corn.
1.30 Shorthand. 2 Robert Smithson came, went a setting[76] with him, got
two partridge. 7.40 Daily examination. 8 Private prayer. 8.15 Supper.
8.30 Walked. 8.20[77] Read Country Parson; ri. 9.15 Family prayers and
private prayer.

Blessings: rose; recollected thrice; prevented from going a fishing and
shooting by seeing Thomas Butterfield[78] drunk.

FRIDAY, AUGUST 9. 5.15 Rose; dressed; psalm; private prayer and meditated. 6 Thought of sporting. 6.15 Composed sermon; ri. 7 Read family
prayers. 7.20 Composed sermon. 7.45 Taught; began to teach Susy Butterfield[79] to read. 8 E; meditated on sins; ri. 8.55 Began to teach Job

---

[75] The problem here seems to focus on vanity, although on 29 April he had in
fact "talked against poets." See 9 November, note 88.

[76] Bird hunting, either with a setter dog or by setting snares.

[77] An obvious error; perhaps should read "8.40."

[78] MS. reads "Butterworth," but Ingham begins using "Butterfield" on the
following day and in monthly summary for August 1734.

[79] MS. reads "Butterworth."

Butterfield to read. 9.15 Private prayer. 9.30 Read Grammar. 10 E; read Grammar; ri. 11 E; at Wilby's; ri. 11.30 Walked. 11.45 Private prayer. 12 Read Law and meditated; ri. 1 Ditto. 2 Made pens for Thomas Thornton. 2.35 Meditated and private prayer. 3 E; breakfast and walked. 4 E; shorthand; ri. 5 E; General Examination of resolutions, etc; ri (idle, went a setting; irrecollected). 6 E; daily examination. 6.30 Resolved to lay in my gloves to prevent scratching my body and my members; not to put my hands into my breeches to prevent unchasteness, for three days;[80] not to go a setting partridge above thrice, if thereby hindered in recollection, for three weeks;[81] to make no snares for a week; N.B. Not to send for Tib nor Joseph to drive partridge at nights; not to throw myself into the temptations of sports. 6.36[82] Taught, and private prayer. 7 E; supper; meditated on Christ, and religious talk with our family; ri. 9 Read family prayers. 9.30 Private prayer; to bed.

Blessings: rose; recollected 9 times; began to teach Job and Susy Butterfield to read; zealous and active in conversation; made resolutions; fervent in family prayers and private prayer.

Sins: thought of setting; trifling thrice.

SATURDAY, AUGUST 10.   5.30 Rose; dressed; wrote diary; psalm. 6 Private prayer. 6.15 Composed sermon; ri. 7 E; read family prayers. 7.20 Composed sermon; ri; taught. 8 E; breakfast; sewed some *A.B.C.s*.[83] 8.50 Private prayer. 9 Offered six *A.B.C.*s and six *Christian Monitors* as part of the vow I made in my journey, to be given to poor people.[84] 10 Read Grammar. 10.30 Got plums,[85] not eat. 11 E; necessary business for my mother; ri. 11.30 Taught. 11.45 With me, Wilby and Jeremy Ellis, read part of *The Christian Monitor*, religious talk and gave them

---

[80] Ingham here struggles to come to grips with his sexuality; cf. 23 April, at note 39.

[81] See "Resolutions 1734," note 11, for a similar resolution made on 13 August.

[82] This is the first instance (and one of the very few) of Ingham indicating the time with a distinction more precise than five-minute intervals.

[83] See *The A.B.C. with the Catechism* (1605) in Appendix 3. The books on the S.P.C.K. list were divided into books already "stitched" and those "in quires" (gatherings) needing to be bound. *An Account of the Origin and Designs of the Society for Promoting Christian Knowledge* (1734), pp. 27ff.

[84] These may be some of the "little books" given to Ingham by Wesley on 23 June. Cf. 23 July, note 47. This offer was extended to John Godley (see daily summary of blessings, below), curate of Ossett.

[85] MS. reads "plumbs."

each one. 1 Dinner. 1.20 Good talk (various) with Jeremy Ellis; ri. 2 E; necessary business; read Law, ri; and wrote diary. 3 Private prayer; finished the first volume of Norris' Discourses.[86] 4.30 Walked, thought how I would act if a priest. 5 E; daily examination; thanksgiving for the blessings, and private prayer; ri. 6 E; meditated on the vanity of the world; ri. 7 E; supper; got shaved. 8 E; read Bible, and religious talk with our family; ri. 9 Read family prayers. 9.15 Began to watch with me, William Wilby, religious talk of watching, and private prayer. 10 Private prayer, read Country Parson, and religious talk. 11 Private prayer; read Country Parson, and religious talk of beginning to learn to read, and to make the Country Parson's resolutions about Christmas;[87] private prayer and thanksgiving.

Blessings: offered six *A.B.C.*s and six *Christian Monitor*s to Godley; religious talk with William Wilby and Jeremy Ellis; watched with me, William Wilby, religious talk; zealous and active.

SUNDAY, AUGUST 11. 6 Rose; dressed. 6.30 Private prayer. 6.45 Read chapter. 7 E; family prayers, and read Country Parson, and religious talk; ri. 8 Thought; breakfast. 9.30 Private prayer and thanksgiving. 9.45 Walked. 10 Public Prayers and Sermon. 12 E; dinner. 1 Taught, and meditated on humility. 2 E; read Country Parson with our family; ri. 3 Public Prayers and Sermon. 4.30 Walked with William Wilby, read Country Parson, and religious talk of observing the Stations, of private prayer, daily examination, and the fear of man. 5.30 Daily examination and private prayer with me, William Wilby. 6 Walked with my mother and meditated on God's perfections; ri. 7 E; supper; taught; read Country Parson, and religious talk with our family. 9.15 Family prayers; private prayer.

Blessings: fervent in private prayer twice; recollected 6 times; zealous to do good.

Sins: dissipated at Public Prayers.

MONDAY, AUGUST 12. 5.45 Dressed. 6 Wrote diary; psalm; private prayer; read Law. 7 E; read family prayers; taught; breakfast. 8 E; read Law; ri; private prayer. 9 Finished Greek Grammar. 11 E; went to see a sick child; ri; came home. 12 Private prayer. 12.15 Dinner. 12.30

---

86 See 15 July, note 36.
87 MS. reads "Xtmass." This refers to the timing of Wilby's intentions, not the content of the resolutions.

Visited again. 1 E; went to see the Park-Miller,[88] learned and useful talk, looked over his books; advised him to study the Greek Testament, promised to assist him; recommended Nelson to him, and private prayer and daily examination; read a chapter of Law, and religious talk; ri. 5.30 Came home; called at Low Laithes; met with old Dame Whitaker,[89] various and useful talk; came home. 6.15 Wrote diary; private prayer. 6.36 Daily examination. 7 Taught. 7.15 Supper. 7.45 Various talk with our family and John Fothergil.[90] 9 Finished the Country Parson with our family and William Wilby. 9.30 Family prayers; sat with our family till 10.30, various talk.

[TUESDAY, AUGUST 13.] 6.45 Dressed. 7 Read Taylor; family prayers; read Taylor on prayer.[91] 8 Taught, and breakfast. 9 Laid on the bed, fretting at myself. 10 Read Law, and Horneck on Vows.[92] 11 Private prayer. 11.15 At Wilby's; ri. 11.45 Psalm and private prayer. 12 Dinner. 12.30 Taught. 1 E; shorthand. 2 Private prayer. 2.10 Began to read the Greek Testament, construing it into Latin. 3 Psalm. 3.15 Trifled.[93] 4 Read Horneck on Watching;[94] ri. 5 E; psalm; meditated on watching; ri. 6 E; daily examination and private prayer. 7 Taught. 7.15 Visited. 7.45 Read Milton. 8 E; supper; read Milton. 8.45 Read Bible and religious talk. 9.15 Family prayers. 9.30 Private prayer. 9.45 Read

---

88   The miller at Low Laithes, part of an area long known as New Park. See 28 July, note 59.

89   "Widow Whittaker" is listed in 1756 as paying a rental of 110 pounds for Low Laithes. *Lord Cardigan's Rents,* 1756 (no. 8), in the Goodchild Loan MSS. (Smithson MSS.) in the Department of Archives and Local Studies at Wakefield Metropolitan District Council Library Headquarters; my appreciation to Mr. John Goodchild, Principal Local Studies Officer and Archivist, for pointing me to the rentals and many other sources of detailed information for the area around Ossett. The old Whitaker home and part of the estate is presently a golf clubhouse and course.

90   MS. reads "Futhergil" here and in subsequent entries of this name.

91   Taylor, *Holy Living,* ch. IV, sec. 7.

92   See Anthony Horneck, *The Happy Ascetick; or The Best Exercise* (1681?), part 2, "The Extraordinary Exercises of Godliness," ch. I, "To enter into solemn vows and promises." See Appendix 3 and "Resolutions 1734," note 11, for a resolution made on this day.

93   The rating for temper of devotion in the Simplicity column for this hour is a relatively low 3.

94   See *The Happy Ascetick,* part 2, ch. III, "To use Watching, or abstinence from sleep."

Law. 10 Psalm and private prayer; read Law; ri. 11 Private prayer and psalm.[95] 11.15 Read Law. 11.45 Private prayer and Thanksgiving.

WEDNESDAY, AUGUST 14. 6 Dressed. 6.15 Psalm, private prayer; vain thoughts. 7.30 Family prayers; vain thoughts. 8 E; taught. 8.15 Meditated on sins; ri. 8.45 Private prayer. 9 Necessary business; wrote diary. 10 E; read Greek Testament; ri. 11 E; at Wilby's; ri. 11.30 Walked. 11.45 Private prayer. 12 Began to meditate, but fell asleep till 3.[96] 3.10 Breakfast, eat apples and nuts. 4 Shorthand; ri. 5 E; meditated, but dissipated. 6 E; daily examination. 6.45 Private prayer. 7 E; taught. 7.30 Visited sick child. 8 Came home; learned talk with our family of lightning,[97] etc. 9 Family prayers; religious talk with William Wilby; private prayer. 10 To bed.

Blessings: fervent in private prayer twice; comforted at night; to bed recollected; no supper.

Sins: Indolent; angry at Nanny Day; eat fruit.

THURSDAY, AUGUST 15. 6 Business and virtue, and wrote diary. 6.30 Private prayer. 6.50 Psalm. 7 E; read chapter. 7.30 Family prayers. 7.45 Read chapter. 8 E; read chapter; breakfast; taught; private prayer. 9 Private prayer and psalm. 9.15 Read Greek Testament; ri. 10 E; read Greek Testament; ri. 11 E; at Wilby's. 11.30 Walked. 11.45 Private prayer. 12 E. 12.10 Dinner. 12.30 Taught. 1 E; shorthand; ri. 2 E; Psalm. 2.10 Read Greek Testament. 3 E; private prayer and psalm. 3.15 Read Greek Testament. 3.40 Psalm and E. 3.50 Greek [Testament]. 4 E; eat fruit. 4.15 Walked; read Hervey's letter; ri. 5 Necessary business. 5.15 E and private prayer; meditated on God's providence; ri. 6 E; daily examination. 6.20 Psalm, private prayer, and psalm. 7 E; supper; taught; read Milton. 8 E; read Milton. 8.30 Various and useful talk with our family. 9 Family prayers. 9.15 Good talk with our family. 9.30 Private prayer. 9.45 To bed. 10 Read Law.

Blessings: recollected 12 times; fervent in private prayer 6 times; regular all the day.[98]

95 Ingham is "watching" this evening. See his resolution on 23 August and his reading earlier this day.
96 The resulting entries in the Simplicity, Recollection, and Resolutions Kept columns for these hours are 0, 0, and 0. Cf. Appendix I(A).
97 MS. reads "lightening." Further indication of Ingham's interest in natural phenomena can be seen on 30 August, where he notes watching a comet.
98 The column in which simplicity is rated hourly contains a 7 or 8 for every hour; the contrast with the previous day was particularly notable.

FRIDAY, AUGUST 16.   7 Dressed. 7.15 Private prayer. 7.30 Meditated on humility. 7.45 Family prayers. 8 E; taught; meditated on my sins; ri. 9 Private prayer and psalm. 9.30 Vain thoughts. 10 E; thought of writing to Hervey. 11.30 Read Law. 12.15 Private prayer. 12.30 Meditated on the nation. 1 Taught. 1.15 Began the Penitential Office for the 16th Day of the Month, made little intermissions twice; ri. 3 E; read Law; ri. 4 E; meditated on the world; ri; private prayer. 5 E; psalm; daily examination; General Examination; private prayer; psalm. 6 E; breakfast. 6.30 Meditated on the Strait Gate. 7 E; taught. 7.30 Read Milton; ri. 8 E; read Milton. 8.30 Began *The Christian Monitor* with our family and William Wilby; ri. 9 Family prayers. 9.15 Mostly religious talk with our family; ri. 10 Private prayer; to bed.

   Blessings: recollected 12 times; fervent in private prayer; fasted till 6. Sins: laid after I was called.

SATURDAY, AUGUST 17.   5.30 Dressed; wrote diary. 6 E; private prayer. 6.25 Thanksgiving for the blessings. 7 E; got sage. 7.25 Read family prayers. 7.45 Breakfast. 8 Walked. 8.20 Taught; necessary business. 9 Psalm; thanksgiving; Collect. 9.15 Wrote a letter to Hervey; ri. 11.30 Went to Wakefield; necessary business. 12.45 Came home. 1.40 Dinner. 2 Walked, and hewed trees. 3.30 Mr Burnell came to see me, learned and useful talk, read a little of Law's *Serious Call,* lent it to him, and *Plain Directions for Reading the Scriptures.* 7 Got shaved and visited a sick child. 8 Read with our family, *Christian Monitor.* 9 Family prayers. 9.15 Private prayer.

   N.B. Troubled with the headache, caused by eating fruit after dinner; very irregular[99] and intemperate.

SUNDAY, AUGUST 18.   N Ps.[100] 7 Dressed. 8 Read family prayers. 8.10 Received a letter from John Wesley,[101] read it, and breakfast. 9 Private prayer. 9.15 Taught and catechized;[102] ri. 10 E and Collect; Public Prayers and Sermon. 12 Private prayer. 12.15 Dinner; delivered from

---

[99]   Hourly recollections are recorded only five times on this day, and all but one (from 6 to 7 a.m.) indicate various levels of being "irrecollected."

[100]   See also 25 August; cf. 22 July (S P); these problematic entries all occur on Sundays.

[101]   This letter is apparently not extant; see reference also in OD IV [Summaries], 24. Ingham and Wesley were arranging for a visit to Epworth; see 26 August et seq.

[102]   This precedes the institution of "Sunday Schools."

going to Thornhill[103] with Fothergil; private prayer. 12.45 Taught. 1 E
and private prayer with William Wilby, began to teach him to learn his
letters; ri. 1.45 Read *Christian Monitor* with our family and Wilby. 2
Various talk with our family. 2.45 Walked to Church. 3 Public Prayers
and Sermon. 4 Came home. 4.15 E; John Armitage came, learned talk,
read a little of Greek Testament. 5.30 Walked with him and William
Wilby, read Country Parson, lent it and Ellis on the Sacrament to Armitage. 6.15 Daily examination; private prayer; with me, William Wilby,
taught him; ri. 7 E; taught. 7.15 Visited. 7.30 Supper. 8 E; read
Christian Monitor with our family. 9.15 Family prayers. 9.30 Various
talk with our family; wrote diary. 10 Private prayer; meditated on uncleanness; ri.

Blessings: received a letter from John Wesley; delivered from going
to Thornhill with Fothergil, and also from going to Robert Smithson;
began to teach William Wilby to learn to read; religious talk with John
Armitage,[104] lent him some books.

Sins: irrecollected at Public Prayers and Sermon.

MONDAY, AUGUST 19. 4.45 Rose; dressed. 5 Wrote diary; psalm;
private prayer; read chapter. 6 Began to compose a sermon on Second
Peter, first chapter, 10th and 11th verses. 7.30 Family prayers and breakfast. 8 E; at Wilby's. 8.30 Walked; taught. 9 Private prayer. 9.15 Read
Greek Testament. 10.30 Thought of letter. 11.15 Walked. 11.45 Private prayer. 12 Dinner; taught. 1.15 Shorthand; ri. 2 Went to see
Rhodes and Dickinson; went a setting with Pickles.[105] 8 Supper at Dickinson's, various talk, and laid there.[106] 12 Private prayer; to bed.

[TUESDAY, AUGUST 20.] 5.30 Private prayer; waited for Pickles. 7
Breakfast with Mr and Mrs[107] Dickinson. 7.45 Went a setting all the
day till 6.30 at night. 7 Supper; taught, and necessary business.[108] 8
Read and religious talk with our family. 9 Family prayers; wrote diary.
9.30.

---

103 Thornhill, three kilometers southwest of Ossett, might have been reached
by fording the River Calder; otherwise, the route was via Horbury Bridge,
Dewsbury. See plate 18.
104 MS. reads "Armtage"; see also 25 August.
105 A common surname in that area.
106 Apparently at or near Batley.
107 MS. reads "Ms."
108 Marginal note in Blessings column reads "serious."

WEDNESDAY, AUGUST 21.   5.45 Dressed. 6 E; private prayer; meditated on the vanity of setting. 7 Meditated. 7.30 Family prayers; taught; at William Wilby's. 8 Thoughts about setting; ri. 8.45 Private prayer. 9 Read the Greek Testament; ri. 10 E; Greek Testament; ri. 11 Walked and meditated; ri. 12 Private prayer; meditated and fell asleep; ri. 1 Read Greek Testament; ri. 2.45 Private prayer. 3 Breakfast; visited sick child. 4 Thoughts of predestination. 5 E; meditated on God's providence; ri. 6 E; daily examination; vain thoughts. 6.45 Private prayer. 7 E; supper; taught; read Milton. 8.30 Finished *The Christian Monitor* with our family and William Wilby. 9 Family prayers. 9.30 Private prayer; to bed.

THURSDAY, AUGUST 22.   5.15 Dressed; psalm; meditated, but slumbered. 6.15 Meditated. 6.30 Wrote diary and private prayer. 7 E; family prayer; necessary business with William Wilby; ri. 8 Taught; breakfast; at Wilby's. 9 Private prayer; forked corn. 12 Private prayer; dinner; at Wilby's, taught. 1 Necessary business. 2.30 Began Ostervald *Of Uncleanness;* ri. 4 Visited a sick child. 5 E; meditated on the vanity of the world; ri. 6 E; daily examination; private prayer; psalm. 6.45 Read Ostervald. 7 E; taught; supper; read Milton. 8.30 Began Beveridge's sermon on the Common Prayer; ri. 9 Family prayers and private prayer.

FRIDAY, AUGUST 23.   6.30 Dressed; wrote diary; private prayer. 7 E and daily examination. 7.15 Family prayers. 7.30 Began to write a letter to Smith; ri. 8 E; at Wilby's; ri; taught. 8.45 Private prayer. 9 Daily examination and E; wrote letter to Smith; ri. 11 Daily examination and E; wrote letter to Smith; ri. 11 E and daily examination; finished letter to Smith. 12.30 Meditated on Christ's sufferings, and private prayer. 1 Taught; began to examine[109] myself, but fell asleep. 3.10 Breakfast and walked. 3.45 General Examination. 4 Walked and visited a sick child; ri. 5 E; meditated on watching; ri. 6 E; daily examination (Resolutions for the following week: to stand one hour in reading the Greek Testament morning and afternoon, and to translate into Greek [Latin?][110] half an hour between 11 and 12; to recollect and use ejaculatory prayer at the beginning of every hour; and if I find myself irrecollected, to lay aside everything, if possible, to regain it;[111] to rise at the first call; if not, to miss my breakfast, or supper, or watch in proportion at night, and lay

---

[109]   The abbreviation here is "Ex" for General Examination.
[110]   See 13 August.
[111]   Cf. Charles Wesley's advice on 20 June.

without bed; to meditate thrice on God's omnipresence); ri. 6.40 Mary France came, mostly religious talk with her. 6.45 Private prayer. 7 E; taught. 7.20 At Wilby's, supper. 8 E; read Milton. 9.15 Family prayers, and various and useful talk with our family. 9.45 Private prayers. 10 Read Ostervald. 11.30 To bed; thoughts of setting, etc.

Blessings: recollected 6 times; wrote resolutions.

SATURDAY, AUGUST 24. 5.45 Dressed. 6 Wrote diary. 6.10 Psalm and private prayer; read chapter. 7 E; read family prayers. 7.15 Breakfast and taught. 8 E; composed sermon, and psalm and private prayer. 9 E; read Greek Testament; ri. 10 E; read Greek Testament; ri. 11 E; translated Greek. 11.30 Walked. 11.45 Private prayer. 12 Read Milton. 12.30 Dinner. 1 Taught. 1.15 Visited sick. 1.30 Went a shooting. 2.30 At Wilby's; came home. 2.45 Read Nelson. 3 Private prayer. 3.15 Read Greek Testament; ri. 4 Walked and eat; ri. 5 E; meditated on God's omnipresence. 6 E; daily examination; private prayer; read chapter. 7 Supper; got shaved. 8 Read Milton. 8.45 Read Beveridge. 9 Family prayers. 9.15 Necessary business; private prayers; to bed.

Blessings:[112]

Sins: loitered most of the afternoon; eat a deal[113] of fruit; intemperate at supper.

[SUNDAY, AUGUST 25.] N P.[114] 6 Wrote diary; private prayer; with me, William Wilby, read Nelson and taught; ri. 7 E; dressed. 7.30 Family prayers. 8 Read Ostervald. 8.15 Catechized. 9 Private prayer and psalm. 9.15 Read Ostervald. 10.15 Public Prayers and Sermon. 12 Private prayer; dinner; taught and catechized. 1.15 Read Ostervald; ri. 2 E; visited; Public Prayers and Sermon. 5 E; meditated on heaven; ri. 6 With me, Armitage and John Brook, learned and useful talk, and read Greek Testament. 7.15 Taught and catechized; supper. 8 E; finished Beveridge's sermon; ri. 9 E; read family prayers and wrote diary. 9.30 Daily examination and private prayer. 10 Read Horneck's *Letter on the Primitive Christians;* ri.

Blessings: catechized, and zealous and active.

Sins: vain thoughts in Public Prayers twice.

112 Nothing is listed by Ingham after this heading; another person has copied over in this place the entry from the Sins column.

113 Meaning "a great deal"; see *O.E.D.,* s.v. "Deal."

114 See 18 August, note 100.

MONDAY, AUGUST 26. 5.20 Dressed; wrote diary; psalm and private prayer. 6 E; dressed. 6.15 Psalm. 6.20 Wrote a letter to Washington. 7 E; family prayers. 7.15 Began a letter to Watson; ri. 8 E; breakfast; at Wilby's, taught. 8.45 Private prayer. 9 Psalm. 9.05 Wrote letter to Watson; ri. 12 Private prayer. 12.15 Finished letter. 12.30 Dinner and taught. 1 At Wilby's. 1.30 Wrote a letter to Washington; ri. 3 Private prayer. 3.15 Wrote a letter to Smyth. 4.30 E and private prayer; went to talk with Dame Fothergil, religious talk, comforted her, and promised to assist her. 5.30 Visited a sick child. 6 E; daily examination and private prayer. 6.30 John Wesley and Charles Wesley came. 7.30 Supper, various and useful talk. 8.30 Family prayers. 9 Private prayer with John Wesley and Charles Wesley; ri.

TUESDAY, AUGUST 27. 4.30 Dressed; private prayer. 5 Breakfast with John and Charles Wesley, various and useful talk. 5.45 Set forward for Epworth with John and Charles Wesley.[115] 6 E; Charles Wesley [read] Greek Testament, and religious talk; ri. 7 E; Charles Wesley read Greek Testament, and religious talk. 8 E; began *The Sincere Convert;*[116] ri. 9 E and Collect; read *The Sincere Convert;* ri. 10.20 Tea at North Elmsall,[117] good talk. 11.20 E; Charles Wesley read Greek Testament, and religious talk; ri. 12 E; and Collect; Charles Wesley read Greek Testament, and religious talk; ri. 1 E; John Wesley delineated a sermon; ri. 1.30 Various and useful talk with a soldier. 2 E; dinner at Doncaster, religious and useful talk. 3 E; Charles Wesley read Greek Testament; ri. 4 Charles Wesley read Greek Testament; ri. 4.45 Various talk. 5.15 Drank. 5.35 Daily examination; Charles Wesley read Greek Testament. 6.30 John Wesley told us the r[eligious] progress of Chapman and Stonehouse of Pembroke College;[118] mostly religious talk. 8.30 At Mr Wes-

---

[115]   The pace of the trip indicates that they walked.

[116]   See Thomas Shepard in Appendix 3.

[117]   Probably at the White Stag, now demolished; see map in Joseph Hunter's *South Yorkshire* (London, 1828), I, frontispiece.

[118]   Wesley spent some time during the spring talking with Walter Chapman (Pembroke College, B.A. 1732) about self-denial, diaries, the Sacrament, the Stations, and other typical Methodist concerns. Chapman's response was somewhat vacillating, but apparently became more consistently positive as the year progressed. George Stonehouse (Pembroke College, B.A. 1733, and vicar of Islington 1738–93) is mentioned only in passing on two or three occasions in the spring and does not appear again in Wesley's Oxford diaries. See OD IV (especially, p. 128) and OD V, passim.

ley's at Epworth. 9 Various and useful talk; supper. 10.15 Private prayer with Charles Wesley. 10.30 To bed.

WEDNESDAY, AUGUST 28. 6 E; dressed; read Kempis; ri. 7 E; wrote diary; ri. 8 Private prayer; E; went into the house; dressed. 9 Various and useful talk with the family; ri; family prayers. 10.30 Religious talk with Mrs Wesley. 10.45 Got shaved. 11.30 Public Prayers.[119] 12.30 Came home; wrote diary. 12.45 Private prayer with John and Charles Wesley, etc. 1 E; meditated on the state of man. 2 Walked with John Wesley, religious talk. 2.45 Private prayer. 3 Pared apples; religious talk. 3.40 Breakfast with John and Charles Wesley, etc. 4 Religious and useful talk with John, Charles Wesley, their mother, and three sisters.[120] 5.24 Read Greek Testament[121] and wrote diary; ri. 6 E; daily examination. 6.15 Private prayer; meditated. 7 E; family prayers and supper; religious talk. 8.30 Read Burkitt on Time. 9 E; trifled with Charles Wesley, etc. 9.30 Private prayer; to bed.

Blessings: preserved from going to the raffle.

THURSDAY, AUGUST 29. 5 E; meditated on the resurrection. 6 E; dressed; wrote diary. 6.30 Read the Scripture. 7 E; read Scripture. 7.15 Private prayer. 7.30 Shorthand. 8 E; breakfast with John and Charles Wesley, etc; ri. 9 Religious and useful talk. 9.30 Walked with John Wesley, religious talk; ri. 10 E; shorthand with Charles Wesley;[122] ri.

---

[119] William Wake, Bishop of Lincoln, had in 1711 urged that the daily prayer services be read in every church in his diocese, as stipulated in the B.C.P. and the "Act for the Uniformity of Publick Prayers" (XIV. Caroli II). Although most priests neglected this daily exercise, Samuel Wesley is typical of some rural clergy who still read the service at least on Stationary days during the week. See John Wickham Legg, *English Church Life from the Restoration to the Tractarian Movement* (London: Longmans, Green and Co., 1914), pp. 83, 90.

[120] Molly (Mary), Kezzy (Kezia), and Patty (Martha). In subsequent entries, Ingham mentions the first two by name, but never Patty, with whom he was apparently falling in love (see Wesley, OD V, 1 [7 September 1734]: "Ingham in love with Sister Patty"). In September 1735, Patty married Westley Hall, who had been simultaneously courting Kezzy. See also note 123 below.

[121] Marginal note ("5 E") indicates ejaculatory prayers on the hour.

[122] This may have been Byrom's shorthand, which Charles was using very proficiently at least as early as February 1736 (see Charles Wesley MS. sermon "Single Intention" and MS. Journal, MA) and may have been learning as early as May 1733. In 1736–37, Ingham applied Byrom's universal shorthand alphabet to the Indian language in Georgia (John Byrom, *The Private Journal and Literary Remains of John Byrom* [Manchester: Chetham Society, 1856], II, 171). Cf. 8 July, note 25.

11 E; began Scougal's *Life of God in the Soul of Man.* 12 Private prayer with Charles Wesley and Molly.[123]   12.15 Meditated. 1 E; trifled. 1.30 Dinner. 2 E; various talk with company.[124] 3.30 Read Scougal; ri. 4 Meditated. 4.30 Went into the fair[125] with John, Charles Wesley, and three sisters. 5.30 Daily examination. 6 Private prayer; family prayers. 7.15 Religious talk with Molly. 8.30 Various talk; sat with Mr Wesley, etc. 9.30 Trifled. 9.45 Private prayer with John Wesley; to bed.

FRIDAY, AUGUST 30.   6 Dressed; E and Collect; read Scougal; private prayer with John Wesley. 7 E; read Scougal; ri. 8 E; finished Scougal's *Life of God.* 9 E and private prayer with John and Charles Wesley. 9.15 Began a sermon. 9.45 Necessary business, and various talk with family. 10 E; read sermon; family prayers. 10.45 With Charles Wesley. 11 E; walked to church; Public Prayers.[126] 12.15 Came home. 12.30 Private prayer with John Wesley, etc. 12.45 Read sermon. 1.15 Walked with John Wesley, religious talk; ri. 2 E; religious talk. 2.30 Meditated. 2.45 Private prayer. 3 E; breakfast; religious talk with John Wesley, Charles Wesley, and their mother. 4 Religious talk with John Wesley and two sisters; ri. 5 E; religious talk with John Wesley. 5.15 Daily examination. 5.45 Private prayer. 6 Went to family prayer, and supper. 7 Various and useful talk with family; looked at the comet.[127] 8 E; religious talk with Molly. 8.30 Heard *The Minute Philosopher.*[128] 9 E; *Minute Philosopher.* 9.30 Necessary business, and trifled. 10 Private prayer; to bed.

[123]   Molly (Mary) Wesley married John Whitelamb in December 1733, causing some turmoil in the Wesley family. She died in childbirth, 31 October 1734. See R. P. Heitzenrater, "Mary Wesley's Marriage," in *Proceedings of the Wesley Historical Society* 40 (October 1976), pp. 153–63.

[124]   Marginal note ("3 E") indicates ejaculatory prayers on the hour.

[125]   The fair was held annually at the end of August in Epworth and during their Oxford years the Wesley brothers were frequently in attendance, being home on vacation. See especially OD I, 73; OD II, 13, 99; OD III, 17.

[126]   See 28 August, note 119.

[127]   There is no record of a comet sighting on this date in the standard listings for this period, such as in Alexandre Guy Pingre, *Cométographie ou traité historique et théoretique des Comètes* (Paris: 1783, 1784), 2 vol. Appreciation to Dr. Brian Marsden, comet specialist at the Smithsonian Museum's Astrophysical Observatory at Cambridge, Massachusetts, and Miss G. A. Edmonds of the Royal Greenwich Observatory, Hailsham, East Sussex, for assistance on this question.

[128]   See George Berkeley, *Alciphron,* in Appendix 3.

SATURDAY, AUGUST 31. 5 Dressed; E; wrote diary; thanksgiving for blessings. 6 Private prayer and E; looked over a sermon of John Wesley;[129] necessary business. 8 E; breakfast; various and useful talk. 9 E and Collect; religious talk with John Wesley, etc. 9.30 Read Dr Cheyne on Health. 10 E. 10.15 Gathered apples; ri. 10.15[130] Went to a wedding. 11 Church. 11.30 Came home; wrote diary; private prayer. 12 E; dinner; good talk (various); ri. 1 E; heard *Minute Philosopher.* 2 E; *Minute Philosopher.* 2.40 Religious and useful talk with Molly, etc. 3 E and Collect; tea; religious and useful talk. 4 E; walked and meditated. 5 E; daily examination; private prayer with John Wesley; religious talk with John Wesley and Kezzy. 6.15 Family prayers and supper. 7 Supper; various talk. 8 E. 8.15 Law, read with the family; ri. 9 Religious and useful talk with Charles Wesley;[131] ri.

129   Although there is no indication which sermon this may have been, Ingham did indicate his degree of attention while reading: "indifferent."
130   Probably should read "10:30." The wedding seems not to have been at Epworth or Wroot as there is none recorded in the parish registers.
131   Perhaps a fitting closing statement for this diary, as Charles seems to have been an important influence on Ingham throughout this period.

Monthly Summaries:
September 1733–August 1734

Following the Wesleyan method of diary keeping, Ingham "cast up" his diary monthly, entering a summary of his activities in the back of the diary dos-à-dos fashion (beginning from the back, turned around as though it were the front). He listed readings by category, noting also which groups had read particular items. He also included lists of writings for the month, both curricular exercises and private correspondence. The most explicit format for these summaries can be seen in the May and June entries.

SEPTEMBER 1733

Religious books.
Transcribed Norris' *Christian Prudence,* and read thrice; read Country Parson twice; read Treatise on the Stationary Fasts twice; read Nelson on the Month,[1] on Fasting[2] thrice, Fridays[3] thrice, Vigils,[4] Sundays;[5] read Secker's Sermon twice; read Bennet's Letter on the Study of Divinity; read and abridged the last half of Brown's *Procedure.*

    Read *Life of Bonnell,* the Stationary Fasts, and Country Parson with Smith.

[1] See Robert Nelson, *A Companion for the Festivals and Fasts of the Church of England* (1704), ch. VIII, "Ember Days in September" (see Appendix 3). Hereinafter cited as *Fasts* or *Festivals.*
[2] Nelson, *Fasts,* "Preliminary Instructions concerning Fasts."
[3] Ibid., ch. XI, "All Fridays in the Year."
[4] Ibid., ch. IX, "The Vigils."
[5] Nelson, *Festivals,* ch. I, "The Lord's Day."

Read Wake's *Catechism* with Atkinson, Washington, Smith, Richardson.

Read 16 sections, first book of Grotius' *De veritas religionis* with Natt.

Read 6 chapters of Brown's *Divine Analogy* with Natt and Knail.

Latin.

Translated the last half of Aldrich's Logic.

Read the 6 last books of Virgil and the first chapter of Aldrich's Logic with Natt.

English.

Read 3 Lives in Plutarch[6] with Natt and Knail.

Letters.

Mother, brother Will, Rhodes.

Acquaintances.

With Natt 8 times, with Charles Wesley twice, with John Wesley twice, with Mr Smith once, with Watson once, with Ford once, with Johnson and Shepard thrice.

OCTOBER 1733

Religious books.

Read Nelson for the Month; Country Parson twice; Bishop Ken's *Meditations;* Norris' *Advice to his Children.*

With Natt 3 chapters of *The Whole Duty of Man;* Ellis' *Christianity in Short.*

With Natt and Knail finished Brown's *Divine Analogy.*

With Natt and Atkinson read Ellis on the Sacrament.

With Smith read Barrow on Industry.

With Smith and Robson read Lucas' *Practical Christianity* and a Sermon [of Atterbury].[7]

With Watson read Country Parson, and a sermon on Indifference.

With Atkinson and Ford read *genesis problematica* on the Stationary Fasts.[8]

---

6 He read the lives of Theseus, Romulus, and Plutarch. See Appendix 3 and 6 and 7 September, notes 13 and 16.
7 See 20 October.
8 John Wesley's treatise; see 14 September, note 22.

Greek.

Read St Matthew and Mark with Natt.

Latin.

Translated Sanderson's Appendix to his Logic.

With Natt finished first book of Grotius, and read second and half the third chapter of Aldrich's Logic.

English.

Read Longinus with Natt.

Letters.

To Mother twice, brother Will, Burton.

Composed.

3 Themes, 4 *geneses thematica,* 2 Oppositions, 4 Suppositions, 3 for Yates.

Acquaintances.

With John Wesley once, Charles Wesley 9 times, Natt 7, Yates twice, Ford twice, Atkinson once, John Whitaker once, with Natt, Atkinson, Washington frequently.

NOVEMBER 1733

Religious books.

Read Brevint on the Sacrament; Thomas à Kempis; Country Parson; two or three Sermons of Norris; St Matthew and St Mark in Greek.

Latin.

Read the 7 first *Prælectiones* of Sanderson's *De conscientiæ obligatione.*[9]

Greek.

Read St Luke and St John.

With Atkinson 7 chapters in Romans.

English.

With Ford, Norris' *Advice,* 'The Great Importance of a Religious Life', and 3 Sermons.

With Ford and Washington, *Christian Prudence.*

---

[9]   Ingham has transposed the words in the title.

With Smith, Robson, and Ford read half of Goodman's *Penitent Pardoned.*

With Atkinson and Washington at Ford's read 6 chapters of Law's *Christian Perfection.*

With Knail read sermon of South's and 10 chapters of first book of Gravesande's Experimental Philosophy.[10]

With Ford, Atkinson, and Washington read first and second chapters of Aldrich's Logic.

Composed.
One Copy of Verses, 2 Themes, one Opposition, one Supposition.

Acquaintances.
At Ford's 12 times, Charles Wesley's 3, John Wesley twice, Natt once, Broughton once, Selby's once. With me Ford twice, Atkinson once, Smyth once. Breakfast at Robson's 4 times, Smith 3, Selby's once, Ford's once; with me twice.

DECEMBER 1733

Religious books.
Read Taylor's *Holy Living,* and *The Whole Duty of Man;* abridged the Prefaces and 5 chapters of St Matthew from Whitby; before private prayer read St Luke, John, and Acts in the Greek Testament.

With Ford read Ken's *Meditations,* and the *Companion to the Altar.*

With Smith, Robson, and Ford finished Goodman's *Penitent Pardoned.*

With Smyth and Washington read Ellis on the Sacrament.

With them [Smyth and Washington] and Watson read a volume of the *Lives of the Fathers.*[11]

With Watson read Norris' sermon on Singularity.

English.
Read one volume of Blackwall's *Sacred Classics.*

Latin.
Finished Sanderson; finished first book of Aldrich with Ford, Atkinson, and Washington.

10 See Willem Jacob van 's Gravesande, *Mathematical Elements of Natural Philosophy* (1720, 1721), in Appendix 3.
11 See William Cave in Appendix 3.

Greek.
Read the Acts.
  With Atkinson finished Romans.

Composed.
Verses, one; Themes, one; one Supposition; one Opposition.

Letters.
Natt, Charles Burton, Brownsword.

Acquaintances.
With John Wesley once, Charles Wesley 4 times, Broughton twice; met with Knail 4 times, with Ford, Atkinson, Washington, Smith frequently. New Acquaintance, Smyth of our own College. With Watson and Broughton.

JANUARY 1733/34

Religious books.
Read Taylor's *Holy Dying;* Ellis on the Sacrament twice; abridged Whitby to [the] 17th chapter of St Luke.
  Read with Ford, Ellis on the Sacrament, and *The Oxford Methodists.*
  With Ford, Smith, and Evans read Goodman's first Conference, and half of *Nicodemus.*[12]
  With Charles Wesley, Smith, and Evans, half of *Nicodemus.*
  With Watson, Secker's sermon.
  With Watson, Washington, and Smyth, Norris' sermon on Singularity, and Lucas' on Company.
  With them [Watson, Washington, and Smyth] and Atkinson, read abridgement of Bull's Life.[13]
  With them [Watson, Washington, Smyth, and Atkinson] and Ford, read two chapters in Law's *Christian Perfection.*
  Read *genesis problematica* on the Stations.

English.
Read second volume of Blackwall's *Sacred Classics.*
  And with Watson, *The History of Charles XII.*[14]

12 See August Hermann Francke, Appendix 3.
13 See Robert Nelson, Appendix 3.
14 See Voltaire, Appendix 3.

And with Knail, *The Provoked Husband,*[15] and finished Gravesande's Mechanics.[16]

With Charles Wesley and Smith, read *Prayers for Every Day in the Week.*[17]

Latin.

With Watson, two and one-half books of Sanderson's Logic.

With Watson, Ford, Atkinson, Washington, and Smyth, one chapter of Aldrich's Logic.

Greek.

St Matthew twice before private prayer.

Composed.

One Declamation; one Theme; one Opposition.

Acquaintances.

Breakfast at John Wesley's twice, at Charles Wesley's 9 [times], at Smith's thrice, at Evans thrice, at Ford's thrice; with me, Smith and Evans thrice, Ford twice, Broughton once, Smyth and Washington once; at nights with Knail thrice, with Watson 7 times, with Ford 7, at Robson's once, at Smith's thrice, at Evans once; with me, Knail 4 times, Smith 4, Ford twice, Evans thrice; visited Gambold with Smith and Evans at Stanton [Harcourt].

FEBRUARY 1733/34

Religious books.

Read sermon on Method[18] twice; read the Prefaces to *Nicodemus.*

With Charles Wesley, Smith and Ford, finished *Nicodemus.*

With Ford, Atkinson, Washington, Smyth, and Watson, finished Law's *Christian Perfection,* and read three chapters of his *Serious Call;* read John Wesley's sermon on the Love of God.

Read first part of *The Christian Monitor* at the Workhouse in St Thomas'.

Abridged Whitby on the New Testament to the Romans.

[15] See John Vanbrugh, Appendix 3.
[16] *Mathematical Elements of Natural Philosophy,* book II, part II, "Of the Motion of Fluids."
[17] See John Wesley, *A Collection of Forms of Prayer for Every Day in the Week* (1733), in Appendix 3.
[18] See *The Way of Living in a Method, and by Rule* (1722), in Appendix 3.

English.
Read two books of Blackmore's *Creation.*

Latin.
Read second and third chapters of Aldrich's Logic with Ford, Atkinson, Washington, Smyth, and Watson.

Greek.
Read St Mark and St Luke before private prayer.

Letters.
To Brownsword one; to Charles Burton one.

Composed.
One Opposition.

Acquaintances.
Breakfast at Charles Wesley's 5 times, at Ford's 7, at Smith's once; with me, Smith and Ford and Evans, once. At nights, at Ford's 9 times, at Watson's twice, at Natt's thrice, at Smith's once; with me, Robson once, Smith and Ford twice; with John Wesley once, with Broughton once, with Gambold once; visited Bolton Sr in his sickness 13 times; at the Workhouse in St Thomas' with Smith 8; at Charles Wesley's on Sunday thrice; walked with Ford, Watson, Washington, Atkinson, Smith,[19] etc, frequently.

MARCH 1734

Religious books.
Finished Francke's *Nicodemus;* read Law of rising,[20] intercession,[21] and fasting,[22] and Miranda's character;[23] at private prayer read Romans, I and II Corinthians, Galatians, and Ephesians.

On Wednesdays and Fridays at 3 at Charles Wesley's with Smith and Carter read almost all Patrick on Repentance and Fasting and Lent; with

19 Ingham has entered the abbreviation for "Smith" but probably meant Smyth, a regular member of that group.
20 William Law, *A Serious Call to a Devout and Holy Life* (1729), ch. XIV; see Appendix 3.
21 Ibid., ch. XX and XXI.
22 William Law, *A Practical Treatise upon Christian Perfection* (1726), ch. VII; see Appendix 3.
23 *Serious Call,* ch. VIII.

them on Sunday at 3 read three of Young's sermons, of Indifferency, and Self-denial, [and] Nature and Grace.

On Friday night with Ford, Atkinson, Watson, Washington, and Smyth read five more chapters of Law's *Serious Call*.

With Ford read the three first Parts of Patrick's *Christian Sacrifice*.

With Ford and Smith on Wednesday, Saturday, and Sunday nights read Goodman's second Conference.

At the Workhouse finished *The Christian Monitor*, and read several chapters [in the Bible].

English.
Abridged Whitby on the New Testament to the Hebrews; read some short treatises.

Latin.
Finished Aldrich's Logic with Watson, Washington, Smyth, Atkinson, (and Ford).

Greek.
Read St John and the Acts at private prayer.

Composed.
Two Themes.

Acquaintances.
At Charles Wesley's thrice a week; with John Wesley twice; breakfast with Natt twice and two nights; breakfast with Ford twice, Smith 4 times, Yates once; with Smith and Ford Wednesday, Saturday, and Sunday nights; at Smith's compared diaries 4 times; with Ford, Atkinson, Watson, Washington, and Smyth every Friday night; at Robson's twice; Watson's once; at the Workhouse thrice a week; visited Bolton Sr frequently; sat up once with Bolton Jr; walked with Watson, Atkinson, Smyth, Washington, etc.

APRIL 1734

Religious books.
Read the Country Parson and resolved;[24] read *Plain Directions for Reading the Holy Scriptures;* read Patrick's *Christian Sacrifice* before the Sacrament.

24 See pp. 165–69.

With Smith, read a Treatise of the 16th Day of the Month, and compared diaries.

With Smith and Ford, finished Goodman's *Winter Evening Conference.*

With Smith, Ford, and Atkinson, began Castañiza's *Spiritual Combat.*[25]

At Charles Wesley's with Smith and Carter, read Hale's Contemplation on Christ Crucified.

With Atkinson, Washington, Watson, Smyth, and Ford on Friday nights, read to the 14th chapter of Law's *Serious Call.*

With Natt, read the 3rd chapter of Law's *Serious Call* and Nelson on three holy days.[26]

With Dixon and Bolton, Sr, read Norris on 'The Importance of a Religious Life', Law on daily examination,[27] and John Wesley's Letter on Company; got them to [have] private prayer and daily examination.

With John Brownsword, read Norris' 'Importance of a Religious Life', John Wesley's Letter of Company; got him to [have] private prayer and daily examination.

With Watson, Washington, Smyth, and Atkinson, all or some of them, read the Country Parson of resolutions, John Wesley's treatise on the Sacrament; Dr. Knight's sermon on the Reformation of Manners, Norris' sermons on Religious Conversation, the Importance of a Religious Life, Love of God, Fear of Death, Successive Vanity of Human Life, etc; read about five of Horneck's sermons on the 5th chapter of St Matthew; read the Lives of St Ignatius, Polycarp, Dionysius,[28] Clemens Romanus, Origen.[29]

With poor people in the Hamel in St Thomas', read half *The Christian Monitor.*

Latin.
Began Francke's *Manuductio ad S. Scripturam.*

Greek.
Began St Clemens Romanus Epistles.

Composed.
One Theme; wrote resolutions; wrote reasons for rising, private prayer, and fasting.

25   See Lorenzo Scupoli in Appendix 3.
26   Easter Eve, Easter Monday, Easter Tuesday.
27   *Serious Call,* ch. XXIII.
28   MS. reads "Dionisius."
29   See William Cave in Appendix 3.

Letters.
One to my mother, and one to Charles Burton.

Acquaintances.
Visited Gambold twice; (John Wesley, Charles Wesley, Broughton, Smith, Ford, Atkinson, Washington, Watson, Smyth); Robson thrice; Natt 4 times. With me, Bolton, Sr, and Dixon 4 times; Brownsword twice; Hervey and Greives of Lincoln College on Monday nights; at the Workhouse in St Thomas' 10 times; visited sick woman 6 times; with John Whitaker once.

THE SUMMARY OF WHAT I READ AND DID, MAY 1734.

Religious books read with myself.
Read Rodriguez on Humility; read Horneck on Fasting, Watching, and making Vows;[30] read Beveridge *De jejuniis quartæ et sextæ feriæ*,[31] and the Canons.

With Others.
Finished Castañiza's *Spiritual Combat* with Smith, Atkinson, Ford, and Hervey; and read Young's *Poem on the Last Day.*

On Friday nights read Law's *Serious Call* with Atkinson, Washington, Watson, Ford, and Smyth.

At Charles Wesley's, read part of Sales' *Introduction to a Holy Life.*

On Saturday night at 9, began Horneck's *Best Exercise*[32] with Atkinson and Washington; watching and praying.

With Hervey, Smith, and Greives, read a sermon of Norris.

With Washington and Watson, read a sermon of Norris; Horneck's *Letter on Primitive Christians*[33] twice, and a sermon.

With Dixon and Bolton, Sr, read several parts of Law's *Serious Call;* began Law's *Christian Perfection.*

With Natt, read a sermon of Tillotson.

[30] Anthony Horneck's *The Happy Ascetick; or, The Best Exercise* (1681?), part 2, ch. II, III, and I; see Appendix 3.
[31] Book III, ch. X, of William Beveridge's *Codex canonum ecclesiæ primitivæ vindicatus ac illustratus* (1678); see Appendix 3.
[32] *The Happy Ascetick.*
[33] Ibid.

With Smith, Ford, Hervey, and Evans, read *The Life of Monsieur de Renty*,[34] and *The Second Spira*.[35]

English.
Read the first volume of Jenkin's *Reasonableness of the Christian Religion* at noons with Washington, Watson, and Smyth.

Latin.
Finished Francke's *Manuductio ad S. Scripturam*.

Composed.
Two Themes; one *problematica* treatise on Matthew 19.17; one Opposition; and one Speech for my degree and to be freed from Exercises.

Acquaintances.
John Wesley, Charles Wesley, Broughton, Gambold, Smith, Hervey, Ford, Atkinson, Watson, Washington, Smyth, Evans, Walker, Greives, Dixon, Bolton, Natt, Brownsword.

JUNE 1734

Religious books, by myself.
Read Dr Waterland on the Nature, Efficacy, and Benefits of the Sacraments; most of Gother on Particular States; *Plain Directions for Reading the Holy Scriptures*.

With others.
With Charles Wesley, Smith, Broughton, and Gambold, read Bishop Hall on Meditation.

Wednesdays, Saturdays, and Sundays with Smith, Ford, Hervey, Atkinson, and Evans, read Deacon's Extracts at the end of his *Collection of Devotions* upon Conforming to the Catholic Church, and the Supplement,[36] etc; Nelson for Sunday.

Mondays and Thursdays with Watson, Smith, Ford, and Hervey, two sermons of Norris.

---

34 See Jean Baptiste de Saint Jure in Appendix 3. Atkinson also participated in this group; see 25 May et seq.
35 See Richard Sault in Appendix 3.
36 Supplement: "An Essay to procure Catholic Communion upon Catholick Principles."

Fridays, finished Law's *Serious Call* with Atkinson, Washington, Watson, Smyth, and Ford.

With Bolton and Dixon, read half of Law's *Christian Perfection,* and *The Second Spira.*

With Natt and Atkinson, read *The Second Spira.*

With Atkinson, Watson, and Bolton, read a sermon of Horneck.

With Mrs Wesley, read Dr Knight's sermon on the Conflagration and Renovation; part of Herbert's Poems,[37] religious talk; part of Country Parson.

With Kezzy [Wesley], religious talk and read part Country Parson.

English.
Read Reeves' translation of Justin Martyr, Tertullian, Minutius Felix, and Vincentius Lirinensis with his prefaces.

With Atkinson, Washington, Watson, and Smyth, read the second volume of Jenkin's *Reasonableness of Christianity.*

Greek.
Finished St Clemens Epistles.

Composed.
Three Lectures on the 10th Satire of Juvenal for my A.B. degree; one Opposition; wrote three Suppositions; one Theme.

Letters.
To Charles Burton; to Joseph Alleine on John Wesley's account.

Acquaintances.
John Wesley, Charles Wesley, Gambold, Broughton, Smith, Evans, Ford, Atkinson, Watson, Washington, Smyth, Bolton, Dixon, Hervey, Walker, Natt.

New.
Mr Wesley, Mrs [Wesley] and Kezzy; walked from Oxford to Ossett, stayed there three days at old Mr Wesley's at Epworth.

37 See George Herbert, *Herbert's Remains* (1652), in Appendix 3.

JULY 1734

Religious books.
Read Nelson's Method of Devotion;[38] Taylor on Chastity; *Plain Directions for Reading the Scriptures;* read Norris' Beatitudes; read several chapters of Law's *Serious Call,* and began it.

With our family and William Wilby, read Bishop [of] Man's *Catechism,*[39] and Alleine's *Sure Guide to Heaven,* and four sermons.

English.
Read Cave's *Primitive Christianity;* read Tully *Of the Nature of the Gods.*

Letters.
To Smith; to John Wesley.

Composed.
Part of a sermon on self-denial.

Acquaintances.
My mother, brothers John and Joseph, and sister Hannah; William Wilby; Jeremy Ellis; Rhodes; relations; began to teach to read James Blackburn,[40] John France, James Fozard, Jonathan, Susy, and Sara Wilby; to write, the three last [Wilbys] and Hannah France.

AUGUST 1734

Religious books.
Read half of Law's *Serious Call;* read half of Ostervald on Uncleanness; read Horneck's *Letter on the Primitive Christians;* read Scougal's *Life of God in the Soul of Man.*

Read the following with our family and William Wilby, Ellis on the Sacrament; the Country Parson; *The Christian Monitor;* Beveridge's sermon on the Common Prayer.

Greek.
Read St Matthew and St Mark.

---

[38] Robert Nelson, *The Practice of True Devotion* (1698), ch. I, "A General Method for the Exercise of True Devotion." See Appendix 3.
[39] See Thomas Wilson in Appendix 3.
[40] MS. reads "Blagburn"; cf. 17 July, and see plate 17.

Letters.
To Charles Burton; to Ford; to Smith; to Watson; to Washington; to Smyth; to Hervey.

English.
Read second and third books of Milton's *Paradise Lost.*

Acquaintances.
At James and Abr[aham] Whitaker's; at Rhodes' and Dickinson's, with Pickles; with Robert Smithson; John Armitage[41] for Richard Burnell; John Brook; Dame Fothergil;[42] first began to teach Job Butterfield, Susy Butterfield, Hannah Cunningham, and William Wilby to read; went to Mr Wesley's at Epworth with John and Charles Wesley, their sisters, and family.

41 MS. reads "Armtage."
42 MS. reads "Futhergil."

Appendixes

1   The "Exacter" Diary Format

A. The "exacter" diary format taught to Benjamin Ingham by Charles Wesley, following John Wesley's pattern, consisted of seven columns within which different kinds of activities and reflections were entered hourly. A central vertical line on the page, drawn with a fold of the previous page as a guide, divided the page in half. On the far left edge, a narrow marginal column listed the hours of the day. The remaining large column on that side received the main entries for the activities of each hour. On the right-hand side of the page were five columns with headings that indicated their use: "D" contains numbers which rate from 1 to 9 his temper of devotion; "Rec" contains the description of his state of spiritual composure or recollection; "Rb" lists resolutions broken, indicated by number and keyed to two basic listings ("Resolutions for Every Day" and "Resolutions for Lent"); "Rk" lists the resolutions kept, based on the same numbering scheme; and "Bl," the right-hand margin in which special blessings were noted, often recapitulating certain entries from the "resolutions kept" column.

As might be expected, the numerical ratings in the Devotion column correlate closely with the descriptive terminology in the Recollection column (especially at first):

D   Rec

9   most zealous
8   more zealous
7   zealous
6   recollected
5   little recollected
4   less recollected
3   irrecollected
2   dissipated
1   dissipated

Thus, any rating of 6 or more in the devotion column was usually associated with a positive state of recollection. See plate 12.

B. On 19 March, two days after an important interview with John Wesley, Ingham added an eighth column to the format in which to indicate additional descriptions of his hourly temper, gleaned through careful recollection. This column, headed "H" (heart?), contains single letter entries which seem to indicate aspects of his demeanor for the preceding hour: d (dull), c (cheerful), s (serious), l (lively). These entries do not correlate quite so closely with the "devotion" ratings noted above. Nevertheless, "serious" almost always appears with a "devotion" rating of 6 or higher, and "dull" usually accompanies a 5 or lower. "Cheerful" and "lively" normally fall within the middle range of 4 to 6. See plate 13.

C. After a three-week reversion to the seven-column format (style A) at the beginning of April, Ingham reinstitutes the H column on 21 April, revising slightly the R and H columns. The Recollection column no longer contains the abbreviations listed above (from "most zealous" to "dissipated"). These are replaced by the single letter "r" each hour, accompanied by a symbol (similar to those used with the digram "ri" in the key to symbols, plate 4) indicating one of the six "degrees of attention": zealous, fervent, attentive, indifferent, cold, and dead.[1] Any of the first three symbols were positive indications that he was "recollected"; the latter three indicated various levels of being "irrecollected." While "zealous" recollection tends to be associated with high rating in temper of devotion (and "dead" with low ratings), the correlation is not nearly so close as it was previously, in style B.

At the same time, he added more abbreviations to the H column: z (zealous), m (mild), h (heavy), vh (very heavy). As before, these entries do not correlate very closely with the D and R columns, although "zealous" and "serious" usually accompany devotion ratings of 6 or more, and "heavy" and "dull" appear with the rating of 5 or less. See plate 14.

D. The last variation of format comes in May, when, after dropping the H column on the ninth, Ingham changed the heading on the D (devotion) column to "S" (simplicity), so that his S and R columns now echo his resolution to be "simple and recollected in everything" (resolution 8). See plate 15.

---

[1] These descriptive analytical terms, as well as those used in the H column, were commonly used within the holy living tradition. See William Woodman's diary (1706–1707), where such terms as "dull, sober, indifferent, hearty, slothful, and lazy" make up a large proportion of his entries. MS., Rawlinson Collection D. 1334, Bodleian Library, Oxford.

2 Biographical Data for Persons Frequently Mentioned

The following information is taken from the Entrance Book, Queen's College, and Joseph Foster, *Alumni Oxonienses* (London: Joseph Foster, 1887), 4 vol.

Alsop, William, of Wickwar, Glos.
Queen's, Batteler;
matric. 14 May 1730, age 18;
B.A. 22 February 1733/34.

Atkinson, Christopher, of Windermere, Westmorland.
Queen's, Batteler;
matric. 3 May 1732, age 19;
B.A. 25 February 1735/36;
Vicar of Thorp-Arch, Yorks.

Bewsher, Mark, of Tirrell, parish Barton, Westmorland.
Queen's, Batteler;
matric. 27 April 1730, age 19;
B.A. 1734.

Black, Simon, of Stroxton, Linc.
Queen's, Batteler;
matric. 27 April 1730, age 19;
B.A. 1733.

Bolton, Richard, of Greystock, Cumb.
Queen's, Batteler;
matric. 4 July 1732, age 19;
B.A. 1737; M.A. 1741; B.D. 1755;
D.D. 1758.

Bolton, Thomas, Jr., of Greystock, Cumb.
Queen's, Batteler;

matric. 10 October 1733, age 16;
B.A. 1737; M.A. 1741; B.D. 1759;
D.D. 1762.

Broughton, Thomas, of Carfax, Ox.
University College;
matric. 17 December 1731, age 19;
B.A. 22 March 1736/37;
Fellow, Exeter College 1734–41;
Rector of Wotton, Surrey 1752–77.

Brownsword, John, of Sussex.
Queen's, Batteler;
matric. 2 March 1731/32, age 17;
B.A. 5 March 1735.

Carter, Richard, of St. Mary's, Ox.
Christ Church;
matric. 12 October 1730, age 17;
B.A. 1734; M.A. New College 1737.

Dixon, George, of Wooloakes, Cumb.
Queen's, Batteler;
matric. 18 March 1728/29, age 19;
B.A. 1734; M.A. 1737; B.D. 1757;
D.D. 1758;
Vicar of Chedworth, Glos. 1759;
Bramley, Hants 1759;
Principal, St. Edmund Hall 1760–87.

Evans, Henry, of Machynlleth, Montgomery.

Christ Church;
matric. 15 March 1732/33, age 19;
B.A. 20 October 1736.

Ford, John, of Farnham, Surrey.
Queen's, Commoner;
matric. 5 July 1733, age 14;
B.A. Corpus Christi 1737; M.A.
1740; B.D. 1748.

Fothergill, Henry, of Ravenstonedale,
Westmorland.
Queen's, Batteler;
matric. 8 July 1730, age 19;
B.A. 1734; M.A. 1737.
Rector of Cheriton Bishop.

Gambold, John, of Pontsheston, Pemb.
Christ Church;
matric. 10 October 1726, age 15;
B.A. 1730; M.A. 1734;
Bishop in the Moravian Church,
Unitas Fratrum.

Greives, Thomas, of Norham, Dur.
Lincoln;
matric. 10 October 1730, age 19;
B.A. 1734.

Hall, Westley, of Salisbury, Wilts.
Lincoln;
matric. 26 January 1730/31, age 20.

Hervey, James, of Hardingstone,
Northants.
Lincoln;
matric. 8 April, 1731, age 17;
B.A. 9 April 1736 [as Harvey].

Knail, William, of Whitehaven, Cumb.
Queen's, Batteler;
matric. 24 March 1728/29, age 16;
B.A. 1734; M.A. 1737; B.D. 1759;
D.D. 1762;
Scholaribus Grindall 1732–33,
1733–34;
Fellow 1751;
Headmaster, Rugby School 1744–51.

Natt, Anthony, of Stepney, Middx.
Queen's, Commoner;
matric. 5 May 1733, age 18;
B.A. Wadham 1736; M.A. 1739;
Fellow 1739;

Rector of Standon, Herts 1747;
of Nettswell, Essex 1766–1801.

Richardson, James, of Brampton,
Westmorland.
Queen's, Batteler;
matric. 8 July 1732, age 18;
Poor Boy 1732–33;
B.A. 1736.

Robson, John, of Sockbourne, Dur.
Lincoln;
matric. 17 May 1732, age 17;
B.A. 1735; M.A. New Inn Hall
1742.

Salmon, Matthew, of Nantwich, Ches.
Brasenose;
matric. 6 February 1729/30, age 16;
B.A. 1733.

Smith, Richard, of Ely, Cambs.
Christ Church;
matric. 30 October 1732, age 18;
B.A. 1736; M.A. 1739.

Smyth, Thomas, of Beetham,
Westmorland.
Queen's, Batteler;
matric. 4 July 1732, age 18;
B.A. 14 February 1737/38.

Thompson, William, of Brough,
Westmorland.
Queen's, Batteler;
matric. 26 March 1731, age 18;
B.A. 1735; M.A. 26 February
1738/39;
Rector of Hampton Poyle with
South Weston.

Walker, James, of Manchester, Lancs.
Brasenose;
matric. 22 February 1733/34, age 14.

Ward, Matthias, of Warcup,
Westmorland.
Queen's, Batteler;
matric. 13 November 1730, age 20.

Washington, Henry, of Penrith, Cumb.
Queen's, Batteler;
matric. 5 July 1733, age 16;
B.A. 1737; M.A. 1741.

Watson, Robert, of Crostard, Cumb.
  Queen's, Batteler;
  matric. 18 March 1729/30, age 18;
  B.A. 1735; M.A. 1738/39;
  Rector of Egdean, Sussex 1759.
Wesley, Charles, of Epworth, Lincs.
  Christ Church;
  matric. 13 June 1726, age 18;
  B.A. 1730; M.A. 1732/33.
Wesley, John, of Epworth, Lincs.
  Christ Church;
  matric. 18 July 1720, age 16;

B.A. 1724; M.A. 1726/27;
  Fellow of Lincoln 1726–51.
Yates, Richard Sutton, of Charleton,
    Ox.
  Queen's, Commoner;
  matric. 7 January 1729/30;
  B.A. 1733; M.A. 1736; B.D. and
    D.D. 1750;
  Rector of Solihull, County Warwick
    1769;
  Vicar of Tardebigge, County
    Worcester 1780–89.

3 Bibliography of Ingham's Reading

The A. B. C. with the Catechism; that is to say, an Instruction to be learned of every person before he is brought to be confirmed by the Bishop (1605).

Aldrich, Henry (1647–1710). *Artis logicæ compendium* (1691).

Alleine, Joseph (1634–1688). *A Sure Guide to Heaven; or, An Earnest Invitation to God, in Order to Their Eternal Salvation, Shewing the Thoughtful Sinner What He Must do to be Saved* (1688).

Atterbury, Francis (1662–1732). A sermon.

Barrow, Isaac (1630–1677). *Of Industry, in Five Discourses. Viz. In General. In Our General Calling, as Christians. In Our Particular Calling, as Gentlemen. In Our Particular Calling, as Scholars* . . . (1693).

Bennet, Thomas (1673–1728). *Directions for Studying. I. A General System or Body of Divinity. II. The Thirty-nine Articles of Religion* (1714).

[Berkeley, George (1685–1753)]. *Alciphron; or The Minute Philosopher* . . . *Containing an Apology for the Christian Religion, Against Those Who Are Called Free-Thinkers* (1732).

Beveridge, William (1637–1708). *Codex canonum ecclesiæ primitivæ vindicatus ac illustratus* (1678).

———. *A Sermon Concerning the Excellency and Usefulness of the Common Prayer* . . . (1682).

Bible (Authorized Version).

Blackmore, Richard (d. 1729). *Creation. A Philosophical Poem, in Seven Books* (1712).

Blackwall, Anthony (1674–1730). *The Sacred Classics Defended and Illustrated; or, An Essay* . . . *Proving the Purity, Propriety and True Eloquence of the Writers of the New Testament*, 2 parts (1725).

Bonnell, James (1653–1699). See William Hamilton.

Bonwicke, Ambrose [the elder] (1652–1722). *A Pattern for Young Students in the University, Set Forth in the Life of Mr. Ambrose Bonwicke, Sometime Scholar of St. John's College in Cambridge* (1729).

The Book of Common Prayer (1662).

Brevint, Daniel (1616–1695). *The Christian Sacrament and Sacrifice; By Way of Discourse, Meditation & Prayer Upon the Nature, Parts, and Blessings of the Holy Communion* (1673).

Browne, Peter (d. 1735). *The Procedure, Extent, and Limits of Human Understanding* (1728).

———. *Things Divine and Supernatural Conceived by Analogy With Things Natural and Human* (1733).

Bull, George (1634–1710). See Robert Nelson.

Burkitt, William (1650–1703). *The Poor Man's Help, and Young Man's Guide: Containing I. Doctrinal Instructions for the Right Informing of His Judgment. II. Practical Directions for the General Course of His Life. III. Particular Advices for the Well-managing of Every Day* (2d ed., 1694).

Castañiza, Juan de (d. 1598). See Lorenzo Scupoli.

Cave, William (1637–1713). *Apostolici: or, the History of the lives, acts, death, and martyrdoms of . . . the most eminent of the Primitive Fathers for the first three hundred years* (1677, 1683).

———. *Primitive Christianity; or, the Religion of the ancient Christians in the first ages of the Gospel* (1673).

Charles XII. See Francois Marie Arouet de Voltaire.

Cheyne, George (1671–1743). *An Essay of Health and Long Life* (1724).

The Christian Monitor. See John Rawlet.

Cicero, Marcus Tullius. *Cicero's Three Books Touching the Nature of the Gods, Done in English; With Notes and Illustrations. Setting Forth, (From All Antiquity,) What Perceptions, Man, by the Only Light of Reason, May Entertein Concerning a Deity* (1st Eng. ed., 1683).

———. *Tully's Offices. In Three Books,* translated into English by Nicolas Grimalde (1556), Roger L'Estrange (1680), and Thomas Cockman (1699).

Clayton, John (1709–1773). Sermons (MSS.?)

Clement I (Clemens Romanus). See Thomas Ittig.

Collier, Jeremy (1650–1726). *Essays upon several Moral Subjects* (1697).

The Country Parson's Advice to His Parishioners . . . (1680).

The Court Convert (?).

Darrell, William (1651–1721). *The Gentleman Instructed in the Conduct of a Virtuous and Happy Life* (2d ed., 1704).

[Deacon, Thomas (1697–1753)]. *A Compleat Collection of Devotions, Both Public and Private: Taken from the Apostolical Constitutions, the Ancient Liturgies, and the Common Prayer Book of the Church of England* (1734).

Death of an Apostate. See Richard Sault, *Second Spira.*

Directions for Reading Religious Books (cf. "Directions how to read this and other religious books with benefit and improvement," appended to John Wesley's published extract of John Norris, *A Treatise on Christian Prudence*).

Ellis, Clement (1630–1700). *Christianity in Short; or, The Way to be a Good Christian* (1682).

————. *The Communicant's Guide: Shewing a Safe and Easie Way to the Lord's Table: in Compassion to the Poorer and Weaker Sort of Christians* (1685).

Ephraem Syrus, Saint (?).

Family Prayers. See *Morning & Evening Prayers for Families.*

Francis de Sales, Saint (1567–1622). *An Introduction to a Devout Life* (1701).

Francke, August Hermann (1633–1727). *Manuductio ad lectionem Scripturæ Sacræ, . . . cum nova præfatione, de impedimentis studii theologici, et appendice, exhibente aliquot ecclesiæ angelicanæ scriptorum loca, ad illustrationem opusculi facientia* (1706).

————. *Nicodemus; or a Treatise Against the Fear of Man. Wherein the Causes and Sad Effects Thereof Are Briefly Described. With Some Remedies Against It. Rendered into English* [by Anthony W. Boehme?] *and Dedicated to the Honourable Society for Reformation of Manners* (2d ed., 1709).

Gentleman Instructed. See William Darrell.

Gerhard, Johann (1582–1637). *Gerard's Meditations and Prayers* (5th ed., 1695).

Glanvill, Joseph (1636–1680). *Some Discourses, Sermons, and Remains of J. G. . . . Collected and Published by A. Horneck* (1681).

Goodman, John (1626?–1690). *The Penitent Pardoned; Or a Discourse of the Nature of Sin, and the Efficacy of Repentance Under the Parable of the Prodigal Son* (1679).

————. *A Winter-Evening Conference Between Neighbours. In three parts* (1684).

[Gother, John (d. 1704?)] *Instructions and Devotions for the Afflicted and Sick* (1697).

————. *Instructions for Particular States* (1689).

Gravesande, Willem Jacob van 's (1688–1742). *Mathematical Elements of Natural Philosophy, Confirmed by Experiments, or an Introduction to Sir Isaac Newton's Philosophy* (1720, 1721).

Greek Grammar, some form of *Græcæ grammatices rudimenta in usum Scholæ Westmonasteriensis* (various editions, 1663–).

Greek Testament. See Johannes Leusden.

Grotius, Hugo. *De veritate religionis Christianæ* (Paris, 1627; Oxonii, 1650).

The Guardian [Richard Steele, Joseph Addison, and others] (1713).

Hale, Matthew (1609–1676). *Contemplations Moral and Divine* (1676).

Hall, Joseph (1574–1656). *The Art of Divine Meditation* (1607).

Hamilton, William (d. 1729). *The Exemplary Life and Character of James Bonnell, Esq., late Accomptant-General of Ireland . . .* (1703).

Hammond, Henry (1605–1660). *A Practical Catechism* (1644).

Herbert, George (1593–1633). *Herbert's Remains; or, Sundry Pieces of that Sweet Singer of the Temple . . .* (1652).

History of Charles XII. See Francois Marie Arouet de Voltaire.

Homer.

Horneck, Anthony (1641–1697). *The Fire of the Altar: or, Certain Directions*

———. *Practical Christianity; or, An Account of the Holiness Which the Gospel Enjoyns, With the Motives to It* (5th ed., 1700).

Meditation, Sermon on (?).

Milton, John (1608–1674). *Paradise Lost, a Poem in Twelve Books* (earlier editions in ten books; 1st ed., 1667).

Minutius Felix. See William Reeves.

Morning and Evening Prayers for Families (S.P.C.K. list, 1734).

Nelson, Robert (1650–1715). *A Companion for the Festivals and Fasts of the Church of England; With Collects and Prayers for Each Solemnity* (1704).

———. *The Great Duty of Frequenting the Christian Sacrifice, and the Nature of the Preparation Required* (2d ed., 1707).

———. *The Life of Dr. George Bull . . . With the History of Those Controversies in Which He Was Engaged; and an Abstract of Those . . . Doctrines Which He Maintained and Defended . . .* (1714).

———. *The Practice of True Devotion, in Relation to the End as Well as the Means of Religion* (1698).

Norris, John (1657–1711). *A Collection of Miscellanies: Consisting of Poems, Essays, etc.* (1687).

———. *Letters Concerning the Love of God, between the author of the Proposal to the Ladies* [Mrs Astell] *and J. Norris* (1695).

———. *Practical Discourses Upon the Beatitudes of Our Lord* (1728); includes the following sermons mentioned by Ingham:

"Christian Blessedness" (eight discourses)

"An Effectual Remedy against the Fear of Death"

"Heavenly-Mindedness"

"The Honour Due to Good Men and the Great Crime of Treating Them With Scorn and Contempt"

"The Importance of a Religious Life Considered from the Happy Conclusion of It"

"The Measure of Divine Love, with the Natural and Moral Grounds upon which it Stands"

"Religious Discourse in Common Conversation"

"Religious Singularity"

"The Successive Vanity of Human Life"

"Worldly and Divine Wisdom"

———. *A Practical Treatise Concerning Humility, designed for the Furtherance and Improvement of that great Christian Virtue both in the Minds and Lives of Men* (1707).

———. *Spiritual Counsel. or, the Father's Advice to his Children* (1694).

———. *A Treatise Concerning Christian Prudence; or, The Principles of Practical Wisdom, Fitted to the Use of Human Life . . .* (1710).

Osterwald, Jean Frédéric (1663–1747). *The Nature of Uncleanness Consider'd . . . to which is Added, A Discourse Concerning the Nature of Chastity, and the Means of Obtaining it* (1708).

The Oxford Methodists: Being Some Account of a Society of Young Gentlemen in that City so Denominated . . . (1733).

Parecbolæ sive excerpta & corpore statutorum Universitatis Oxoniensis (1729).

[Patrick, Simon (1626–1707)]. *The Christian Sacrifice. A Treatise Shewing the Necessity, End and Manner of Receiving Holy Communion: Together With Suitable Prayers and Meditations for Every Month in the Year, and the Principal Festivals* . . . (1671).

————. *The Devout Christian Instructed How to Pray and Give Thanks to God; or, A Book of Devotions for Families* (11th ed., 1700).

————. *A Treatise of Repentance, and of Fasting, Especially of the Lent-Fast* (1686).

The Penitential Office for the Sixteenth Day of the Month, [Treatise on].

Plain Directions for Reading the Holy Scriptures. Homily Upon Reading the Holy Scriptures . . . *the 7th ed. cor*ᵈ. (175?).

Plutarch. *The Lives of the Noble Grecians, and Romans, the Most of them Compared Together by* . . . *Plutarch of Chæronea.* Englished by Th. North; tr. by John Dryden (1603).

Pope, Alexander (1688–1744). *The First Satire of the Second Book of Horace, Imitated in a Dialogue Between Alexander Pope on the One Part, and His Learned Council on the Other* (1733).

The Provoked Husband. See John Vanbrugh.

Rawlet, John (1642–1686). *The Christian Monitor, Containing an Earnest Exhortation to an Holy Life* . . . (1686).

[Reeves, William (1667–1726)]. *The Apologies of Justin Martyr, Tertullian, & Minutius Felix, in Defence of the Christian Religion, With the Commonitory of Vincentius Lirinensis Concerning the Primitive Rule of Faith* . . . *Translated, With Notes, by W. Reeves* . . . *And a Preliminary Discourse Upon Each Author. Together With a Prefatory Dissertation About the Right Use of the Fathers* . . . (1709).

Rodriguez, Alonso (1526–1616). *A Treatise of* [*the Virtue of*] *Humilitie* (1631).

Saint Jure, Jean Baptiste de (1588–1657). *The Holy Life of Mons*ʳ *de Renty, a Late Nobleman of France, and Sometimes Councellor to King Lewis the 13th* (1658).

Sanderson, Robert (1587–1633). *Logicæ artis compendium* (1615).

————. *De obligatione conscientiæ, prælectiones decem* . . . (Oxon, 1660; London, 1661).

[Sault, Richard (d. 1702)]. *The Second Spira, Being a Fearful Example of an Atheist, who had Apostatized from the Christian Religion, and Died in Despair at Westminster, Dec. 8, 1692. By J. S.* [Richard Sault] (6th ed., 1693).

Scougal, Henry (1650–1678). *Life of God in the Soul of Man; or, The Nature and Excellency of the Christian Religion* (1677).

Scupoli, Lorenzo (1530–1610). *The Spiritual Combat: or, The Christian Pilgrim in His Spiritual Conflict and Conquest* (1698).

Secker, Thomas (1693–1768). *A Sermon* [on Deut. 32:46, 47] *Preached before the University of Oxford* . . . *on Act Sunday* . . . *July 8, 1733* ["On the Advantages and Duties of an Academical Education"] (1733).

Second Spira. See Richard Sault.

Self-Denial, Treatise on (?).

Shepard, Thomas (1604–1649). *The Sincere Convert, Concerning the Small Number of True Believers* . . . (1659).

Sherlock, William (1641–1707). *A Practical Discourse Concerning Death* (1689).

Smalridge, George (1663–1719). *A Sermon* [on Gen. 49:6] *Preached Before the Commons* . . . *Jan. 30, 1701/2, Being the Anniversary Fast of the Martyrdom of King Ch. I* (1702).

———. *A Sermon* [on Judg. 13:30] *Preached Before the Court of Aldermen* . . . *Jan. 31, 1708/9, Being the Anniversary of* . . . (1709).

South, Robert (1634–1716). A sermon.

The Spectator [Joseph Addison, Richard Steele, and others] (1711–1714).

Stationary Fasts. See John Wesley.

Statutes. See *Parecobolæ* . . .

Stearne, John (1660–1745). *Tractatus de visitatione infirmorum, seu de eis parochorum officiis, quæ informos et moribundos respiciunt* (Dublin, 1687; London, 1700).

The Tatler. By Isaac Bickerstaff, Esq. [Richard Steele, Joseph Addison, and others] (1709–1711).

Taylor, Jeremy (1613–1667). *The Rule and Exercises of Holy Dying* (1651).

———. *The Rule and Exercises of Holy Living* . . . *Together With Prayers Containing the Whole Duty of a Christian* (1650).

———. *The Worthy Communicant; or a Discourse of the Nature, Effects, and Blessings Consequent to the Worthy Receiving of the Lord's Supper* (1660).

Tertullian. See William Reeves.

Theseus and Romulus, lives of. See Plutarch.

[Thomas à Kempis, Saint (1380–1471)]. *De imitatione Christi.*

Tillotson, John (1630–1694). A sermon.

Trapp, Joseph (1679–1747). *The Duties of Private, Domestic, and Public Devotion; on Josh. 24:15* (1717).

Vanbrugh, John (1664–1726). *The Provoked Husband, or, a Journey to London. A Comedy* . . . *written by Sir J. Vanbrugh and Mr.* [Colley] *Cibber* [after Vanbrugh died] (1728).

[Vickers, William.] *A Companion to the Altar; Shewing the Nature and Necessity of a Sacramental Preparation, in Order to Our Worthy Receiving the Holy Communion* (6th ed., 1707).

Vincent, of Lerins, Saint (Vincentius Lirinensis). See William Reeves.

Virgilius Maro, Publius. *Æneis.*

Voltaire, Francois Marie Arouet de (1694–1778). *The History of Charles XII, King of Sweden* (1732).

Wake, William (1657–1737). *The Principles of the Christian Religion Explained: in a Brief Commentary upon the Church-Catechism* (1699).

Waterland, Daniel (1683–1740). *The Nature, Obligation, and Efficacy, of the Christian Sacraments, Considered; in Reply to a Pamphlet* [by A. A. Sykes] *Intituled, An Answer To the Remarks Upon Dr. Clarke's Exposition of the Church-Catechism* (1730).

The Way of Living in a Method, and by Rule: or, a Regular Way of Employing Our Time [By a Presbyter of the Church of England] (1722).

Welchman, Edward (1665–1739). *XXXIX Articuli ecclesiæ anglicanæ, textibus e sacra Scriptura depromptis confirmati, brevibusque notis illustratii; cum Appendice de Doctrina Patrum* (1713).

Wesley, John (1703–1791). *A Collection of Forms of Prayer for Every Day in the Week* (1733).

————. "Essay upon the Stationary Fasts," MS., 1733, MA.

————. Sermon on the Love of God (Mark 12:30), MS., 1733, MA.

————. Sermon (Treatise) on the Sacrament, MS. 1732, MA.

Wesley, Samuel (1662–1735). *A Letter from a Country Divine to His Friend in London, Concerning the Education of Dissenters in their Private Academies* (1703).

————. "A Letter Concerning the Religious Societies," Appendix to *The Pious Communicant Rightly Prepared* (1700).

Weston, James. *Stenography Compleated, or the Art of Short-hand Brought to Perfection . . .* (1727).

Whitby, Daniel (1638–1726). *A Paraphrase and Commentary on the New Testament* (1703).

The Whole Duty of Man [Richard Allestree? (1619–1681)] (1659).

Wilson, Thomas (1663–1755). *The Principles and Duties of Christianity; Being a Further Instruction for Such as Have Learned the Church-Catechism* (1707).

Young, Edward (1643–1705). "The Danger of Indifferency" [on Matt. 6:24], in *Sermons on Several Occasions* (1703).

————. "The Nature and Use of Self-Denial" [on Matt. 16:24], in *Sermons on Several Occasions* (1703).

————. *Two Sermons Concerning Nature and Grace* [on Matt. 26:35] (1700).

Young, Edward (1683–1765). *A Poem on the Last Day* (1713).

4 Text of Ingham's Letter to John Wesley Dated July 27, 1734

Reverend Sir,

I meet with many cases of conscience in the country, though I can find no casuist to resolve them. I did not altogether know the advantage of living at Oxford so well before as I do now. Those that have it in their power to reside there are wise if they do so. To act well in the country requires more knowledge and prudence and a great deal more zeal. Tis scarce possible to imagine how wicked the world is. The generality are dead in trespasses and sins, and even those who pass for good Christians are sunk deep in a dead indifferency. Sincerity is as rare a thing as a black swan. Since I left your good mother [see 1 July], I've not met with one person that is in good earnest for heaven, except the poor rug-maker [William Wilby]; God indeed is chief ruler in his heart. The most zealous conversation and the best discourses have no effect upon most people; they are no more moved or concerned than a stone. Reflecting frequently on this has confirmed my belief of an election of grace. I should be glad to know your thoughts on this subject at a convenient opportunity.

Since my coming into the country I've for the most part been fervent and zealous in private prayer and frequently very much affected with lively meditation, which hath comforted me much and made me easy and cheerful. What dejects me most is when I lay long or am idle, or in company where I can do no good. I desire to know how I ought to act when I'm in company with superiors that talk only about trifles. Alas, sir, I'm vastly deficient in rising regularly and early, which is the very material point, though blessed be God I've now got a woman [Molly Harrup] to call me who rises pretty early, so that I hope to mend. I've methodized my time according to the following scheme. Supposing I rise at 5 or sooner, I spend till 6 in devotion, repeating the hymn in dressing, then write diary, afterward chant a psalm, then private prayer, and then meditate or read the Holy Scriptures; at 6 compose treatises; at 7 we have family prayers, I first read the lesson out of the New Testament using a collect before and after, then most of the Common Prayer, the rest of the hour I compose; 8 breakfast; 8.15 two poor children [John France and James Blackburn] come to me to read; 8.45 private prayer, I propose to observe the three ancient hours of prayer when at home; from 9 to 11 I read the Greek Testament according to Francke's [directions]; at 11 I go to teach the rug-maker's children to read; 11.45 private prayer for myself and friends; 12 dinner, read Norris [*Practical Discourses*]; 1 shorthand; 2 Greek Testament; 4 walk; 5 devotion; 6 meditation, I choose the subject beforehand; 7 supper, read Milton [*Paradise Lost*]; 8 read religious books with our family; 9 read family prayers; 9.30 private prayer for perseverance in behalf of myself and friends, for death, etc. On Wednesday and Friday from 8 to 9, meditate on my sins, and private prayer; 12 to 1 meditate on Christ's sufferings and private prayer; 2.45 private prayer; 3 breakfast, read Norris. On Sunday I propose to meditate two hours from 6 to 7 [morning and evening]; to read and [have] religious talk with our family or some poor neighbours at spare time. I shall readily submit to your better directions in any thing. I've begun to teach four poor children to write [Jonathan, Susy, and Sarah Wilby, and Hannah France], which takes up a little time, and I wait upon them whenever they come. It's a hard thing to be so regular in the country as at Oxford. By my mother I'm tempted to indulge; by my relations and friends to visit them often. Should I do it? Supposing a friend was to visit me on a Stationary day, how must I behave myself? In eating and drinking should I confine myself to such a quantity when with strangers? [Cf. pp. 119, 167.] Your directions in these cases will be very useful.

My hearty love to your brother and all our friends. I've received a letter from Mr Smyth; he says he'll acquaint his tutor with all his concerns. I design shortly to write to Mr Ford and Watson. I earnestly desire the hearty prayers of all our friends.

From your most obliged and affectionate friend and servant,

Ben. Ingham

Direct for me of Ossett to be left / at Ed Stringer's Stationer in / Wakefield, Yorkshire.

[Address] For the Reverend Mr John Wesley / Fellow of Lincoln College / Oxford

Selected Bibliography

An Account of the Origin and Designs of the Society for Promoting Christian Knowledge. [London,] 1734.

An Account of Several Workhouses for Employing and Maintaining the Poor. London: J. Downing, 1732.

Allison, Christopher FitzSimons. *The Rise of Moralism; the Proclamation of the Gospel from Hooker to Baxter.* New York: Seabury Press, 1966.

Amhurst, Nicholas. *Terræ Filius; or, The Secret History of the University of Oxford.* London, 1726. 2 vols.

Ayliffe, John. *The Antient and Present State of the University of Oxford.* London: E. Curll, 1714. 2 vols.

Batty, William. "An Account of Benjamin Ingham and His Work." Eng. MSS. 1062, The John Rylands University Library of Manchester.

Bouyer, Louis. *A History of Christian Spirituality.* London: Burns & Oates, 1969. 3 vols.

Byrom, John. *The Private Journal and Literary Remains of John Byrom.* Manchester: Chetham Society, 1856. 2 vols.

Foster, Joseph. *Alumni Oxonienses.* London: Joseph Foster, 1887. 4 vols.

Gambold, John. "The Character of Mr. John Wesley." *Methodist Magazine* 21 (March 1798), pp. 117–21, 168–72.

Hearne, Thomas. *Remarks and Collections of Thomas Hearne,* ed. H. E. Salter. Oxford: Clarendon Press, 1914–21. Vols. 9–11 of 11 vols.

Heitzenrater, Richard P. *John Wesley and the Oxford Methodists, 1725–1735.* Ph.D. diss., Duke University. Ann Arbor, Mich.: University Microfilms, 1972.

Hodgkin, Robert Howard. *Six Centuries of an Oxford College; a History of the Queen's College, 1340–1940.* Oxford: Basil Blackwell, 1949.

Legg, John Wickham. *English Church Life from the Restoration to the Tractarian Movement.* London: Longmans, Green and Co., 1914.

Magrath, John Richard. *The Flemings in Oxford.* Oxford: Oxford Historical Society, 1904–24. 3 vols.

———. *The Queen's College.* Oxford: Clarendon Press, 1921. 2 vols.

Mallet, Charles Edward. *A History of the University of Oxford.* New York: Longmans, Green and Co., 1924–27. 3 vols.

Martz, Louis. *The Poetry of Meditation.* New Haven: Yale University Press, 1954.

Orcibal, Jean. "The Theological Originality of John Wesley," in *A History of the Methodist Church in Great Britain.* London: Epworth Press, 1965. Vol. 1 of 4 vols.

Outler, Albert C. *John Wesley.* New York: Oxford University Press, 1964.

Pointer, John. *Oxoniensis academia; . . . or the Antiquities and Curiosities of the University of Oxford.* London: S. Birt, 1749.

The Present State of the New Buildings of Queen's College in Oxford. [Oxford,] 1730.

Robinson, Howard. *The British Post Office.* Princeton, N.J.: Princeton University Press, 1948.

Salmon, Thomas. *The Present State of the Universities.* London: J. Roberts, 1744.

Squires, Thomas W. *In West Oxford.* London: A. R. Mowbray, 1928.

Thompson, Richard W. *Benjamin Ingham (Yorkshire Evangelist) and the Inghamites.* Kendal, Cumbria: Privately published, 1958.

Thornton, Catherine, and Frances McLaughlin, eds. *The Fothergills of Ravenstonedale.* London: William Heinemann, 1906.

Tyerman, Luke. *The Oxford Methodists.* London: Hodder and Stoughton, 1873.

Ward, W. R. *Georgian Oxford, University Politics in the Eighteenth Century.* Oxford: Clarendon Press, 1958.

Wesley, John. *The Journal of the Rev. John Wesley,* edited by Nehemiah Curnock. London: Epworth Press, 1909–16. 8 vols.

Whitefield, George. *A Short Account of God's Dealings with the Reverend Mr. Whitefield.* London: W. Strahan, 1740.

Willey, Basil. *The English Moralists.* London: Chatto & Windus, 1964.

Wilson, Thomas. *The Diaries of Thomas Wilson, D.D., 1731–37 and 1750,* ed. by C. L. S. Linnell. London: S.P.C.K., 1964.

Wood, Anthony. *The Life and Times of Anthony Wood, Antiquary, at Oxford 1632–1695, Described by Himself,* edited by Andrew Clark. Oxford: Oxford Historical Society, 1891–95. 5 vols.

Index

The text of the Diary is indexed by date; other matter, chiefly editorial, is indexed by italicized page numbers. (n) following a date indicates a diary reference that is made explicit only by a footnote; n or nn refers to other footnote material. *Passim* indicates one or more short gaps in an otherwise unbroken sequence of dates. Material in the monthly summaries that duplicates the main diary text is not separately indexed.